Land Tenure in Sierra Leone

The Law, Dualism and the Making of a Land Policy

Ade Renner-Thomas

authorHOUSE®

AuthorHouse™ UK Ltd.
500 Avebury Boulevard
Central Milton Keynes, MK9 2BE
www.authorhouse.co.uk
Phone: 08001974150

First published by AuthorHouse 8/12/2010

ISBN: 978-1-4490-5868-5 (e)
ISBN: 978-1-4490-5866-1 (sc)
ISBN: 978-1-4490-5867-8 (hc)

Land Tenure in Sierra Leone

Contents

PART 2 LAND LAW IN THE WESTERN AREA

PART 5 MAKING OF A LAND POLICY: CRITIQUE AND PROPOSALS FOR REFORM

APPENDICES

TABLE OF STATUTES
SIERRA LEONE STATUTES

ENGLISH STATUTES

GHANA STATUTES

TABLE OF CASES

Page

PREFACE

This book is intended to serve several purposes. The first objective is didactic. The book is primarily for law students who need to know the laws governing land tenure in Sierra Leone. To enable the reader to understand the dual system of land tenure in force in Sierra Leone – English tenure in the Western Area and customary tenure in the Provinces – the work starts by giving an account of the background to this duality of tenure. It attempts to explain why this dualism, which arose because of the different colonial experiences of the former Western Area and the former Protectorate, still persists almost fifty years after the two entities were merged to form the unitary State of Sierra Leone. The book explains for the benefit of students the main features of the English-derived land law in the Western Area and the land tenure structure in the Provinces which is governed predominantly by customary law, influenced to a limited extent by the received English law.

The book also aims to assist the legal practitioner who may not have undertaken detailed, or indeed any, formal study of the dual system of land tenure in force in Sierra Leone. This it does by illuminating the practical problems that may confront them as they advise their clients or draft legal documents for the creation or transfer of interest in land in different parts of Sierra Leone. It is hoped that the legal practitioner, by reading this work, will appreciate the diversity of the land tenure system in Sierra Leone of which he is required to have an intimate if not specialist knowledge.

It is my view that no study of land tenure in Sierra Leone would be complete or of value to the student or legal practitioner if it omitted constructive criticism of the system and consideration and appraisal of proposals for land tenure changes in the light of stated policies. By giving an account of the development of policy initiatives and setting out the achievements and shortcomings of land tenure reform to date the book aims to stimulate debate on current proposals not only among students and practitioners of the law but also among members of the wider non-legal community such as politicians, traditional rulers, private landowners in both the Western Area and the Provinces, financial institutions (for whom land is often the only form of collateral for the loans they may want to make), local and foreign investors, environmentalists, civil society activists (seeking to protect the marginalized landless and poor members of society) and countless other stakeholders.

Part 1 which contains two chapters provides a general introduction, outlining the geographical, social and cultural background and political and legal history (Chapter 1); and explaining the present pluralistic legal system (Chapter 2), knowledge of which is indispensable for an understanding of the operation of the dual system of tenure.

Part 2 gives an account of English or non-customary tenure and the application of the English law of real property as part of the general law which almost exclusively governs land tenure in the Western Area. Chapter 3 traces the origins and legal basis of title to land in the Western Area. Chapter 4 illustrates the application of the received English land law in specific areas of the land law in force in the Western Area. Part 2 ends with a discussion of the methods of acquisition and proof of title to land in this part of the country (Chapter 5).

Part 3, which consists of four chapters, discusses customary land tenure which is in force only in the Provinces. Chapter 6 introduces the concepts of ownership and title to land under customary law. Chapter 7 then highlights the different forms of tenure under customary law. Chapter 8 examines and analyses the nature of interests in land held by various entities under customary law, while Chapter 9 states the law governing the disposition and acquisition of interests in land held under customary tenure.

Part 4 focuses on the problems arising from the interaction of the two systems (Chapter 10).

Finally, Part 5 provides an appraisal of developments since the year 2000 towards the making of a national land policy (Chapter 11) and the work concludes with a critique of the dual land tenure system and some proposals for its reform (Chapter 12).

With the paucity of data and published literature on land tenure in Sierra Leone a work of this nature could not have been undertaken without the assistance of so many persons that it is impossible for me to mention them all by name. For this reason, I take this opportunity to express my profound gratitude to all those who have contributed in one way or another to making this book a reality.

I am especially indebted to Susan Faircloth for all her guidance at the later stages of the preparation of this work, without which I would have had great difficulty with the overall presentation.

However, I owe especial gratitude to certain people who took time out of their busy schedules to read this work in the draft stage and enormously improved the quality of its content by making suggestions for revisions and corrections. In this regard, mention should be made of Dr Abdulai Conteh, Mr. Berthan Macaulay Jnr and Mr. Abdul Tejan-Cole. I must also express appreciation to Dr. Armand Thomas for the great benefit of endless discussions with him on a great number of topics covered in this work and on its general presentation.

Ms Hassatu Jalloh, Confidential Secretary in the office of the Chief Justice, and Mrs Fatmata Koroma, my secretary and personal assistant, contributed immensely in the preparation of the manuscript for this work and helped me avoid many pitfalls that I would have fallen into had I persisted in my attempt to do the typing myself.

Finally, it is with love and profound gratitude that I acknowledge the patience, encouragement and counselling of my dear wife and lovely daughters during the many years that it took to complete this work.

A. RENNER-THOMAS
Freetown
2010

TABLE OF ABBREVIATIONS

A.C.	Appeal Cases
All. N.L.R.	All Nigeria Law Report
ALR S.L.	African Law Reports [Sierra Leone]
App. Cas.	Appeal Cases
C.A.	Court of Appeal [Sierra Leone]
Cap.	Chapter
C.C.	Civil Case in former Supreme Court (now High Court)
CH.	Chancery Division
Ch. D.	Chancery. Division
Civ. App.	Civil Appeal [Sierra Leone]
D.A.C.	District Appeal Court [Sierra Leone]
F.S.C.	Federal Supreme Court Reports [Nigeria]
G.L.A.C.	Group Local Appeal Court [Sierra Leone]
H.L.	House of Lords
H.C.	High Court [Sierra Leone]
J.A.L.	Journal of African Law
K.B.	King's Bench
L.C.	Local Court [Sierra Leone]
L.J. Ch.	Law Journal Chancery
L.L.R.	Lagos Law Reports
Lofft	King's Bench Law Reports (1751–1824) by Capel Lofft, now reported in Vol. 98 of English Reports
L.R.App.Cas.	Law Reports Appeal Cases
M + W	Meeson and Welsby
N.L.R.	Nigerian Law Reports
N.M.L.R.	Nigerian Monthly Law Reports
P.C.	Privy Council
S.	Section
S.C.	Supreme Court [Sierra Leone]
S.L. Law. Rec.	Sierra Leone Law Recorder
SLLR	Sierra Leone Law Reports (1960–63)
S.L.S.(O.S.)	Sierra Leone Studies (Old Series)
S.L.S. (N.S.)	Sierra Leone Studies (New Series)

Sar, F.L.R.	Fanti Law Reports (2nd Selection, by Sarbah)
Ves.	Vesey
W.A.C.A.	West African Court of Appeal Reports
W.L.R.	Weekly Law Reports
W.N.L.R.	Western Nigeria Law Reports
W.R.N.L.R.	Western Region of Nigeria Law Reports

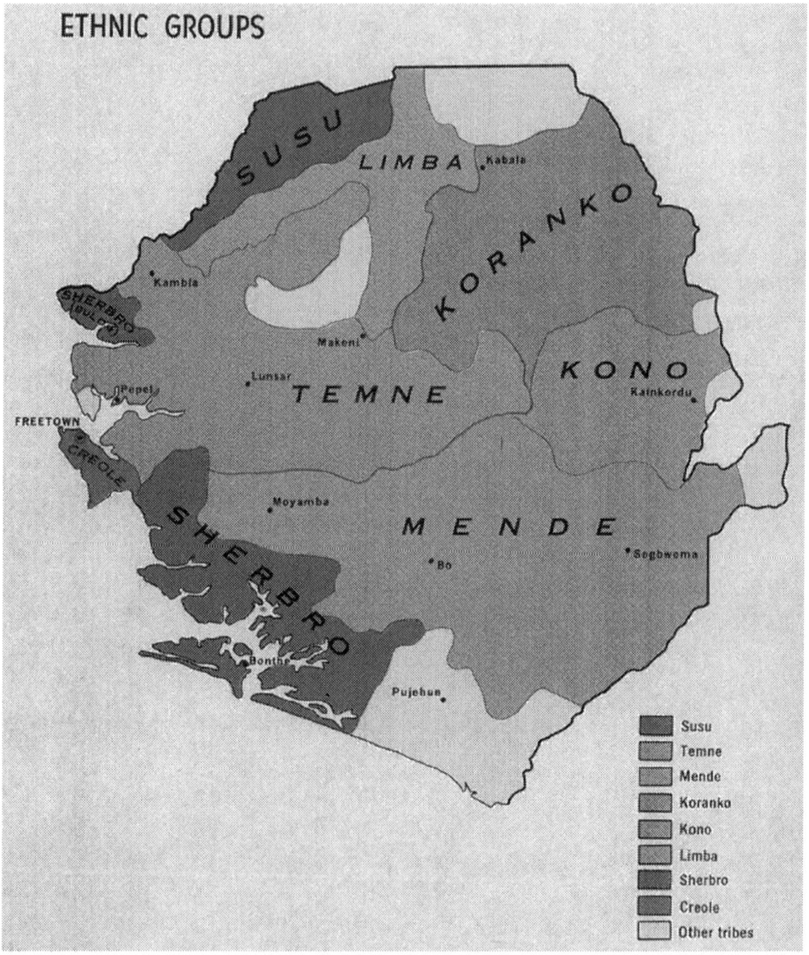

Map 1 Distribution of ethnic groups
Map courtesy of the University of Texas Libraries,
The University of Texas at Austin.

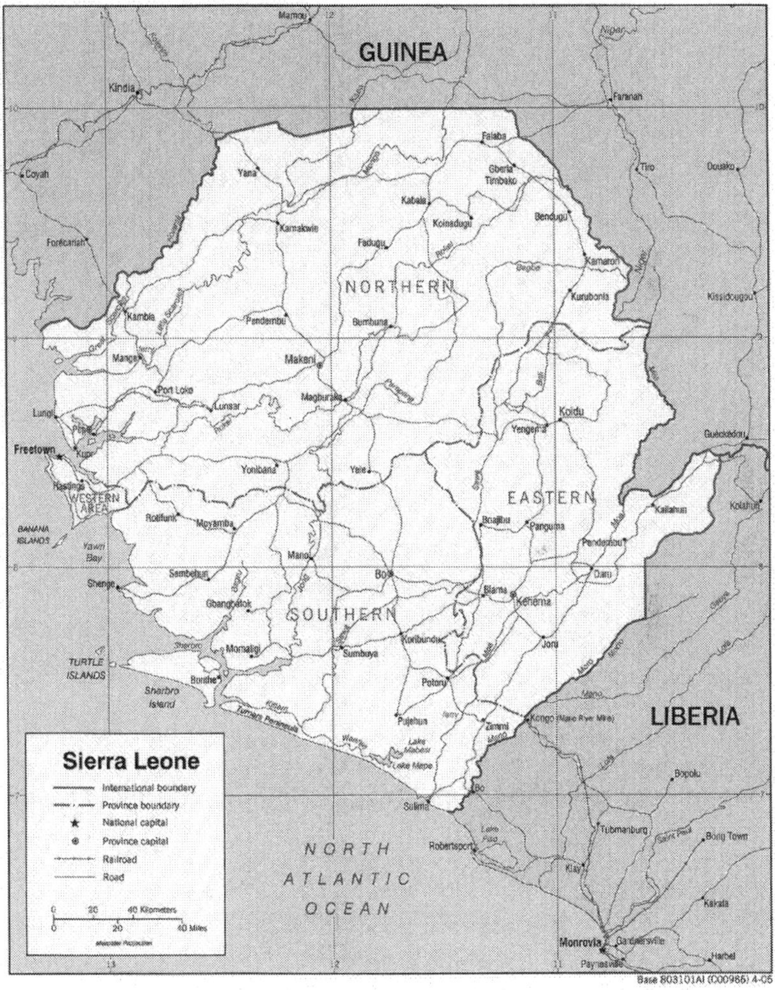

Map 2 Administrative divisions
Map courtesy of the University of Texas Libraries, The University of Texas at Austin.

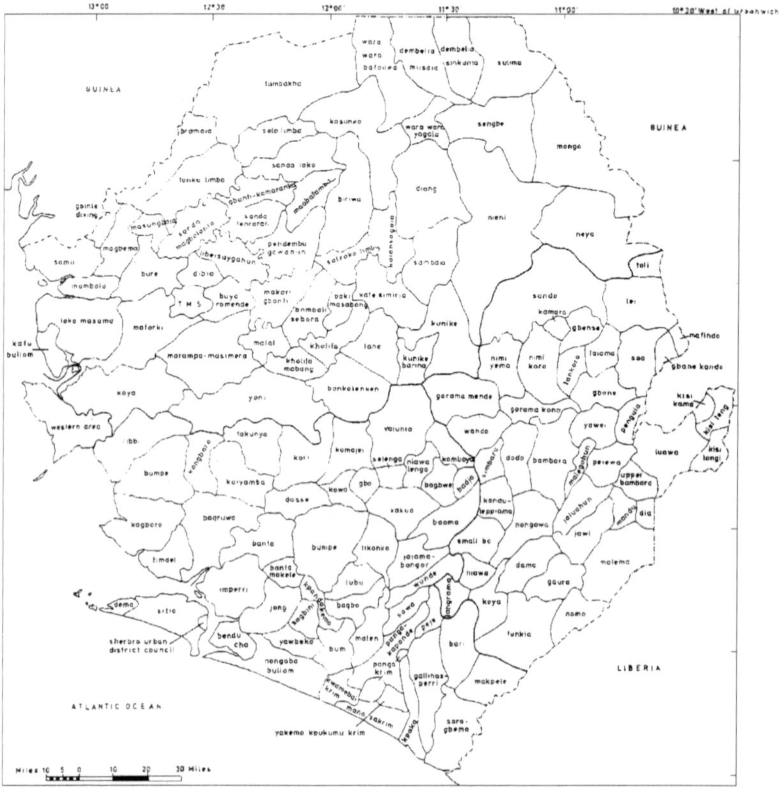

Map 3 Chiefdom boundaries

PART 1
GENERAL INTRODUCTION

CHAPTER 1
BACKGROUND TO LAND TENURE IN SIERRA LEONE

1.1 THE COUNTRY AND ITS PEOPLE
1.1.1 The Country
1.1.2 Name and Location

The name Sierra Leone now uniformly applies to the two distinct territories that formerly constituted the British Crown Colony of Sierra Leone and the Sierra Leone Protectorate and which were united on the attainment of independence in 1961 to form the present sovereign State.[1] Sierra Leone is located on the West Coast of Africa between 6°66′ and 10°00′ north latitude, and 10°16′ and 13°18′ west longitude, bound on the north and north-east by the Republic of Guinea and on the south-east by the Republic of Liberia. The total land area of Sierra Leone is approximately 45,000 square kilometres.[2]

1.1.3 Vegetation and Land Use

The southern half of the country is within the heavy tropical forest belt while the northern interior, with relatively less rainfall, is characterized, to a large extent, by open savannah woodland or grassland mixed with mangrove swamps and featuring the estuaries of seven major rivers. The greater proportion of the land area of Sierra Leone (approximately 26,700 square kilometres) is under closed forest, including a large portion of secondary forest caused by shifting cultivation.

The primary use of the land throughout Sierra Leone is for agricultural exploitation. It is however significant that though an estimated 80 per cent of the population depends on the land for their living, the majority still engage in farming only for subsistence. Traditionally, the average individual farm size did not exceed five or six acres and the use of mechanical or even animal powered cultivators and harvesters is still

1 In the early history of the country the name "Sierra Leone" and its derivative "Sierra Leonean" referred only to the former Crown Colony and its inhabitants.

2 For a more detailed geographical description see: J.T. Clarke, *Sierra Leone in Maps*.

relatively uncommon. Farmers tend to cultivate only such areas as they can effectively manage. Another reason for the relatively small size of individual farms is that farmers depend, in most cases, on the seasonal distribution of family or communal lands, and it would be unusual for an individual's allocation to be at great variance with the average.

In areas where the family as a unit cultivates a farm as a sort of joint venture, the farms tend to be much larger. This is also true of areas where swamplands have been reclaimed for farming and where plantation-type crops, such as coffee, ginger or cocoa, are grown, whether by individuals, family groups or co-operatives. Finally, the recent drive by Government to increase agricultural production has led to large-scale exploitations on land leased to individuals and other entities.

Perhaps the single most important factor affecting agricultural production and land use in Sierra Leone is the practice of "*bush fallow*" or shifting cultivation. In practice, this means that at any one time a vast expanse of agricultural land is left to lie fallow without any form of active cultivation in an attempt to get the soil to regain its fertility. This process not only significantly reduces the amount of agricultural land available for allocation to families and individuals but is also very demanding on human resources. Technically, shifting cultivation involves the annual brushing of "new" patches of secondary bush followed by the burning of the cleared dry bush before the usual cultivation process starts.

The duration and pattern of bush fallow vary from area to area and are largely dependent on the type of crops grown and the inherent fertility of the particular farm territory. Thus, in the relatively fertile western lowlands, the fallow period ranges from six to ten years. In the south and east of the country, the increase in cash crops production and the adoption of modern farming methods have tended to lead to the reduction in the fallow periods as lands once left under fallow are progressively being put under permanent cash crop plantations. Finally, the trend towards enlarging the traditional farm bush[3] usually leads either to shorter periods of bush fallow or to migration in search of fresh farm lands outside the traditional areas.

In particular, the practice of shifting cultivation and the resulting shortages of suitable farm land have led to an increase in demand for inland valley swamps. Enterprising individuals who fail to secure an allocation of communal or family lands sufficient for their personal needs resort to acquiring their own farms, a trend which is partly responsible

3 Farm lands are usually expressed and measured in terms of "farm bushes".

for the individualization of tenure. However, as indicated below, the population drift from the rural to urban areas has meant that the pressure on agricultural land has not reached such alarming proportions as would have otherwise been expected.

1.2 THE POPULATION OF SIERRA LEONE

1.2.1 Population Size and Growth

It is estimated that the present (2009) total population of Sierra Leone is over five million. According to the last population census in 2004 the total was fixed at 4,976,871.[4]

In 2006 the growth rate of the population was estimated at about 2.0 per cent,[5] per annum but this is probably much higher now due to the decrease in infant mortality and the overall improvement of health facilities throughout the country. Another significant feature of the population statistics of Sierra Leone is that the urban population appears to be increasing much more rapidly than that of the rural areas, due mainly to net migration to the cities. Thus, the Western Area, with only 694 square kilometres of territory, has a population density of 1,244 persons per square kilometre as compared with Koinadugu District in the Northern Province with a population density of only 21.4 persons per square kilometre over a total area of 12,399 square kilometres.

As shown later in this work, such imbalances in the distribution of the population and the disparities and anomalies in respect of access to land in different areas have had an adverse effect on the agricultural production of the country and on its overall economic development. In particular, the scarcity of arable land in some parts, for example the Western Area, and its inaccessibility in others have contributed to a large extent to the marked decline in agricultural production which Sierra Leone is experiencing today.

The main population movements also tend to be in response to shifting economic opportunities. Thus, after the discovery of diamonds in Kono and iron ore in Tonkolili, these districts presented new opportunities for wage earning and employment outside the agricultural sector and therefore attracted large numbers of migrants from other areas.

4 Unpublished figures obtained from Statistics Sierra Leone.

5 Cf. the figure for 1967 cited by Ralph Saylor, *The Economic System of Sierra Leone.*

1.2.2 Ethnic Distribution

Despite these movements from the rural and agricultural areas to the urban and mining areas, the distribution of population according to ethnic grouping is fairly well settled today. With the exception of the nomadic Foulah, who consistently cross and re-cross the northern border between Guinea and Sierra Leone, no large scale tribal migrations have occurred in recent years.

The indigenous population is composed of thirteen different ethnic groups. The two main groups are the Mende and the Temne, who together constitute approximately 63 per cent of the population. These are followed in terms of numbers by the Limba and Kono. The rest of the indigenous population is accounted for by nine other minor ethnic groups, viz. the Susu, Yalunka, Loko, Sherbro, Krim, Gola Gallina, Koranko and Kissi.[6]

The Creoles, the detribalized descendants of the heterogeneous group of early settlers in the former Colony, are generally regarded as non-indigenous and constitute less than 4 per cent of the population. Their status with regard to rights in provincial lands will be discussed at other stages of this work.

1.3 POLITICAL AND ADMINISTRATIVE DIVISIONS

1.3.1 Administrative Divisions

Sierra Leone is divided for administrative purposes[7] into four main regions as follows:

i. The Western Area;
ii. The Northern Province;
iii. The Southern Province; and
iv. The Eastern Province.

The three Provinces are in turn sub-divided into twelve districts:

i. Bombali, Kambia, Koinadugu, Port Loko and Tonkolili in the Northern Province;
ii. Bo, Bonthe, Moyamba and Pujehun in the Southern Province; and

---

6 See Map 1 showing the distribution of the ethnic groups at p. xxxvi

7 See Map 2 showing administrative divisions at p. xxxvii.

iii. Kailahun, Kenema and Kono in the Eastern Province.

Under the Local Government Act, No. 1 of 2004, each of the twelve districts is declared to be a locality within the meaning of the Act. The corresponding locality in the Western Area, for this purpose, is described as the Western Area Rural District. In addition to these thirteen localities, for local government purposes, there are five towns (Bo, Bonthe, Kenema, Koidu/New Sembehun and Makeni Town), and the capital City of Freetown, which are municipalities. The provincial districts are in turn divided into 149 chiefdoms – the basic units of native administration in the Provinces – each headed politically by a paramount chief.

1.3.2 The Western Area

Geographically, this region corresponds to the territory of the former Colony of Sierra Leone. It includes the capital city, Freetown, and a number of suburban villages scattered around the peninsula, as well as the islands of Banana and Plantain and the enclave located within the Bonthe Town Council. The Western Area is unique and distinct from the Provinces in many respects. As will be shown below, its peculiar colonial history and political development have led to the absence from this region of the usual traditional African institutions. Secondly, though the Western Area has an admixture of population and is now settled by all the indigenous ethnic groups, yet over the years, it has come to be regarded as the traditional home of the Creoles. The Creoles are distinguishable from the other indigenous ethnic groups by the fact that they speak no African language and have always lived a detribalized mode of life.[8]

1.3.3 Natives and Non-Natives

This difference in social background between the Creoles and the rest of the indigenous population has been further widened by the fact that the Creoles are classified by certain statutes as "non-natives", as in the case of the Provinces Land Act, Cap. 122 as amended by the Act No. 20 of 1972, for the purpose of land tenure in the Provinces. This statute defines a non-native as any person "*not entitled under customary law to rights in land in a Province*". As will be shown later, entitlement to rights in land

8 The Creoles speak a dialect known locally as "Krio" which is the lingua franca used throughout Sierra Leone.

in the Provinces under customary law is determined on the basis of patri-descent, so that, since the majority of Creoles have no patrilineal affinity with indigenous Sierra Leoneans, they are classified as non-natives for the purposes of land holding under the Provinces Land Act and are therefore precluded by its provisions from acquiring any interest in land in the Provinces greater than a tenancy for a term of fifty years.[9]

Joko Smart has argued in a contribution to the *Annual Survey of African Law*,[10] that the distinction between "natives" and "non natives" no longer applies to the Creoles as a result of the provisions of the Sierra Leone Citizenship Act 1973, which now defines a "native" as:

> *"a citizen of Sierra Leone who is a member of a race, tribe or community settled in Sierra Leone, other than a race, tribe or community which is of European or Asiatic or American origin".*[11]

This definition amends and replaces that contained in Section 4(1) of the Interpretation Act, No. 8 of 1971, which excluded from the classification of natives persons "*whose principal place of settlement* [was] *in the Western Area*", that is Creoles.

Though we agree with Joko Smart that Creoles could now be classified as natives for some purposes, we most respectfully do not share the view that they are to be regarded as natives "*for all purposes*". Though the Interpretation Act defines a non-native as "*any person other than a native*", the term "*non-native*" for the purpose of the Province Land Act, Cap. 122 has a specific meaning, that is "*any person not entitled under customary law to rights in land in a Province*". This definition was inserted into the Provinces Land Act by an amendment contained in Act No. 29 of 1972. Since this amending statute was enacted later than the Interpretation Act of 1971 the presumption is that the legislature intended to provide a specific definition of a non-native for the purpose of the Provinces Land Act different from the existing definition contained in the Interpretation Act. Moreover, since the Sierra Leone Citizenship Act 1973 does not purport to alter this definition of a non-native it follows that Creoles could still be classified as non-natives except where they can show that they are entitled under customary law, that is by birth, to rights in lands in a Province.

9 This is the effect of section 4 of the Provinces Land Act, Cap. 122.

10 (1973), Vol. viii, p.82.

11 Section 29 of Sierra Leone Citizenship Act, No. 4 of 1973.

To revert to the distinction between the Western Area and the Provinces, whereas there is a statutory restriction on the nature and quantum of interests which non-natives may acquire in land in the Provinces, there is no such restriction imposed on natives in respect of lands in the Western Area.

This partly accounts for the fact that the Western Area, as a region, has the highest concentration of population per square kilometre. Moreover, the fact that the total land area of the Western Area only covers 346 square kilometres has meant that there is an ever increasing pressure on land for residential and other purposes. This scarcity of land has led to much speculation and an escalation in the value of development land, with hardly any or no land being reserved for agriculture. Agricultural production in the Western Area is thus confined to vegetable and market farming, as well as small scale plantations of fruit trees in some of the suburban villages. The continued existence of vast tracts of land classified as "*State land*" and "*Forest Reserves*" has also helped to aggravate the land problem in the Western Area.

1.3.4 Local Government in the Western Area

For local government purposes the Western Area is divided into two localities:

1. First, the Municipality of Freetown established by Statutory Instrument No. 15 of 2005 made by the President pursuant to powers vested in him by section 2(2) of the Local Government Act, No.1 of 2004. The City of Freetown comprises an area set out in the Schedule to the Statutory Instrument and is virtually coterminous with the former Municipality of Freetown established by the now repealed Freetown Municipality Act 1973; and
2. The Western Area Rural District established by Statutory Instrument No. 16 of 2005 made by the President pursuant to powers vested in him by section 2(2) of the Local Government Act 2004 and comprising an area set out in the Schedule to the said Statutory Instrument. This territory is virtually coterminous with the former Rural Area established under the

now repealed Rural Area Act, Cap. 75 of the Laws of Sierra Leone 1960.

The City of Freetown is administered by the Freetown City Council consisting of 32 elected Councillors, four for each ward in the City.

The 2004 Act provides for the election of a Mayor in addition to the Councillors. The functions of the City Council are however very limited and have no direct bearing on land use and policy in the Western Area. The Western Area Rural District is now administered by the Western Area District Council consisting of sixteen elected Councillors, one from each ward in the District. In addition to the Councillors, there is elected for every village or town set out in the fourth column of the Schedule to the Statutory Instrument No.16 of 2005 a head whose functions include co-operating "*with the Western Area District Council or such other relevant body in the surveying, registration or leasing of land in the village or town*". The functions of the village or town head in respect of lands in the Western Area should be distinguished from those of the chiefdom council in respect of provincial lands by virtue of the Provinces Land Act, Cap. 122.

Though there is no provision for a system of native administration as such in the Western Area, under the Tribal Administration (Western Area) Act, Cap. 78, each ethnic group resident in the Western Area may elect a tribal head recognized by the Central Government. The duties of these tribal headmen include assistance in the collection of local taxes; liaison between the Government and the various tribal communities in matters of local as well as national concern; and adjudication in disputes arising out of customary marriages.[12] There is also provision in the Administration of Estates Act, Cap. 45,[13] for the Administrator-General to seek guidance from tribal headmen in the Western Area in the ascertainment of the persons entitled under customary law to share in the residue of the estate of a native who dies intestate leaving assets in the Western Area which, pursuant to the Act, should be distributed in accordance with customary law. Subject to what has been stated above, the Tribal Administration (Western Area) Act, Cap. 78, expressly provides that no tribal headman in the Western Area is to exercise any jurisdiction, civil or criminal, of any nature whatsoever in respect of members of his tribe. Contravention of this provision is an offence. However, the traditional courts established under

12 See section 10(2) of Cap. 78 as amended

13 Section 43(2) as amended by Act No. 16 of 1976.

the Local Courts Act, No. 20 of 1963, have no jurisdiction in the Western Area nor is customary law applicable therein.

Before leaving the Western Area, a word ought to be said about the Bonthe Town Council. This Council, formerly the Sherbro Urban District Council, was administered as part of the Western Area, but geographically was in the Southern Province. The new Bonthe Town Council was established by Statutory Instrument No. 26 of 2005 made by the President pursuant to powers vested in him by section 2(2) of the Local Government Act 2004 and comprising an area set out in the Schedule to the said Statutory Instrument and virtually coterminous with the former Sherbro Urban District established by the now repealed Sherbro Urban District Council Act, Cap. 76 of the Laws of Sierra Leone 1960. The Sherbro Urban Council consists of twelve Councillors elected from the three wards in Bonthe Town. Its population is for the most part made up of Sherbro and Mende, with a small proportion of members from the other ethnic groups. There are no native chiefs and no system of native administration.

1.3.5 The Provinces

As stated above,[14] the bulk of the land area, and the majority of the population, of Sierra Leone are to be found within the territorial limits of the Provinces. The area covered by the Provinces is approximately the same as that of the former Protectorate. The three Provinces are divided into twelve districts and further sub-divided into 149 chiefdoms.

1.3.6 Provincial Administration

In addition to the system of native administration centred around the institution of chieftaincy, there is a system of local administration undertaken by the central government with a Provincial Secretary responsible for co-ordinating the activities of government officials throughout each Province. The most important official in terms of local administration is now the Local Council Chief Administrator appointed pursuant to section 31 of the Local Government Act 2004. This is so because since the coming into force of the latter statute it has been generally assumed that the Chief Administrators of each of the twelve District Councils in the Provinces are meant to replace and perform the functions of the District Officers. It is

14 See page 5.

doubtful whether there is any legal basis for this assumption particularly when one considers the functions of a District Officer as far as matters relating to land tenure in the Provinces are concerned. According to the Provinces Act, Cap. 60[15] (which incidentally was not expressly repealed by the Local Government Act 2004), a District Officer and his superior, the Provincial Secretary, were vested by that statute with authority to control native institutions, and in this regard, they played a key role in the implementation of the land policy of the Government. In particular, section 28 of Cap. 60 provides, inter alia, as follows:

> *"A District Officer shall have power and authority to inquire into and decide as hereafter provided any matters which have their origin in poro[16] laws, native rites or customs, land disputes, including land disputes arising between paramount chiefs, or any other disputes which, if not promptly settled, might lead to breaches of the peace."*

Under subsection (4) of the latter section the Provincial Secretary had power to review, vary or set aside the decision of the District Officer. Otherwise the decision was to be transcribed into the District Decree Book and remain binding on all interested parties.

More importantly, for the purpose of access to land in the Provinces, section 3(2) of the Provinces Land Act, Cap. 122, stipulates that the approval of the District Officer is a prerequisite for the occupation of land by non-natives within a district. The District Officer is also vested with power under the latter statute to review the amount paid as rent in respect of leases granted under the Act and to supervise and authenticate the execution of all such leases, if made by deed. Since the enactment of the Local Government Act 2004 it is now common practice for the Chief Administrator of the local council where the land is located to perform the latter functions vested in the District Officer. This is despite the fact that under the Local Government Act 2004, the functions of the Local Council Chief Administrator is limited to the following (section 31(4)):

15 See section 2 of the Provinces Act, Cap. 60 where it is provided that a Provinces Secretary shall be *virtute officii* a District Officer and shall have all the powers of a District Officer for every District within his Province.

16 "Poro" is a traditional male secret cultural society with much influence in land matters.

> *"(a) … the financial and other resource management and the day-to-day administration of the local council;*
> *(b) … the implementation of all lawful decisions of the local council;*
> *(c) … assist and advise the Chairperson in the performance of his functions;*
> *(d) [supervision and co-ordination of] the activities of the other staff and Departments of the local council;*
> *(e) … custody of all documents and records of the local council;*
> *(f) … such other functions as the local council or Chairperson may determine; and*
> *(g) [to] ensure that staff performance standards are met."*

Under the District Council Act, Cap. 79, which was repealed by the Local Government Act 2004, there was no such office as Local Council Chief Administrator. The nearest equivalent was the Secretary of the District Council appointed pursuant to section 35(1) of Cap. 79 with very limited powers. Indeed, it is clear from section 41(1) that the District Officer who was appointed by the central government rather than being accountable to the former District Council exercised authority over its members. Thus section 41(1) empowered a District Officer to appoint one or more members of a District Council "*to inquire into and report upon* [inter alia] *any boundary dispute within his district*".

In the absence of any express provision in the Local Government Act 2004 empowering the Local Council Chief Administrator to exercise the above and other statutory functions of the former District Officer in respect of provincial land matters, it is submitted that the present practice is without any legal foundation.

1.3.7 The Chiefdoms

The basic unit of local and native administration in the Provinces is the Chiefdom. Each chiefdom is an autonomous, territorial, as well as socio-political unit, headed by a paramount chief who traditionally is chosen from one of the "ruling houses", that is one of the descent groups whose ancestors are reputed to have "founded" the chiefdom. [17]

17 See Map 3 on p. xxxviii for the chiefdom boundaries.

However, in recent times it is not unheard of for persons totally unconnected with ruling houses to be elected as paramount chiefs because of their wealth, personal influence or political connections.

The chiefdoms vary in size in terms of their land area and of their population. However, even the largest chiefdoms nowhere approach the size and political organizations of, for example, the highly centralized Ashanti or Yoruba states in Ghana and Nigeria respectively. Structurally, each chiefdom is composed of a number of "*sections*", each section being headed by a section-chief or sub-chief subordinate to the paramount chief. Again, the number of constituent sections within any chiefdom may vary according to its size and population. The area of the section-chief's jurisdiction constitutes, as it were, a sub-chiefdom, and is governed on similar lines to the parent unit.

Each section of a chiefdom is further sub-divided into smaller units of "*towns*" or villages under the traditional rule of a town chief or village headman responsible immediately to the section chief, but owing ultimate allegiance to the paramount chief.

The socio-legal significance of the typical "*town*" or village within a chiefdom lies in the fact that it is both a political as well as a kinship organization made up of several descent groups with its members linked by bonds of affinity or consanguinity to a common ancestor, the reputed founder of the "*town*" or village. Thus, though the chiefdom is not strictly a kinship organization, membership thereof is derived by birth and descent traced patrilineally or matrilineally to one of the founding ancestors of the towns and villages which together constitute the chiefdom.

Each member of the chiefdom therefore becomes entitled to succeed to rights in land or to hold elective office by virtue of his birth into one of the families which originally settled in the chiefdom.

1.3.8 Paramount Chiefs

The chiefdom is also a political unit over which the paramount chief exercises political jurisdiction, with each member of the chiefdom ultimately owing allegiance to the paramount chief, even if specific acts of allegiance are sometimes translated through a hierarchy of subordinate traditional rulers. By tradition, allegiance to the chief was expressed in a number of ways, such as the payment of customary tribute in the form of a proportion of one's farm produce, or by joining in communal chiefdom labour (*nd-yenge* in Mende). In former times, the paramount chief, in turn, acted as a military protector of his people and was also responsible for the civil administration of his chiefdom. He combined legislative, judicial and executive powers in his rule and was generally responsible for the maintenance of social and political order within his chiefdom. In this, he was assisted by the principal elders in the chiefdom and various other officials, such as the Chiefdom Speaker[18] who also acted as Regent Chief during an interregnum.

Together with section chiefs, town chiefs and village headmen, these officials and elders served as the paramount chief's council, and the paramount chief was supposed to consult them as a body over matters affecting the chiefdom as a whole, such as the alienation of communal lands to an outsider. However, invariably, the paramount chief always acted after consultation with only a smaller group, or inner council consisting of the speaker, the section chiefs and a varying number of influential elders within the chiefdom. In the modern chiefdom, however, most of the powers and duties of the paramount chief have been transferred to the statutory body known as the chiefdom council (formally known as the Tribal Authority). Matters such as legislation, administration of justice and finance are now within the purview of the chiefdom councils. In particular, the right to hear and determine cases arising under customary law has been taken away from the traditional courts of the chiefs and sub-chiefs and transferred to the Local Courts. The role of chiefs in the adjudication of disputes arising within their chiefdoms is now limited to informal arbitration with the consent of the parties, and to their membership of the panel of the Group Local Appeal Courts set up by statute. The power of control, management and protection of communal/chiefdom lands is now shared with the chiefdom council of which the paramount chief is merely a chief executive. The social and political authority of the paramount chief has considerably diminished due mainly to the fact that the office is no longer exclusively hereditary but is now, to a very large extent, elective. Moreover, chieftaincy elections are increasingly being dominated by wider political considerations that sometimes have no bearing on matters relating to the particular chiefdom, but are merely extensions of issues from the national political scene. Paramount chiefs are now increasingly being regarded as an arm of the central Government, especially as they depend on the latter for their basic emoluments, having lost many of the rights and privileges to demand or receive various forms of customary tributes in cash or kind and other perquisites of office.

---

18 *Lavalie* in Mende or *Kumrabai* in Temne.

Yet, despite this relative decline of the authority of the paramount chiefs, the political and social organization of the indigenous population is centred around the chiefdom and, to a large extent, both still hinge on the institution of chieftaincy, particularly in relation to the acquisition and preservation of rights and interests in land within the chiefdom.

Finally, the importance of the chiefdom lies in the fact that each chiefdom is an independent and autonomous unit for the purposes of the administration of justice under the traditional system. There is a Local Court established for each chiefdom, with jurisdiction co-extensive territorially with that of the chiefdom for which it is established. Moreover, rules of customary law are by statute defined with reference to chiefdoms and are only applicable within a particular chiefdom if they have been recognized as having the force of law therein. However, this does not mean the existence of separate and distinct bodies of law for the various chiefdoms, rather, customary law has evolved along tribal lines, with local variations arising out of the particular needs and circumstances of individual chiefdoms. It is therefore more usual to speak of Mende or Temne customary law that to speak of the customary law of *X* or *Y* chiefdom.

1.4 HISTORICAL BACKGROUND TO THE DUAL LAND TENURE SYSTEM

1.4.1 Introduction

This historical account does not seek to relate the detailed history of the former Colony and Protectorate of Sierra Leone but merely to present, as briefly as possible, certain landmarks in the political history of the country, a knowledge of which should assist the reader to fully understand the origins of the present dual land tenure system of Sierra Leone.[19] The main emphasis for our purposes, therefore, will be on the contrasting colonial experiences of the two territories that came together to make up independent Sierra Leone. As will be shown below, what is now the Western Area was until independence a British Colony, an integral part of the British Empire, with its entire territory considered as a British possession, and its inhabitants British subjects. On the other hand, the former Protectorate (now Provinces) was essentially considered as foreign territory over which the British Crown exercised limited sovereignty,

19 For a detailed historical account the reader is referred to standard texts such as Christopher Fyfe's *History of Sierra Leone*.

without ever claiming *dominium* over its lands. As a result, its inhabitants only acquired the status of British protected persons.

1.4.2 From Settlement to Crown Colony

The founding of the Colony was inextricably linked with the campaign for the abolition of the slave trade and with the work of certain British humanitarians and philanthropists such as William Wilberforce, Granville Sharpe and Henry Thornton, towards the end of the 18th century.

The British had previously established fortified trading stations along the "*Guinea Coast*" of West Africa near the area of the Sierra Leone Peninsula. These "*factories*" (so called because they were manned by factors and agents) were built on lands that had been rented from the native African rulers. This was the period of the "*landlord-stranger*" relationship between the Europeans and the Africans.[20] The coastal region of Sierra Leone, with its natural harbour facilities, and the well populated adjacent territories provided ideal conditions for the trade in goods and slaves carried on by European agents and African rulers alike. British Chartered Companies[21] had established factories in places like Sherbro, Bunce and Tasso Islands off the Sierra Leone mainland.

An important event for the anti-slavery movement was the judgment delivered in England by Lord Mansfield in the case of *Somerset v. Steward*[22] in which he asserted that the institution of slavery was unknown to the laws of England. As a result of this decision, a large number of ex-slaves from the West Indies and elsewhere were attracted into Britain, thus aggravating the social problem caused by the already large number of blacks then in Britain.[23] To relieve the situation a scheme was devised, on the advice of a Dr. Henry Smeathan,[24] whereby those "*black poor*" were to be settled on a territory to be acquired somewhere in the area of the Sierra Leone Peninsula.

---

20 See article by V.R. Dorjahan and C. Fyfe in *Journal of African History*, 1962(3), pp. 391–7.

21 For example, the Company of Adventurers, the Royal Company, and the Company of Merchants Trading in Africa, to name only a few.

22 (1772) Lofft 1.

23 These were the so-called "Black Poor" see Fyfe, op. cit.

24 Smeathan was a naturalist who had spent four years working in the vicinity of Sierra Leone.

1.4.3 Acquisition of the Settlement

With assistance from the British Government and a few philanthropists, the first batch of settlers consisting of 351 freed slaves and 60 Europeans, mostly women, left England in 1786 for Sierra Leone. On arrival the leader of the expedition, a British naval captain named Thompson, concluded a treaty with one of the local rulers, King Tom of the Temne kingdom of Koya, whereby the latter purported to grant a piece of territory, measuring 20 square miles (32 square kilometres) approximately, as the site for the new settlement.

Though the grant was said to be made "*on behalf of and for the sole benefit of the free community of settlers*", the status of the land so acquired was not immediately clear. The settlement itself, however, was intended by its founders to be self-governing.[25] This attempt to establish an independent settlement soon failed in the face of hostility from the neighbouring natives.

1.4.4 The Company Government

In the meantime, in 1791, Granville Sharpe, William Wilberforce, Thomas Clarkson and other philanthropists, who had been associated with abolition of the slave trade and the relief of the "*black poor*", formed the Saint Georges Bay Association, later incorporated as the Saint Georges Bay Company. Among the declared objects of the new Company was a desire "*to colonize a small part of the coast of Africa ... to introduce civilization among the natives ... and to govern all equally according to the laws of England*". Henceforth, all settlers arriving from Great Britain were to be allotted plots of land in the settlement against a payment of an annual quit rent with the usual reservations respecting mines and minerals being made in favour of the Company.[26]

The fortunes of the settlement improved with the arrival, in 1792, of a group of 1,100 so-called Nova Scotians. The Nova Scotians[27] soon took up arms in protest against the imposition by the Company of the quit rent.

25 The settlement was named Province of Freedom.

26 See "Terms of Sierra Leone Company to the Settlers, 3 November, 1791" C.O. 267/34.

27 The Nova Scotians referred to here were ex-slaves who had previously been settled in Nova Scotia, Canada, after fighting on the side of the British in the American war of Independence.

This revolt was put down by the Company with the assistance of a group of 550 Maroons, ex-slaves newly arrived from Jamaica. This brought a definite end to the experiment of local self-government.

1.4.5 The Crown Colony

In 1799, the Company was granted a royal charter, with a Governor-in-Council having legislative powers. At the same time, so much of the peninsula as was vested in the Crown was granted to the Company:

> *"with full power to purchase from all having right to make sale thereof, so much land in addition thereto as shall include the whole tract commonly known by the name of the Peninsula of Sierra Leone, all which lands so granted are hereby created one independent Colony, by the name of the 'Colony of Sierra Leone'."*[28]

However, the Company suffered many setbacks and was unable to administer the new Colony without substantial financial assistance from the British Government. In 1807, the Sierra Leone Company relinquished the government and management of the Colony and surrendered to the British Crown all its possessions and rights over lands in the Sierra Leone Peninsula.[29] In 1808, Sierra Leone became a Crown Colony.

Further campaigns mounted in England by the Abolitionists had led to an Act of Parliament, in 1807, declaring the slave trade illegal. Freetown was chosen as the site for a Vice-Admiralty Court with jurisdiction to try the owners and crew of captured slave ships. The slaves from the captured ships were settled in Freetown where they became known as "*Re-Captives*" or "*Liberated Africans*". This necessitated the expansion of the Colony and the acquisition of further territory in the immediate neighbourhood of Freetown. Between 1809 and 1819 several settlements sprang up in places still bearing such names as Leicester, Wilberforce, Regent, Gloucester, Charlotte, York and Kent. These developments were made possible because, in 1807, a peace treaty had been signed between the Government of the Colony and the neighbouring Temne rulers to bring an end to the incessant attacks by the Temne seeking to dislodge the settlers and repossess their lands.

28 See C. Newbury, *British Policy Towards West Africa: Selected Documents 1786–1874*.

29 See the Sierra Leone Company Transfer Act 1807 (47 Geo. III C. 44).

The territory of the Colony was further enlarged by the acquisition of the Sherbro, Banana and York Islands by treaties of cession made with local chiefs. By 1820, the Colony's population consisted of the survivors of the original settlers, the Nova Scotians, Maroons and Re-Captives, whose title to lands allotted by the Company had been not only confirmed by the new administration but also converted into a form of freehold by the issue of Crown Grants in fee simple. To these there came to be added an ever-increasing number of the indigenous population from the neighbouring tribes such as the Temne, Mende, Madingos, Susu, Foulah and Kroo who simply occupied available lands within the Colony without any formal grants or other claims of right. This was the beginning of the squatter problem which is still prevalent in the Western Area today.

1.4.6 Towards the Declaration of a Protectorate over Territories Adjacent to the Colony

The importance of a study of the early history of the Protectorate lies in the insight it gives one into the land policy of the colonial administration, which consisted broadly of a retention of the indigenous land tenure structure combined with the imposition of administrative controls on alienation of lands by natives.

Original contact with the hinterland was through trade which the peoples of the Colony came to depend on as farming did not yield much profit for them. These contacts by the Creole settlers soon went further into the interior than the immediate Temne territory of Koya. Later, the Government of the Colony, in an effort to improve the Colony's trade, also sent trade missions into the interior and even went so far, sometimes, as to interfere in the local politics of the indigenous peoples. In particular, it was anxious to halt the inter-tribal wars that had hitherto been actively encouraged by the slave traders. However despite these periodic incursions, the Colony Government found it increasingly difficult to give protection to its subjects who frequently encountered open hostility and suffered serious economic losses in these neighbouring territories. As a result, there were repeated but unsuccessful demands by certain leading Creole spokesmen in the Colony for the extension of British influence and control over the neighbouring country by the annexation of more territory. The official British colonial policy remained opposed to such extension, largely, it would seem, because of the added responsibilities and expense that this would have entailed.

However, another factor that hastened the declaration of a Protectorate was the presence and policy of the French in the neighbouring territories in West Africa. From their base in Senegal, they were active in expanding their influence by the signing of so-called treaties of "*sovereignty and protection*" with local rulers.

The interests of the two colonial powers were also likely to clash as the French pursued the defeated Samori Toure, a Madingo warrior, who had overrun large sections of territory in the Sierra Leone hinterland between 1870 and 1890. The threat of Freetown being hemmed in prompted the British to hold consultations with the French in 1882 that led to a convention that fixed a boundary between the Scarcies and Malacoure rivers demarcating their respective spheres of influence. This was also the period of the "Scramble for Africa" when European powers with interests in Africa signed treaties that were to define most of the present boundaries of African States. One such treaty signed between the French and the British delimited their respective spheres of influence in the Sierra Leone hinterland and fixed the eastern boundary at 14° west longitude.

Meanwhile, the British had modified their original policy of non-expansion and went on to sign treaties of "*peace unity and commerce*" with local rulers within their sphere on influence. There were no more treaties of cession of territories. The standard treaty, however, did contain a clause that no native ruler was to cede his territory "*except through and with the consent of the Government of Her Majesty*". In August 1895, by an Order-in-Council made under the Foreign Jurisdiction Act, 1890, the British Crown "*acquired jurisdiction in foreign countries adjoining the* [Sierra Leone] *Colony*". This was followed by a Proclamation issued on 31 August 1896 declaring a Protectorate over an area of territory about 43,400 square kilometres within the British sphere of influence in the Sierra Leone hinterland.

The immediate legal consequence of the proclamation of a Protectorate was that, henceforth, the inhabitants acquired the status of British protected persons under the sovereignty of the British Crown. The Legislative Council of the Colony was also to be the legislative authority for the Protectorate. One of the first laws to be enacted was the Protectorate Ordinance 1896. This defined the administrative and judicial system which was to apply in the Protectorate. It recognized the jurisdiction of the native chiefs and their courts but also introduced a series of British-type courts to handle serious crimes and specific civil matters. The same Ordinance of 1896 asserted the right of the Crown to all rights in minerals, metals and precious stones but did not claim any specific rights of "superior" ownership over native lands in the Protectorate.

1.4.7 British Policy on Protectorate Land

Between 1901 and 1945 the Colonial Government had adopted a policy of *indirect rule* of the Protectorate that was to continue right up to independence in 1961. Throughout this period hardly any attempt was made by legislation or otherwise to alter the status of Protectorate lands. In 1927 the Protectorate Land Ordinance (now the Provinces Land Act, Cap. 122) was enacted to regulate the exercise by the former Tribal Authorities (now chiefdom councils) of their power to permit the use and occupation of Protectorate land by non-natives. In the preamble to this Ordinance it was declared, for the first time, that all lands in the Protectorate were vested in the Tribal Authority who held such land for and on behalf of the native communities concerned. "*Tribal Authority*" was defined by the Ordinance as the "*Paramount Chiefs and their Councilors and men of note, or sub-chiefs and their Councilors, and men of note*". Save for minor amendments, the provisions of this Ordinance continue to be in force and this is virtually the only legislation relating to land tenure in the Provinces.

The Concessions Ordinance of 1937 (now Concessions Act, Cap. 121), which applied both to Colony and Protectorate, was also intended to restrict the freedom of the Tribal Authorities to grant concessions of Protectorate land for agricultural purposes. It was laid down that no Tribal Authority or any other native was to have the power to alienate land for the purpose of cultivation except under the provisions of this Ordinance and the Protectorate Land Ordinance of 1927. The Governor's consent was necessary for any grants or dispositions and he was only to sanction concessions of up to 1,000 acres if he was satisfied that the grant was for the benefit of the chiefdom, or in respect of larger areas, if for the benefit of the whole country. The Concessions Ordinance also provided that under no circumstances may a Tribal Authority or any native alienate land exceeding fifty acres for any longer term than ninety-nine years, unless it was to the Colonial Government for a public purpose.

1.4.8 Towards Political Unification of the Colony and Protectorate

After the failure of the attempt at local self-rule for the Province of Freedom and following the period of transition under the Sierra Leone Company, the Colony, from 1808 onwards, was administered by a Governor assisted by a Council. The Governor-in-Council acted as both the legislative and executive arm of government until 1863 when a new constitution separated the two functions by creating two distinct Councils, the Legislative and the Executive. This constitution with slight amendments continued in force till 1924 when the so-called "Slater" constitution was introduced. The 1924 constitution enlarged and reconstituted the Legislative Council bringing in for the first time Protectorate representation. This was part of a series of moves aimed at bringing the two entities of Colony and Protectorate closer together politically.

As far as the Protectorate was concerned, the next major development was the enactment of Ordinance No. 27 of 1945 which provided for the establishment of District Councils and a Protectorate Assembly. Further, by Ordinance No. 2 of 1954, every Ordinance enacted on or after 1 July 1953 was to apply to both Colony and Protectorate unless otherwise stated therein. The Legislative Council had been reconstituted in 1951 to reflect an increased Protectorate representation. However, while the elected members from the Colony were elected directly by popular vote those from the Protectorate were elected indirectly through the District Councils and the Protectorate Assembly.

1.4.9 Independence and Republican Status

Independence was granted by the British to both the Colony and the Protectorate on 27 April 1961.[30] By the Independence Constitution of 1961 a common Sierra Leonean citizenship was created in respect of all persons who had been born in the former Colony or Protectorate of Sierra Leone and who were on 26 April 1961 citizens of the United Kingdom and Colonies or British Protected Persons.[31] Elections to the House of Representatives were held in 1962 and 1967 on the basis of universal adult suffrage. The aftermath of the 1967 elections marked a change in the

30 See the Sierra Leone Independence Act 1961 (9 & 10 Eliz. II C. 16.)

31 See section 1 of the Sierra Leone (Constitution) Order in Council, Public Notice No. 78 of 1961.

political direction of the country as a democratic change of government was rendered impossible by a military coup. After the military interregnum ended in 1968, the All People's Congress, which had narrowly defeated the Sierra Leone's Peoples Party in the 1967 elections, quickly consolidated its hold over the country, transforming it into a Republic in 1971, and into a one-party system of Government in 1978, under the 1978 Constitution.

However, despite the departure from "*Westminster-type*" democracy the 1978 Constitution still preserved all the so-called fundamental rights and freedoms of the individual including the freedom to hold property and protection from the expropriation without payment of adequate compensation.

The year 1991 was a turning point in the political and constitutional history of Sierra Leone. It marked the commencement of the brutal civil war when a group of Revolutionary United Forces (RUF) rebels under the leadership of the notorious Foday Sankoh invaded the country from Liberia. In that same year the ruling All People's Congress renounced the one-party system of government and introduced a new constitution enacted as Act No.6 of 1991. However, even before the projected multi-party elections could be held the Joseph Saidu Momoh regime was ousted in a military coup organized by a group of young officers who had been deployed to drive out the rebels.

The National Provisional Ruling Council (NPRC) interregnum ended in 1996 without the military regime fulfilling its promise to end the rebel war which by then had spread to most of the Provinces. Almost a year after being elected to office the Sierra Leone People's Party (SLPP) government under the leadership of Ahmad Tejan Kabbah was toppled in yet another *coup d'état* that saw the installation of the Armed Forces Revolutionary Council (AFRC) junta. Unlike the NPRC junta the AFRC coup met with widespread resistance right from the start, mainly because of the brutality unleashed upon innocent civilians by the members of the AFRC and the RUF rebel forces, who had been invited into Freetown by the AFRC with whom they had formed an unholy alliance.

The AFRC interregnum came to a brutal end and the Kabbah regime was reinstalled following an invasion in February 1998 by so-called ECOMOG forces consisting mostly of the Nigerian military. In January 1999 remnants of the AFRC and the RUF attempted to re-take Freetown but were repelled by the combined efforts of ECOMOG and a British expeditionary force. Since 2001, when the war was formally declared at an end, the country has enjoyed relative peace and stability, which has made it possible for two Presidential and Parliamentary elections to be held in accordance with the provisions of the 1991 Constitution in 2002 and 2007.

The 2002 elections saw the Kabbah-led SLPP Government being returned to power whilst the 2007 elections signalled the first handover of power by one civilian administration to another since independence and the installation of an APC regime under the leadership of Ernest Bai Koroma supported in an informal coalition by the Peoples's Democratic Movement (PMDC) under the leadership of Charles Margai who had broken away from the SLPP.

CHAPTER 2
THE LEGAL SYSTEM AND SOURCES OF LAND LAW IN SIERRA LEONE

2.1 THE LEGAL SYSTEM IN PERSPECTIVE

2.1.1 Introduction

A key factor in the duality of land tenure in Sierra Leone today is the existence within the same jurisdiction of two separate but parallel systems of courts and laws. Sierra Leone is not unique in this respect, as a plural legal system is to be found in most other African countries, such as Ghana and Nigeria, which also have in force a dual system of land tenure. The distinction is that in most other African countries the two systems of tenure tend to exist and even overlap within the same geographical area. In addition, they are invariably administered by an integrated system of courts which apply the various systems of law in accordance with well-defined choice of law rules.

The present legal system in force in Sierra Leone is the product of the different political, historical, social and cultural background of the former Colony and Protectorate. Prior to the colonial era the administration of justice, and the exercise of legislative authority throughout the territory that is now Sierra Leone were centred exclusively in the hands of the native chiefs and other traditional rulers. The common thread which ran through the entire legal system was that it was based entirely on the customs and traditions of the people. Since these customs and traditions varied from tribe to tribe, and from locality to locality, one would expect the traditional legal system to have been marked by a great many disparities and complexities. On the contrary, the legal institutions to be found then were characterized by their relative similarities and simplicity. Disputes, whether regarding land or other matters, were subjected to informal arbitration rather than formal adjudication in courts of law as under the English tradition. Moreover, the laws that were then applied, though unwritten, and therefore not easily accessible and ascertainable, were nonetheless derived from well-established and recognized customs and usages.

These customs and traditions, if not uniform throughout, had significant similarities. For example, in the field of land tenure, the fundamental traditional basis of claims to rights in land, and the methods of transferring interests therein, were basically the same. This situation was destined to change dramatically with the advent of the African settlers and English colonizers in the territory that later became known as the Colony of Sierra Leone.

2.1.2 Introduction of English Legal Institutions in the Former Colony

There appears to be no specific or direct authority for the initial introduction of English law and the establishment of English-type courts in the former Colony. Notions of English law had been first introduced by the early settlers and later by the company government between 1787 and 1808. The English-type courts which were established in the Colony during this period applied the common law then in force in England as well as local Ordinances and Orders-in-Council. Authority for the exercise of legislative power first came from various Charters granted by the English Parliament between 1791 and 1821.[32] In particular, a Charter of 1799 expressly vested in the Directors of the Sierra Leone Company power to make laws (for the Colony) "*not repugnant to those of England*" and to appoint a Governor and Council vested with similar legislative authority.

It was not until 1857 that it was recognized by statute[33] that the laws, that is, the common law and doctrines of equity and the statutes, in force in England, were also to be in force in the Colony. The reception date of 1 January 1857 was advanced by subsequent Ordinances until it was finally fixed at the present date of 1 January 1880.[34]

Once English law had been thus introduced into the Colony, it came to be applied by English-type courts to the exclusion of customary law. Though the customary courts of the native chiefs, which were in existence before the establishment of the settlement, were never formally abolished, there is certainly no evidence that they were ever recognized or retained by the Company or the Colonial Government.

---

32 See, for example, the Charter of Incorporation of the Sierra Leone Company, 31 Geo. III, C. 55.

33 Ordinance No. 96 of 1857.

34 See section 74 of the Courts Act, No. 31 of 1965.

This situation has persisted even after independence. Under the Courts Act 1965, only English-type courts have jurisdiction within the Western Area, and customary law is only applicable by these courts in limited circumstances outlined in section 76 of the Courts Act 1965. Even though the Government recognizes headmen elected by members of the various ethnic groups in the Western Area, their role in the administration of justice is limited to adjudication of disputes arising out of customary marriages.[35] All other matters, whether arising between two natives, or between a native and a non-native, in the Western Area, are subject to the general law as administered exclusively by the English-type courts.

2.1.3 The Protectorate and the Introduction of the English Legal System

Unlike the situation that existed in the former Colony, when English law and legal institutions were introduced in the Sierra Leone hinterland, the indigenous legal system was allowed to co-exist and develop alongside the imported one. The first step in the process of British intervention was an Order-in-Council of 24 August 1895, made under the Foreign Jurisdiction Act 1890, empowering the Legislative Council of the Colony of Sierra Leone to exercise jurisdiction in the territories adjacent to the Colony.[36] This was followed by the proclamation of 31 August 1896, by which the British Government assumed a Protectorate over these territories.

The first piece of legislation relating to the administration of justice in the Protectorate was the Protectorate Ordinance, No. 20 of 1896.[37] This Ordinance among other things formally recognized the jurisdiction of the traditional courts then existing, according to native law and custom at the time and provided for the establishment of three types of courts, namely, the Court of the Native Chiefs; the Court of the District Commissioner and Native Chiefs; and the Court of the District Commissioner. The jurisdiction of the Courts of Native Chiefs, established under the Protectorate Ordinance 1896, extended in civil matters to all cases between natives governed by customary law other than cases involving title to land. In criminal matters, serious offences such as those of

35 See section 10(2) of the Tribal Administration (Western Area) Act, Cap. 78, as amended.

36 See Hertslet's *Map of Africa by Treaties*, Vol. 20, p. 172.

37 Its short title being "an Ordinance to determine the mode of exercising Her Majesty's jurisdiction in the territories adjacent to the Colony of Sierra Leone".

murder, culpable homicide, slave-trading and cannibalism were excluded from the jurisdiction of these Courts. The combined Courts of District Commissioner and Native Chiefs had jurisdiction in all criminal matters excluded from the Courts of Native Chiefs, and though they were allowed to apply customary law in cases between natives, it was provided that they were to be guided, as far as possible, by the laws in force in the Colony, that is, English law. Finally, the Court of the District Commissioner had jurisdiction, inter alia, to hear and determine all civil cases between non-natives or between a native and a non-native, and all cases involving a question of title to land, although arising exclusively between natives.

There was provision for the District Commissioners to be assisted by Assessors who were selected from a list of reputed local experts in the relevant customary law. The jurisdiction to hear cases involving title to land was eventually to be transferred to the reconstituted native courts, subject to the exclusion of cases between two or more paramount chiefs or tribal authorities. Disputes involving paramount chiefs or tribal authorities have continued to be excluded from the jurisdiction of both the traditional and the English-type courts, and were until the enactment of the Local Government Act 2004 mostly within the purview of the District Officers who resolved such disputes by the means of administrative inquiries.

On the whole, the policy of allowing the two legal systems to develop separately, but in parallel, continued throughout the period of British administration of the Protectorate. As will be shown later in this chapter, this policy has been retained even after independence, and the unification of the former Colony and Protectorate under a single constitution.

2.2 THE COURTS AND SETTLEMENT OF LAND DISPUTES

2.2.1 The Present Court System

Though under the present 1991 Constitution of Sierra Leone[38] there is established a single unified judiciary with jurisdiction throughout Sierra Leone, it recognizes and retains the distinction between the so-called English-type courts and the traditional courts. The English-type courts are, in order of hierarchy, the Supreme Court of Sierra Leone, the Court of Appeal and the High Court of Justice, as the superior courts of record, with Magistrates' Courts as inferior courts of record. At the other end of the judicial hierarchy are the traditional courts consisting of the Local

38 Act No. 6 of 1991.

Courts and the Group Local Appeal Courts established under the Local Courts Act 1963.

2.2.2 Jurisdiction of the English-Type Courts in Land Matters

Though the English-type courts are established throughout Sierra Leone, their jurisdiction in matters relating to land tenure is restricted in many significant respects. Thus, section 21 of the Courts Act 1965 specifically excludes from the High Court's jurisdiction "*any action or original proceedings to determine the title to land situated in the Provinces other than leasehold granted under the Provinces Land Act, Cap. 122*".

The question of the jurisdiction of the High Court in land matters in the Provinces was raised by the Supreme Court in the case of *Caulker v. Kangama*[39] in which the subject matter of the action was a house in Kono District, Eastern Province. The action had been instituted in the High Court by the plaintiff respondent for recovery of possession of the house. The appellant in his defence had disputed the ownership of the respondent and averred, in effect, that he was the owner having purchased the said premises. Though the question of the court's jurisdiction was not taken up either in the High Court or the Court of Appeal, in delivering the judgment of the Supreme Court Cole C.J. said inter alia:

> *"It is clear therefore that at the close of pleadings, one of the main issues which had to be determined by the trial Judge was ownership of the premises. This naturally involves the question of title to the said premises".*

The learned Chief Justice then read and construed sections 18 and 21 of the Courts Act 1965, dealing with the jurisdiction of the High Court, and went on to observe that the expression "*title to land*" was not defined in the 1965 Act or any other statute. He however relied on section 4 of the Interpretation Act 1971 which defines "land" as including "*any house, building or structure whatsoever, and any estate, interest or right in land*" and went to hold that, in the circumstances, the High Court did not have jurisdiction under the aforementioned provisions of the Courts Act 1965 to hear the action. The trial was therefore declared a nullity.

39 S.C. Civ. App. 2/74, judgment delivered on 18 June 1975, unreported.

The effect of this exclusion is that the role of the superior courts in the settlement of disputes involving question of title to land held under customary tenure in the Provinces is restricted to that of review on appeal. Since the bulk of land disputes that arise in the Provinces revolve around a question of title, this is a very significant limitation. The High Court has, whenever possible, sought to justify its right to hear and determine land disputes, in its original jurisdiction, by making a distinction between matters which merely touch and concern title to land, such as an action for recovery of possession, and those which actually involve a declaration of title, or a determination of ownership *simpliciter*, and are therefore excluded from its original jurisdiction under the provisions of section 21 of the Courts Act 1965.

In theory, there is no similar restriction upon the original jurisdiction of Magistrates' Courts in respect of land matters. Section 7(1) of the Courts Act provides as follows:

> *"In addition to any civil jurisdiction which may be conferred upon Magistrates Courts by any other enactment every such Court shall have jurisdiction to hear and determine any cause or matter other than an action founded upon libel, slander, false imprisonment, malicious prosecution, seduction or breach of promise of marriage, which may be lawfully brought before it and wherein the claim, debt, duty or matter in dispute does not exceed five million leones in value, whether on balance of account or otherwise."*

Section 7(2) then goes on to stipulate that apart, from certain matters listed in the Third Schedule to the Act, the parties to an action may agree in writing to vest jurisdiction in a Magistrates' Court to hear a matter which could not otherwise be lawfully brought before it. Actions relating to title to and/or recovery of possession of land are not among those listed in the Third Schedule. The question that arises then is whether such actions could be properly brought before Magistrates' Courts. This point came up for determination by the West African Court of Appeal in the Sierra Leone case of *Dupigny v. Blell*.[40] In delivering the judgment of the Court Verity, Ag.P had this to say:

40 (1957–60) ALR S.L. 66.

> *"Although I am aware that in certain territories in West Africa it is expressly provided that Magistrates Courts shall not exercise jurisdiction in any case in which questions of title to land or to any interest to land are raised, no such exception is to be found in Section 29 of the Courts Ordinance*[41] *nor in any statute to which I have been able to refer".*

It is submitted that in making this assertion the learned Acting President did not consider the provision of section 11 of the Summary Ejectment Act, Cap. 49 of the Laws of Sierra Leone 1960, which limits the jurisdiction of Magistrates' Courts in the former Colony to deal with land matters in the following terms:

> *"Nothing in this Act contained shall be deemed to abridge or affect … the jurisdiction vested, or hereafter to be vested in the Courts of the Colony in taking cognizance of, and adjudicating upon, questions of title and matters relating to land, tenements and hereditament, nor shall anything in this Act be deemed to deprive any person of any right or remedy as landlord or tenant, or otherwise, or in respect of rent, possession or other relief save only as to actions and proceedings against persons exercising the powers conferred by this Act as in this Act expressly provided, and any person may, save as aforesaid, pursue his rights and remedies in the Courts of the Colony irrespective of this Act, or of any decision of the Magistrate hereunder."*

In contrast, the corresponding statute, the Summary Ejectment (Provinces) Act, Cap. 50, which vests jurisdiction in Magistrates' Courts in the Provinces to deal with actions brought by a chiefdom council to recover possession of any land within a chiefdom does not contain any such restriction on the jurisdiction of the Magistrate. Indeed, section 4(1) of Cap 50 expressly provides that the "*Court shall have jurisdiction to deal with* [the matter] *notwithstanding any* claim *of right or title.*"

Mention should also be made of the provisions of section 16(2) of the Local Courts Act, No. 20 of 1963, which state that Customary Law Officers or District Appeal Courts may of their own motion, or on the application

41 This statute was Cap. 50 in the 1946 edition of the Laws of Sierra Leone.

of a Local Court or any party to the proceeding, for reasonable cause, transfer any proceedings initiated before a Local Court to a Magistrates' Court or a District Appeal Court. There is no clear guidance in the Act as to what may amount to "*reasonable cause*". However, it would appear that such transfers are in fact effected mainly to bypass the provisions of the Act which prevent legal practitioners from appearing before Local Courts, or where complex questions of law may be involved. The practical effect of such transfers is that the original jurisdiction of Magistrates' Courts may thus be extended on an ad hoc basis to deal with all land cases governed by customary law, including cases involving a question of title to land.

However, it is submitted that since section 21 of the Courts Act deprives the High Court of jurisdiction to determine the title of land situated in the Provinces, a fortiori, *no* Magistrate can exercise a similar jurisdiction in the Provinces.

2.2.3 Jurisdiction of Local Courts in Land Matters

Jurisdiction to hear and determine matters involving a question of title to land arising in the Provinces is expressly vested in the Local Courts as part of their general jurisdiction to hear and determine all civil cases governed by customary law. However, these Courts are deprived of jurisdiction where the case is one between two or more paramount chiefs or chiefdom councils involving a question of title to land.

This exclusion may be explained by the fact that the jurisdiction of the Local Court is limited territorially to the particular chiefdom in and for which it is established. This in fact creates an important lacuna in the available machinery for the settlement of land disputes by judicial means in the Provinces.

2.2.4 Appeals from Local Courts

There is a right of appeal from Local Courts to the English-type courts. According to section 29(1) of the Local Courts Act, there is constituted for each District of the Provinces a District Appeal Court consisting of the Magistrate for the District who sits with two Assessors, selected by him from a list of experts in customary law drawn up by the District Officer where the matter involves a question of customary law. In theory, any person aggrieved by an order or decision of a Local Court may appeal either to the District Appeal Court or to the Group Local Appeal Court consisting of paramount chiefs within the District other than the one from whose chiefdom the appeal emanated. In practice, this provision of the Local Courts Act is seldom invoked and in recent times hardly any appeals are filed in the Group Local Appeal Court.

An appeal at the District Appeal Court is by way of a complete rehearing and any party may be represented by a legal practitioner before the District Appeal Court, unlike the Local Court or the Group Local Courts where lawyers have no right of audience.

Appeals from the District Appeal Courts go to the Local Appeals Division of the High Court constituted by Judge of the High Court sitting with two Assessors where a question of customary law is in issue. As in the District Appeal Court the role of the Assessors is only advisory on questions of customary law. Finally, there is a right of further appeal from the Local Appeals Division of the High Court to the Court of Appeal, and then to the Supreme Court.

2.3 SETTLEMENT OF LAND DISPUTES OUTSIDE THE COURT SYSTEM

2.3.1 The Role of District Officers

As stated earlier in this chapter, land disputes arising in the Provinces which are excluded from the jurisdiction of Local Courts, that is those involving a question of title to land between two or more paramount chiefs or chiefdom councils, have in the past invariably been the subject of an inquiry conducted by District Officers in accordance with powers vested in them by the Provinces Act, Cap. 60. The exact status of such inquiries is not clear from the provisions of the Act. However, though District Officers were essentially administrators who may or may not be familiar with the relevant customary laws of their District, yet, they tended to conduct such inquiries on a quasi-judicial basis.

The Provinces Act, Cap. 60, which, as stated earlier, was not repealed by the Local Government Act 2004, provides that District Officers may be assisted by Assessors whose opinions on questions of customary law become part of the record of the inquiry without being binding on the District Officer. Responsibility for the ultimate findings of the inquiry rested exclusively with the latter. A search of the records of inquiries held in accordance with the Act, however, reveals that District Officers relied, to a large extent, on the opinion of the Assessors in reaching a decision.

Decisions reached in such inquiries were entered in a "Decree Book" kept in the District Office and, unless varied or reversed in review, were conclusive evidence of the right of the respective parties with regard to the land in dispute. A power of review is vested, first, in the Provincial Secretary under section 28(4) of the Act.

2.3.2 The Role of the Provincial Secretary

A person aggrieved by any decision set aside or varied by the Provincial Secretary may further complain to the Resident Minister for the Province. Such complaint is considered as an appeal against the decision. The Minister may, if so called upon, or on his own motion, revoke any decision, or order a District Officer, to hold a fresh inquiry. There are no laid-down guidelines on which either a Provincial Secretary or a Minister may act in reviewing a decision of a District Officer. Suffice it to say that these officials in most cases do not limit themselves to legal considerations but allow themselves to be influenced by political factors such as government policy on chiefdom boundaries, and thus, sometimes, to the prejudice of the vested legal rights of the parties involved in the dispute.

Needless to say, this is a rather unsatisfactory way of resolving land disputes whose outcome may well mean the dispossession of a whole community within a particular chiefdom, or the involuntary transfer of their allegiance from one chiefdom to another. It is also significant that the Provinces Act, Cap. 60, is particularly silent on the question of a judicial review of what in essence are administrative decisions. This situation presumably has been allowed to continue because of the political implications of such disputes.

2.3.3 The Role of the Customary Law Officer

Another provision of the Local Courts Act 1963 gives authority to a Customary Law Officer or a District Officer to review any decision of the Local Courts or the Group Appeal Courts where, in their opinion, a prima facie case of miscarriage of justice is disclosed or an obvious error is to be corrected. Again, the Act does not provide any assistance as to the principles by which the reviewing officer should be guided. However, in exercise of the power of review, the Customary Law Officer may, inter alia, order any case to be retried by the same or any other court of like jurisdiction, or before a Magistrates' Court. This is yet another opportunity for an ad hoc extension of the jurisdiction of Magistrates' Courts.

2.4 THE SOURCES OF LAND LAW IN SIERRA LEONE

2.4.1 Introduction

In the preceding section of this chapter, it was sought to establish how, as a result of the introduction of English judicial institutions during the colonial era, and their retention after independence alongside modified versions of indigenous judicial institutions, there is in operation in Sierra Leone a dual system of courts: the English-type courts which have jurisdiction throughout the country and the Local Courts with jurisdiction only in the Provinces. This dualism in the court system is also reflected in the system of laws which the two systems of courts apply.

2.4.2 Classification of the Sources of Law

Though the present Constitution of Sierra Leone lists five different "sources" of laws, yet, these could be classified for present purposes under two broad headings:

i. "General Law", meaning the rules of common law and the doctrines of equity referred to in section 170(2) of the Constitution and all enactments in force in Sierra Leone; and
ii. "Customary Law" which is defined in section 170(3) of the Constitution, Act No. 6 of 1991 as "*rules of law which by custom are applicable to particular communities in Sierra Leone*".

We shall now proceed to analyse the content of the general law and customary law respectively, and examine the authority for their application by the various courts in Sierra Leone.

2.4.3 The General Law

As already indicated, the general law in force in Sierra Leone consists basically of the received English law. Both English statute and non-statute law have been imported into Sierra Leone. Thus, for our purpose the general law of Sierra Leone is made up of the following:

i. Statutes of general application in force in England at the reception date, that is 1 January 1880, for example, the Wills Act 1837;
ii. Imperial legislation, for example, Orders in Council and Acts of the United Kingdom Parliament made expressly applicable to Sierra Leone during the colonial period;
iii. Post-reception-date English statutes specifically adopted by the local legislation, such as those listed in the Schedule to the Imperial Statutes (Law of Property), Adoption Act, Cap. 18, for example, the English Conveyancing Act 1881;[42]
iv. Enactments of the local legislature (both colonial and post-independence) including adaptations and re-enactments of extraneous law as local law; such as the Limitation Act, No. 51 of 1961, which is an adaptation of the English Limitation Act of 1939;
v. The English-derived common law, that is, the rules of law generally known as the common law and the principles of law generally known as the doctrines of equity.

2.4.4 Statutes of General Application

Though this phrase is to be found in the formulation of the reception clauses of virtually all the former English colonies in Africa, yet there has never been any statutory definition of what constitutes a statute of general application. There is a considerable amount of literature and judicial dicta on the meaning of the phrase[43] but each time a particular statute comes up for initial determination of its status, the matter is very much left to the discretion of the particular judge or court. Thus, until the matter has been ruled on, one cannot say with any certainty whether a particular statute is of general application, and hence received, or not. Moreover, the lists of statutes which have been held to be of general application in the various jurisdictions differ.

As far as Sierra Leone is concerned, the list includes such an assortment of statutes as the Statute of Frauds 1677, applied in *Terry v. Aribaut*[44] and

42 For a full list of post-1880 English property statutes adopted by Cap. 18, see Appendix 1 at p.314.

43 See, for example, A.E.W. Park, *The Sources of Nigerian Law*, pp. 24–29; W.C.E. Daniels, *The Common Law in West Africa*, pp. 319–46; A.N. Allott, *New Essays in African Law*, p. 48 ff.

44 (1964–66) ALR S.L. 427.

Thomas v. Johnson;[45] the Statutory Declaration Act 1835, applied in *Bright v. Roberts*;[46] the Wills Act 1837, applied in *John v. Khalil*[47] and *Bangura v. Davies*;[48] the Real Property Act 1845 applied in *Davies v. Bickersteth*[49]and the Leases Act 1849 applied in *Khalil v. John*.[50] There is on the other hand only one reported case from Sierra Leone where a statute was held not to be of general application.[51]

What guidelines then are the courts to use in determining whether or not a particular English statute is of general application and therefore imported under the general reception clause? There appears to be no set formula.[52] However, it seems to be generally agreed that a statute may still be applicable even though, subsequent to the reception date, it has been amended or even repealed in England.

Further, in *Attorney-General v. Margai*,[53] in holding that the English Summary Jurisdiction Act 1848, was in force in Sierra Leone the trial Judge had this to say:

> *"... It is not necessary that every section of an English Act in force on January 1, 1880, should be applicable to Sierra Leone. Such an English Act is subject to the provisions (or any provision) of a local ordinance".*

This would tend to lend support to the view that, where an English statute of general application conflicts with a local statute on the same subject matter, the local statute will prevail to the extent of the inconsistency, the English statute being deemed repealed pro tanto by necessary implication.

Finally, a ruling given in one case that a statute is, or is not, of general application is not necessarily irreversible either way, for circumstances and conditions in the receiving country may have so changed as to make the statute no longer applicable or vice versa. This latter factor is, to a large extent, left with the discretion of the courts to reflect changes in local

45 (1968–69) ALR S.L.380.
46 (1964–66) ALR S.L.156.
47 (1957–60) ALR S.L 336.
48 (1964–66) ALR S.L.52.
49 (1964–60) ALR S.L.403.
50 (1960–61) 1 SLLR 176.
51 See *In the Matter of the Public Lands Acquisition Ordinances* (1945) W.A.C.A. 31
52 For a list of ten suggested requirements see A.N. Allott, op.cit, pp. 50–4
53 (1960–61) 1 SLLR 17.

conditions by their rejection of received statutes that are ill suited to such changed conditions.

2.4.5 Reception of Other English Statutes

Under this heading fall two further categories of legislation that have been imported into Sierra Leone. First, there are those pieces of Imperial legislation made by virtue of prerogative powers conferred, for example, by the British Settlements Act 1887 or the Foreign Jurisdiction Act 1890, under which the Merchant Shipping Act 1894 was made applicable to Sierra Leone and other countries. For our purposes this type of received law is not very important as no measure affecting the status of land in Sierra Leone was enacted by the Imperial legislature.

Next in this category are what we may described as "*adopted*" statutes. According to section 4(1) of the Interpretation Act, the phrase "*adopted law*" is used to describe:

> *"any Act of the United Kingdom or English Parliament or an Order in Council or other legislative instrument made thereunder otherwise than by an authority in Sierra Leone which has an effect in Sierra Leone".*

During the colonial era there was a practice whereby named English statutes, or particular sections thereof, were adopted by the local legislature and so given the force of law in Sierra Leone. Thus, by the Imperial Statutes (Law of Property) Adoption Act, Cap. 18, statutes listed in the Second Schedule to the Act were specifically adopted to the extent stated therein. Among statutes thus adopted were the Conveyancing and Law of Property Act 1881, the Settled Land Act 1882 and the Trustee Act 1888.

It is, however, a matter of regret that though these English property statutes were only adopted in 1932, long after the series of 1925 English property statutes which significantly reformed and modernized English land law, yet, the opportunity was not taken to introduce some of those reforming measures into Sierra Leone by adopting any of the latter statutes. As may be seen from the list in Appendix 1, the latest in date of the statutes adopted under the Imperial Statutes (Law of Property) Adoption Act, Cap 18, is the Conveyancing Act 1911. Even after Independence in 1961, the local legislature has not been particularly active in enacting reforming statutes in the field of the law of property. Thus, Sierra Leone is still lumbered with the bulk of pre-1925 English property statutes originally enacted to suit the peculiar socio-political and economic conditions of pre-twentieth-century English society. The paradox and contradictions arising from the application of these statutes become more apparent when we examine the substance and the grammar of these statutes, which for the most part are not only archaic but invariably irrelevant to the realities of present-day Sierra Leone. Furthermore, there is very little leeway allowed the Sierra Leone judiciary to introduce modifications in the construction of these statutes. The only guidance given to the Sierra Leonean courts is to be found in section 11 of the Interpretation Act 1971, No. 8 of 1971, which simply enjoins the court to read an adopted law:

> *"with such verbal alterations to names, localities, courts, officers, persons, moneys and otherwise as may be necessary to make the same applicable in all circumstances".*

2.4.6 Local Statutes

Finally, as part of the general law in force in Sierra Leone we have what we have termed purely local enactments. These also fall into two categories. First, there are those statutes which are adaptations and re-enactments of non-received English statutes, example, the English Sale of Goods Act 1839 enacted as Cap 225; the English Companies Act 1929 enacted as Cap. 249; and the English Limitation Act 1939 enacted as Act No. 51 of 1961. This method of legislating, in principle, afforded the local legislature ample opportunity to select what was suitable and ideal for local conditions, and to prune off those provisions of the imported law which, for any good reason, may be deemed unsuitable for introduction into the local society. However, in the field of law of property, in general, and of land tenure in particular, the local legislature has not grasped this opportunity. Thus, we still have in our statute books today references to such concepts as "*socage tenure*", "*fee tail*" and "*escheat*".

The main reason for this is that the local legislature has not only failed to do any effective pruning before adapting and re-enacting English statutes but also failed to keep pace with the process of review and modernization of the local statute law, a process which is constantly going on in other countries such as Ghana and Nigeria. Thus, to take a random example, the rules for the distribution of residual assets on deceased intestate persons under the general law contained in the Schedule to the Administration of Estates Act, Cap. 45, were adopted from the English Statute of Distribution 1670–85 and remained unchanged until 2007 when the Devolution of Estates Act was enacted.

The second category of local enactments is what may be termed purely local statutes in the sense that they are initiated and conceived locally, without being based on (at least not directly) or inspired by any extraneous laws. It is remarkable that in this regard there has hardly been any significant legislative activity in the field of the law of property in general. As far as the Provinces are concerned, the only local enactment worthy of note in the field of land law is the Provinces Land Act, Cap. 122, which was enacted as far back as 1927. This might be understandable in view of the fact that land tenure in this part of the country is and has always been governed predominantly by customary law which has so far remained unmodified.

However, when we turn to the Western Area, where customary law has no place in the system of land tenure, the role of the local legislature has been relatively insignificant. Moreover, most of the important statutes relating to land, such as the Unoccupied Lands (Ascertainment of Title) Act, Cap. 117, The Public Lands Act, Cap. 117, the Town and Country Planning Act, Cap. 81, and the State Lands Act 1960, were enacted during the colonial era. Since Independence in 1961, apart from minor amendments to existing local statutes, the only major enactment in the field of land law that has been passed by the local legislature is the Non-Citizens (Interest in Land) Act 1966. This lack of legislative activity is surely not because there are no areas of the Sierra Leone land law in need of reform or modernization.

Finally, on this aspect of this work, reference should be made to the provisions of the Interpretation Act which prevented any statute passed before 1 July 1953 from applying to the Provinces "*unless it is provided by the Act itself or is extended thereto by an Act*".[54] It would appear that this provision only affected adopted and local statutes, as pre-1880 statutes of general application are in force throughout Sierra Leone by virtue of the general reception clause.[55]

54 Section 8(1) of Act No. 8 of 1971. However, the effect of this provision has been negated to a large extent by the provision of section 4(2) of the Laws (Adaptation) Act, No. 29 of 1972. See fn 33 at p. 27.

55 See section 74 of the Courts Act 1965.

2.4.7 Which Common Law?

According to section 170(1) of the Constitution[56] "*the common law*" is listed as one of the sources of the laws of Sierra Leone. The Constitution then goes on to provide that:

> "*the common law of Sierra Leone shall comprise rules of law generally known as the common law, the rules of law generally known as the doctrines of equity, and the rules of customary law including those determined by the Superior Court of Judicature*".[57]

Clearly, the term "*common law*" here must have a different meaning from those in English law. Usually "*common law*" refers to all the non-statute laws of England, including those rules which were formerly administered by the Court of Chancery in England, and now known as doctrines of equity. In another, narrower, sense it refers to the rules derived from custom and administered by the Common Law Courts in England as opposed to the doctrines of equity. This latter meaning is that adopted by section 4(1) of the Interpretation Act 1971. The "*common law*" is therein defined as "the common law of England, as referred to in Section 74 of the Courts Act 1965".

This section of the Courts Act 1965 is the general reception clause providing as follows:

> "*subject to the provisions of the Constitution and any other enactment, the common law, the doctrines of equity, and statutes of general application in force in England on the first day of January 1880, shall be in force in Sierra Leone*".

This section is clear authority for the application of both the English common law in the narrower sense of the word, and the doctrines of equity, by the courts in Sierra Leone.

56 Act No. 6 of 1921.
57 Ibid., section 125(2).

What is not very clear however is whether the limitation in the reception clause to pre-1880 laws refers only to statutes of general application, or whether it applies equally to the common law and doctrines of equity. In other words, which rules of common law and doctrines of equity are the courts in Sierra Leone to give effect to: those currently in force in England or those that were in force as at 1 January 1880?

The interpretation of similarly worded reception clauses in Ghana and Nigeria has led to a great deal of controversy among jurists and academics.[58] Without being drawn into this rather theoretical debate, it is submitted, with respect, that a closer reading of section 74 of the Courts Act 1965 would tend to indicate that the reception date only applies to the received statutes of general application and not to the common law and doctrines of equity. The punctuation of the section suggests such a reading, though this per se would not justify such a conclusion. However, this view is strengthened by the practice of the courts in Sierra Leone which seldom, if ever, draw any distinction between pre- and post-1880 English cases in applying rules of common law or doctrines of equity.

This practice persists despite judicial pronouncements that the only decisions of English courts, on principles of common law and doctrines of equity as well as on the construction of statute, which are to be treated as binding authority in the Sierra Leone courts are those given before 1880, whilst all post-1880 decisions of the English courts on similar points are merely of persuasive authority, though invariably treated with the highest respect.[59]

In this regard, it should be noted that it is not only English decisions that are treated as being of persuasive authority. The same treatment is reserved for decisions of the superior courts of all Commonwealth countries.[60] However, the courts in Sierra Leone have tended to adhere very strictly to English precedents, particularly those elaborating rules of the common law and the doctrines of equity.

In principle, the courts still have a discretion to either apply, or reject, post-1880 English decisions on principles of common law or doctrines of equity. However, between the two extremes lies a third possibility, that of applying such decisions in a modified form where necessary, to suit the peculiar local conditions of Sierra Leone. In this way, the courts would be helping to develop a truly Sierra Leonean "*common law*" in

58 For a summary and review of the leading arguments on either side, see Allott, op. cit., pp. 60 ff.

59 See *Hamed v. White Cross Insurance Company* (1957–60) ALR SL 276.

60 See *Akar v. Attorney-General* (1967–68) ALR S.L. 283.

the broader sense of the term. So far there are hardly any signs of such a development.

2.4.8 Customary Law

Customary law, or Native law and Custom (as it is sometimes referred to), was the law that was in force throughout the territory of Sierra Leone before the advent of the British colonizers. As has been pointed out earlier in this chapter, when a Protectorate was declared over the Sierra Leone hinterland, the British recognized traditional institutions then existing according to customary law, and permitted this law to co-exist alongside the English laws which had been earlier introduced into the Sierra Leone Colony. This policy of permitting customary law to co-exist, and develop alongside the received English law, was continued even after the colonial era.

Though the general law, as defined above, and customary law remain the two major sources of law in Sierra Leone, as far as land tenure in the Provinces is concerned, customary law is still the predominant law that regulates rights to and interests in land. However, it should be re-emphasized at this stage that though it is convenient to talk about "*customary law*" as a source of law in Sierra Leone, yet there is not just a single body of laws that can be labelled "the customary law of Sierra Leone".

On the contrary, there are numerous separate customary laws based on the traditions, culture and customs of the various ethnic groups, such customary laws differing more or less from one another in substance or in detail. Even within a particular ethnic group, such as the Mende or the Temne, there are local variations of its customary law at the chiefdom or some other level. How then can one identify what customary law is to be applied by the courts in Sierra Leone? This leads us to the statutory definition of customary law.

2.4.9 Definition of Customary Law

The two main statutes that define customary law are the Constitution and the Local Courts Act 1963. The Constitution defines customary law as "*the rules of law which by custom are applicable to particular communities in Sierra Leone.*"[61] This definition, without more, is not very helpful in determining which customary law is to be applied in any given situation as

61 Section 170 of the Constitution, Act No. 6 of 1991.

it does not indicate whether the communities referred to are ethnic, social, cultural, political or territorial groupings. Moreover, most communities in Sierra Leone would be found to be culturally heterogeneous, often with conflicting and contrasting customs and traditions.

A more comprehensive definition of customary law is that contained in section 2 of the Local Courts Act 1963 which defines customary law as:

> *"any rule other than a rule of general law having the force of law in any chiefdom of the Provinces, whereby rights and correlative duties have been acquired and imposed which is applicable in any particular case, and conforms which natural justice and equity, and not incompatible either directly or indirectly with any enactment applying to the Provinces, and includes any amendments of customary law made in accordance with the provisions of any enactment."*

Implicit in the above definition is the fact that, even though the roots of any particular rule of customary law may be grounded in the custom or tradition of a particular ethnic group, yet such rule only acquires the status of a rule of law by being generally accepted and recognized as having the force of law by any community of that ethnic group settled within the territorial confines of any chiefdom of the Provinces. In other words, every rule of customary law must be identified with a particular group or community within a chiefdom. In practice, however, the major principles of customary law transcend chiefdom boundaries, and despite the scattered character of ethnic distribution in the Provinces of Sierra Leone today, it is still possible and meaningful to identify, analyse and distinguish the rules of customary law on a tribal basis.

The next point that emerges from the definition of customary law in the Local Courts Act 1963 is that rules of customary law are subject to several qualifications and restrictions in their application. Thus, according to the definition in the Act, a rule of customary law must conform to natural justice and equity, and must not be incompatible with any statute law in force in the area of its application. These and other restrictions in the application of rules of customary law will be considered below. Let us first of all examine the rules governing the application of customary law by the courts in Sierra Leone.

2.4.10 Rules for the Application of Customary Law

There is a clear distinction to be drawn here between the traditional courts on the one hand and the English-type courts on the other. Though it is generally assumed by both legal and non-legal persons in Sierra Leone that customary law is the primary law to be applied by the traditional courts, yet there is no direct or express provision to this effect in the Local Courts Act 1963, which is the only statute that deals with the jurisdiction of the traditional courts. Section 13(1) of this Act is relevant in the regard. Firstly, it gives Local Courts jurisdiction to administer the estates of deceased natives within their territorial jurisdiction where such administration is governed by customary law. Secondly, the section provides that the Local Courts have jurisdiction to administer the estates of deceased natives within their territorial jurisdiction where such administration is governed by customary law. Thirdly, the section provides that Local Courts have jurisdiction to hear and determine other civil matters governed by either customary law or the general law, the latter to be applied only within certain prescribed limits. The jurisdiction conferred on Local Courts in respect of criminal cases is simply "t*o hear and determine all criminal cases*" subject to certain limitations on the courts' powers of punishment without any indication of what system of law is to apply.

Notwithstanding these rather vague and imprecise provisions of the Local Courts Act 1963, relating to the application of customary law by the traditional courts, yet the inference could safely be drawn that the intention of the legislature was to enjoin the Local Courts to apply customary law as their primary or basic law. This inference is supported by the stipulation contained in section 13(2) of the Act to the effect that "*where there is no provision of customary law the general law shall apply*". It is submitted that the only logical interpretation that could be placed on this subsection is that customary law is to be the primary law of these courts and the general law is only to apply as a secondary or residual law, where, for any reason, there is a gap in the customary law, or it is excluded because of repugnancy or incompatibility, as laid down in section 2.

In contrast with the Local Courts, the English-type courts have a more clear-cut authority vested in them to apply customary law. The existing provisions are contained in section 76 of the Courts Act 1965. Section 76(1) of this Act permits these courts to apply customary law "*when determining matters arising in the Provinces*" in their civil jurisdiction only, provided such customary law is not

> *"repugnant to natural justice, equity and good conscience, nor incompatible, either directly or by necessary implication, with any Act applying to the Provinces".*

Section 76(2) further provides that such customary law shall be deemed applicable in all causes and matters where, in the opinion of the Court, substantial injustice would be done to any party by a strict adherence to the rules of any law other than customary law, *"except where the circumstances, nature or justice of the case shall otherwise require"*. Thus, while section 76(1) is a general enabling provision, section 76(2) narrows the field down by giving particular instances when customary law should be applied in preference to the general law. Presumably, substantial injustice would be done by the application of the general law in a case where the claim or subject matter in dispute is one which originated under customary law, or is otherwise governed by customary law, or where either party being a native, customary law, as his personal law, is relevant to the claim or subject matter in dispute. However, section 76(2) is specifically made subject to section 76(3) of the Act which provides as follows:

> *"No party shall be entitled to claim the benefit of any customary law if it shall appear either from the express contract, or from the nature of the transaction out of which any cause or matter may have arisen, that such party agreed that this obligation in connection with such transaction should be regulated exclusively by any law referred to in Section 74 [that is, the received English law] or any Act of Sierra Leone; and in cases where no express rule is applicable to any matter in controversy, the Court shall be governed by the principles of justice equity and good conscience".*

Thus, it becomes evident that at least some guidance is given to the English-type courts (unlike the traditional courts) in making a choice between the two systems of law. However, despite such clear-cut authority for these courts to apply customary law, where appropriate, in determining matters arising in the Provinces within their civil jurisdiction, yet in practice this authority is seldom invoked in the court's original jurisdiction. Most of the cases coming before the Magistrates' Courts and the Superior

Courts of Judicature, that is the High Court, the Court of Appeal and the Supreme Court, requiring the application of customary law, as opposed to the general law, are for determination under those Courts' appellate jurisdiction. Besides, section 21 of the Courts Act 1965 divests the High Court of original jurisdiction over certain matters governed by customary law, such as the question of title to land situated in the Provinces. Even where the courts have determined that the relevant law to apply is customary law, such application is made subject to certain restrictions and limitations.

2.4.11 Factors Affecting the Application of Customary Law

Having examined the definition of customary law and the rules governing its application by the two systems of courts, that is, the traditional courts and the English-type courts, we should now focus our attention more closely on the factors which might limit its application in particular cases.

The first and most obvious limitation is that customary law is basically applicable only to the Provinces. This is particularly true of the customary law relating to land tenure. The only exception envisaged by statute where customary law may apply outside the Provinces is under in section 41 of the Administration of Estates Act, Cap. 45. Where a native dies intestate leaving assets in the Western Area prior to the coming into force of the Devolution Act 2007, the distribution of his estate is to be in accordance with the relevant rules of customary law of intestate succession. Another possible exception is where Tribal Headmen apply customary law to settle matrimonial disputes between members of their tribe resident in the Western Area. This is provided for by section 12 of the Tribal Administration (Western Area) Act, Cap. 78. In such cases the process is more in the nature of an arbitration than an adjudication.

Another limitation on the application of customary law is that, by definition, it must conform with "*natural justice and equity*". Section 76(1) adds the words "*good conscience*". It is submitted that these words do not impose any further qualification as "equity" in this context subsumes among other concepts "good conscience".[62] In theory, the courts can refuse to apply any rule of customary law which is repugnant to the known principles of natural justice, equity or good conscience. There are however

62 For a full discussion of the concepts of natural justice, equity and good conscience, see Allott, op. cit., pp. 60 ff.

very few reported Sierra Leone cases where the repugnancy test has been applied to invalidate a rule of customary law.[63]

The next restriction on the application of a rule of customary law is that it should not be incompatible, either directly or by necessary implication, with any Act applying to the Provinces. It should be noted here that the incompatibility is with statutes applying to the Provinces only. This reduces the possibility of conflict in the field of land law. As we have seen, very little of the local property legislation applies to the Provinces, and the bulk of the received property statutes will be inapplicable to the Provinces for the simple reason that customary law is still the predominant law that governs land tenure in the Provinces. In the absence of any decided cases, where the point has been taken, it is difficult to predict the attitude of the courts on the question of the incompatibility of customary law with statute law. It is suggested that where the transaction or subject matter is one governed by customary law, the courts should not construe a statute so as to avoid the transaction or to affect the subject matter, unless the statute was enacted, expressly or by necessary implication, to alter the relevant rule of customary law.

Another restriction on the application of customary law is that where there is evidence that the parties to a dispute, either by express agreement, or by the nature or form of the transaction involved, have evinced an intention to exclude customary law. This is provided for by section 76(3) of the Courts Act 1965. However, the wording of the provision suggests that the courts have a discretion as it is only where the above factors are apparent to the court that a party is deprived of his entitlement to claim the benefit of customary law.

Further, the exclusion of customary law must have been total so that the intention must have been that the "*transaction should be regulated exclusively*" by some other law.[64] Thus, where the transaction is regulated partly by customary law, and partly by the general law, then the court has a discretion to apply either system of law depending on all the circumstances. For example, where there has been an *inter vivos* gift of land under customary tenure made to **A** followed by a devise of the same land to **A** by a will in English form, in the event that the validity of the transfer is questioned, which system of law should apply? Such problems of internal conflict of law that are likely to arise because of the co-existence of the two systems of law will be discussed more fully later in this work.

63 See *Fulla v. Kondowa* (1970–71) ALR S.L. 306.

64 Emphasis added.

2.4.12 Conclusion

The exposition in this chapter has demonstrated that the dual system of land tenure in Sierra Leone today hinges to a large extent on the duality of the legal system and, in many ways, the former is a product of the latter. The picture that emerges from the above review of the legal system is that the Western Area has its own distinct legal system, based largely on the received law which is applied by English-type courts. This part of the country which is geographically distinct from the other parts features a system of land tenure derived exclusively from English law. In the Western Area there is hardly any room for interaction with the other system of land tenure in the country. On the other hand, the Provinces stand in contrast with the Western Area in that, though the system of land tenure in the Provinces is governed predominantly by customary law, there is room for the two systems of courts and laws to co-exist, thus creating the possibility of interaction and, at the same time, producing potential areas of conflict between the two systems. There are thus two levels of dualism. At the national level there is dualism between English tenure in the Western Area and customary tenure in the Provinces. At the internal level, that is within the Provinces themselves, the dualism of the legal system exercises a great deal of influence on the system of customary tenure, which is still the predominant form of tenure in that part of the country.

PART 2
LAND LAW IN THE WESTERN AREA

CHAPTER 3
THE ORIGINS AND LEGAL BASES OF TITLE TO LAND IN THE WESTERN AREA

3.1 BACKGROUND TO THE ACQUISITION OF TERRITORY BY THE BRITISH IN THE FORMER COLONY (NOW WESTERN AREA)

3.1.1 Introduction

As has been demonstrated in the first part of this work, the dual system of land tenure in force in Sierra Leone today is the product of the historical, political and legal developments in the former Colony and Protectorate of Sierra Leone during the colonial era. This Chapter will be devoted to a closer and more detailed examination and analysis of those events associated with the founding and political development of the Colony which were, directly or indirectly, responsible for the introduction and retention of the concept of Crown (later State) land in the former Colony (now Western Area) of Sierra Leone. In particular, such analysis will focus on the legal effect of the various treaties of cession signed by the local rulers during the colonial era with a view to establishing the legal bases of title to State and private lands in the Western Area today.

The following are the key events which call for such detailed analysis:

i. The conclusion of the treaty of 1787 for the acquisition of the territory that was used for the establishment of the Province of Freedom, a self-governing entity for the settlement of freed slaves;
ii. The incorporation of the Sierra Leone Company under Royal Charter in 1791 and the grant of land by the Company to occupiers of the settlement;
iii. The transfer of all rights to landed property which had been acquired by the Sierra Leone Company to the British, and the establishment of the Crown Colony in 1808; and

iv. The expansion of the Colony, consequent on the acquisition and annexation of further territories by the British between 1808 and 1883.

These events were important stages in the assumption of British sovereignty and *dominium* over the territories involved, and it was against this background that English law in general, and the English system of land tenure in particular, were introduced into Sierra Leone. This was done mainly by the making of Crown grants to the settlers and other persons in the former Colony of Sierra Leone. This process of colonization in Sierra Leone was rather unusual, for unlike the process of colonization in Ghana and Nigeria, one of its direct consequences was that the English system of land tenure was not simply superimposed on the existing system of customary tenure. Instead, the system of customary tenure was completely eradicated and replaced by the English system of tenure. As a result the only interests and rights which could be now be created, or subsist in or over the land in the Western Area today, are those derived from, and based on, the received English law of property.

3.1.2 The Treaty of 1787

The most logical point to start our examination and analysis is the execution of the treaty of cession in 1787 between King Tom, one of the Temne rulers of Koya in the then Sierra Leone Peninsula, and Thompson, the leader of the English expedition that had brought the first group of freed slaves to be settled in Sierra Leone.

Though the execution of the treaty was by Thompson, a British subject, according to the exact words of the treaty, the 20 square miles (32 square kilometres) of territory that was thus acquired was:

> *"for and on behalf of and for the sole benefit of the free community of settlers, their heirs and successors now lately arrived from England and under the protection of the British Government ... for the settling of the said free community to be theirs, their heirs and successors for ever".*[65]

65 For a full text of this treaty see Hertslet's *Map of Africa by Treaties*, Vol. 1, p. 26.

The intention of Granville Sharp and others who had initiated the founding of the settlement was that it was to be independent and self-governing though the settlers were to be considered as British subjects. According to the historian Fyfe,[66] the leader of the expedition, Thompson, was to take the settlers to Sierra Leone, acquire a settlement from the native chiefs and "*stay in the river to help them as long as provisions and the crew's health allowed*".[67] The land thus acquired was indeed allotted to the initial group of settlers but there is no clear evidence on which one can judge the legal basis of these initial allotments. Presumably they were outright grants made on the basis of English common law which was the law the settlers had brought with them.[68]

Whatever might have been the basis of the initial allotments, the settlers' occupation of these lands did not go unchallenged by the native chiefs. As stated in Chapter 1, Naimbana repudiated the treaty of 1787 on the grounds that King Tom, a subordinate chief, had no authority to sign it. He followed this up with a notice to quit issued to the settlers. However, the grant of land was later confirmed by Naimbana in a new treaty signed in 1788. This treaty was in almost the same terms as that of 1787 and was also expressed to be "*on behalf of and for the sole benefit of the free community of settlers, their heirs and successors*".[69] It is submitted that, even though the initial settlers were considered as British subjects, it was at this stage still not clear whether the new settlement was an English territory and the lands ceded a Crown possession.

As far as the native chiefs were concerned, there is no doubt that they did not appreciate, or at least did not accept, the outright alienation of their lands. Even after the treaty was signed by Naimbana in 1788, there was an attack on the settlement launched by King Jimmy, a neighbouring Temne chief, in 1789. This was followed by further confrontations prompted mainly by the expansion of the Colony beyond the coastal strip. An attempt by Clarkson, the then Governor, in 1792, to settle the boundary of the Colony with Naimbana and his chiefs did not prevent yet more attacks by the Temnes in 1807, after the Temne had been defeated militarily.

66 C. Fyfe, op. cit., p. 19.

67 In fact, Thompson left the settlement a few months after September 1787.

68 See extract quoted from Granville Sharp's 'Short Sketch of Temporary Regulations for the Intended Settlement on the Grain Coast of Africa near Sierra Leone' cited by C.W. Newbury, *British Policy Towards West Africa: Selected Documents 1786–1874*, p. 401.

69 For the full text of the 1788 treaty see J.J. Crooks, *A History of the Colony of Sierra Leone*, 1903, p. 361.

This process of subjugation took place during the rule of the Company Government.

3.1.3 The Sierra Leone Company

After the attack and destruction of the settlement in 1789, attempts were made in England by Sharp and others to salvage the situation. Having failed to get the support of the British Government of the day, Sharp managed to get certain private philanthropists to invest in a Company which was, in 1791, to receive a Charter of incorporation under the name of the Sierra Leone Company. The Charter gave the Company authority to carry on trade and to hold, from the Crown, the lands originally granted by the native chiefs and any other lands they might acquire on the Sierra Leone Peninsula.

The Sierra Leone Company Act 1791 confirmed the land grant to the Company and designated the territory held by the Company, "*one independent Colony by the name of 'Colony of Sierra Leone*'". The Directors of the Company were at the same time empowered to legislate for the Colony provided that such legislation was not repugnant to the laws of England. The new settlers who were brought by the Sierra Leone Company, came subject to certain prescribed conditions.[70] Among these conditions were the grant of land to them subject to the payment of a "quit rent", and an undertaking to cultivate the land within two years from the date of the grant.

The land tax thus levied by the Company and named "Q R" (quit rent) should be differentiated from the quit rent which had survived in England as a relict of medieval land tenure, or the levy, known by the same name, imposed on lands granted in other Crown colonies for the purpose of safeguarding Crown rights. The quit rent imposed by the Sierra Leone Company on land granted to the settlers was simply a land tax to yield revenue for the Company. It is ironic that the collection of quit rent which had to be abandoned by the Company Government in the face of open resistance and non-compliance by the Nova Scotians, and the Maroons, was only resumed after the territory became a Crown Colony in 1808.

70 See C.O. 267/34, '… Terms of the Sierra Leone Company to the Settlers, 3rd November, 1791', reproduced by Newbury, op. cit., p. 611.

3.1.4 The Transfer of the Possessions of the Sierra Leone Company to the Crown

Various factors, including the refusal of the settlers to pay the quit rent, and the hostility of the neighbouring Temne, prevented the Sierra Leone Company from attaining its objectives. As the Colony became increasingly dependent on grants from the British Parliament for its survival, a recommendation was made for the transfer of the Colony to the Crown. The Sierra Leone Company Transfer Act 1807 provided inter alia:

> *"that the said Company shall be and they are hereby divested of and from all that tract or district of land commonly called and known by the name of description of The Peninsula of Sierra Leone... and the same and every of them are and is hereby declared and enacted to be fully and absolutely vested in His Majesty, his heirs and successors, for ever" [emphasis added].*

On 1 January 1808 Sierra Leone became a Crown Colony. Following the establishment of the Crown Colony, steps were taken by the British Government to ensure that all engagements by the Sierra Leone Company to the settlers, on the subject of land grants, and between the Company and the native chiefs, were to be respected.[71] Thus, an attempt was made in 1808, by the appointment of Land Commissions, to hear claims and to place on a legal footing existing grants of land in the Colony. According to Crooks:

> *"It was found that both cultivation, and the improvement of the settlement, was impeded owing to the absence of legal and decisive grants, and the impossibility of producing titles to property".*[72]

The new Government, therefore, invited all claims to be lodged before January 1810. This date was subsequently extended to the end of that year. An Ordinance had been passed in 1809 which provided that any lands, not in use or occupation and which might be cultivated before

71 See Newbury, op. cit., p. 479 and C.O. 267/24.

72 J.J. Crooks, op. cit., p. 76.

1 January 1810, should become the freehold property of the cultivator and his heirs free from all claims. As a result of the great impact of this statute on agricultural production, a further statute was passed in January 1810 granting to all persons who had cultivated and hedged in any land, then in the possession of the Governor and the Council, the freehold for themselves and their successors.

Moreover, Maxwell[73] was later instructed to settle all outstanding claims to land, to grant the remaining allotment promised the settlers since 1792 and to give landholders a secure title. Accordingly, a proclamation was made in June 1812 that the Governor and Council were ready to confirm the title of holders of land from the Sierra Leone Company. The grants were made subject to an oath of allegiance to the British Monarch, the payment of quit rent and an undertaking to cultivate the land granted within a specified period. The grants were to contain the reservation of a right of resumption by the Crown for public purposes. Thus, subject to the above conditions, those settlers who availed themselves of the opportunity afforded for the confirmation of their title henceforth had a secure freehold title to their lands.[74]

3.1.5 The Cession of Further Territories to the British Crown between 1808 and 1885

Apart from the various territories ceded by treaty to the Sierra Leone Company (or conquered from the Temne), several other territories were later ceded directly to the British Crown and thus became part of the Crown Colony. In particular, Bunce, Tasso, and other islands and the territory extending one mile inland on the northern bank of the Sierra Leone River were ceded in 1924 by Bey Mauro, King of the Bulloms. Other important treaties of cession were those of 1825 and 1861 by which the territories of Bacca Lokoh (part of the present Port Loko District, Northern Province) and the Islands of Bonthe, Sherbro and Turtle were ceded to the British Crown.

The significance of these latter treaties is that, unlike the earlier ones referred to, by which territories forming part of the Sierra Leone Peninsula

73 Lt. Col. C.W. Maxwell was Governor of Sierra Leone, 1811–14.

74 According to the Report of the Commissioners who inquired into Land Grants, published in 1827, very few settlers availed themselves of the opportunity to confirm their titles, mainly because of the reintroduction of the quit rent and the heavy fees charged by those who made out the grants. See Newbury, op.cit., p. 64 ff.

were ceded or annexed, in most cases they were not to vest absolute ownership of the lands in question in the British Crown. In other words, in respect of certain of those territories in the hinterland, for example Bacca Loko, the British exercised sovereignty, but did not claim *dominium*, over the lands involved. The only exception was a tiny enclave geographically part of the Bonthe District, Southern Province. The rest of these territories, though they should, *de jure*, have been considered as part of the Colony, were later administered as part of the Protectorate and this situation has continued even after independence.

The practical result of this anomalous situation is that, though these territories were, strictly speaking, part of the Colony, the lands comprised therein were never made subject exclusively to English law but, like other lands in the former Protectorate, have been governed predominantly by customary law.

3.2 THE LEGAL IMPLICATIONS OF THE TRANSFER AND ACQUISITION OF TERRITORY IN THE FORMER COLONY

3.2.1 Introduction

In the light of the foregoing historical data, what inferences could be drawn about the legal basis of title to land in the former Colony (now Western Area) of Sierra Leone? It is suggested that this question can be viewed from two perspectives. On the one hand, that of the native chiefs and the indigenous communities whose rights or claims to the territories involved had been thus extinguished, and on the other, that of the British Crown and persons deriving, or claiming through it, absolute title to the newly acquired lands.

3.2.2 The Perspective of the Native Chiefs

From the above historical account this work has shown that, from the outset, that is, from the treaty of 1787, the native chiefs involved did not appreciate the conclusive effect of the grants they were making to the British, purportedly on behalf of the settlers. Even after the treaty of 1787, which was supposed to have confirmed the outright grant of land made by King Tom in 1787, Naimbana continued to act as the Colony's "landlord".

Moreover, there appears to have been no legal power vested in the native chiefs to alienate such lands outright.

Thus, after the death of Naimbana in 1793, his successors, including Bai Farama, refused to consider themselves bound by the treaties made by their predecessors and continued to maintain that the lands were inalienable. This is one of the factors that can help to render understandable the attitude of the Temne in seeking to repossess the lands ceded by constant attacks on the settlement until 1807 when they were finally subjugated.

But even the British were not insensitive to the arguments and contentions of the native chiefs. Thus, despite the Treaty of Peace and Alliance signed in 1807, between the Governor of Sierra Leone and Bai Farama, King Tom and other Temne Chiefs, Bai Farama was allowed to retain a few native towns and was to continue to receive regular payments from the Sierra Leone Company of 100 bars. He was also to receive dues from ships watering in the harbour, other than ships belonging to the settlement and the proprietors of Bunce Island. Besides, as far back as 1792, the Sierra Leone Company had agreed to indemnify natives who lost their crops as a result of the activity of Pepys[75] in laying out avenues to the west of the settlement which necessitated cutting through farms and villages owned and occupied by the neighbouring indigenous populations.[76]

Thus, as far as the native chiefs and their peoples were concerned the transfer of territories was not altogether a voluntary act. Moreover, it is doubtful whether the native chiefs who signed the so-called treaties of cession were fully aware of the long-term legal implications. It is quite reasonable to assume that they genuinely believed they were not parting with the ultimate title for good, but were only making a temporary grant, albeit on a more regular basis than the usual "*landlord-stranger*" relationship to which they had been accustomed. It is significant to note in this regard that Sierra Leone was the first Colony in the strict sense of the word to be established by the British in West Africa. It differed in its origins from other West African Colonies, which were all originally formed as trading stations.[77]

75 This was an English surveyor sent out to the settlement by the Sierra Leone Company.

76 See Fyfe, op. cit., p. 47.

77 According to Crooks, op. cit., p. 32, when the first settlers arrived in Sierra Leone the only territory in West Africa under British rule or protection was the trading establishments on the Gold Coast belonging to the Africa Company of Merchants. The settlement of Bathurst, Gambia dated from 1816, and the Colony of Lagos, Nigeria from 1861.

3.2.3 The Perspective of the British Crown

From the standpoint of the British and settlers, there was no doubt that they considered the grants of land made between 1787 and 1883 as, indeed, effecting the transfer of the absolute ownership of the lands involved from the natives to the new occupants. What was not very clear was whether the intention, initially, was to consider the earlier territories ceded as British possessions, or as independent domains under the protection of the British Monarch. However, as the constitutional status of the settlement changed it became more and more obvious that the territories ceded were being treated as British possessions. Thus, in the Charter of Incorporation of the Sierra Leone Company, the grant of land made thereunder to the Company was in respect of lands already

> *"vested in His Majesty, his heirs, and successors with full power, liberty and privilege to and for the said Company to purchase of and from all Kings, Princes and chiefs, or other power, having the right to make sale thereof [any land within the Sierra Leone Peninsula and to hold the same] upon such terms, conditions and reservation to be inserted in the said grant as His Majesty, his heirs and successors respectively shall judge expedient".*[78]

The Charter of Incorporation of 1791 was followed by the Charter of 1799, which confirmed the grant of land to the Company and also constituted the lands so granted the independent Colony of Sierra Leone. Though the territory was thus declared an independent Colony, the government established by the Company, as well as the settlers and other colonists, owed direct allegiance to the British Crown. If the Company and the inhabitants of the Colony were thus subject, at least indirectly, to British sovereignty, it was never made evident that the territory itself was under British *dominium*. Grants of land were made to the settlers and other individuals (some of them Europeans) but they were not at this stage made in the name of or on behalf of the Monarch and could not by any stretch of the imagination be termed Crown grants. The next and final stage in the process of establishing British sovereignty and *dominium* over the territories ceded was the enactment of the Sierra Leone Company

78 The Sierra Leone Company Act 1791, see Newbury, op. cit., p. 463.

Transfer Act 1807, under which the Colony was transferred to the British Government and became a Crown Colony.

Under this Act, all lands which had been granted, purchased or otherwise acquired, possessed, enjoyed or claimed by the Company were declared to be "*fully and absolutely vested in His Majesty, his heirs and successors, for ever*". From this point on, all the territory comprised in the Colony was considered a British possession and the lands as Crown lands. As we have seen, the British Government, at the same time, took over responsibility for grants of lands to the settlers, and such grants were thenceforth made in the name of the Crown.

However, though such vesting of the title to absolute ownership of the lands within the Crown Colony of Sierra Leone was in line with British constitutional theory in respect of Crown rights over British possessions overseas, it conflicts with leading judicial opinion on the effect of similar treaties of cession in West Africa. Thus, Viscount Haldane, in delivering the opinion of the Privy Council in the oft-quoted case of *Amodu Tijani v. Secretary, Southern Nigeria*[79] put forward the following proposition with regard to the treaty by which King Docemo ceded Lagos to the British in 1861:

> *"As a result of the cession to the British Crown by former potentates the radical title [in Lagos lands] is now in the British Sovereign. But that title is throughout qualified by the usufructuary rights of the communities, rights which as the outcome of deliberate policy, have been respected and recognized".*

Having thus held that the cession of the radical or ultimate title to the Lagos lands to the British Crown was made on the footing that the rights of property of the inhabitants were to be fully respected, Viscount Haldane then went on to assert that

> *"this principle is the usual one under British policy and law when such occupations take place. The general words of the cession are construed as having related primarily to sovereign rights only".*[80]

79 (1921) 1 A.C. 399 at p. 404.

80 Ibid., at p. 411.

It is submitted, with respect, that this principle which is stated to be the usual one "*under British policy*" does not apply in the case of the cession of territories in Sierra Leone by the native rulers to the British. This difference or departure from the usual principle could presumably be attributed to the methods and purpose of occupation and settlement of the territories in Sierra Leone. From the outset, the lands acquired from the chiefs were intended to be outright purchases to be used as permanent homes for the community of freed slaves who were being sent out from Britain. This is evidenced by the fact that once the lands had been ceded neither the settlers nor the British Colonizers observed any of the familiar usages between landlord and stranger. No rent was paid for the land nor was tribute offered to the former owners. Further, on the death of the rulers who had first ceded the lands no new treaties were signed as recognition of the subsisting rights of their successors, a practice which was usual in the landlord-stranger relationship. Finally, where necessary, the British were prepared to use superior military force to safeguard or impose any rights to which they thought they were entitled under the treaties of cession.

3.2.4 Conclusion

Thus, the claim of the British Crown, and of those deriving title through or under it to ownership of the lands that came to comprise the territory of the former Colony, was absolute. There were none of the usual reservations of rights to the ultimate or radical title made in favour of the indigenous population. Whatever vested rights these latter held over these lands were completely and effectively extinguished and were replaced by rights and interests based exclusively on English law, which henceforth came to govern land tenure within the Colony (now Western Area) of Sierra Leone. Despite any doubt which might be entertained about the initial validity of the claim to absolute ownership maintained by the Crown this theory has come to be generally accepted as the legal basis of all title to land in the Western Area today.

CHAPTER 4
ASPECTS OF THE APPLICATION OF THE RECEIVED ENGLISH LAND LAW IN THE WESTERN AREA

4.1 INTRODUCTION

This chapter is devoted to setting out, in outline only, the manner in which certain key concepts, doctrines and fundamental principles of English land law were received in the Colony of Sierra Leone, and the extent to which they are still in force in the Western Area of Sierra Leone even though in the process of reform and modernization of English property law most of them have been amended and/or repealed in England.

There has been hardly any attempt by the local legislature to adopt or to adapt the major statutory reforms that were introduced into the English law of property by the legislation enacted in England in 1925. In this regard, virtually all the statutory provisions discussed in this work are from pre-1925 English property legislation. In short, to a very large extent, the land law currently in force in Sierra Leone consists basically of the English common law, the doctrines of equity and English property statutes enacted prior to 1911.

Of all the areas of English law received in Sierra Leone, the law of property is probably the most complex. For this reason, and because of the need to keep a proper balance between this and other parts of this work, it is intended to limit the present discussion to only certain basic doctrines, and important aspects of the received land law, which tend, in a typical way, to reveal the impact and the continued influence of the received English law of property on the system of land tenure in Sierra Leone as a whole. Since a comprehensive statement of the received English law may be accessed in older editions of standard works on English law of property, only important and frequently encountered aspects of the received land law are discussed below:

i. the doctrines of tenures and estates;
ii. equity and the law of trusts;
iii. co-ownership;

iv. the law of landlord and tenant; and
v. the law of mortgages.

4.2 THE DOCTRINES OF TENURES AND ESTATES

The doctrine of tenures and the doctrine of estates are two of the most fundamental doctrines of the English law of real property. In order to assess the significance of these doctrines in the land law of Sierra Leone it is necessary to trace briefly their evolution in the English legal system up to the date English law was introduced into Sierra Leone.

The origins of the doctrines may be traced back to the introduction of the feudal system in England after the Norman Conquest in 1066. Under this system all lands in England came to be regarded as owned by the Crown; a subject could not own land but was deemed to be a tenant, holding his land of the Crown, either directly or indirectly, under one or other of the various tenures. Thus, what the tenant owned was not the land itself but interests in it. The term "*tenure*" was used to describe the quality or manner of the tenant's holding, and the term "*estate*" described the quantum or the extent of his interest in the land.

At the early stages of the system there were two main categories of tenure:

i. Free tenure consisting of tenures in chivalry (or military tenure), tenures in socage and spiritual tenures; and
ii. Unfree tenures – villainage or copyhold.

Each tenancy stipulated the services, such as military service, to be performed by the tenant. Apart from these services, there were certain incidents of tenure such as relief, wardship, escheat and forfeiture. Another peculiarity of the early feudal system was that each time the land was transferred a new tenancy was created. This was known as the process of sub-infeudation.

However, by the time English law came to be introduced into Sierra Leone there had been certain important changes in the feudal system of tenure in England. Firstly, by the Statute of Quia Emptores, 1290, alienation by sub-infeudation had been prohibited and no new tenures could thenceforth be created except by the Crown. Secondly, and more importantly, the Tenures Abolition Act 1660, converted all free tenures into socage tenure, and abolished the most burdensome incidents of tenure, leaving only escheat, reliefs and fealty.

The doctrine of tenure was introduced into Sierra Leone almost imperceptibly through the making of Crown grants of lands in the former Colony. As mentioned in Chapter 1, when Sierra Leone became a Crown Colony in 1808, all lands within the territory became theoretically the absolute property of the Crown. Thus, when the Colonial Government came to confirm existing grants of land and to issue new ones, lands were conveyed to be held by the grantees "*by the tenure of free and common socage*", or freehold, as it is more commonly called. Though from the wording of these grants, the grantees could be considered as tenants of the Crown, in practice, they held their lands as absolute owners. In fact, freehold tenure in Sierra Leone has always been considered as being free from virtually all the incidents of tenure to which we have already referred. However, at the early stages of the Colony's history, land grants were made subject to the payment of quit rent, the oath of allegiance and an undertaking by the grantee to cultivate or otherwise develop the land. One incident of the tenurial relationship that was introduced directly, and has survived in Sierra Leone, is the right of escheat and forfeiture enjoyed by the Crown. This deduction may be made from the fact that in 1886 it was considered necessary for the local legislature to enact the Escheat Ordinance (now Cap. 20) which according to its long title was intended:

> *"to provide for the appropriation of the casual revenue of the Crown arising from escheated estates, and to declare the law and practice in cases of escheat".*

Ironically, this particular piece of legislation has survived in the statute book, even though the right of escheat has been superseded by the right of the State to take the unclaimed assets of persons dying instestate as *bona vacantia* under the provisions of the Administration of Estates Act, Cap. 45. Strictly speaking, forfeiture, which was also provided for in the Escheat Ordinance, was a right of the Crown, dependent upon the Royal Prerogative rather than upon tenure, to seize and keep the land of any person attainted of high treason or felony.

Thus, though in theory there was nothing to prevent the Crown from reserving tenurial incidents when it made the grants of land in the Colony, it is submitted that it was only an attenuated form of the doctrine of tenure that was introduced into Sierra Leone. Unlike the position in England where, "*despite the sweeping changes made by statute, the fundamental principles of ownership of land remain the same as before the legislation of 1925*", that is, the Sovereign remains the lord paramount of all land within the realm, in Sierra Leone today, there is no trace of any tenurial relationship between the State, which succeeded to the land rights of the Crown, and the private owner of freehold land. It could therefore be said that as far as ownership of land in Sierra Leone is concerned the doctrine of tenure is only of academic interest.

In contrast, the doctrine of estates, which in effect is an offshoot of the doctrine of tenure, is still of great significance in the system of land tenure in the Western Area of Sierra Leone. Just as under English law, interests in land are classified according to their quantum or duration, the maximum time before which the interest or tenancy must come to an end is termed the estate for which the tenant holds the land. The two main categories of estates which could subsist in land are:

i. estates of freehold; and
ii. estates of less than freehold, or leasehold estates.

4.2.1 Freehold Estates

Freehold estates could be created either in fee (called fee simple or an entailed estate), or for life (called a life estate). Similarly, estates of less than freehold also rank according to their duration, from a term of years to a lease from year to year or other periodic tenancies. Another feature of the doctrine of estates, which applies in Sierra Leone as part of the received English law, is that the various estates can exist simultaneously in land in one of three different ways:

i. in possession,
ii. in remainder; or
iii. in reversion.

Estates which are held in possession are said to be present estates, meaning that, in the absence of any other restriction in the instrument which created the estate, the holder of the estate can enjoy the fruits and benefits accruing from the property from the moment the grant takes effect. In contrast, estates which are held in remainder, or in reversion, are said to be future estates because the right of the holder of the estate, to enjoy the fruits and benefits accruing therefrom, is postponed to some time in the future on the expiry of the prior estate or interest. The distinction between the three types of estates could be illustrated by the following grant made by a settlor, **S**:

> *"To* ***A*** *for life; after the death of* ***A****, to* ***B*** *for life; and after the death of* ***B****, to* ***C*** *in fee simple provided he is already married at the death of* ***B****."*

A holds an estate in possession because his interest vests at the date of the grant. **B** holds a future estate in remainder because his interest only vests in possession in the future after the expiry of **A**'s estate, that is, when **A** dies. **C** also holds a future estate like **B** but, as we shall illustrate below, with a slight difference. Although it is apparently the intention of **S** to dispose of all of his interest in the property which he has given to **A**, **B** and **C**, because he has made the gift to **C** subject to a condition, **S** still retains an interest in the property which could vest in possession in the future in the event that **C** does not fulfil the condition for the gift to him. The interest which **S** thus retains in the property is known as a reversion, because the property will revert to him in the event of the gift to **C** failing.

The above illustration also discloses another peculiarity of future estates in land under English law, that is, that estates either could be vested in interest like that held by **B** above, or could be contingent like that held by **C** and **S** above. The vesting of a contingent interest is predicated upon an uncertain event or the fulfilment of an uncertain condition. As we shall see below, a contingent interest may fail even if the event actually occurs before it is due to vest in interest or the condition is fulfilled because when the grant is made, the particular gift offends against the English common law rule against perpetuities. Put briefly, the rule against perpetuities states that a contingent interest is void *ab initio* unless it is certain that the interest will vest, if it vests at all, within the lifetime of persons living when the grant comes into operation, plus a further period of twenty-one years from the expiry of the last life in being, at the time of the grant coming into effect, plus any gestation period.

A further complication could arise if the grantor or settlor, instead of making the gift absolute, decides to make it conditional or determinable.

Thus, a gift "*to **A***" without more will be an absolute gift, but one to "***A** provided he marries **C***" will be a conditional gift, whilst one to "***A** until she remarries*" will be a determinable gift. As pointed out earlier, there are strict rules of the common law governing the creation of the various estates which, unlike the position in England today, are still applicable in Sierra Leone.

It is, in our view, useful to take a closer look at the various estates so as to give us an insight into how and when they are usually created, and the form in which they can subsist under the land law of Sierra Leone. We shall deal first with the three types of freehold estates: the fee simple, the fee tail and the life estate, before looking at leasehold estates.

4.2.2 The Fee Simple

According to section 8 of the Imperial Statutes (Law of Property) Adoption Act, Cap. 18 of the Laws of Sierra Leone 1960, a conveyance of freehold land to any person without words of limitation, or any equivalent expression, operates to pass to the grantee the fee simple or the whole interest which the grantor has to convey in such land, unless a contrary intention appears in the conveyance. Thus, in a grant "*to **A***" without more, if the grantor has a fee simple, **A** gets a fee simple; if the grantor has only a life interest, **A** gets a life interest, in this case an interest which will last for the life of the grantor, otherwise known as an interest *pur autre vie*. The Wills Act 1837, which is in force in Sierra Leone as a statute of general application, contains a provision to the same effect in respect of a devise of real property by any will made or confirmed after 1837.[81] Thus, the statutory provisions dealing with the methods of creation of a fee simple in Sierra Leone are similar to those under English law.

Under English law a "*fee*" implies an interest in land held of some lord in whom a superior title is vested and is the opposite of "*allodium*" or allodial ownership. Thus, though it is said that the fee simple is the most ample estate which can exist in land under English law, strictly speaking, it is still held in tenure and therefore falls short of absolute ownership.

Thus to say that a person owns land in fee simple really means that he holds it of somebody else (his lord) "*by the tenure of free and common socage for an estate in fee simple*". However, if we accept that the doctrine of tenure is not fully applicable in Sierra Leone, then the fee simple in Sierra Leone should be considered as the equivalent, both in law and in fact, of

81 See sections 28 and 34.

absolute ownership, since it is the persistence of the doctrine of tenure which has precluded the fee simple in England from being recognized as such. It follows that the fee simple owner of land in Sierra Leone enjoys all the advantages of absolute ownership. As it is put by the editors of Megarry and Wade's Law of Property,

> *"[The fee simple owner's] powers of 'using abusing' his land are indeed limited in many ways by statute and by the right of his neighbours .... They are not limited by any inherent narrowness in the concept of property in land."*[82]

This absolute nature of the fee simple ownership of land in Sierra Leone has always been recognized and upheld by the courts.[83]

It should be added that the fee simple not only is a concept recognized by the statute and case law of Sierra Leone, but also forms part of the established legal terminology in current and common use throughout the country in the field of conveyancing.

4.2.3 The Fee Tail

The main distinguishing feature between a fee simple and a fee tail is that at common law where the holder of a fee simple died intestate his interest would pass to his issue or, if he had no issue to his ascendants or, failing ascendants, to collaterals, such as brothers or sisters or nephews or nieces. On the other hand if the holder of fee tail interest in land dies, his interest will pass only to his issue, and only to the eldest male in each generation, or as an exception to the females equally, failing which the interest will revert to the grantor. It is this restricted succession that gave the fee tail its name, which is derived from the Latin *feodum taillatum*, literally a fee that is cut down or truncated.

Despite the fact that the fee tail is not an estate which is commonly created in grants *inter vivos* or by will, it has often been recognized by the courts in Sierra Leone as an estate which could be created and subsist in land held under English-type tenure in the Western Area of Sierra Leone. The rule at common law, which remains unaltered in Sierra Leone, is that the estate could be created by the use in a will of any words which show an

82 R.E. Megarry and H.W.R. Wade, *The Law of Real Property*, 4th edn, pp. 66–67.

83 See for example *Jaber v. Radar* (1950–56) ALR S.L. 87.

intent to create an entail, even if no technical expressions such as, "*to **A** and the heirs of his body*", or "*to **A** in tail male*", have been used. By applying this rule in construing the wills of certain Sierra Leonean testators, the courts have often declared that an estate tail had been created in circumstances where the testators probably had no such intention. Thus, in *Williams v. Bollingbroke King*[84], a Sierra Leonean testator devised real property to:

> *"**B**, his heirs and assigns for ever, as tenants in common, but in the event of **B** dying without issue, to **C** and **D**, the sons of **A**, as tenants in common, and after the death of **C** and **D**, to their heirs and assigns for ever".*

There was also a provision in the will that the property was to be for the separate use of **B**. **B** subsequently got married, and with her husband as co-mortgagor, mortgaged the property to **E** but did not acknowledge the deed before a judge.[85] **E**, in exercise of the power of sale under the mortgage, sold the property to **F** who, on discovering that there had been no acknowledgement of the mortgage deed by **B** before a judge, and that there was a gift over in the event of **B** dying without issue, repudiated the sale by **E**. In an action by **F** to recover the purchase price the West African Court of Appeal, per Michelin J, upheld the construction of the devise by the trial judge that the devise to **B** was of an estate tail, and therefore the provision of the English Fines and Recoveries Act 1833 applied to **B** who was a married woman at the date the mortgage deed was executed. **F** was therefore justified in repudiating the sale.

Another case in which the liberal rule of construction of a will was used to create an entail is *May v. Williams.*[86] The testator in that case had devised property to his widow, his children "*and their legitimate children after them for ever*". Kingsley, Ag. C.J. held that the words "*for ever*" were words of limitation and construed the devise as creating an entail confined to those legitimate children of the persons named in the devise. Similarly in *Sawyer v. Rose,*[87] a devise to **A** with limitation that the property devised was to descend "*from children to children*" was held to create an estate tail.

---

84 (1922–45) 2 S.L. Law Rec. 21.

85 As was then required under section 40 of the Fines and Recoveries Act 1833. This Act was repealed by the Imperial Statutes (Law of Property) Adoption Act, Cap. 18 of the Laws of Sierra Leone 1960.

86 (1950–56) ALR S.L. 55.

87 (1960–61) 1 SLLR 107.

This approach of the courts in construing wills in such a way that has sometimes led to the creation of an entail was explained by Bankole Jones, P. in the Court of Appeal in the case of *George v. George*[88] when he stated *obiter* that in construing the will of a Creole the Court would take notice of the long-established Creole practice of devising estates so as to descend from one generation to another with the object of preserving them as family property for as long as possible. In that particular case, the Court had to construe a devise in the will of a Creole testator to his son "*and* [the son's] *issue as tenants in common*". The trial judge, Cole, Ag. C.J. (as he then was), had construed the term "*issue*" to mean "*children*".[89] Ironically, the Court of Appeal upheld this construction and further held that on the face of the will the expression "*issue*" was a *word of purchase* and, distinguishing *Wild's case*,[90] concluded that the devise was to the son and all his children as tenants in common.

In a dissenting judgment Marcus-Jones, J.A. took the view that in such devises as in that particular case the word "*issue*" was prima facie to be construed as a word of limitation and not as a word of purchase and was equivalent to "*heirs of the body*". He therefore concluded, quite rightly it is submitted, that on a proper construction of the will the word "*issue*" had been used as a word of limitation creating in the devisee an estate tail, (the words "*tenants in common*" or the gift over notwithstanding), and that since no steps had been taken by the devisee either by deed or by will to bar the entail, the property devolved on his intestacy on all his heritable issue as tenants in common.

Apart from such instances, where the courts in construing a will have recognized the concept of the fee tail as part of the received English land law, there is no evidence that it features in any significant way in the land law of Sierra Leone. Sierra Leoneans who wish to tie up land in the family tend to create a settlement involving the grant of successive life interests up to the limit allowed by the rule against perpetuities.

4.2.4 The Life Estate

For the reason just stated, this type of freehold estate is frequently created in land either by deed *inter vivos* or by will. Prior to the enactment of the Imperial Statutes (Law of Property) Adoption Act, Cap 18, a life estate

88 (1967–68) ALR S.L. 86.
89 The High Court judgment is reported as *George v. George* (1964–60) ALR S.L. 480.
90 (1599), 6 Co. Rep. 16b.

could arise by operation of law in the case of curtesy or dower.[91] Of the two types of life estates, the life estate for the life of the tenant and the estate *pur autre vie*, only the former is commonly created in Sierra Leone. Finally, it should be noted that, in Sierra Leone, an interest in land for life can still exist as a legal estate. Apart from this distinction, the law of life estates is the same as that applicable under English law to the corresponding equitable life interests.

It should be noted for completeness, that where the life estate is created as part of a settlement, the powers of the life tenant are still governed in Sierra Leone by the Settled Land Acts 1882–1890 adopted under the Imperial Statutes (Law of Property) Adoption Act, Cap. 18.

4.2.5 Leasehold Estates

All the various forms of leasehold interests could be created in land in Sierra Leone. In practice, leaseholds are probably of greater importance than some of the freehold estates such as the fee tail and the life estate. Their main characteristic, in contrast with freehold estates, is that their maximum duration is fixed in time. Another distinction is based on the fact that leaseholds are still classified as personalty at law whereas freehold estates are classified as realty. However, this distinction is of little practical importance as, for virtually all purposes, leaseholds are now recognized as interests in land, thus leading to their further classification under the heading of "*chattels real*".

As under English law, leasehold interests are created either by contract or by operation of law. The principal categories of leasehold estates which could subsist in land in Sierra Leone are the term of year or fixed term, and the periodic tenancy

4.2.6 The Fixed Term

The main characteristic of this form of leasehold estate is the certainty of its duration. The term for which the tenant holds the land must be fixed and definite in the sense that it must have a certain beginning and a certain ending. The fact that the term might be curtailed (for example, by forfeiture) under some stipulation to this effect in the lease does not alter the basic conception, that is, that of certainty of duration. The term may be

91 See section 5 of Cap. 18.

for as short a period as one year, or for as long as three thousand years, and may therefore, potentially, last longer than a life estate but the former will still be classified as a leasehold. The duration of the term as well as other incidents of the tenancy are matters for agreement between the parties to the transaction. A lease, therefore, falls into two major areas of substantive law: "*property*" in so far as it is an estate in land, and "*contract*", regulating the respective rights and duties of the parties.

4.2.7 Periodic Tenancies

The main distinction between the fixed term and a periodic tenancy is that whereas the former determines automatically the periodic tenancy continues until proper steps are taken to determine it. Thus if it is from year to year, it must be determined by six months' notice expiring on the anniversary of the tenancy, and if it is for a lesser period, by notice equal to the length of the successive terms. Though a periodic tenancy may thus continue indefinitely, at any given moment the tenant's estate has a fixed term which may be renewed by tacit mutual consent if no notice to determine is given by either party.

4.2.8 Tenancies at Will and at Sufferance

Though these tenancies are generally treated as being subject to the law governing leasehold estates it has been said of the tenancy at will that it

> *"involves tenure (that is a relationship of landlord and tenant) but no definite estate, for there is no defined duration of the interest".*[92]

However, the payment of rent by a tenant at will, on a yearly basis or at other periodic interval, makes him a tenant from year to year or some other periodic tenant.

In the case of a tenancy at sufferance, since this only arises where a tenancy has determined but the tenant remains in possession without the landlord's assent or dissent, it involves neither an estate nor any real tenure. Strictly speaking, therefore, neither tenancies at will nor tenancies at sufferance should be classified as estates in land.

92 Megarry and Wade, op. cit., p. 45 .

4.3 EQUITY AND THE LAW OF TRUSTS

4.3.1 Introduction

Throughout this section, the word "*equity*" will be used in its narrow technical sense; that is meaning the body of rules which, before 1873, was formulated and administered by the English Court of Chancery and which, as we saw in Chapter 2 of this work, is one of the main sources of law applied by the courts in Sierra Leone. Like the entire English common law, equity was formally received into Sierra Leone and now forms part of Sierra Leonean law, by virtue of the reception clause contained in section 74 of the Courts Act 1965.

For the equitable jurisdiction of the High Court we have to refer to a provision of the repealed Courts Act, Cap. 7, according to which the former Supreme Court was:

> *"to possess and exercise all the jurisdiction, powers and authorities, which are vested in or capable of being exercised by Her Majesty's High Court of Justice in England".*[93]

Though the rest of the Act has been repealed this particular provision was saved by section 18(2) of the Courts Act 1965, which provides, inter alia, that:

> *"the High Court shall exercise unlimited original and supervisory jurisdiction in all causes and matters in the same manner and with the same powers and authorities as immediately before the commencement of this Act".*

The effect of the above provisions, therefore, is that the High Court of Sierra Leone has the same equitable jurisdiction as the High Court of Justice in England.

In order to assess the extent of the equitable jurisdiction of the Sierra Leonean courts generally, and the significance of equity in Sierra Leonean law in particular, it is necessary to trace the history of English equity and the development of the institution of the trust. For obvious reasons, a detailed account of such history and development is outside the scope of this work. Only a very brief outline will be given here.[94]

93 See section 11.

94 For a fuller exposition the reader is referred to standard works on the subject such as:

4.3.2 The Growth of Equity

The period immediately after the Norman Conquest had seen the birth and the early growth of the common law in England. However, by about 1250 the common law had failed to be an entirely efficient system as a result partly of the injustice of some of its rules themselves, and partly because of the rigidity of the writ system. Parties aggrieved by such injustices had to turn to the King as the fountain of justice, with a prayer that he should intervene to see that justice was done. Such petitions were referred to the Chancellor who drew upon his own sense of what justice required in each particular case. By the end of the 15th century these petitions were addressed directly to the Chancellor, the issues were tried in his own court and decrees were made in his name. This, put briefly, was the beginning of the equitable jurisdiction of the Court of Chancery in England.

When equity was first introduced, there were no set rules or procedures. Successive Chancellors decided each case on its merits and according to "conscience", and their judgments were founded not on precedence but on their own individual sense of right and wrong. Modern equity, that is the body of rules now enforced in Sierra Leone as part of the received English law, is generally dated from the Restoration and may be said to have evolved from the judgments given in the English Court of Chancery from the Chancellorship of Lord Nottingham (1673–82) down to that of Lord Eldon. By the end of the Chancellorship of Lord Eldon in 1827 almost all the principles of equity had been firmly established and the equitable jurisdiction of the English courts had expanded to its present-day proportions. It was this modern equity that was introduced into Sierra Leone by Ordinance No. 20 of 1857.

In Sierra Leone, both the common law and equitable jurisdictions have always been exercised by the same court, for when, in 1858, the Court of Quarter Sessions and the Court of Recorder of Freetown were abolished, and replaced by the former Supreme Court, the latter was vested inter alia with the same original jurisdiction as the Common Law Courts and the Courts of Chancery in England.

4.3.3 The Development of the Trust

Holdsworth, *History of English Laws*; Plucknett, *Concise History of English Laws*; and Potter, *Historical Introduction to English Law.*

The concept of the trust is perhaps the most important single contribution of equity to the substantive law of England. The original form of trust was the "*use*", employed in England in the Middle Ages for various reasons, such as to escape the burdens of feudal tenure, to give power of testamentary disposition over land (before this was provided by statute), or even to facilitate a fraud. The essence of the "*use*" was that land was conveyed to **A** (the *feofee to uses*) who was to hold it for the benefit of **B** (the *cestui que use*). But whatever the purpose for which the use was created, the position was that the common law did not recognize the rights of **B** at all, but regarded **A** as alone beneficially entitled. It was here that the Chancellor interfered to compel **A** to hold the property for the benefit of **B**, the person rightfully entitled. Thus, English law came to distinguish between two types of ownership over the same property: **A** was said to be the owner at law, and **B** the owner in equity.

Both **A** and **B** owned an interest in the same land. Since **B**'s interest was protected by the Chancellor in the exercise of his equitable jurisdiction, it became known as the equitable estate, in contrast to **A**'s interest, which, since it was protected by the common law courts, came to be known as the legal estate.

4.3.4 Legal and Equitable Estates

Since the medieval English legal system was dominated by the land law, it was in the field of land law that the intervention of equity made its greatest impact, an impact which is best illustrated by the institution of the trust and the distinction between legal and equitable rights in land. The intervention of equity in this regard followed exactly in the footsteps of the common law, so that where the interest conveyed to the trustee is a fee simple, life interest or lease, equity recognized an equivalent interest in the beneficiaries. Thus, the legal fee simple could be conveyed by the owner:

> *"to **A** in trust for **B** for life with remainder to **C** in tail with remainder to **D** in fee simple"; or "upon trust for **B** until he should die or become bankrupt; or upon trust for **B** for 99 years."*

Equitable life interests, entails, leases, reversions, and remainders, and any other interest recognized at common law, could thus be created under trusts; the maxim being "*Equity follows the law*".

As a result of the 1925 property legislation only two kinds of legal estates can now exist under English law, that is the fee simple absolute in possession and the lease.[95] Since these statutes do not apply in Sierra Leone it is still possible for a fee simple owner to make a settlement (for example, *to **A** for life with remainder to **B** in fee simple*) by which the legal estate is split up into portions. Thus, all the estates recognized at common law could still subsist in equity under a trust and be recognized as equitable estates.

Originally, an equitable ownership of land differed quite markedly from a legal ownership. Thus, the interest conferred upon the beneficiaries of a trust was at first only a right *in personam*, a right to proceed against the trustee personally to compel him to carry out his trust. It followed, therefore, that any person other than the trustee into whose hands the trust property might come was not amenable to the jurisdiction of equity. In contrast, legal ownership confers rights *in rem*, rights of property in the land itself, which can be enforced against anyone. According to Megarry and Wade,

> *"the Chancellors solved this problem by extending the categories of persons upon whom performance of the trust would be enjoined".*[96]

This involved the application of two basic equitable principles. The first is that a person who takes trust property without giving value in exchange (such as an heir, executor or donee) must take it with all its burdens, equitable as well as legal, for it is said, equity does not assist volunteers. The second is a corollary of the principle of conscience which forms the basis of equitable intervention. A person who takes trust property knowing that the property is being transferred to him, in breach of trust, is bound by the trust, and it does not matter that he has given value. In the view of equity he becomes a constructive trustee. Such a purchaser need not have actual notice of the trust but he may be fixed with constructive notice if he would have known of the trust had he taken in the matter all such steps as a reasonable man would have taken.

95 See section 1 of the English Law of Property Act 1925.
96 Megarry and Wade, op. cit., p. 113.

The above two principles are summed up in the cardinal maxim in which is expressed the true difference between legal and equitable rights:

> *"Legal rights are good against all the world; equitable rights are good against all persons except a bona fide purchaser of a legal estate for value without notice and those claiming under such a purchaser".*[97]

The effect of this development is that equitable rights in land are advanced almost to the status of legal rights though they remain vulnerable against a person who had bought the land from the legal owner in genuine ignorance of the existence of the trust.

However, even though the transferee may have given value for the trust property, and was without notice that the transfer was in breach of trust, he is nevertheless bound by the trust if the interest he has acquired under the transfer is not a legal interest but only an equitable one: for the maxim is, where the equities are equal the first in time prevails. Equitable interests under English law are therefore much more than rights *in personam* against trustees: they are species of property right, that is, rights *in rem*,

> *"but exceptional because of their peculiar infirmity, that they would be lost if the legal title came to a bona fide purchaser without notice".*

This distinction between legal and equitable interests could be further illustrated by reference to some decided cases. In *Kabba v. Young*[98] the respondent brought an action in the former Supreme Court against the appellant for possession of a house and also for *mesne profit* in respect thereof. The respondent had purchased the house from the vendor at a time when the second appellant had an equitable interest in it, the latter already having paid a substantial proportion of an agreed purchase price to the vendor for the same house and being in receipt of rental payments from the first appellant who occupied it as a tenant. The respondent instituted proceedings for possession of the house as its legal owner and the appellants resisted the respondent's claim on the bases, firstly, that the second appellant was a prior purchaser of the house who had fulfilled the

97 Megarry and Wade, op. cit., p. 114.

98 (1944) 10 W.A.C.A. 135.

conditions of purchase and had been put into possession by the vendor, his tenant, the first appellant; and, secondly, that the respondent, being a purchaser with notice, was bound by all the equities which the appellant could enforce against the vendor, one of them being the right to relief against a claim for possession.

The Court, per Kingdom C.J., held that:

> *"There can be no doubt that the defence would be a complete answer to an action by a vendor who brought an action against a purchaser who was in possession, who had paid part of the purchase price and had fulfilled his part of the bargain by tendering the balance within the time stipulated for full payment, as was unquestionably done in the present case. It is indeed difficult to imagine such a futile action being brought by a vendor".*[99]

In considering the position of the respondent as a second purchaser for value with notice the Court relied on a passage from Dart, *The Law of Vendors and Purchasers,*[100] to the effect that notice of land being in the occupation of a person other than the vendor is notice to a purchaser that the person in possession has some interest in the land and a purchaser having notice of that fact is bound either to enquire what that interest is or to give effect to it whatever it may be.

According to Dart:

> *"On this principle a purchaser is bound by all the equities which the tenant could enforce against the vendor".*

In the Nigerian case of *Ogunbabi v. Abowaba,*[101] the West African Court of Appeal had to consider the situation where land had been sold informally and without a conveyance to **A**, and some years later the same land was sold and conveyed to **B**. The principle that emerges from this case is that if the first purchaser can produce a purchase receipt evidencing the sale, and show that he was let into possession of the land, he will be deemed to have acquired an equitable interest in the land analogous to an estate contract, which can be converted into a legal estate by a decree of specific

99 Ibid., at p. 136.
100 6th edn (1888) at p. 975.
101 (1951) 13 W.A.C.A. 222.

performance. As the defendant in this case could have acquired knowledge of this equitable interest but for his gross or culpable negligence, he was therefore presumed to have had notice of the plaintiff's equitable interest, and as a result, could not claim to be a bona fide purchaser of the legal estate without notice.

With these cases may be contrasted the case of *Turay v. Kamara*[102] illustrating the other side of the doctrine of bona fide purchaser of the legal estate without notice. In that case, the Court of Appeal held that a purchaser for value of the legal estate in property which had been acquired fraudulently by the vendor still obtained a good title as he had no notice of the fraud. Similarly, in the Nigerian case of *Griffin v. Talabi*[103] the West African Court of Appeal held that the plaintiff who had acquired the legal title to land without notice of the defendant's equitable interest took free from it. In that case, the defendant had a conveyance from someone who had earlier bought the land in dispute but without having a conveyance executed in his favour by the original owners.

Before the sale to the defendant, the same land had been sold by way of execution to another person who sold and conveyed it to the plaintiff. There was no evidence that the defendant's predecessor, after the sale to him, ever entered into possession or, if at all he did, that he remained in continuous possession up to the time of the sale to the plaintiff. The Court held that the defendant's predecessor in title had only obtained an equitable interest in the land leaving the legal title still in the owners and which the plaintiff's predecessor took under the sale by way of execution.

4.3.5 The Effect of Registration

There is at present no enactment in Sierra Leone comparable with the English Land Charges Act 1925. This has considerably reduced the importance of the doctrine of the bona fide purchaser for value without notice by providing that those equitable interests registrable under the Act, as land charges, were to be void as against a subsequent purchaser of the legal estate unless they were registered, whether the subsequent purchaser had notice of the equitable interests or not. The only mechanism available in Sierra Leone is the system of registration of instruments, the relevant statute being the Registration of Instruments Act, Cap. 256.

102 (1968–69) ALR S.L. 89.
103 (1948) 12 W.A.C.A. 371.

The main distinction between the two systems is that under the Sierra Leone statute, it is not the interests themselves which are registrable but the instruments creating them, and secondly, no distinction is made in this statute between an instrument transferring or creating an equitable interest and one transferring or creating a legal interest. Moreover, it is not even clear that registration of an instrument is constructive notice of the contents of that instrument for it is nowhere so stated in the Sierra Leone statute.

Nigerian authorities construing legislation with provisions identical to those of the Sierra Leone statute are at variance on this point with *Foloshade v. Duroshola*[104] holding that registration of a deed is not notice of its contents, whereas in *Akinbade v. Elemosho*[105] the Court treated the registration of an earlier conveyance as one of the factors fixing a subsequent purchaser with notice.

It is submitted that the latter of these two conflicting cases is to preferred, as it is consistent with the general principle that a purchaser will have constructive notice of any prior interest which would have come to his knowledge had he made due inquiries, and will therefore have constructive notice of the contents of any registered instrument.

4.3.6 The Creation of Trusts in Sierra Leone

Despite the peculiar infirmity of equitable estates, in that they could be lost if the legal title was transferred to a bona fide purchaser without notice, these estates are regularly created in Sierra Leone mainly because of the advantages afforded by the institution of the trust to a settlor or a testator who wishes for various reasons to keep the ownership, and the management of a property, apart especially where it is to be preserved for the benefit of several generations. Trusts of land may fall under any one of following three heads:

i. Settled land;
ii. Trusts for sale; and
iii. Charitable trusts.

4.3.7 Settled Land

104 (1961) 1 All N.L.R. 87.
105 (1966) N.L.Q. 42.

The strict settlement in origin denoted a complicated restrictive type of family settlement designed to tie up land in the settlor's family. In its simplest form, it might be a gift by will "*to **A** for life with remainder to **B**, the son of **A**, in tail*". A life interest followed by an entail was the most effective limitation for tying up land, since anything more restrictive would violate the rule against perpetuity. In such cases, the land was substantially inalienable until **B** was able to bar the entail on attaining his majority. However, under the provisions of the English Settled Land Act 1882, which is in force in Sierra Leone, any arrangement whereby any land, or any estate or interest in land, is limited to, or in trust for, any persons by way of succession becomes a settlement and the land becomes settled land. Thus, if freehold or leasehold land is conveyed by deed or given by will,

> *"unto and to the use of A and his heirs in trust for X for life, remainder in trust for Y and his heirs"*

or freehold land is conveyed

> *"to A for life remainder to B and his heirs"* or *"to X and his heirs to the use of Y and the heirs of his body"*,

in each case, the land becomes settled land. Every grant or devise of a limited interest creates a succession and therefore a settlement. It makes no difference whether the interests are legal or equitable.

Though a settlement could thus be created by deed or by will, in Sierra Leone, virtually all settlements arise as a result of land being given by will to several beneficiaries in succession, the intention of the testator being that it should remain inalienable as long as possible. We may recall the remarks of Bankole Jones, President of the Court of Appeal, in the case of *George v. George*[106] to the effect that the general practice of the Sierra Leone Creoles in particular is to devise their family estates "*so as to descend from one generation to another*" and in such a manner as to ensure that the entire estate would be preserved as family property as long as possible. Ironically, such a desire conflicts with the general scheme of the Settled Land Act 1882 which still governs such devises that create a settlement within the meaning of the Act.

106 (1967–68) ALR S.L. 93.

The main purpose of the English legislation was to give the tenant for life under the settlement wide powers of dealing with the land – by sale, exchange, leasing, mortgaging or otherwise – without the consent of the other beneficiaries or an order of court, just as if he were the owner in fee simple, the rights of the beneficiaries being protected in the case of a sale by shifting the settlement from the land to the purchase money which has to be paid into court or into the hands of at least two trustees of the settlement.

The powers and duties of the tenant for life in granting a lease under the Settled Land Act 1882 were considered by the Court of Appeal in the case of *Khalil v. John*[107]. In particular, the Court held that in construing the words "*best rent*", as used in section 53 of the Act, there is no set formula for arriving at a desired figure.

What is the best rent, is in each case, a question of fact and a matter for negotiation. Provided the tenant for life has not acted mala fide, a lease which is invalid for failing to secure the best rent may be saved under the relevant provisions of the Leases Act, 1849, which was held to be in force in Sierra Leone as a statute of general application.

The Act also applies to land held by or in trust for infants; and this is so even where there is no succession, as for example, where a testator devises land to his infant son in fee simple. Again, contrary to the desire of most Sierra Leonean testators, the Act enables an infant's land to be sold irrevocably by the trustees of the settlement acting on his behalf, even without the consent of his parents or guardians, but with the usual safeguard that the purchase-money has to be held by the trustees until the infant comes of age. The only case in which the Act does not apply is where a simple or bare trust is created by the testator – where one or more persons of full age are entitled to the property devised in possession absolutely – that is, where there is no element of succession and no infancy, whether there is a trust for sale or not.

4.3.8 Trusts for Sale

The main object of a trust for sale is normally to provide the beneficiaries with an income. It is a settlement which directs the trustee to sell the property, invest the proceeds, and hold the resulting fund upon the trusts declared by the settlor. The effect of creating such a settlement is that even before sale, the rights of the beneficiaries are deemed to be rights in

107 (1960–61) 1 SLLR 167.

personalty, for equity treats that as done which ought to be done. Since the average Sierra Leonean settlor's intention is to preserve his property *in specie*, this form of settlement is not very common in Sierra Leone. Moreover, in the present state of the country's economy, there are relatively few investment opportunities other than investments in real property.

For this reason also, the provisions of the Settled Land Act 1882, which give the tenant for life wide powers of sale, exchange, leasing, mortgaging and otherwise dealing with the settled land free from the trusts, are seldom invoked for the purposes of a sale.

The usual practice is for the tenant for life to lease out the property if it is not needed for occupation by the testator's family or, in the case where it consists of undeveloped land, to grant a building lease in accordance with the provisions of the Act.

4.3.9 Perpetuities and Charitable Trusts

Apart from trusts of real property intended for the benefit of named individuals or group of individuals, such as members of the settlor's or testator's family, or for some private purpose, a trust may be created which has as its object to promote public welfare. The main distinction between the two is that a private trust must comply with the rule against perpetuities whereas a public trust, otherwise known as a charitable trust, is not void even if it infringes the perpetuity rule. Under English law the rule against perpetuities is intended to guard against the remote vesting in interest of property, the assumption being that the control of remote vesting would preserve the alienability of land.

The English common law rule against perpetuities which applies in Sierra Leone may be stated briefly as follows:

> *"Every limitation of a future interest, in real or personal property, to arise on a contingency is void, unless the contingency is such that it must happen, if it happens at all, within the period of a life or lives in being and 21 years after. If the limitation is made without reference to lives in being the period is 21 years".*

In the case of *In Re Allie (Deceased)*[108] the former Supreme Court had to consider the validity of a devise of certain properties by a Sierra Leonean testator to his executors,

> *"upon trust that they shall put them out to rent and utilize the rent accruing therefrom [inter alia] to defray the traveling expenses and maintenance of any member of my family who may come to Freetown on a visit from home at Jaber".*

In construing this clause of the will Smith C.J. observed that:

> *"The trust, on the face of it, is in perpetuity, and it is plain that if English law is to be applied it is void on this account unless it is a valid charitable trust"*[109].

The learned Chief Justice then went on to hold that English law was the applicable law. He then considered at length the English law on charitable trusts. In particular, he relied on the case of *Income Tax Special Purposes Commissioners v. Pemsel*[110] in which, according to the learned Chief Justice, Lord Macnaghten set out what has since been accepted as the classical definition of a charity in these words:

> *"Charity in its legal sense comprises four principal divisions: trusts for the relief of poverty; trusts for the advancement of education; trusts for the advancement of religion; and trusts for other purposes beneficial to the community".*[111]

The nature of a charitable trust was also considered by the former Supreme Court in the case of *In Re Thomas Charitable Trust*[112]. In that case, the Court applied the *cy-pres* doctrine where a testator, by his will made in 1900, had left money to trustees to found an agricultural college, "*for the education of male natives of the Colony*". Due in part to a lack of

108 (1950–56) ALR S.L. 338.
109 Ibid., at p. 341.
110 (1891) A.C. 531.
111 Ibid., at p. 538.
112 (1950–56) ALR S.L. 12.

candidates from the Colony, the work of the college had to be suspended. The plaintiffs applied for the Court to construe the will as relating to male natives of the Protectorate as well as males of the Colony. They contended inter alia, that under the *cy-pres* doctrine the grant should be extended to admit to the benefit of the trusts of the charity male natives of the Protectorate. Beoku-Betts, J. considered the circumstances in which the doctrine may be applied in English law and relied in particular on the dicta of Evershed, J. the case of *In Re Dominion Students Hall Trust, Dominion Students' Hall Trust v. Attorney-General*[113] where the *cy-pres* doctrine was extended "*to include persons who if excluded, would create an undesirable and unnecessary discrimination*".

4.3.10 Implied, Resulting and Constructive Trusts

Finally, mention should be made of the fact that apart from express trusts, as under English law, other trusts may arise in Sierra Leone as a result of the operation of equity. Thus, an implied trust is said to arise where, without any conveyance of the property in question having been made, two people enter into such a relationship with each other that equity implies therefrom that one holds on trust for the other. A resulting trust may also arise by operation of equity where there is a conveyance of property in any of the following circumstances:

i. Where the beneficial interest under an express trust is not fully disposed of or exhausted.
ii. Where property is purchased in the name of another; except where the presumption of a resulting trust is rebutted by evidence of an intention to benefit the person named in the conveyance or where the presumption of advancement (itself rebuttable) applies; and
iii. Where a person makes a voluntary conveyance of his property and the presumption of advancement does not apply.

Constructive trusts are imposed by equity from a fiduciary relationship already in existence. Thus, in *Issac v. John*[114] an agent who had bought property in his own name with money provided by his principal was held to be a constructive trustee of the property for the benefit of the principal.

113 (1947) Ch. 183 at p. 186.
114 (1957–60) ALR S.L. 208.

Similarly, if by virtue of his position a trustee obtains any valuable interest in the trust property for himself, the general rule is that he holds it on a constructive trust for the beneficiaries. The same applies to a person to whom trust property is conveyed if he knew that the conveyance was in breach of trust or if, without being protected by the plea of purchaser without notice, he afterwards deals with the property in a way inconsistent with the trust.

4.4 CO-OWNERSHIP OF LAND

4.4.1 Introduction

It has been shown earlier in this work that under English law it is possible for several interests in land to co-exist simultaneously. It is equally possible for two or more persons to hold an estate or interest in land simultaneously. The English common law relating to co-ownership of land, which governed such concurrent interests, was introduced into Sierra Leone as part of the received law, and is still applicable in the same form that it was introduced several years ago. It is also important to distinguish it from communal tenure which is a characteristic feature of customary land law.

The English common law recognized four types of co-ownership:

i. Tenancy in common;
ii. Joint tenancy;
iii. Tenancy by entireties; and
iv. Coparcenary.

4.4.2 Joint Tenancy and Tenancy in Common

Both the joint tenancy and the tenancy in common could still subsist at common law in Sierra Leone. The main distinction between these two types of co-ownership is the right of survivorship (*jus accrescendi*). Where a joint tenant dies without having severed his interest in the joint tenancy his share accrues on his death to the surviving joint tenants so that the last surviving joint tenant ultimately becomes the sole or absolute owner. In contrast, when a tenant in common dies, his share passes to his successors, whether by will or on an intestacy.

Another distinction which in way could be said to explain the first relates to the nature of the interest held by a tenant in common as opposed to a joint tenant .Whereas tenants in common are regarded as holding undivided shares in the land, each share being capable of being alienated *inter vivos* or by will, joint tenants do not own any identifiable shares by themselves, but each joint tenant owns the whole, subject to the concurrent ownership of the other joint tenants.

Thus, if land is transferred to **A**, **B**, and **C** as joint tenants, or without any additional words, they take as joint tenants because there is nothing to show what shares they are to have in the property. But if the property is given to them, with the addition of words, which show what shares they are to have in it, such as for instance "*equally*", "*share and share alike*", "*in equal shares*", "*between A and B*" or "*amongst A, B and C*" they take as tenants in common.

In any event, in order for co-owners to hold as joint tenants certain conditions must be satisfied. There must be evidence in the grant of the "Four Unities": interest, title, time and possession:

i. Unity of interest requires that the nature and duration of the interest held by each joint tenant must be the same. There would be no unity of interest in a grant "*to A for life and to B for 30 years*";
ii. Unity of title means that the co-owners must have derived their title from the same instrument or the same act. There would be none if one co-owner derives his title from a grant *inter vivos* and the other under a will;
iii. Unity of time means that the interest of the co-owners must have vested at the same time. Thus, in a grant *inter vivos, to A for life remainder to B for life*, the grant evidences unity of interest and of title as between **A** and **B** but not unity of time as the vesting of **B**'s interest is postponed till after the death of **A**; and
iv. Unity of possession is necessary for there to exist any type of co-ownership whether joint tenancy or tenancy in common. This requirement is satisfied, irrespective of whether the estate is a present or future Thus in a grant, *to A for life remainder to B and C for 30 years thereafter to C absolutely*, there is unity of possession but not unity of interest between the co-owners and **C**. Therefore, their co-ownership during the period of 30 years after the death of **A** is a tenancy in common.

Even if all the four unities are present, the co-ownership may not necessarily give rise to a joint tenancy. It merely means that the co-ownership is capable of being a joint tenancy depending on a variety of factors such as the intention of the grantor.

Thus, in the absence of fraud or mistake, if the grantor uses the words "*as joint tenants*" or "*as tenants in common*" to qualify the grant effect must be given to his intention as expressed. As stated earlier, where the grantor uses words of severance this would indicate that the co-owners are to take as tenants in common. Further, equity leans against a joint tenancy because of the doctrine of survivorship. As a result, in certain circumstances, consistent with the equitable maxim "*equality is equity*", it may be presumed in equity that the co-owners are to hold as tenants in common rather than as joint tenants. The presumption, which is rebuttable, will arise:

i. Where two or more persons purchase land and contribute to the purchase price in unequal shares;
ii. Where two or more persons hold land as part of a formal or informal partnership; and
iii. Where two or more persons lend money and take land as security for the loan. Irrespective of whether the lenders advanced the same or different amounts they hold their interest in the mortgaged property as tenants in common.

4.4.3 Determination of a Co-Ownership

At common law, a joint tenancy may be determined by any of the following acts:

i. Total or partial alienation by one joint tenant to a stranger;
ii. Acquisition by one joint tenant of a greater interest than that held by his co-owners;
iii. Partition;
iv. Sale;
v. Severance by mutual agreement; and
vi. Any course of dealing which would tend to indicate that the co-owners intend to hold their interests as tenants in common rather than as joint tenants.

Similarly, a tenancy in common could be determined by sale, partition or acquisition by one tenant of the shares of his co-tenant.

4.4.4 Tenancy by Entireties and Coparcenary

We can dispose of the last two forms of co-ownership very briefly as they are seldom encountered in practice in Sierra Leone. Prior to the enactment of the Married Women's Property Act 1882, a husband and wife were considered as one for the purpose of acquisition of interest in land. A tenancy by entireties arose where an estate was conveyed or devised to a married couple in circumstances that would have dictated that they take as joint tenants had they not been married. However, unlike a joint tenancy, the interest could not be severed and the survivor became the absolute owner on the death of one of the two. This situation could not possibly arise in Sierra Leone today because by section 4 of the Imperial Statutes (Law of Property) Adoption Act, Cap. 18:

> *"so much of English law as restricts the acquisition holding or disposition of ... real or personal property by a married woman as such"*

is no longer in force in the Western Area.

Under English law prior to 1926, a coparcenary existed where two or more persons together constitute a single heir, for example, where a tenant in tail died intestate leaving female heirs only. Though the successors enjoyed unity of possession, interest and title, the right of survivorship did apply. The co-ownership could have been determined by partition or transfer to a coparcener or a stranger.

4.5 THE LAW OF LANDLORD AND TENANT

4.5.1 Introduction

This is yet another area of the received English law of property that continues to apply with very little or no modification by local legislation. The only local statute of significance in this field is the Rent Restrictions Act, Cap. 52, which, as we shall see, gives some protection to tenants but without necessarily creating statutory tenancies. Though the English law of landlord and tenant consists basically of common law rules from the law of real property and the law of contract, in recent years there has been a great deal of statutory intervention in England, often prompted by social considerations such as the need for rent control and protection of certain categories of tenancies. However, most of these statutes were enacted in England after 1911 and therefore do not apply in Sierra Leone. The relationship of landlord and tenant in Sierra Leone is therefore to a very large extent still governed by the English common law rules in this field, which developed as a special branch of the law of contract. Mainly for this reason, this work does not give a detailed account of the substantive law but merely illustrates its application in such aspects as the creation, the incidents, and the determination of leases and tenancies.

4.5.2 Creation of Leases and Tenancies

At common law, a parole lease was sufficient to create the relationship of landlord and tenant in the case of corporeal hereditaments. There was no necessity to employ either a deed or writing. This is still the law with regard to leases not exceeding three years and other periodic tenancies. Thus, a periodic tenancy for an indefinite period, such as one from year to year, or week to week, may be validly created by a parole lease, the rationale being that though it may endure for much longer than three years it may also be determined at an earlier date.

The requirement that a lease, which exceeds three years, must be made by deed is part of the received English statute law in force in Sierra Leone. Firstly, section 1 of the Statute of Frauds 1677, provides that:

> *"All leases … or term of years … made or created … by parole, and not put in writing and signed by the parties so making or creating the same, or their agents thereunto lawfully authorized in writing, shall have the force and effect of leases and estates at will only".*

Section 2 of the Act exempts leases not exceeding three years at a rent of two-thirds at least of the full improved value of the land. Secondly, section 3 of the Real Property Act 1845, provides that a lease required by law to be in writing shall be void at law if made after 1 October 1845, unless also made by deed.

The courts in Sierra Leone have consistently held that both these statutes are of general application and therefore received into Sierra Leone and have applied the provisions referred to above in a long line of cases. However, though the effect at law of non-compliance with these provisions is to render the lease incapable of passing the term agreed upon by the parties the courts in their equitable jurisdiction have held that the abortive lease must be regarded as a contract for a lease, provided the constituents for a specifically enforceable contract are present. The agreement for the lease must not only be legally binding, there must be evidence of either a memorandum in writing, as required by section 4 of the Statutes of Frauds 1677, or an act of part-performance by the plaintiff. Thus, in *Ibrahim v. Solomon*,[115] the plaintiff and the defendant entered into a verbal agreement whereby the plaintiff, as tenant from year to year of certain premises owned by the defendant, agreed to give up possession of the premises so that they could be rebuilt, on the understanding that he would be granted a lease of part of the rebuilt premises for a term of five years. The plaintiff paid a year's rent in advance but the defendants failed to grant him a lease on the agreed terms. The plaintiff then instituted an action for the specific performance of the verbal agreement. The court considered whether there had been sufficient acts of part-performance on which it could decree specific performance and held that mere payment of rent by the plaintiff was not sufficient part-performance to take the agreement out of the statute.

It would appear, however, that even where a lease exceeding three years has been made by deed it will be void unless the deed is registered within the period prescribed by the Registration of Instruments Act, Cap. 256.

The effect of non-registration is to render the agreement void at law but not necessarily in equities. Therefore, neither party may enforce any of its terms unless the relationship of landlord and tenant has arisen by operation of law where, for example, the tenant has been let into possession and rent paid calculated periodically. This in fact is one of the ways that a periodic tenancy often arises where it is not created by express grant. As stated above, a periodic tenancy will arise by operation, or presumption of law, whenever a person is in occupation of land with the permission of the owner, not as a licensee nor for an agreed period, and rent measured, by reference to a particular period, for example yearly, monthly or weekly, is paid and accepted. In *Samuels v. Dialdas & Sons*[116] the Court held that

115 (1950–56) ALR S.L. 331.

116 (1960–61) 1 SLLR 21.

a periodic tenancy had arisen by operation of law where the plaintiffs permitted the defendants to hold over after the expiry of a fixed term lease and accepted rent from them.[117]

However, in *Katah v. Chellaram & Sons*,[118] Verity, Ag. J.A. explained that:

> *"It is not to be assumed that from a mere holding over and acceptance of rent a tenancy from year to year is to be implied".*

According to the learned Judge, it is in each case a question of fact whether, in the particular circumstances, it is shown to have been the intention of the parties to create such a tenancy, or whether the facts go to show no such intention. On the facts of this particular case, the Court held that there was no such intention, and thus a periodic tenancy had not arisen by operation of law.

A tenancy at will may be created either expressly or by implication, as, for example, where a tenant with the consent of his landlord, holds over after the expiry of the lease; or where he goes into possession under a contract for a lease or under a void lease. A tenancy at sufferance, in contrast, arises for example where a tenant for a fixed term remains in possession without the consent of the landlord, after the term has come to an end.

4.5.3 Terms of Leases and Other Tenancies

The terms and conditions of a lease, or of any other type of tenancy, is almost always a matter of agreement between the parties. In Sierra Leone, there is absolute freedom of contract in this regard for there is no law, statutory or otherwise, which prevents parties from including any stipulation or condition, however onerous or one-sided, as a term of the lease or tenancy agreement. However, where the parties have not expressly provided for certain essential terms these will be implied to give effect to their presumed but unexpressed intention. Thus, the relationship of landlord and tenant automatically implies a covenant for quiet enjoyment

117 See also *Johnson v. Zachariah* (1957–60) ALR S.L. 118.
118 (1957–60) ALR S.L. 7.

by the tenant.[119] On the other hand there is no implied undertaking on the part of the landlord that the premises are or will be fit for habitation, or for any particular use.[120]

Apart from the covenant and conditions, which will be implied by law under a lease or tenancy agreement, there are certain covenants which are usual in leases and tenancy agreements. Among these the most commonly encountered are the following.

On the part of the tenant:

i. A covenant to pay rent;
ii. A covenant to pay all charges for service and utilities such as electricity, water and telephone;
iii. A covenant to keep the premises in repair and deliver them up in a state of repair at the end of the term;
iv. a covenant not to assign sublet or part with possession of the premises either unconditionally or without the consent of the landlord;
v. A covenant to permit the landlord to enter and view the state of the premises; and
vi. A covenant of re-entry and forfeiture for non-payment of rent or breach of any other covenant.

4.5.4 Covenant to Pay Rent

The obligation of the tenant to pay rent, the quantum and manner of payment are invariably the subject of express agreement. Where there is no such express stipulation the obligation to pay is itself the corollary of a common law right of the landlord founded on implied contract. This common law right has been given statutory force by the provision of section 4 of the Distress for Rent Act 1737, (applicable in Sierra Leone) which entitles an owner to recover from any person occupying his land a reasonable sum for use and occupation of the land, unless otherwise agreed.

However, even where the quantum of rent payable has been fixed by agreement, this could be modified on the application of either party to have the rental value of the demised premises determined by the Rent Assessment Committee in accordance with the provisions of the Rent Restriction Act, Cap. 52.

119 See *Budd-Scott v. Daniel* (1902) 2 K.B. 351; and *Markam v. Paget* (1908) 1 Ch. 697.
120 See *Hart v. Windsor* (1843) 12 M&W 68.

The application could be made either by the owner or the tenant of any dwelling house or shop, or by a prospective tenant to whom an offer to let any dwelling house or shop has been made (section 5 Rent Restriction Act, Cap. 52). For the purposes of the Act, a dwelling house is defined as a house let for human habitation but excludes a house bona fide let at a rent which includes payment in respect of board or service or both board and service. A shop is defined to include any stores, warehouses or other premises let for professional, trade and business purposes. In assessing the rental value of such premises, the Committee is to take into account, inter alia, the rent obtaining in the same locality in respect of similar accommodation, and it is to make adjustment for improvements or deterioration of the premises or increase in the ratable value of the premises.

Though the Act enables either the landlord or the tenant to apply for an assessment, virtually all the applications to the Committee on record so far have been made by tenants with a view to securing a reduction in the rent. The landlord would inevitably be more interested in an increase than in a reduction of the rent and would normally achieve this by simply increasing the rent at the end of the term. However, in theory, where a landlord has made improvements during the course of the tenancy, provided he did so with the consent of the tenant, he may be entitled to have the rent increased by the Committee in accordance with the provisions of the Act. Outside the limits of this Act a tenant in the Western Area of Sierra Leone today has no protection against prohibitive and unconscionable increases in rent by his landlord.

4.5.5 Covenant to Repair

At common law, a tenant for a fixed term of years is liable for both voluntary and permissive waste.[121] However, it is usual to insert a covenant obliging the tenant to keep the premises in "good tenantable repair" or "in good and tenantable order and repair:; in "good and substantial repair"; or even in "perfect repair". In *Johnson v. Zachariah*[122] Bairaman C.J. defined the tenant's obligation to repair as being:

121 See *Westham v. East London Waterworks Co.* (1900) 1 Ch. 624.
122 (1957–60) ALR S.L. 118.

> *"a duty to keep the premises wind and water tight but no duty to sustain and uphold the premises nor is he responsible for natural wear and tear",*[123]

citing in support of this proposition the cases of *Wedd v. Porter*[124] and *Marsden v. Edward Heyes Limited.*[125] In *Jaber v. Jaber*[126] Boeku-Betts, relying on a passage from Williams and Yates,[127] stated that the covenant to repair is performed if the tenant keeps the premises substantially in repair and does all he reasonably ought to do in performance of the covenant.

According to Beoku-Betts, J., the question of whether the tenant has well and substantially maintained and kept the premises in good condition and repair according to the agreement is a matter of evidence. The yardstick is that of a reasonably minded owner. Material factors to be taken into consideration are the locality, character and age of the premises.

4.5.6 Covenant by the Tenant not to Assign or Sublet

At common law a tenant enjoys the right of free disposition of his holding. He may do this either by assignment, which involves a grant of his whole interest in the demised premises, or by granting an estate for a term shorter than his own in the form of an underlease or subtenancy. It is, however, usual to provide for the matter of assignment or subletting by express agreement. Such a covenant may be expressed in an absolute form, imposing an unconditional prohibition against assignment or subletting upon the tenant, or it may be in a qualified form, merely prohibiting assignment or subletting "*without the (written) consent of the lessor*". There is frequently a proviso added to the qualified form that the landlord's consent "*shall not be arbitrarily or unreasonably withheld*".

The English Courts have tended to construe such covenants very strictly, insisting that the prohibition imposed on the tenant should not be allowed to go beyond the letter of the agreement.[128]This policy has also been adopted by the courts in Sierra Leone and in the case of *Macfoy v.*

123 Ibid., at p. 121.

124 (1916) 2 K.B. 91.

125 (1927) 2 K.B. 2.

126 (1950–56) ALR S.L. 97.

127 *The Law of Ejectment*, 2nd edn, 1911 at p. 92.

128 See, for example *Church v. Brown* (1808), 15 Ves. 258 at p. 265 per Lord Eldon; and *Grove v. Portal* (1902) 1 Ch. 727.

U.A.C. of Sierra Leone Limited[129] the Court of Appeal applied the case of *Chaplin v. Smith*[130] and held that a lessee who had covenanted not to part with possession of the demised premises was not in breach of that covenant where he merely permitted another person to have use of the premises whilst he retained possession as lessee.

4.5.7 Determination of Leases and Tenancies

At common law a lease or tenancy for a fixed term automatically determines at the end of the term granted. In Sierra Leone, there are no statutes in force comparable with such English statutes as the Agriculture Act 1947, the Landlord and Tenant Act 1957, the Rent Acts 1957–68 and the Leasehold Reform Act 1967 which in various ways give a tenant security of tenure (even where his tenancy has expired or has been duly determined) by creating a statutory tenancy, or even going to the extent of enabling the tenant to acquire the freehold as is possible under the Leasehold Reform Act 1967. The nearest the Sierra Leonean tenant can come to acquiring security of tenure is by invoking the provisions of the Rent Restrictions Act, Cap. 52. We have already considered earlier in the chapter[131] the circumstances in which the Act could be invoked for the assessment of the rental value of certain demised premises. The Act further provides security of tenure for the tenant by prohibiting the making of any order for possession where the rental value of the demised premises has been determined or is in the course of being determined, except on six specified grounds.

The grounds on which possession may be ordered could be summarized under the following headings:

i. Breach: where any rent lawfully due from the tenant has not been paid or an obligation of any tenancy has not been fulfilled, such as the covenant to repair;[132]
ii. Nuisance: where the tenant or any other occupant is guilty of conduct which is a nuisance or annoyance to adjoining occupiers or is guilty of illegal or immoral user of the premises;[133]

129 (1964–66) ALR S.L. 3.
130 (1926) 1 K.B. 198.
131 Above, p. 92.
132 See *Williams v. Boyle* (1942) S.L. Law Rec. 30.
133 See *Mohyeddin v. Nicol* (1968–69) ALR S.L. 247.

iii. Tenant's Notice to Repair: where the tenant has given notice to quit and the landlord has acted on it to his detriment;
iv. Premises required for the landlord or his family: where, in the case of a dwelling house, it is required by the landlord for himself or his family or for some other person engaged in his full-time employment, or in the case of a shop the landlord requires it for his own profession, trade or business and no other reasonable accommodation is available to him for such purposes;[134]
v. Public interest: where the premises are required for any purpose which in the opinion of the court is in the public interest;
vi. Alternative accommodation: where the landlord is willing to provide alternative accommodation for the tenant at such rent and on such terms as the Rent Assessment Committee considers reasonable and in the case of a shop as would reasonably preserve the goodwill of the tenant's business.

The Act is however silent as to how long the tenant may thus remain in possession after the rental value of the premises has been determined. No case has yet come up for decision where the courts have had cause to give an indication of what sort of period should expire before an order for possession could be made where the above six grounds are relied on. It has, however, been held that a tenant who ceases to be in physical or actual occupation of the premises cannot rely on the protection of the Act.[135]

Where the Act does not apply, even a fixed-term tenancy could be determined prematurely by the landlord, invoking a condition for re-entry and forfeiture. In such a case, there must be a clear intention expressed on the part of the landlord to determine the tenancy upon the tenant's breach of the stipulated condition. Though such clauses normally provide that upon re-entry the lease shall determine and be forfeited, there is authority to support that proposition that the effect of a breach of condition is to make the lease voidable and not void.[136] The landlord in such a case has the option whether or not to terminate the tenancy, and only some act which shows an intention to end it will avoid the lease or the agreement.

134 See *Spencer v. Gibson* (1962) 2 SLLR 84.
135 See *Wilson v. Guerrier* (1922–45) 3 S.L. Law Rec. 28.
136 See *Davenport v. R.* (1877) 3 App.Cas. 115 at 128.

4.5.8 Relief against Forfeiture

Under sections 210–212 of the English Common Law Procedure Act 1852 the Sierra Leone courts have a wide discretion to grant relief against forfeiture. Where the breach alleged is non-payment of rent, relief will normally be granted if the tenant pays or tenders the rent to the landlord, or pays the same into court together with the costs of the proceedings before the trial. A tenant is also afforded an opportunity to petition the court for relief from forfeiture under the provisions of the Conveyancing Act 1881. Under this Act, before a landlord can enforce forfeiture, he must first serve a notice on the tenant specifying the particular breach complained of, and requiring that it be remedied, if possible, or reasonable compensation paid therefor. Even where the tenant has failed to comply with such a notice the court may still grant him relief.

The question of relief from forfeiture is entirely at the court's discretion. In the exercise of this discretion the court is to take into account all the circumstances of the case including the nature of the breach, the frequency or otherwise of its occurrence, and the conduct of the tenant. Thus, in *Jaber v. Jaber*[137] the plaintiff sought to have the defendant's lease forfeited on the ground that he had failed to repair the demised premises. The defendant as part of his defence pleaded that the plaintiff was not the owner of the premises and that the notice to repair served on him was insufficient. Beoku-Betts, J. held that the discretion to grant relief from forfeiture must be exercised judicially and:

> *"in doing so the conduct of the defendant must be considered. If the defendant relies on the discretion of the court, his conduct must be such as entitles him to favourable consideration".*[138]

In the *Jaber* case, because of the conduct of the defendant in impugning his landlord's title, and his persistent refusal to observe the covenant to repair, relief against forfeiture was refused.

In another case, *Basma v. Noureldine*[139] decided a year later, Beoku-Betts, J. laid emphasis on the very wide discretion which section 14 of the Conveyance Act 1881 gives the courts. The learned Judge cited with

137 (1950–56) ALR S.L. 97.

138 Ibid., at 106.

139 (1950–56) ALR S.L. 234.

approval the dicta of Earl Loreburn, L.C. in *Hyman v. Rose*[140] to the effect that it was not advisable to lay down any rigid rules for guiding the court in the exercise of its discretion. In that case, Beoku-Betts, J. exercised his discretion in favour of granting relief against forfeiture for breach of covenant to repair but did so subject to a condition that the defendant agreed to employ the plaintiff's architect to do all the repairs necessary to put the property in a good and tenantable state. Similarly, in *Zion Church Trust Board v. Charaf*[141] though the trial Judge, Tejan-Sie, C.J. thought the conduct of the defendant had been "*most irresponsible*" because of the deliberate disregard of his obligations under the lease, he concluded that he was satisfied that "*on just reasonable grounds*" there was no case for forfeiting the lease. However, this case, decided on its peculiar facts, should be viewed as exceptional, especially in view of some of the factors which the judge took into account in exercising his discretion in favour of the defendant, such as the fact that the lease was a building lease and the property would eventually revert to the plaintiff, and that the particular breach – non-payment of rent – was capable of remedy. In contrast, in *Garrick v. Withfield,*[142] the defendant was refused relief against forfeiture mainly because his defence amounted to a denial of the landlord's title, even though the pleading was amended before the end of the trial

4.6 THE LAW OF MORTGAGES

4.6.1 Introduction

As in England, the law of mortgages in Sierra Leone is the product of the common law, equity and statute. The relevant statute is, in the case of Sierra Leone, still the Conveyancing Acts 1881 and 1911, adopted as part of the statutory law of Sierra Leone by virtue of the Imperial Statutes (Law of Property) Act, Cap. 18.

The traditional concept of a mortgage under English law is the conveyance or other disposition of land as security for the payment of a debt or the discharge of some obligation for which it is given. This form of secured credit transaction has always been of great appeal as much to the average landowner in the Western Area as to banks, other financial institutions and even to non-institutionalized moneylenders. This is mainly due to the fact that in Sierra Leone land has for long been regarded as

140 (1912) A.C. 623 at 631.
141 (1967–68) ALR S.L. 248.
142 (1950–56) ALR S.L. 394.

the principal resource for most people and affords the only investment opportunity as well as the most acceptable security for the raising of financial credit. There is hardly a land-owning family in Freetown that has not, at one time or another, used its landed property as security for various forms of loan either in the formal or the informal sector.

However, in view of what has been stated about the essential similarity between the English law of mortgages and the law as applied in Sierra Leone, at least as far as the common law and equity are concerned, this aspect of this work shall be limited to merely highlighting certain aspects of the repealed English law still in force in Sierra Leone, such as those governing the modes of creating mortgages in Sierra Leone, and the rights and remedies, of the respective parties under the transaction.

4.6.2 Creation of Mortgages

The earliest form of mortgage under English law was a mere pledge, either a *vivum vadium* (a living pledge) in which the entire debt was discharged by means of the creditor entering into possession of the property of the debtor and using the rent and profits accruing therefrom to offset both principal and interest, or a *mort vadium* (a dead pledge) in which the creditor used the rents and profits accruing from the property in his possession to offset only the interest, leaving the principal to be paid from other sources by the debtor.

In Sierra Leone a mortgage could be created in one of four ways:

i. By adopting the statutory form to be found in the schedule to the Conveyancing Act 1881;
ii. By a deed of conveyance from the mortgagor to the mortgagee;
iii. By a charge by way of legal mortgage created over the property of a company in accordance with the provisions of the Companies Act, Cap. 249; or simply
iv. By the deposit of the title deed of the mortgagor, which fact may be evidenced in a memorandum of deposit.

However, the form of the mortgage to be used and the method of its creation will invariably depend on, firstly, the nature of the interest which is being mortgaged, whether freehold or leasehold, and, secondly, on whether it is a legal or equitable mortgage that is to be created.

4.6.3 The Statutory Mortgage

Statutory mortgages could be created in accordance with the provisions of the Conveyancing Act 1881. Section 26(1) of this Act provides that a mortgage of freehold or leasehold land may be made by a deed expressed to be by way of statutory mortgage. The form of such mortgage is that given in Part 1 of the Third Schedule to the Act, subject to such variations and additions, if any, as circumstances may require. The section also provides that certain covenants shall be deemed included and implied in the deed by virtue of the Act. These are, firstly, that the mortgagor will pay the principal debt on the agreed date and, in the meantime, will pay interest as and when due, and, secondly, that on repayment of the principal and interest, the mortgagee shall, at the request of the mortgagor, reconvey the mortgaged property to the mortgagor, or as he shall direct. In either case, where the mortgage is made in accordance with the common law, or with statute, the mortgage deed to be valid at law must be registered within the prescribed time limit laid down by section 4 of the Registration of Instruments Act, Cap. 256. The statutory form of mortgage is seldom utilised in Sierra Leone.

4.6.4 The Non-Statutory Mortgage

The common law or non-statutory form of mortgage, which had gone through a number of changes by the time it came to be introduced in Sierra Leone, still survives in Sierra Leone today, and involves the conveyance of the mortgagor's interest in the land to the mortgagee. A typical mortgage document of a freehold land would recite the interest of the mortgagor in the property intended to be used as the security, the terms of the loan, the agreement of the mortgagor to create the mortgage followed by a conveyance of the fee simple to the mortgagee, subject to a proviso for redemption by the mortgagor on payment of the principal and agreed interest and a reconveyance of the fee simple by the mortgagee.

Unlike the charge by way of legal mortgage, which is the form of mortgage currently in use in England and other former British colonies, a mortgage created by the conveyance of the fee simple to the mortgagee deprives the mortgagor of the opportunity of creating subsequent mortgages, irrespective of the fact that the value of the property is several times higher than the amount of the loan secured by the mortgage.

A legal mortgage of leasehold property on the other hand could be made in either of two ways:

i. By assignment of the unexpired term of the lease accompanied by a covenant for re-assignment on redemption; or
ii. By a sublease of the mortgagor's term, granting the mortgagee a sub-term at least a day less than the mortgagor's term, on condition that the mortgagee surrenders the sub-term when the debt is repaid.

It is usual to grant a sub-term, less a number of days, to enable the mortgagor to create subsequent mortgages, if necessary, by other sub-terms, each being longer than the previous ones. In this way it is always possible to create several legal mortgages of leasehold property.

4.6.5 Creation of Equitable Mortgages

The above methods are only applicable to the making of a legal mortgage. An equitable mortgage on the other hand can arise either as a result of express agreement or by operation of law. The following is a summary of the circumstances under which an equitable mortgage could be created in Sierra Leone today.

i. Where there is a contract to create a legal mortgage: If **A** agrees that, in consideration of money advanced, he will execute a legal mortgage in favour of **B**, an equitable mortgage is created in favour of **B** and he can enforce the execution of a legal mortgage by suing in equity for specific performance. In theory, the mortgagee may call for a legal mortgage, but in practice, he is content to rest upon his equitable rights, for equity treats the contract as an actual mortgage.
ii. Mortgage of an equitable interest: Where the mortgagor has only an equitable interest in the property to be mortgaged, any mortgage he creates must necessarily be equitable. Thus, where a legal mortgage of the fee simple in land has already been created, the mortgagor retains only an equity of redemption, which is an estate in equity, and therefore all subsequent mortgages of the same land are merely equitable. Similarly, beneficiaries under a

trust only have equitable interests in the property and can therefore create only equitable mortgages thereof.

iii. Defect of form: Where a document purporting to be a legal mortgage is not in the form required by law, it creates an equitable mortgage. In such a case, parol evidence is admissible to establish the intention of the parties as to the terms and extent of the security. Similarly, a document charging a property for a debt may operate as an equitable charge, entitling the holder to payment out of the property, but it does not amount to an agreement to give a legal mortgage and the strict mode of enforcing it is by sale and not by foreclosure.[143]

iv. Deposit of Title Deeds: A deposit of title deeds of property for the purpose of security creates an equitable mortgage. This is based on the common law principle that an agreement concerning land accompanied by adequate part-performance is enforceable by an order of specific performance. Such an equitable mortgage, by deposit of title deeds, may or may not be accompanied by a written document setting out the terms agreed on by the parties. This is the form of mortgage that is most often used by the banks and moneylenders in Sierra Leone to secure small loans. It is usual for the banks to have executed a memorandum under seal since a mortgage by deed confers on the creditor the statutory power of sale.[144]

4.6.6 The Rights and Remedies of the Mortgagee

One of the immediate legal effects of the creation of a legal mortgage, involving the transfer of the mortgagor's legal estate in the land to the mortgagee, is to give the mortgagee a right to possession of the mortgaged property, and to the appropriation of the rents and profits accruing therefrom.[145] A mortgagor remaining in possession of the mortgaged property is, at law, in no better position than a tenant at sufferance and could be ousted at the pleasure of the mortgagee either by peaceful entry or by an action for possession. However, in practice, this right of the mortgagee is never enforced. This is due mainly to the fact that equity

143 See *Mathews v. Goodday* (1861) 31 L.J. Ch. 282.
144 See *Barclays Bank D.C.O. v. Khalil* (1972–73) ALR S.L. 14.
145 See *Smith v. Walker* (1968–69) ALR S.L. 115.

imposes a duty on the mortgagee to account strictly to the mortgagor for rents and profits realized while in possession of the mortgaged property.

The most important of the mortgagee's rights over the property are those which arise on non-payment of the principal and interest on the agreed date. Strictly, at law, if the mortgagor failed to repay his debt on the date stated in the instrument, he lost his land forever to the mortgagee and yet remained liable for the debt. This situation has however been altered by the intervention of equity which gives the mortgagor an equitable right of redemption after the contractual date has passed. Provided the mortgagee receives all that is due him from the mortgagor he can always be compelled by equity to restore the property to the mortgagor. But the recognition of this equitable right of redemption in the mortgagor has also led to the recognition of a right in the mortgagee to maintain an action for foreclosure, that is to insist on the mortgagor exercising his equitable right to redeem his property within a reasonable time, or be forever precluded from exercising it.

Where foreclosure is ordered, the mortgagor's equitable right to redeem is declared by the court to be extinguished[146] and the full beneficial title of the mortgagor in the mortgaged land becomes vested in the mortgagee. The remedy of foreclosure is also open to an equitable mortgagee and it is immaterial whether his mortgage is made merely by deposit of title deeds or is accompanied by a written memorandum.[147]

The next remedy of the mortgagee, in the event of non-payment of the debt by the mortgagor, is the power to sell the mortgaged property. This may be expressly provided for in the mortgage deed, or may arise under the provisions of the Conveyancing Act 1881. The more usual practice is for the statutory power of sale to be incorporated in the mortgage document. Under the Act, the power arises where the mortgage was made by deed (it could therefore apply to equitable mortgages made by deed) and the mortgage money is due, that is the legal date for redemption has passed. Even where the power has arisen under the Act, it does not become exercisable unless one of the following three conditions has been fulfilled:

i. Notice requiring payment of the mortgage money has been served on the mortgagor and default has been made in payment of part or all of it for three months thereafter; and

146 See *Sawyer v. Rose* (1960–61) 1 SLLR 107.

147 Cf. *Barclays Bank D.C.O. v. Khalil* above, dicta of Cole C.J. at p. 20.

ii. Some interest under the mortgage is in arrear for at least two months;
iii. There has been non-compliance with some provisions contained in the Act or in the mortgage deed (other than the covenant for payment of the mortgage money or interest) by the mortgagor or by someone who concurred in making the mortgage.

The effect of a valid sale is to vest all the estate and interest of the mortgagor in the purchaser subject to prior unredeemed mortgages, if any, but free from the vendor's and subsequent mortgages and the equity of redemption. As was pointed out earlier, the statutory power of sale is available to an equitable mortgagee only where the mortgage was by deed. Even in such a case, since the power vested in the mortgagee by the Act is to sell "the mortgaged property", it has been held that an equitable mortgagee can sell no more than he has, that is an equitable interest.[148]

A right of the mortgagee, which is probably the least utilized, is the right to appoint a receiver. Where the mortgage is by deed, a mortgagee, legal or equitable, has a statutory power to appoint a receiver.[149] This power arises, and becomes exercisable, in similar circumstances as the power of sale. The court may also in certain circumstances appoint a receiver to take possession of the property.[150]

These remedies of the mortgagee are cumulative and are in addition to his right to sue on the covenant for repayment except where he has foreclosed. The usual practice in Sierra Leone, especially where the mortgagee is a bank, is to first sue to enforce the covenant for repayment.

When this yields no result, then the machinery provided by the Execution Against Real Property Act, Cap. 22 is utilized to effect a sale of the property. The advantage of this procedure is that the responsibility to ensure that the sale is conducted in compliance with the Act is shifted from the mortgagee to the sheriff.

4.6.7 The Rights and Remedies of the Mortgagor

The mortgagor's basic right is the legal right to redeem. The legal right is contractual and arises by virtue of the agreement of the parties and from

148 See *Re Hodson & Howes Contract* (1887) 35 Ch. D 688; cf. *Re White Rose Cottage* (1965) Ch. 940 at 951 per Lord Denning.

149 See section 19(1) and (3) of the Conveyancing Act 1881.

150 See *Barclays Bank D.C.O. v. Khalil*, above.

the very nature of the transaction. The equitable right to redeem on the other hand does not arise until after the legal date of redemption has passed. This latter right is a creature of equity and is protected by equity in two ways: firstly, by the principle that if a transaction is found to be a mortgage then "*once a mortgage, always a mortgage*"[151] and, therefore, redeemable notwithstanding any agreement to the contrary; secondly, by the rule that a mortgagee should not stipulate for a collateral advantage which would make the right of redemption illusory or render the equity of redemption valueless by clogging it. However, as has been shown above, this equitable right of redemption may be extinguished against the mortgagor's will by foreclosure, sale, or even lapse of time where the mortgagee remains in possession of the mortgaged land for twelve years, without giving any written acknowledgement of the title of the mortgagor, or of his equitable right to redeem, and without receiving any payment on account of principal and interest made by or on behalf of the mortgagor.[152]

The mortgagor's most valuable asset is probably his equity of redemption. This is the sum total of a mortgagor's right in his property, and it is a recognition of the fact that equity regards the mortgagor as owner of the mortgaged property, subject to the mortgage. A useful account of the nature of an equity of redemption is given in the dictum of Lord Hardwick in *Casborne v. Scarfe* as follows:

> *"An equity of redemption has always been considered as an estate in land, for it may be devised granted, or entailed with remainders, and such entail and remainders may be barred by a fine and recovery, and therefore cannot be considered as a mere right only, but such an estate, whereof there may be a seisin; the person, therefore, entitled to the equity of redemption is considered one owner of the land".*[153]

A Sierra Leonean case of some importance which raises several issues relating to the mortgagor's equity of redemption is *Alie Bundu v. Grant Sallu Bundu Kamara*.[154] The respondent had mortgaged his freehold property in Freetown to **D** to secure a loan of two thousand leones. The mortgage was effected by a conveyance of the said property to **D** subject

151 See *Seton v. Elade* (1802) 7 Ves. 265 at 273 per Lord Eldon, L.C.
152 Section 13 of the Limitation Act, No. 51 of 1961.
153 (1737) 1 ALK 603 at 605.
154 1976 Judgment of the Supreme Court (unreported).

to a proviso for redemption on an agreed date. Before the date fixed for redemption, the appellant, a judgment creditor of the respondent, in execution of the judgment debt, purported to purchase the respondent's equity of redemption at an auction sale undertaken by the sheriff pursuant to section 5 of the Execution against Real Property Act, Cap. 22. The appellant subsequently obtained an order from the High Court directing **D** to execute a deed of release of the mortgage in his favour, after payment of the outstanding principal and interest by the Sheriff out of the balance of the proceeds of sale of the equity of redemption. The appellant thereafter went into possession of the mortgaged property, and the present action was brought by the respondent claiming a reconveyance of the mortgaged property to him. The trial judge dismissed the claim but his decision was reversed by the Court of Appeal. The Supreme Court upheld the decision of the Court of Appeal on the following grounds:

i. That, by utilizing the proceeds of sale in the hands of the Sheriff not only to satisfy the judgment debt but also to obtain for himself the reconveyance of the legal estate, the appellant had purported to purchase both the equitable and the legal estate in the mortgaged premises when all he was entitled to was the equitable estate vested in the respondent, that is the equity of redemption;
ii. There was no evidence that the procedure laid down by the Execution Against Real Property Act, Cap. 22, had been followed by the Sheriff. The sale was therefore to be set aside;
iii. The release of the mortgaged property was as a result improperly obtained and was also to be set aside;
iv. In view of (ii) and (iii) above the legal estate had reverted to **D**; and
v. As it had been held that the sale by the Sheriff as well as the release were a nullity the respondent's right to redeem the mortgage had never been extinguished and he was therefore entitled to the mortgaged property.

It is submitted with respect, that the decision of the Supreme Court could be criticized on several grounds. The Court seems to have placed much reliance on the effect of the purported sale of the respondent's equity of redemption by the Sheriff under the Execution Against Real Property Act, Cap. 22. Indeed, the Supreme Court correctly applied the proposition that there is nothing in law to prevent a judgment creditor purchasing the assets of a judgment debtor sold in execution. Secondly, the Court also upheld the decision in *Porter v. Khoury*[155] that a mortgagor's equity of redemption could properly be sold in execution under the provisions of the Execution Against Real Property Act, Cap. 22, section 2 of which makes "*the house, lands and other hereditaments and real estate situated or being within any part of the Western Area*" and belonging to a judgment debtor liable to be sold in execution. The only reason, therefore, it would appear, why the sale of the equity of redemption was set aside was because, in the words of Harding, J.S.C.,

> "*it was not proved that the conditions precedent to sale as contained in Sections 7, 9 and 10 of the Execution Against Real Property Act, Cap. 22, were complied with by the Sheriff before he purported to sell the property in question*".

Harding, J.S.C. therefore concluded that in such circumstances he was not satisfied that the sale was bona fide and therefore was to be set aside. It is submitted, with respect, that there was no obligation on the appellant in the case to prove that the sale was regular and bona fide, nor, indeed, does the Act impose any burden on a purchaser to prove that a sale is regular and bona fide. In the absence of proof to the contrary, the sale should have been presumed valid – *omni praesummuntur rite et solemniter esse acta.*

Another criticism that can be made of the Supreme Court's decision is that the Court seemed to have acted on the basis that the appellant, as an assignee of the mortgagor's equity of redemption, needed a court order before he could secure the release or reconveyance of the mortgage property. If this inference is wrong, then the ruling that the order for the release of the property was irregular and was therefore to be set aside was, in the opinion of the present writer, *per incuriam*, since it does not necessarily support the final decision.

Fourthly, even if the purported sale of the mortgagor's equity of redemption by the Sheriff was irregular and, therefore, the subsequent release or reconveyance by **B** to the appellant was also of no effect, this per se did not entitle the mortgagor to a reconveyance of the mortgaged property.

155 (1937–49) ALR S.L. 128.

The only way he could have been entitled was by duly redeeming the property, that is by paying off the outstanding principal and interest. The sale of the equity of redemption having been set aside, the appellant was entitled to a refund of the price thereof and all the parties were to be returned to the position in which they stood when the appellant purported to purchase the mortgagor's equity of redemption.

To revert to the analysis of the rights of a mortgagor, it should be added that where he is left in possession of the property he can sue at common law to protect that possession, and to recover the land from anyone other than the mortgagee or someone claiming through him. Since equity regards the mortgagor as owner of the mortgaged property subject to the mortgage, the mortgagor can bring an action and obtain equitable remedies against any person, for example to prevent injury to the property or to enforce a restrictive covenant.

Under the provisions of the Conveyancing Acts 1881 and 1911, the mortgagor is also authorized to grant an occupation lease for a term not exceeding twenty-one years, or in the case of a building lease, for a term not exceeding ninety-nine years, unless a contrary intention is expressed by the parties, or a receiver has been appointed and is duly acting. Usually, the parties stipulate that the mortgagor should not exercise his statutory powers of leasing at all, or without the consent of the mortgagee, as was the case in *Barclays Bank D.C.O. v. Khalil.*[156]

Finally, the mortgagor has the right to request the court, in foreclosure proceedings, to order a sale of the mortgaged property in lieu of foreclosure.[157] This is a most important safeguard where, as is usually the case, the value of the property mortgaged far exceeds the amount of the mortgage debt. Even where a foreclosure order absolute has been made, the court has a discretion, in special circumstances, to reopen the foreclosure. Such circumstances may include where an unexpected event at the last moment prevents the mortgagor from raising the money, or where the property has some special value to the mortgagor (for example an old family house) or there is a wide gap between the real value of the property and the mortgage debt.[158]

156 Above.

157 See section 25(2) Conveyancing Act 1881.

158 See *Campbell v. Holyland* (1877) 7 Ch. D. 166 per Jessel, M.R. at 172–5.

4.7 IMPACT OF THE RECEIVED ENGLISH LAW

What has emerged from this review of certain aspects of the received land law in force in the Western Area of Sierra Leone is that, because it is based almost exclusively on the received English law of property as at the reception date of 1880, several anachronisms exist, particularly in the area of statute law. Besides, apart from the fact that most of the reform introduced by the 1925 English legislation are not in force in Sierra Leone, there has been a marked absence of local legislative intervention in the field of land law generally. However, it would be inadvisable to undertake any review or reform of the received English law relating to land tenure in the Western Area of Sierra Leone without taking the opportunity to explore the possibility of harmonizing it with customary law which, to a large extent, still governs land tenure in the Provinces of Sierra Leone. The feasibility of such harmonization, as well as the advantages and disadvantages thereof, will be examined later in this work.

CHAPTER 5
ACQUISITION AND TRANSFER OF TITLE TO LAND IN THE WESTERN AREA

5.1 INTRODUCTION

In Chapter 3 we traced the origins and legal bases of title to land in the Western Area back to the establishment of the self-governing entity for the settlement of freed slaves up to the declaration of the Crown Colony of Sierra Leone. This chapter will examine the various types of title which subsist today, and analyse the process of acquisition and transfer of such title, as well as the evidence and degree of proof required for the judicial confirmation of these titles. In particular, we shall be considering the problems associated with the concept of possessory title, a form of title which has become predominant in the Western Area today for reasons which will be outlined below. For the purposes of our present analysis, lands in the Western Area are classified into two broad categories, namely, State lands and private lands.

The law as stated in this chapter should be read subject to the provisions of the Non-Citizens (Interests in Land) Act, No. 30 of 1966, which restricts the right of non-citizens of Sierra Leone to acquire the freehold of land in the Western Area. It also provides that no non-citizen shall purchase or receive in exchange or as a gift any reserved leasehold, that is a leasehold of which the unexpired term exceeds twenty-one years, without first obtaining the consent of a Board set up under the Act. The significance of these statutory provisions, and those of the Provinces Land Act, Cap. 122 of the Laws of Sierra Leone 1960, which impose similar restrictions on the acquisition of land in the Provinces by non-natives, is discussed in Part 4 below.

5.2 STATE LANDS

According to the interpretation section of the State Lands Act, No. 19 of 1960 (formerly the Crown Lands Ordinance), State lands are defined to include:

> *"all lands which belong to the State by virtue of any treaty, cession, convention or agreement, and all lands which have been or may hereafter be acquired by or on behalf of the State, for any public purpose or otherwise whosoever and land acquired under the provisions of the Public Lands Act and includes all shores, beaches, lagoons, creeks, rivers, estuaries and other places and waters whatsoever belonging to, acquired by, or which may be lawfully disposed of by or on behalf of the State."*[159]

Indeed, this definition is wide and all embracing. Theoretically, all the lands which together constituted the territory of the former Colony of Sierra Leone, and which are not held by private individuals, or other entities, by virtue of the provisions of certain statutes or grants from the State or its predecessor in title, the Crown, are to be considered State lands.

With regard to the lands to which the State succeeded, on the attainment of independence from the British, we need not go over the process of acquisition of title thereto as this has been exhaustively dealt with in Chapter 3. It should however be emphasized that not even the Government of Sierra Leone knows the exact extent, in terms of acreage, of the lands that could properly be classified as "State lands". This is because there has never been a comprehensive survey of the lands involved, nor are there any existing accurate and reliable records of the total number of grants of land so far made by the Crown and later the State.

However, it is possible to identify specific parcels of land which had been surveyed, for one purpose or the other, during the Colonial era, and which were later transferred to the Sierra Leone Government with proper records. These lands include:

i. The Defence Lands (under the Defence Lands Acquisition Act, Cap.119);

159 See Act No. 19 of 1960, section 2.

ii. Admiralty Lands (under the Admiralty Lands Act, Cap. 123);
iii. War Department Lands (under the War Department (Kortright Hill and Kennedy Ridge) Act, Cap. 124);
iv. Former Ordinance Lands (under the Ordnance Lands Act, Cap. 125);and
v. The Kroo Reservation (under the Kroo Reservation Act, Cap. 127).

The title of the State over such lands and other identifiable State lands as defined by the State Lands Act 1960, is equivalent to absolute ownership. The use of the expression "absolute ownership" is proper because, in the case of State ownership of land in the Western Area, there is no reservation of rights of any kind in favour of individuals or communities in diminution of the State's title, other than those rights expressly disposed of by the State by grant or otherwise.

Apart from lands thus acquired by the State, as successor in title of the British Crown, there are various statutes which enable the State either to acquire title to lands compulsorily or to have title thereto declared vested in the State by executive proclamation or by judicial pronouncement. The following statutes fall into the first category:

i. The Public Lands Act, Cap. 116;
ii. The Town and Country Planning Act, Cap. 81;
iii. The Forestry Act, Cap. 189; and
iv. The Defence Lands Acquisition Act, Cap. 119;

Of these statutes, the Public Lands Act, Cap. 116, which originally provided for the compulsory acquisition of land by the State in the Western Area only but is now deemed to be applicable throughout the Provinces also,[160] is the one most commonly utilized by the State to acquire title to land for public use. Besides, the relevant provisions dealing with the procedure for the appropriation of the land and for the assessment and payment of compensation contained in the Public Lands Act, Cap. 116,

160 This is the effect of section 4(2) of the Laws (Adaptation) Act, No. 29 of 1972 which provides that notwithstanding the provisions of section 8 of the Interpretation Act 1971, every existing law shall be deemed to apply throughout Sierra Leone unless expressly or by necessary implication limited by law to a specified area or part of Sierra Leone.

are applicable whenever the State acquires title to land under any of the other statutes for use by the State.

5.2.1 Compulsory Acquisition of Land by the State under the Public Lands Act, Cap. 116

The Public Lands Act dates back to 1898 and, apart from a few minor amendments over the years, has withstood the test of time. Part I, that is sections 3–14 of the Act, lays down the procedure for giving notice to the owner or occupier of the land identified for acquisition, the survey and the eventual appropriation. Part II, that is sections 14–20, provides the machinery for the assessment and payment of compensation as well as for the determination of cases of disputed compensation and conflicting claims to ownership of any land acquired under the Act. These latter provisions of the Act have often come up for judicial interpretation. A review of the decided cases reveals certain propositions which are of relevance to this aspect of this work. Thus, *In Re Public Lands Ordinance*[161] is authority for the proposition that a claimant for compensation under the Act does not have to show that he has a good root of title to the land acquired. According to Macquarrie Ag. L.J.:

> *"all that the section [s. 17] requires is that a claimant in such a case shall show a title such as would be held valid if unchallenged."*

Another proposition which emerges from *In Re Public Lands Ordinance*[162] relates to the interpretation of section 18 of the Act which deals with the time limit within which claims for compensation should be brought. According to the West African Court of Appeal's interpretation of this section, failure to bring an action claiming compensation within one year of the notice of acquisition would deprive even an undisputed owner of his right to compensation. The narrowness of such an interpretation is evident from the following dicta of Foster-Sutton, P. in delivering the judgment of the West African Court of Appeal in the instant case. The learned President said inter alia:

161 (1920–36) ALR S.L. 340.
162 Ibid. at 344.

> *"In considering the construction and effect of this Ordinance the court must be guided by the well-known principle that a statute should not be held to take away private rights of property without compensation unless the intention to do so is expressed in clear and unambiguous term but it seems to me that, applied to the present case, the language o f the provision in question clearly leads to that conclusion."*[163]

There is no doubt, however, about the intention of the legislature with regard to section 17(9) of the Act, which stipulates that no compensation is payable where the land has been unoccupied for the period of twelve years prior to the acquisition.[164]

The effect of this provision is that a person who is unable to prove beneficial user of his land for the prescribed period may well find himself being expropriated without receiving any compensation, even though he was otherwise in actual possession or entitled to possession of the land in question at the time of its acquisition by the State.[165]

As far as the State is concerned, the registration of a plan of the land appropriated, together with a certificate, in the office of the Registrar-General within eight days of any such appropriation, is conclusive evidence that such land has been set out, appropriated and taken for the service of the State under the provisions of the Act. Payment in accordance with the provisions of section 20(4) of the Act operates as a complete discharge and acquittance of such compensation, and of all claims, in respect of the land, or any interest therein, without prejudice to any subsequent proceeding at the instance of any persons having, or alleging, a better right thereto as against the person to whom such payment may have been made.[166]

5.2.2 Non-Compulsory Acquisition of Title to Land by the State

Unlike the Public Lands Act, Cap. 116, which provides for the compulsory acquisition of title by the State making use of the simple process of

163 Ibid. at 403.

164 The word "unoccupied" here has the same meaning as under the Unoccupied Lands (Ascertainment of Title) Act, Cap. 117, see below.

165 See *In Re Public Lands Ordinance* (1937–49) ALR S.L. 264 for an application of section 17(a) of Cap. 117.

166 See section 20(4) of the Public Lands Act, Cap. 116.

appropriation and registration of a certificate, the Unoccupied Lands (Ascertainment of Title) Act, Cap. 117, and the Escheat Act, Cap. 20, require a declaration by the courts or some other competent authority before the State can claim title to land thereunder. Under the provisions of Cap.117, the Director of Survey and Lands may claim any piece of land as State land if, in his opinion, such land is unoccupied land within the meaning of the Act. For the purposes of the Act:

> *"all land shall be deemed to be unoccupied land where it is not proved by the person claiming the same that beneficial user thereof for cultivation or inhabitation, or for collecting or storing water, or for any industrial purposes, has been made for twelve years next prior to the commencement of this Act".*[167]

No such action can be taken by the Director of Surveys and Lands however where the person claiming the land is able to produce documentary evidence of title extending over a period of twelve years, nor where the land is planted with economic trees, such as banana, coffee, cocoa, gum, kola or plantain. In addition, lands which are included in the Public Register, and plans of town lots of Freetown (essentially, lands presently within the central business district of Freetown), Bonthe and York Island, are excluded from the operation of Cap. 117.

Where there is prima facie evidence that any person is wrongfully claiming any unoccupied land the Attorney-General may apply to the High Court for a summons to be issued for service upon the claimant requiring him to appear and produce documentary evidence of his title or to otherwise prove his claim of right to the land in question. The principles by which the High Court is to be guided in reaching a decision are expressly made less stringent than those applicable in the usual case of a disputed title to land. Thus, section 7 of the Act stipulates that:

> *"the court shall be guided by equity and good conscience only, and by the best evidence that can be produced, although not such as may be required or be admissible in ordinary cases, nor shall it be bound by the strict rules of evidence or*

167 See section 4 of Cap. 117.

> *procedure or by any case or by technicalities or legal forms whatever".*

The effect of this provision is that the claimant's task of proving his title as against the State is made much lighter. By relaxing the rules of evidence and procedure, and by inviting the court to act on principles of equity and good conscience, the section allows the court to take into account factors which otherwise might not have been relevant in the ascertainment of the claimant's title. Thus, a claimant, it is submitted, need not prove a good or valid title in law, but only needs to convince the court that, on a balance of justice, he ought to be allowed to continue in possession of the land. A decision in favour of a claimant, however, does not necessarily confer title in him, it only allows him to retain possession, and prevents the State from claiming entitlement thereto. On the other hand, section 8(1) of the Act specifically provides that if the land is not unoccupied, but the claimant is unable to produce documentary evidence of his title extending over a period of twelve years, then a report of the facts of the case should be sent to the President who may, thereupon, make a grant of the land to the claimant subject to such reservations and conditions as the President shall determine.

When this statute was originally enacted in 1911, it was, as indicated in its subtitle, intended to be "*an Act for readily ascertaining the ownership of unoccupied lands*". No doubt, if its provisions had been "applied" with any consistency and regularity it would have contributed, in no small measure, to the eradication of the present uncertainty surrounding the ownership of State lands, particularly in the suburbs of Freetown. It would also have, in a way, filled in some of the gaps caused by the absence of a system of registration of title. However, as it has turned out, in practice, the Director of Surveys and Lands has made little use of its provisions in recent years. Maybe this is a tacit recognition of the rather unfair advantage given to the claimant who might well be, and invariably is, a squatter under the provisions of the Act in general, and by section 7 in particular, which reduce the chances of the State succeeding in such actions.

The Escheat Act, Cap. 20, is another piece of dead wood in the statute books in the sense that its provisions have never been invoked in recent years. However, since it has not been repealed and, theoretically, remains a channel through which the State may acquire title to land, it ought to be discussed in this work. This statute was originally enacted in 1886 as Ordinance No. 19 of 1886:

> *"to provide for the appropriation of ... the revenue to arise from the estates and effects of persons who have died intestate without heirs or next of kin".*

In fact, it does declare the law and practice in cases of escheat, and specifically provides that the Attorney-General is empowered, or may be directed, in any case in which lands or tenements have escheated, or become forfeited to the State, to file a claim on behalf of the State, for a declaration by the court vesting the land in question in the State. The effect of such a declaration vesting the land in the State is the same as if there had been a trial, and judgment had been given in favour of the State in respect of the said land. However, any person claiming title to land, respecting which a declaration in favour of the State has been made, may challenge the same on an appeal to the Court of Appeal.

However, as pointed out earlier, this statute has not been utilized in recent years as a means of acquiring title to land by the State. It is suggested that there are two reasons for this failure to invoke the provisions of a statute which, technically, still remains in force. Firstly, the incidence of forfeiture by the State of the real estate of a private citizen is virtually non-existent in recent years. Secondly, the practice of escheat has been superseded by the right of the State to *bona vacantia* as provided for under section 31 of the Administration of Estates Act, Cap. 45, whereby all the assets of an intestate which remain unclaimed after two years from the date of publication of the required notice[168] lapse to the State.

5.2.3 Acquisition of Land by the State by Private Treaty

Finally, there is nothing in the law which prevents the State from acquiring title to land under private ownership by the process of a voluntary transfer of title thereto by any person having the right or authority to effect the same. In such a case, the disposition will be subject to the same rules as are applicable under the general law for the acquisition and transfer of title to land owned by private persons or entities.

---

168 See section 29 of the Administration of Estates Act, Cap. 45.

5.3 PRIVATE LANDS

5.3.1 Introduction

There are basically two main methods by which title to lands may be acquired by private owners in the Western Area, namely:

i. By a direct grant from the State (formerly the Crown) or from someone who had derived title directly or indirectly from the State; and

v. By adverse possession which, when combined with the effect of the Limitation Act, No. 51 of 1961, may extinguish the title of the former owner.

5.3.2 Acquisition of Land from the State under the State Lands Act, No. 19 of 1960

We have already analysed the historical background to the present form of State grants in Chapter 3, and have demonstrated that the initial dispositions made by the Company Government, and later the Crown, to the early settlers were not made on any sound legal basis. However, when the settlement became a Crown Colony, steps were taken by the Colonial Government to regularize these dispositions and to put them on a proper footing. Grants were thenceforth made in the name of the Crown, and conveyed either the freehold or any lesser interest in the land. They were also made subject to the payment of quit rent, the taking of an oath of allegiance by the grantee and an undertaking to have the land cultivated or developed within a prescribed time limit. The condition regarding beneficial user has survived under the provisions of the State Lands Act[169] which currently governs grants of land made by the State. The other two conditions have since been discarded.

In the very early stages of the Colony, there was also a requirement that all grants made by the Crown were to be registered. However, initially, there were no sanctions for failure to register, nor did non-registration affect the validity of the grant. Registration was in fact used as a device to keep track of those persons from whom quit rent was due. However, by 1857, largely because of the large-scale evasion of the quit rent, a Registration Ordinance[170] was enacted which provided that all Crown grants not

169 No. 19 of 1960.

170 No. 94 of 1857.

registered within one year, from the date thereof, were to be void. Even this legal sanction, which in principle invalidated Crown grants in case of non-registration, was not strong enough to compel holders of such grants to comply with the requirements of registration. The Ordinance of 1857, having proved ineffective and largely inoperative, was eventually repealed in 1867.

This work has already established that the present legislation dealing with grants of land by the State is the State Lands Act.[171] In this Act, a grant is defined to include:

> *"a grant for an estate in fee simple, a lease or any license to the grantee to hold and occupy State land".*[172]

Authority for the making of grants of State land is now vested in the Minister of Lands, Country Planning and the Environment. Sections 3 and 4 of the Act provide as follows:

> *"3. The Minister may make grants of State Lands in such manner and subject to such conditions as may be required and as he may deem proper.*
> *4. Every grant shall be executed by the Minister or a public officer authorised by him in that behalf".*

In practice, depending on the nature and duration of the grant and the size of the land to be disposed of, the grant may actually be made by the Minister, or even the Permanent Secretary of the Ministry. The lack of consistency in this practice is often the source of much confusion frequently leading to litigation by competing claimants of the same parcel of State land.

The policy of successive governments in recent times has been to refrain from making an outright grant in fee simple in the first instance. Initially, grants are made, sometimes not even by deed but by a mere letter signed by the Permanent Secretary, subject to the payment of a yearly rent, and a condition to develop the land by the erection of a building within three years of the grant. Provided the grantee has complied in some measure with the provisions of the grant, by either erecting some structure on the

171 No. 19 of 1960.

172 See section 2 of Act No. 19 of 1960.

land or, in the case of a development lease, by undertaking the agreed improvements on the land to the satisfaction of the relevant authorities, the lease may be converted to a grant for an estate in fee simple.

In this regard, there is a provision in the Act to the effect that, where any land granted under the Act appears to the State to have been unoccupied for a period exceeding twelve months, the land shall revert to the State, and all money paid in consideration of the grant shall be forfeited, unless, after due notice, the grantee affords proof that he intends to use and develop the land, to a reasonable extent, within a reasonable time.[173] Information received from the Director of Surveys and Lands would tend to indicate that this provision is seldom enforced.

There is also a provision that the State reserves the right to enter the land granted for the purpose of prospecting, mining and removal of mineral and mineral oil and, except in the case of a building lease, to remove any stone, gravel, soil or other substances required for the construction or repair of any road, government building, or public work.[174] Where the State enters and resumes possession of any part of State land sold or leased under the Act, compensation is payable only for buildings or crops destroyed or damaged thereon and not for the land itself unless the land in question exceeds two hundred acres. In such a case, compensation is payable for any portion in excess of 4 per cent of the total acreage thus repossessed. Such compensation is to be assessed on the same principles as those laid down in the Public Lands Act, Cap. 116.

Finally, section 6 of the Act provides that subject to the above conditions every grant of State land, executed by or on behalf of the President, and expressed to be made in conformity with the provisions of the Act, is to be deemed valid and effectual for the purpose of conferring and assuring any proprietary, possessory or other right expressed or intending to be thereby conferred.

Indeed, until relatively recently a Crown or State grant was the safest way to acquire title to land in the Western Area of Sierra Leone. The production of such a grant as evidence of title was almost conclusive proof of ownership of whatever interest or estate was granted or conveyed therein. This was based on the widespread assumption that all lands in the Western Area, which had not been disposed of by a grant from the Crown or the State remained vested in the State, in keeping with the principle of the Crown's claim to absolute ownership of all lands within the former

173 Section 28 of Act No. 19 of 1960.

174 Ibid., section 7(2).

Colony, a British possession. However, over the years two main factors have contributed to undermine the basis of this assumption, and to render a title based on a Crown or State grant just as precarious as a title acquired from any other source.

The first factor is the absence of a system of registration of title and, apart from judicial action, the lack of any other machinery or process, such as a comprehensive survey, whereby the title of the State to any particular land may be established with any reasonable degree of certainty. A second factor is the incidence of squatting on unoccupied State lands which has increased to such an extent that it has now become almost uncontrollable. This latter factor has been due mainly to the steep increase in the population of the Western Area since the end of the civil war, and the resulting scarcity of land and other resources. In certain cases, some of these squatters, and their ascendants, might have occupied the land in question over several generations and in recent times, in lieu of a State grant, have been arming themselves with Statutory Declarations purporting to establish their possessory title to such lands.[175]

As we have mentioned above, although the State Lands Act and other statutes contain provisions for judicial action to recover State lands unlawfully occupied by squatters and other unauthorized persons, these provisions are seldom, if ever, invoked. Apparently, quite often, officials of the Ministry of Lands, Country Planning and the Environment are in possession of information indicating that vast stretches of State lands are being unlawfully occupied or claimed by squatters and/or land grabbers. However they are reluctant to act, because of the threat, or the actual use, of life-threatening violence, that has led in the recent past to fatal consequences. If the authorities have been inactive, the unlawful claimants of State lands have not been sitting idly by. Several cases are now pending before the courts where claimants, without any title derived from the State or the Crown, are seeking to have a declaration of title with the State and grantees of the State as defendants.

One point which will eventually have to be clarified by the courts is whether the State is bound by the provisions of the Limitation Act, No. 51 of 1961. Section 30 of this Act stipulates that the provisions of the Act shall apply to proceedings by and against the State in like manner as it applies to proceedings between private citizens. However, this provision

---

175 See pp. 135ff. for a discussion of the practice of using Statutory Declarations to establish possessory titles.

would appear to be in direct conflict with that contained in section 32 of the State Lands Act 1960, which stipulates that:

> *"the right of the State to sue for the recovery of State land shall not be barred or affected by any statute, Act or other law of limitation".*

It might be argued that, since the Limitation Act was passed in 1961 and the State Lands Act in 1960, there is implied repeal of the conflicting provision in the earlier Act. On the other hand, it could be argued that since the Limitation Act is more or less a consolidating statute, and since the law as to limitation remains substantially the same after 1961 as it was before 1960, the inference to be drawn is that Parliament did not intend to repeal the provision of the State Lands Act; otherwise it would have done so expressly. It is submitted that the former interpretation is to be preferred since section 30 of the Limitation Act deals specifically with limitation in so far as it affects State lands.

5.4 LONG POSSESSION AND THE ACQUISITION OF TITLE TO LAND IN THE WESTERN AREA

5.4.1 Introduction

An appropriate background for our discussion under this sub-heading would be the following comment by Livesey-Luke, C.J. in the course of his judgment in the Supreme Court in the case of *Seymour Wilson v. Musa Abess:*[176]

> *"... It is a matter of common knowledge that most of the lands in the Western Area outside the City of Freetown are based on possessory title and most of them are not covered by any title deeds. That situation is the result of the history of landholding established in the Western Area about two centuries ago. The system which has been in operation in the Western Area since founding of the Colony (Now Western Area) is that land passes within the same family from one generation to another in many cases without the existence of any document of title ... Indeed the courts in Sierra Leone*

176 S.C. Civ. App. 5/79, judgment delivered 19 June 1981, unreported.

> *have on innumerable occasions decided in favour of owners of a possessory title without documents of titles as against the holders or registered conveyances".*

These very revealing words of the learned Chief Justice confirm the fact that in the Western Area of Sierra Leone judicial recognition has long been given to evidence of possession as a means of establishing title to land in this part of the country. They also highlight the predominance, in terms of numbers, of possessory title over documentary titles, especially in the suburban parts of the Western Area. However, the historical explanation offered by the learned Chief Justice for the present situation is only a limited one.

Indeed, at the origin of every possessory title is the fact of long adverse possession, or "squatting", to use the more popular expression. The incidence of squatting goes as far back as the founding of the Colony. This work has already shown that most of the early settlers turned down the invitation of the Colonial Government to have their grants confirmed and registered or to have fresh grants issued where none existed, mainly because of their reluctance to pay any land tax (or quit rent as it was called). Writing to the Duke of Chandos as far back as 14 September 1868, Sir Arthur Kennedy, then Governor of the Colony of Sierra Leone, had this to say on the problem of squatting:

> *"Your grace is aware that there are numerous villages in this settlement [sic]; and by a reference to the office of the Registrar I find not five per cent of those occupying Crown Lands and allotments, have any grants or title at all, and may have obtained and held their allotments by fraud".*[177]

It is not possible to estimate the number of persons presently squatting on lands in the Western Area as against holders of grants but, whatever the real figure eventually turns out to be, the seriousness of the problem at present in the Western Area calls for immediate remedial action as squatting now takes place not only on State lands but also on private lands. Not only does this phenomenon constitute a serious threat to the law and order situation in the country but it also serves as a serious set-back to the use of land as a resource for the economic development of the country.

177 See Newbury op. cit., p. 634 reproduced from C.O. 267/295.

It is against this background that we come to examine more closely the question of acquisition of title by virtue of long possession, the existing statutory provisions on limitation of action in land matters and judicial attitude in respect of the ascertainment and establishment of possessory title to land generally.

5.4.2 The Effect of Adverse Possession and the Limitation Act 1961

It is a generally accepted and well-established principle of the common law that the mere possession of a piece of land may in certain circumstances raise a presumption of entitlement to such possession or at least of lawful occupation of the same. Such a presumption is rebuttable by proof of a superior title thereto. However, the presumption gets stronger and more difficult to rebut as the duration of the possession gets longer and the chances of proving a superior title otherwise diminish. However, it is the combination of adverse possession and the effect of limitation that is the foundation of possessory title. Limitation is a creature of statute. Where the provisions of the Act apply, by barring the original owner's right of action to recover possession, and by extinguishing his title to the land, it leaves the new owner with a title based simply on adverse possession. What then are the relevant provisions of the Act, and how have the courts in Sierra Leone interpreted them?

The first provision of importance is that which states that, where an owner of land is entitled in possession, time does not begin to run against him for the purposes of the Act unless he has been dispossessed or has discontinued his possession and adverse possession has been taken by some other person.[178]

What amounts to dispossession and discontinuance of possession as a basis for adverse possession was considered by Beoku-Betts, J. in the case of *Pratt v. Nicol*.[179] According to the learned Judge "*dispossession*" suggests some active steps by the claimant to take over possession from the owner or to drive him from possession. "*Discontinuance*", on the other hand, implies that the owner has abandoned his possession and some other person has taken over possession. However, as Beoku-Betts, J. emphasized in *Pratt*

178 See section 1(1) of the Limitation Act, No. 51 of 1961 and compare it with section 10(1) of the English Limitation Act 1939. The local statute is an adaptation of the English statute.

179 (1937–49) ALR S.L. 377.

v. Nicol it is not sufficient that the owner goes out of physical occupation of the land. For discontinuance to be effective the intention to abandon must be clear and

> *"the evidence must show that it was complete and that the defendant after such discontinuance obtained exclusive possession for the statutory period."*[180]

Thus, in the instant case, where the owner of the house allowed the defendant to occupy a portion of it after he had himself ceased occupying the house, but manifested his intention of not giving him exclusive possession by retaining one room for himself and sending other persons to reside in the house from time to time, it was held that there was no discontinuance of possession by the owner.[181]

Adverse possession, as used in section 11(1) of the Act, does not bear a technical meaning but has been construed to mean simply possession inconsistent with the title of the true owner. There must be evidence of acts of the claimant inconsistent with the possession of the owner. For, in the words of Beoku-Betts, J. in *Pratt v. Nicol*:[182]

> *"if the defendant's acts are consonant with his recognition of the continued possession of the owner, he or she could not be said to have exclusive possession, though, in fact, he or she occupied the premises".*

Thus, in the case of *Mansaray v. Williams*[183] the Court of Appeal, per Bankole-Jones, C.J., held that despite the fact that it was found that the appellant had been in possession of the premises for a considerable length of time without paying rent, he failed to prove adverse possession (and was therefore disentitled from relying on section11(1) of the Limitation Act), because there was evidence that in earlier proceedings, brought by the respondent claiming arrears of rent and ejectment respectively, it had been established that the relationship of landlord and tenant still subsisted between the parties and the appellant had continued to recognize the

180 Ibid., p. 281.
181 See also *Rahman v. Elba* (1950–56) ALR S.L. 88.
182 Above at p. 281.
183 (1968–69) ALR S.L. 326.

respondent as landlord. It is trite law that a tenant cannot impugn the title of his landlord.[184]

Where, however, there is evidence of continuous and undisturbed adverse possession for the prescribed statutory period, the effect is to extinguish the true owner's right of action for recovery of possession of the land, as well as his title thereto. This is the effect of section 16 of the Limitation Act. It is submitted that, in this regard, limitation only operates negatively. Whilst it eliminates the claim of the former owner it does not per se entitle the person left in possession to succeed in an action for a declaration of title. It is common practice in Sierra Leone for litigants seeking a declaration of title either as plaintiff or by way of counter-claim to plead merely the fact of long possession and to attempt to rely on the provision of the Limitation Act for such a declaration. There is, however, a long line of authorities which have established the basic principle that in an action for declaration of title, the plaintiff must succeed on the strength of his title, and not on the weakness of that of his defendant.[185] The most frequently cited of such authorities is the case of *Seymour Wilson v. Musa Abess*.[186]

In that case Livesey-Luke, C.J. cited with approval the dicta of Weber, C.J. in support of this principle, in the case of *Kodilinye v. Odu*[187] and then went on to reassert the principle in these terms:

> "*... In a case for a declaration of title, the plaintiff must succeed by the strength of his title. He must prove a valid title to the land. So if he claims a fee simple title he must prove it to entitle him to a declaration*".

In *Seymour Wilson*, the plaintiff based his claim partly on long possession and partly on documentary evidence of title, so it was not necessary, for the purpose of the decision, for the learned Chief Justice to lay down what degree of proof was required by the plaintiff who was seeking a declaration of title based on mere possession. However, there are dicta of Ken During, J.A. in the case of *Wyse v. Turay*[188] tending to suggest

184 See also *Pratt v. Kamara* (1964–66) ALR S.L. 72.

185 See *England v. Official Administrator* (1964–66) ALR S.L. 315; *Venn v. Cole* (1968–69) ALR S.L. 331; and *Swill v. Caramba-Coker* (1972–73) ALR S.L. 277.

186 Above.

187 (1935) 2 W.A.C.A. 336 at 337–8.

188 Civ. App. 10/79; judgment delivered by the Court of Appeal on 22 October 1980, unreported.

that adverse possession even for the statutory period would not entitle a claimant to a declaration of title based on long possession. The learned Justice of Appeal then went on to cite a passage from *Cheshire's Modern Law of Real Property*,[189] dealing with the subject of good root of title as required to be shown by a vendor under English law. Part of the passage quoted by During, J.A. reads as follows:

> *"Even the rule under the Limitation Act, that title is extinguished after 12 years adverse possession by a stranger, does not in itself enable a vendor to show a good title by proving possession for even 30 years [or 40 years in Sierra Leone] in himself. He must go further and show what persons were entitled to the land when he took possession, and prove that their claims have been barred by his continuance in possession".*

The inference to be drawn from the court's citation of this passage from Cheshire, and its reliance on the statement of law contained therein, is that the court was equating the degree of proof required to establish good title imposed by statute on a vendor with that required of a plaintiff or claimant for a declaration of title based on long and adverse possession. It is submitted, with respect, that the law as stated in the passage cited from Cheshire properly applies in an action between a purchaser and a vendor for breach of covenant of title but does not necessarily apply in an action for declaration of title based on long and adverse possession. It is possible that a claimant may be able to prove continuous and undisturbed adverse possession for over 40 years, but would still not be entitled to a declaration of title if he is unable to show that, not only has the defendant's title been extinguished by operation of the Limitation Act, but also that the title of all persons who may be entitled after the defendant, for example a reversioner or a remainderman under a settlement, has also been extinguished.

On the other hand, one can envisage a situation where a claimant may become entitled to a declaration of title by proving that the defendant was the absolute owner of the land in question, and that the latter's title has been extinguished in favour of the claimant, even though he has not been in adverse possession for up to forty years. Thus, in the case of *Nathan Cole v. Abdulai Betts and another*[190] the court granted a declaration of title

189 6th edn, 1949.

190 CC 342/56 – unreported decision of a civil case in the former Supreme Court.

to the plaintiff where it was proved that he had been in continuous and undisturbed possession for only fourteen years, and had by his adverse possession extinguished the title of the defendant, who was then the owner in fee simple of the property in question.[191]

It is also established law that the onus lies on the claimant for a declaration of title to satisfy the court that he is entitled on the evidence brought before the court to a declaration of title. This principle relating to the evidential burden was laid down by Weber, C.J. (Sierra Leone) in delivering the judgment of the West African Court of Appeal in the case of *Kodilinye v. Odu.*[192] The dicta of Weber, C.J. were adopted and applied by the Supreme Court in *Macauley v. Stafford*[193] and *Seymour Wilson v. Musa Abess.*[194] The standard of proof required to discharge the burden placed on the plaintiff in an action for a declaration of title would appear to be a very high one.

The courts have tended to compare and contrast it with that required in an action for trespass. Beoku-Betts, J.S.C. did so in *Macauley v. Stafford*[195] in the following terms:

> *"As a legal concept a claim for a declaratory [sic] title demands a much higher degree of proof than that required for a claim for trespass".*

Livesey-Luke, C.J. elaborated on this theme even further in *Seymour Wilson v. Musa Abess*[196] when he stated:

> *"In a case of trespass, what the plaintiff has to prove is a better right of possession than the defendant. One of the ways he may do this is to prove that he has a better title to the land than the defendant. But 'better' title in the context of an action for trespass is not necessarily a 'valid' title. In the case of trespass the court is concerned only with the relative strengths of the titles or possession proved by the rival claimants. The*

191 See also *Allen v. Gooding*, judgment of the West African Court of Appeal on appeal from the former Supreme Court of Sierra Leone delivered 27 March 1945, unreported.

192 Above, at 337–8.

193 S.C. Civ. App. 1/75 judgment delivered by the Supreme Court in 1975, unreported.

194 Above.

195 Above.

196 Above.

> *party who proves a better title or a better right to possession succeeds, even though there may be another person, not a party, who has a better title than him. But in a case for a declaration of title, the plaintiff must succeed by the strength of his title. He must prove a valid title to the land."*

Further on in the judgment, Livesey-Luke, C.J. cited with approval the dicta of Lord Hetherly in the case of *Bristow v. Carmican*[197] to the effect that the slightest amount of possession would be sufficient to entitle the person who is so in possession, or who claims under those who have been or are in possession, to maintain an action for trespass against anyone who cannot show a better title. In contrast, to succeed in an action for a declaration of title based on adverse possession the claimant not only must prove exclusive, undisturbed and continuous possession, for the prescribed period under the Limitation Act to bar the particular defendant, but also must show that there is no other person with a title superior to the possessory title that he is relying on.

5.4.3 Acquisition and Proof of Possessory Title to State Land

The question of proof of title to land by long possession takes a different dimension where the land is alleged or deemed to be State land. Reference has already been in this chapter to the apparent conflict between the provisions of section 32 of the State Lands Act 1960 and section 30 of the Limitation Act 1961 as to whether the Limitation Act can operate to bar the right of the State to sue for the recovery of possession of State land. It has been argued that because of the express and specific nature of the provisions of section 30 of the Limitation Act 1961, the title of the State to State lands could be extinguished by the combination of adverse possession and the effect of section 19 of the Limitation Act. However, this does not prevent a person from acquiring a possessory title to such lands albeit one always subject to the superior title of the State. The question that does arise here, in view of the unreliability of available data on existing State lands, is how easy is it, as a matter of fact and law, for the State to maintain an action for the recovery of possession of State land over which a squatter or some other person has acquired some sort of possessory title. As a matter of law, quite apart from the common law right of the State to maintain an action for the recovery of possession of State land as the legal owner

197 (1878) 3 App.Cas. 641, H.L.

thereof, there exist certain statutory provisions which, in theory at least, should enable the State to recover possession of land which is in fact State land or merely claimed as State land.

This work has already examined the provisions of the Unoccupied Lands (Ascertainment of Title) Act, Cap. 117, under which the Director of Surveys and Lands could claim as State land any land which, in his opinion, is unoccupied within the meaning of the Act. There are provisions under this Act for proceedings to be instituted against any person laying claim to the land in question, requiring him to prove his title thereto, failing which the land would be declared to be State land, and the claimant ordered to give up possession of the same. The practical difficulties preventing the enforcement of the provisions of that Act have also been considered.[198]

The State Land Act of 1960 also contains provisions similar to those already highlighted in the Unoccupied Lands (Ascertainment of Title) Act, Cap. 117. According to section 30(1) of the Act, where any person without right, or whose title or licence has expired or been forfeited or cancelled, is in occupation of State land, the Attorney-General or his representative, or the Director of Survey and Lands, may institute proceedings either in the Magistrates' Court or the High Court for recovery of possession of such land. The onus to prove that his occupation is lawful rests on the defendant. Section 31 of the Act further provides that in such proceedings, and in every action against the Government in which title shall be in issue the mere averment that land is State land is sufficient proof of such fact. If the defendant fails to discharge the burden thus cast upon him the Court is empowered to order that possession be given by the defendant to the plaintiff on behalf of the State, either forthwith, or after such reasonable time as the court may think fit to allow the defendant to remove buildings and harvest such crops as he may have on the land. In addition, it is a criminal offence to unlawfully occupy or use State land and any person found guilty of the offence is liable to a fine not exceeding one hundred leones.

However, just as in the case of the Unoccupied Lands (Ascertainment of Title) Act, Cap. 117, the provisions of the State Lands Act 1960 discussed above are hardly ever invoked before the courts. At any rate, there is no known case which has been decided under the Act. This again might seem surprising in the light of the available evidence of widespread unlawful occupation of State lands, particularly in the suburban part of the Western Area. There are, in the opinion of the present writer, two main factors for

---

See pp. 118-19.

this apparent neglect or refusal by the authority to enforce the existing law.

Firstly, the practice of the Surveys and Lands Department when it identifies any State land being unlawfully occupied is, as an initial move, to serve a notice upon the unlawful occupier informing him that the land is State land and requiring him to quit the same within a specified time. The notice also normally threatens the occupier with both civil and criminal proceedings in the event of non-compliance. In addition, where there are any buildings or other permanent structures on the land, these would invariably have been built without the necessary permit required under the Town and Country Planning Act, Cap. 81, so the notice to quit would be backed up by a notice to demolish the offending building or structure within a specified time limit. It is only in the case of neglect or refusal to comply with the terms of these notices that the Department of Survey and Lands would contemplate initiating judicial proceedings. Even in such an eventuality the mere issue and service of the summons on the unlawful occupier is normally sufficient to ensure his departure from the land, and thus prevent the necessity for a court action.

The second factor responsible for this marked absence of court action, and therefore of decided cases, is the policy of Government to order action under the statutes only in exceptional cases, either where the land is either urgently needed for public or some Government-sponsored project, or where the fact of the unlawful occupation and the presence of squatters create some special problems such as a security risk or health hazard. This inactivity, as we have indicated before, is also attributable to a lack of political will on the part of successive governments, as very often, the political implications of moving whole communities of squatters from State lands when there is no alternative site to resettle them are too serious for any government to overlook. As it is, Government has no consistent or dynamic housing policy nor is there any adequate alternative services offered by the private sector. For most persons newly arriving from the Provinces it is much easier and more practicable to take possession of any unoccupied land and build a cheap temporary structure on it than to look for accommodation that is most of the time just not available in a fast-growing and overcrowded city. In this regard, the solution to the problem of squatting would seem to lie more in political and social action than in the enforcement of the existing laws.

5.5 STATUTORY DECLARATION AS EVIDENCE OF POSSESSORY TITLE TO LAND IN THE WESTERN AREA

5.5.1 Introduction

Mention should be made at this stage of the fast-developing trend whereby attempts are made to convert what is in effect a possessory title into a documentary title by the making of a Statutory Declaration under the provisions of the Statutory Declarations Act 1835. These documents invariably recite the fact that the main declarant whose title is sought to be established thereby had been in possession of the particular land for a period of time either by himself or through his predecessors in title. This is followed by a joint declaration by two witnesses who invariably depose to the reputed ownership of the first declarant. The land involved is delineated on a survey plan drawn and attached to the document and a description of the boundaries is inserted in a schedule to the main declaration. The declaration is then made on oath in the presence of a Commissioner for Oaths. The document is then registered in accordance with the provisions of the Registration of Instruments Act, Cap. 256.

5.5.2 Status of Statutory Declarations before the Courts

Doubt was expressed by the Court of Appeal in the case of *Roberts v. Bright*[199] as to the status of these documents and whether they are registrable and admissible in evidence by virtue of the provisions of section 15 of the Registration of Instruments Act, Cap. 256.

The Court concluded in that case that the document may be admissible in evidence by virtue of the provisions of the Evidence (Documentary) Act, Cap. 26. This latter view was confirmed by Livesey-Luke, C.J. in *Seymour Wilson v. Musa Abess.*[200] In the opinion of the learned Chief Justice there was no doubt that a Statutory Declaration "*is a statement made by a person in a document and is therefore governed by the provisions of the Act*", that is section 3 of the Evidence (Documentary) Act, Cap. 26. This section makes provision for the admission of evidence of any statement made by a person in a document tending to establish a fact, if direct oral evidence of that fact would be admissible provided certain conditions are fulfilled. Among the conditions are that the maker of the statement had personal knowledge of

199 (1964–66) ALR S.L. 156 per Ames. P.

200 Above.

the matters contained in the document and that he is called as a witness at the trial unless he was dead, or unfit to attend as a witness, or he was out of the jurisdiction.

It is submitted, however, that even when such a document is admitted in evidence it is not conclusive proof of the facts stated therein and should therefore not be treated as a document of title. Support for this view is to be found in the case of *Kamara v. Fofana*.[201] In that case the plaintiff instituted an action for a declaration of title based on long possession. The two defendants also counter-claimed for a declaration of title in respect of separate portions of the same land. The first defendant relied, for evidence of title, on a conveyance from the Administrator-General, and the second defendant, on a Statutory Declaration. In dismissing the counter-claim of the second defendant Livesey-Luke, Ag. J. as he then was, stated unequivocally that "*a statutory declaration is no proof of title*".

The second defendant had in fact purported to establish his possessory title by means of the Statutory Declaration but none of the declarants gave evidence at the trial. The trial Judge, however, found as a fact that the second defendant was not in occupation of the part of the land she was claiming to be entitled to nor had she ever exercised any rights of a person entitled to possession. Therefore, in the absence of any other independent evidence the Statutory Declaration was treated as a useless piece of document.

The conclusion to be drawn from the *Kamara* case is that where a claimant for a declaration of title based on long possession relies on a statutory declaration in support of his claim, if the same is admitted in evidence, it is not to be treated as a document of title, but only as evidence that tends to establish title and is to evaluated on the same basis as any other evidence whether oral or documentary. Having said this, it should be pointed out that an increasing number of purchasers of land in the Western Area are finding that they have no choice but to accept a vendor's possessory title as evidenced in such Statutory Declarations. At least, they have the advantage of preserving in a written form the evidence that the vendor or his predecessor in title purports to rely on to establish such title. This, however, is no guarantee that the facts deposed to in the Statutory Declaration are true and the purchaser, as so often happens, might well be buying a law-suit.

201 (1964–66) ALR S.L. 413.

5.6 PROBLEMS ASSOCIATED WITH THE ACQUISITION AND ASCERTAINMENT OF TITLE TO LAND IN THE WESTERN AREA

What emerges, therefore, from the review of the present situation relating to the acquisition and ascertainment of title to land in the Western Area is that, short of judicial proceedings to obtain a declaration of title, there are hardly any other means open to a title holder to prove that he is the indisputable owner of any piece of land. As we have demonstrated above, not even the State can always give the assurance that its title to State lands is sound and unimpeachable. A fortiori, the private citizen is even more vulnerable, and particularly so where he is obliged to acquire title from a vendor who himself has nothing to offer but an untested possessory title. As a pointer to the future and in anticipation of our proposals for reform of the present land tenure system as a whole, it is fitting to conclude this chapter with the thoughts of Livesey-Luke, C.J. expressed in the case of *Seymour Wilson v. Musa Abess*:[202]

> *"In view of the present trends and practices in dealings relating to land in the Western Area it may be desirable to introduce a system of compulsory land registration in the Western Area. Such a measure may have the effect of putting an end to or of discouraging undesirable speculation and fraudulent dealings in land. It would protect innocent purchasers against fraudulent and unscrupulous dealers in land. It would also simplify conveyancing and create certainty and security in the ownership of the land, and it would relieve potential purchasers from the risk of buying lawsuits".*

We shall examine more closely the proposals put forward by the learned Chief Justice later in this work.

202 Above.

PART 3

LAND LAW IN THE PROVINCES

CHAPTER 6
THE CONCEPTS OF OWNERSHIP AND TITLE TO LAND UNDER CUSTOMARY LAW

6.1 APPLICATION OF THE CONCEPTS OF TITLE AND OWNERSHIP TO CUSTOMARY LAND TENURE

6.1.1 Introduction

At this stage of this work, it is necessary to explain the use of some terms and concepts in the context of the examination and analysis of certain aspects of customary land tenure. In discussing the various forms of tenure this work will show that one of the characteristic features of customary tenure is the vesting of the "paramount title" in some entity or group. Thus, under family tenure title to lands held by the family is vested in the family as a unit, while in the case of communal tenure, title to communal lands is not vested in the community as such, but in the traditional or socio-political heads of each community. What then is the true significance of the concept of "title" under customary law?

6.1.2 The Notion of Title to Land under English Law

The word "title" in its primary sense evokes a right, and, generally, a "legal title" means a right or a claim to property, especially a right to possession of property. Under English law, indeed under most other legal systems, there are various kinds of title to property, particularly where that property is land. Thus, the lowest and most imperfect title consists of mere or naked possession or physical occupation of property without any apparent right or any claim of right to hold and continue such possession. On the other hand, a complete legal title exists where the right of possession is joined with the right of property. In another context, for example. for registration purposes under the English Land Registration Act 1925, a person entitled to land in England may prove and register an absolute title, a qualified title or a possessory title, each type indicating the degree of proof of ownership the registered owner has been able establish in the land at the time of registration. In this regard, "title" is the same as "ownership". Thus, an "absolute title" is a title good against all the world, and is virtually equivalent to "absolute ownership". It is in this sense that we use the word "title" in the context of our examination and analysis of interests held in land under customary tenure.

6.1.3 The Concept of Title to Land under Customary Tenure

Though it has often been doubted whether there is any "real" or "true" ownership of land under African customary law generally,[203] there is no doubt that African societies, like human societies everywhere, acknowledge and protect legal rights to property and recognize a relation between a particular property and the person in whom it is vested. This notion of a legal right also involves the cluster of claims, privileges, powers and immunities generally associated with ownership. Under customary land tenure, it is the aggregation of "rights" vested in the holder (which may be a community, a family or an individual), with respect to a particular parcel of land, that gives the holder title thereto. There may exist simultaneously, and in relation to the same piece of land, various rights and differing interests vested in and held by several different entities.

The range of interests in land capable of existing under customary law is very wide and could include such interests as the interest of control and supervision frequently based on jurisdictional authority; the interest of management such as that vested in the head of family under family tenure; the interest of occupation; and the interest of mere user. In this regard, the term "ownership" is sometimes loosely used to describe the relation between a particular interest and the entity in which it is vested. According to Bentsi-Enchill,[204]

> *"this is what makes it possible for it to be said of the same land, concurrently and with truth, that it belongs to the community, that is belongs to C's family and that it belongs to X. This may be confusing, but it is intelligible".*[205]

Although it is more appropriate to refer to various entities as "holding" named interests in land, it is more usual to use the term ownership in the

203 See Allott, "Towards a Definition of Absolute Ownership". (1965), *J.A.L.* 99.

204 "Do African Systems of Land Tenure Require a Special Terminology?" (1965), *J.A.L.* 114.

205 Ibid., p.119.

sense illustrated above by the passage from Bentsi-Enchill's article. Where the interest "owned" accords the "owner" the fullest cluster of rights, including the maximum right of user and disposal, then it amounts to absolute or allodial ownership.

Thus, the allodial or absolute owner of property, in this sense, could be described as the person or group of persons, recognized under a particular system of tenure as having the maximum cluster of rights in, and over the property in question subject, of course, to other interests in the same property which may be held by other persons or entities. This implies that the various interests, which could subsist in land, held under customary tenure, can be classified in an ascending or descending order of amplitude and range, with allodial ownership at the apex. In such a scheme, allodial ownership becomes the standard by which all other interests in property are measured and defined.

6.1.4 Provincial Land and Use of the Term Ownership

In the light of the foregoing analysis, is it then correct and appropriate to talk about ownership or about absolute allodial ownership of land held under customary law in the Provinces of Sierra Leone being vested in any entities? As to the first part of the question, the answer is clearly in the affirmative, in the sense that "ownership" is the term commonly used to describe the relation between an interest, and the person or group of persons in whom that interest is vested. The relation for which the term "holder" is also sometimes used. This is because customary law is sophisticated enough to recognize varying types of interests in land that can be "owned" or "held" by different persons or groups of persons simultaneously.

With regard to the second part of the question, the answer is not so clear-cut for the simple reason that it is impossible to generalize in view of the fact that there exist different forms of tenure. The nearest we come to absolute or allodial ownership of land is the title vested in the individual under individual tenure. This is because an individual's interest in such lands embraces the maximum cluster of rights, of which the most important are those of user and disposal, which enable him, for example, to cultivate the land, to build on it, to dispose of it by will, sale or gift and to carve out lesser interests in favour of others, such as when the land is loaned or leased or pledged, and to pass his interest on to heirs on his death. These rights, to which an individual holding the paramount interest in land under individual tenure is entitled, are enjoyed without prejudice to, and despite the interests held by, other entities in the same land, such as the interest of control and supervision vested in the chiefdom council and the paramount chief based on their jurisdictional authority over all lands within the chiefdom.

The individual's interest in such lands amounts to absolute or allodial ownership also because it is an original interest, in the sense that it is held of no-one nor is it dependent on, nor derived from, any other interest.

Where paramount title to land is vested in or claimed by, or on behalf of, a collectivity, such as a family or a community, it may appear less appropriate to describe such a title as absolute or allodial ownership. This is due to the fact that one of the most important rights flowing from allodial ownership, that is the right to use and enjoy the property owned, is exercised, not by the group as an entity, but by individuals or groups of individuals who together constitute the owning group, whether the family or the community. However, though such individuals or groups of individuals may hold an interest in group-owned land, which entitles them to certain rights of user and enjoyment, yet their interest falls short of that plenary title which constitutes absolute or allodial ownership. This is because their interest is not an original interest but one derived from, and dependent on, the group's title. This title is in fact the paramount title amounting to absolute or allodial ownership. However, even if we cannot describe the community's or the family's title to land in terms of absolute ownership as defined above, yet it still remains the paramount interest which is capable of being owned or held in land under these types of tenure. It is an original interest not held of anyone nor dependent upon or derived from any other interest.

CHAPTER 7
FORMS OF TENURE UNDER CUSTOMARY LAW IN THE PROVINCES OF SIERRA LEONE

7.1 BACKGROUND TO THE VARIOUS FORMS OF TENURE UNDER CUSTOMARY LAW

Though it is usual to talk of customary land tenure as a single and uniform system with characteristic features different from, for example, those of English forms of tenure, yet, a closer examination of the system of customary tenure in the Provinces of Sierra Leone will reveal that the system is marked by a high degree of complexity. This intricacy stems, firstly, from the fact that the system of landholding in the Provinces is inextricably linked with the historical, political, socio-economic and cultural background of the various native communities. Secondly, this complexity could be traced to the fact that there is not just a single body of customary laws governing land tenure in the Provinces but in theory at least, there exist as many customary laws as there are ethnic groups in Sierra Leone, each with its own characteristic features in particular areas of the law relating to land tenure. This complexity is principally manifested by the existence, within the system of customary tenure itself, of not just one single and uniform type of tenure, but of at least two distinct forms of tenure: communal tenure and family tenure.

The main basis of the distinction between these two forms of tenure is that the origins of title to land are traditionally traced to two entirely different sources. Communal tenure features in areas where lands were, by tradition, initially appropriated on behalf of the whole community by conquest, annexation, settlement or some other means. On the other hand, family tenure tends to exist in areas where the initial appropriation of lands within that particular area is traditionally attributed to individuals, who first cleared and settled upon virgin territory for the benefit of themselves and their immediate retinue, rather than for the benefit of the larger community to which they formerly belonged.

Apart from this traditional distinction between communal tenure and family tenure we have found it necessary to distinguish a third type of tenure which has, virtually, grown out of the two traditional forms of tenure.

This third form we have described as "individual tenure", because its main characteristic is that of the vesting of the title to the lands in question and all the attributes of ownership in individuals, as opposed to the traditional groups, such as the community or the family. Because of the manner in which individual tenure has emerged, it is not possible to associate it with any particular region or chiefdom of the Provinces. Rather, as we shall see, it tends to be prevalent in virtually all the urbanized areas of the Provinces.

We shall now examine the main features of these various types of tenure so as to determine how they each fit into the general framework of customary land tenure in the Provinces of Sierra Leone.

7.2 FAMILY TENURE

The logical starting point is family tenure because this is the most common form of tenure to be found throughout the Provinces of Sierra Leone. It is practised by the two major tribes, the Mende and the Temne, who between them occupy the majority of the 149 chiefdoms, and, to a lesser extent, by other minor ethnic groups such as the Sherbro and the Susu.

7.2.1 Definition of Family in the Context of Land Tenure

It is desirable first to define the term "family" as used in this context. The word has several different connotations depending on the context and the field of study in which it is being used. Thus, the sociologists would refer to a "simple", "elementary" or "nuclear" family in describing a group of relations consisting of a man, his wife and children living together.[206] Where the group extends to include a man's immediate ascendants and descendants and other consanguine and affinal relations, it is described by sociologists as an "extended family".[207] Basically, therefore, a family is a kinship group marked by kinship relationship.

However in using the term "family" in a legal context one has to be more precise, for obvious reasons, especially where property rights are concerned. In Sierra Leone customary law the term "family" is generally

206 See Royal Anthropological Institute of Great Britain and Ireland, *Notes and Queries on Anthropology*, 6th edn, p. 70; Bohannan, *Social Anthropology*, 1963, p. 73.

207 See Radcliff-Brown and Forde, *African Systems of Kinship and Marriage*, p. 5.

used to describe a variety of groupings, which Joko Smart[208] has classified into two main categories:

i. The residential family units or households; and
ii. The unilateral descent groups, such as clans and lineages.

Both the household and the wider descent group are relevant as far as rights to property, particularly land, are concerned under customary law. However, for our present purposes, when we use the expression "family" in relation to land generally, and to the form of tenure in particular, we are referring to the unilateral descent group, claiming descent from a common ancestor, either patrilineally or matrilineally, sometimes also referred to as kindred, a lineage, or loosely, as a clan.

Thus, among the Mende the basic family unit for the purposes of land tenure is the *ndehun blaa* (as opposed to the *mawei*, the household) which has been defined by Little as:

> *"a group of persons standing in close blood relationship with each other, mainly on the patrilineal side, who constitute a descent group for the purposes of the inheritance of land and other forms of collective property".*[209]

In a typical Mende village, members of the *ndehun blaa* would be the direct patrilineal descendants of the "founder" of the particular village. They would normally occupy several *kuwui* (literally: compounds) within the village or town. Invariably, the *ndehun blaa* would also claim "ownership" of adjoining satellite villages and unoccupied farm bushes.

This combination of villages "owned" by a common *ndehun blaa* would normally constitute the socio-political unit known as a "section" which, as we have already explained, is the main sub-division of every chiefdom. This same distinction between the "family" as a descent group, lineage or clan, as opposed to a "household", or a simple/compound family, is to be found in the social structure of some other ethnic groups such as the Temne, Susu, Loko and Limba.[210]

208 Joko Smart, *Sierra Leone Customary Family Law*, p. 11.
209 Little, *The Mende of Sierra Leone*, revised edn, p. 101.
210 See McCulloch, *Peoples of Sierra Leone*, p. 89.

Thus, for the limited purpose of land tenure under customary law in the Provinces of Sierra Leone, a "family" may be defined as a group of persons tracing descent from a common ancestor, either patrilineally or matrilineally, and claiming title to lands within a particular chiefdom. Since virtually all the ethnic groups of Sierra Leone adopt the rule of patrilineal descent,[211] this implies that in those chiefdoms where family tenure is practised, rights in land are only claimed on the basis of both patri-descent and patri-succession. Patri-descent in this context refers to the political aspect of patri-lineage, for a person can only claim to be a subject of a chiefdom, and therefore entitled to rights in land therein, if he is able to trace a kinship relationship with any particular family within the chiefdom. Similarly, it is membership of a particular family that entitles that member, on the basis of patri-succession, to succeed to and enjoy rights in property or any hereditary office within the chiefdom. Family tenure, therefore, could be described as the system of customary tenure in which titles to land within a particular chiefdom are claimed by various descent groups, each with a common ancestor, and who constitute family units as described above. These family units, apart from being socio-political entities, are also endowed by customary law with corporate legal personality for the purpose of land tenure. As demonstrated below,[212] the family has the capacity to claim and hold lands under customary law, to have title vested in itself as an entity and to enjoy the fullest cluster of rights recognized by customary law over the lands in question. The family's title to such lands and its rights therein may be subject to the interests held by other entities in the same lands, some of these interests being dependent upon and others independent of the family's title. Despite such qualifications of the family's title to such lands, we are able to describe the form of tenure under which they are held as family tenure because the family's title is paramount and original and is not dependent on or derived from that of any other entity.

In view of the above account, "*family lands*" may be described broadly as lands held under family tenure. Where necessary, l a distinction should be made between such family lands and lands held by family groups as members of a community in areas where communal tenure is the predominant and generally recognized form of tenure.

211 The exception is possibly the Sherbro. See Hall, *The Sherbro of Sierra Leone*, passim; and H.M. Joko Smart, 'Sierra Leone Family Law', unpublished PhD thesis, London, 1973, p. 107.

212 See pp. 176ff.

Another point of clarification about the family's title to family lands is that, though the paramount title may be regarded as being vested in the family as a group, beneath the umbrella of this group title are varying degrees of lesser interests held in specific, or particular portions of, the "group-owned" land, and vested in sub-family groups and individuals. As with every corporate entity endowed with capacity to own property, responsibility for the management of the group-owned property is vested in a particular group organization. In the case of family lands under family tenure that organization is the head of family aided, to a certain extent, by principal members of the family. Without going into any detail, at this stage, about the responsibilities of the head of family we can state outright that it is only those unapportioned or unappropriated areas of family lands that are under the direct supervision and control of the head of the family. Over the apportioned or appropriated areas the family basically retains only a reversionary or residual interest manifested in the form of ultimate control.

7.3 COMMUNAL TENURE

The main feature of communal tenure is that title to lands, in a given area in the chiefdom, is claimed by, or on behalf of, the community as a whole, and not by or on behalf of families, sub-family groups or individuals.

Like the descent group which has been designated in this work as a family for the purposes of title to land under family tenure, the community is also a corporate entity endowed with legal capacity to enforce and defend its claims and rights to communal lands vis-à-vis other communities. However, unlike the family, it is not a kinship group but a socio-political entity. There is also a similarity between the two entities in that membership of a community, and a member's right to claim an interest in communal lands, are based on descent from some kinship group within the community, which in patrilineal communities is based exclusively on patri-descent, as explained above.[213]

213 Above, p. 148.

7.3.1 The Community and Communal Tenure

As a socio-political unit the community occupies an identifiable land territory with precise boundaries. At its broadest and highest level the community is co-extensive with the chiefdom. Viewed externally, such a community presents an appearance of a monolithic unit holding all the lands comprising its territory under a communal form of tenure, but viewed internally, it consists of several sub-communities, villages, families and other groups, and even individuals, holding varying degrees of interests in specific portions of communal lands.

Another feature of communal tenure is that the title to communal lands as a whole is not vested directly in the community as an entity but in the socio-political head of the particular community. Thus at the highest level, that is the chiefdom level, title to communal lands is vested in the paramount chief as representative of the community as a whole. This is why it is still possible for paramount chiefs in the Kono chiefdoms where communal tenure is prevalent to be referred to, in popular parlance, as the "owners" of all lands in their chiefdom. This position contrasts starkly with that obtaining in areas under family tenure where title to family lands is vested directly in the family itself as a unit, and the head of a family is only vested with rights of management, control and supervision.

The other feature of communal tenure, which in certain respects makes it similar to family tenure, is that it is only unapportioned and unappropriated portions of communal lands, and those lands which are strictly public lands, such as sacred bushes, common grazing lands and communal farms where these still exist, that are subject to direct management, control and supervision of the socio-political head of the community at any level. As regards apportioned or appropriated areas of communal lands, the community retains a reversionary or residual interest and this is manifested not only in the supervision and administrative control exercised by the socio-political head, but also in the latter's exercise of jurisdictional authority over the area. The degree of supervision, and the amount of control, vary depending on the quantum and nature of interests held by members of the community, such as families, sub-family groups or even individuals, in the apportioned or appropriated parts of communal lands but the extent of jurisdictional authority exercised by the socio-political head is constant throughout the community.

Communal lands could thus be broadly defined as lands held under communal tenure, title to which is claimed by a community as a unit occupying an identifiable territory with the title thereto actually vested in the socio-political head of the community, such as a paramount chief, section chief, village headman or other subordinate traditional ruler (depending on the level of the communal hierarchy that one is concerned with) in a representative capacity for the benefit of the community as a whole. Traditionally, within any given community there existed no boundaries between portions of communal lands held or occupied by various sub-groups or individuals, and access to communal lands, for members of the community, was virtually unrestricted, and dependent only on choice and availability. However, with the increasing scarcity of cultivable land due to the practice of shifting cultivation, the increasing commercialization of communal lands due to extensive urbanization in some areas, the emphasis on large-scale exploitations and plantations of cash-crops and economic trees, and finally, because of the trend towards individualization, it is now not unusual to find well-defined boundaries demarcating portions of communal lands claimed or occupied exclusively by family groups or individuals.

Despite the above factors which tend to undermine the traditional basis of communal tenure, and despite the apparent similarities with family tenure, communal tenure is still identifiable as a distinct form of tenure under which lands within any given community, as defined above, are claimed by the community as a whole, with some held by members as groups or individually, and with the ultimate title, and overall rights, or supervision and control being vested in the socio-political head of the community.

From the ethnic perspective, this form of tenure is prevalent in the Kono, Koranko and Yalunka chiefdoms and, to a limited extent, in the Susu, Limba and Kissi areas of certain chiefdoms.

7.4 INDIVIDUAL TENURE

7.4.1 Introduction

The proposition has often been advanced, sometimes by the highest judicial authority and by the most eminent jurists, that the notion of individual ownership of land is a concept foreign to African customary law. In this regard, we may recall the well-known and oft-quoted words of Rayner, C.J. relied on by Lord Haldane in giving the opinion of the Privy Council in *Amodu Tijani v. Secretary, Southern Nigeria*,[214] as follows:

214 (1921) 2 A.C. 399.

> *"The next fact which is important to bear in mind in order to understand the native land law is that the notion of individual ownership is quite foreign to native ideas. Land belongs to the community, the village, or the family, never to the individual".*

Lord Haldane then went on to assert that this was pure native custom along the whole of the West African coast. However, he conceded the fact of individual ownership of certain lands, as in Lagos, though he attributed this to the "*introduction of English ideas*". Despite the obvious inexactitude of the assertion that land never belonged to the individual under customary tenure, this passage from Lord Haldane's judgment has often been relied on, judicially, as laying down a cardinal principle of customary law in Ghana and Nigeria.[215] On the other hand, Rayner's statement has been criticized by several African writers amongst them Ollennu,[216] Bentsi-Enchill[217] and Kludze.[218] In discussing Rayner's observation, Kludze contends that it could only relate to an earlier stage of Ghanaian society, for at the time Rayner was writing, in 1896, land was being purchased freely by individuals out of their own resources and held as private property. Kludze concludes that the statement that "individual ownership" was "foreign to native ideas" was therefore to be understood to mean that the notion was unknown until comparatively recently.

In the case of customary tenure in Sierra Leone, it is true that the increasing emphasis on the concept of individual ownership is a product of modern times, due mainly to the process of urbanization and the introduction of a cash economy and English legal ideas. However, even before the colonial era, there had always been a trend towards individualization of certain types of landholding. The very basis of family tenure, described above, implies the acknowledgement of an initial appropriation, clearing and settlement of virgin forest by an individual, the actual or reputed founder of the family.

Mende folklore, in particular, is full of stories of pioneering ancestors, such as a farmer or a hunter, who reputedly cleared stretches of virgin and

215 See *Kuma v. Kuma* (P.C.) (1936), 5 W.A.C.A. 1; *Hammond v. Randolph* (P.C) (1936), 5 W.A.C.A. 12.

216 *Principles of Customary Law in Ghana*, pp. 25–9.

217 *Ghana Land Law*, pp. 80–1.

218 *The Ewe Law of Property*, pp. 138–9.

other unoccupied land and laid claim thereto on behalf of himself, his immediate family and his followers. Reference has already been made to the fact that these basic units of settlement have today become the nuclei of the average village or town around which have grown satellite villages all claimed or occupied by the patrilineal descendants of the founder.

The process of individualization of ownership also has its origins in the Temne custom of the head of the household allotting plots of appropriated family farmlands to each of his wives and to their respective children. This fragmentation among the various branches of a man's household was invariably persisted in, even after the death of the parents, and as the children grew up to establish their own household. However, in traditional Temne society the process was not taken to its logical conclusion for, after several generations, such individually held lands would normally come to be considered as family lands as the number of descendants entitled to inherit the same multiplied.

There is, however, permanency in the Mende practice whereby a family owning large tracts of lands would allocate "blocks" or portions of such family lands to several brothers to assist them in setting up independent *maweisia* or farming households. Though the paramount title to such lands remains vested in the ancestral family, each individual member in time acquires a distinct and exclusive proprietary interest holding which lasts for his lifetime, and which he can alienate *inter vivos* to other members of the ancestral family, subject to ratification by the family head. Such interest is also inheritable on his death by members of his immediate or nuclear family as next of kin, instead of by the wider descent group, in accordance with the relevant customary law rules of distribution on intestacy.

Whether or not the land thus allocated continues to be held apart, and independent of the rest of the ancestral family lands, would depend on a number of factors, such as whether the process of fragmentation continues, the permanency of the form of exploitation and the type of use thereof by the allocatee and his successors.

In more recent times, the process of individualization of tenure has taken on a rather permanent and distinguishable character in chiefdoms where there are large urban centres, in areas of the reclaimed mangrove swamps around the Scarcies River and in parts of the rural area where large-scale plantations tend to be replacing subsistence farming and shifting cultivation.

The various ways in which an individual may now come to acquire the paramount title to land in the Provinces can be listed as follows.

7.4.2 Individual Acquiring Title by Clearing Virgin Forests

This was one of the traditional methods of gaining access to land, and to some extent is still of importance today. In densely populated areas, where family tenure is practised, most of the lands have now been appropriated by family groups. However, in sparsely populated areas, such as exist in the Limba chiefdoms of Koinadugu District where communal tenure is still prevalent, there have been instances in more recent times of individuals claiming title to land by clearing portions of communal forest or bush for the purpose of making a farm or establishing a new residential area. There is no general rule that land so carved out of virgin forest, previously held under communal tenure, is automatically considered as individual property. However, if such land cleared by individual effort is cultivated, or settled on by the same person and his descendants for several generations, it gradually acquires the status of land subject to individual ownership, and the interest thus acquired endures for as long as there are heirs to succeed the original occupier.

On the other hand, if the appropriated land is not cultivated or settled on permanently it reverts to the pool of communal land, and is held by the head of the community for the use and benefit of the community as a whole, or may be appropriated and occupied by other family group or individuals within the community.

7.4.3 Individual Acquiring Title by Purchase

The sale of land is now a recognized transaction in all the chiefdoms of the Provinces. This is now invariably the only method by which individuals, especially persons who are from outside a particular chiefdom, and therefore not entitled to rights in land therein, may acquire title to land in the Provinces. However, this general statement is subject to the qualification that the concept of an outright alienation of the family's interest in its land by sale to a stranger, that is, to a person from outside the chiefdom where the land is situated, is not recognized by Temne customary law. Even the concept of an absolute sale to a kinsman of the same chiefdom is a relatively modern development restricted to urban areas.

Where an outright sale of land is permitted by the relevant customary law, and the transaction is duly concluded with the owning group, if such a sale is to an individual, it will operate to pass on the paramount or other title in such land originally vested in the vendors and thus change the status of the land to one subject to individual tenure. The individual as holder of the paramount title becomes competent to deal with his property in every way permitted by the relevant customary law independent of his ancestral family or the community of origin.

7.4.4 Individual Acquiring Title by Gift

Another common method by which individuals, particularly strangers in a chiefdom, acquire title to land is by gift. Land is frequently given to a stranger on his marriage to a female member of a land-owning family, or as a sign of appreciation for services rendered to the family or to the community as a whole. The nature of the title thus acquired by the grantee will depend both on the applicable customary law and on the conditions, if any, imposed by the grantor when making the gift. So, for instance, under Mende customary law, a grantee of land in consideration of marriage acquires a proprietary interest in the use and occupation of the land which continues in perpetuity after the death of his spouse without issue. The grantor may however recover possession of the land if the grantee disputes or challenges the title of the grantor to the "reversion", or if he effectively abandons the land or his line becomes extinct.

However, there is nothing in principle to prevent a land-owning family, community or even an individual owner of self-acquired property from making an outright gift of land, which is recognized as having the same legal effect under customary law as an outright sale. In fact, this is the device now frequently employed in many Temne chiefdoms where the people have refused to come to terms with the phenomenon of an outright sale. What should normally be regarded as the purchase price is received as a "*shakehand*" on the pretext that it is given not as consideration for the purchase but for the purpose of thanking the "donor" for making the grant.

7.4.5 Individual Acquiring Title by Long Possession

It is a fundamental doctrine of most African customary laws that original title to land cannot be ousted by extinctive prescription or adverse possession.[219] Thus, under customary law, land granted merely for a grantee's occupation and use, even without a fixed duration, can never be prescribed

219 See *Fulla v. Kondowa* (1970–71) ALR S.L. 300, discussed more fully at p. 212.

by the grantee against the reversionary grantor.[220] No period of limitation operates under customary law to bar the grantor's right to recover the land where, for example, any of the conditions of occupancy are broken. However, in certain circumstances, the courts will apply the equitable principles of laches, acquiescence or proprietary estoppel to prevent the grantor from reasserting ownership of the land in question.

Thus, according to the full Court of the then Gold Coast in the *Bokitsi* case[221] where persons in possession had occupied the land:

> *"under such circumstances ... as would cause them to believe themselves to be the owners of the land and to incur pecuniary responsibilities in consequences of that belief, we think it right to state that in our opinion it would be contrary to the principles of equity to allow the native law to apply in its entirety".*

Through the constant application of such equitable principles, the force of the customary law rule against acquisition of prescriptive title has come to be attenuated and we can now safely state that it is possible, in appropriate circumstances, for title to be acquired without a positive grant.[222]

7.4.6 Individual Acquiring Title by Partition

In cases of dispute, or break-up of the traditional family link, it is not unusual for the various factions to agree on a partition of family lands, especially where all efforts at arbitration and other traditional methods of settlement of the dispute have failed.

Reference has also been made to the block system of apportioning lands peculiar to the Mende whereby a member can acquire, by mere long user, exclusive right to occupy, virtually in perpetuity, a portion of family land which has been apportioned to him. An individual's interest thus acquired by partitioning alters the status of the land in question to one subject to individual ownership at least for the duration of the life of the original

220 See *Agyeman v. Yarmoah* (1913) D and F 1911–16; *Epelle v. Ojo,* 7 N.L.R. 96; and *Kargbo v. Kanu* (1970–71) ALR S.L. 378.

221 (1902) Sar. F.L.R. 148 at 160.

222 See *Fiscian v. Nelson* (1946) 12 W.A.C.A. 21; *Abbey v. Ollenu* (1954) 14 W.A.C.A. 567; *Akuru v. Olubadan-in-Council* (1954) W.A.C.A. 523; *Nwakobi v. Nzekwu* (1964) W.N.L.R 1019; cf. *Sithia Tribal Authority v. Official Administrator of Intestate Estates* (1937–49) ALR S.L. 411.

grantee. This status may continue indefinitely where the paramount title to the land is transferred either *inter vivos*, or by testamentary disposition, to another individual. However the status is lost, in most cases, where the holder of the title dies intestate. Because of the rules of distribution under customary law, the title would invariably revert to the deceased's immediate or extended family as a group.

7.4.7 Individual Acquiring Title by Succession

The interest that an individual acquires in land by way of succession depends on whether the land is ancestral family land, communal land, or self-acquired property. As a rule, the successors to self-acquired property acquire the same quantum of right and interest as their predecessor had in the property.

The paramount interest in land could therefore be acquired where that was the interest held in the property by the deceased. Thus, where an individual owner dies intestate leaving a sole heir, though this is a rare occurrence, in principle such a successor acquires the absolute rights and interests of the deceased. If there are several heirs, as is invariably the case, then the status of individual ownership of the land may only be preserved on a partition as described above.

As the concept of testate succession is gradually being accepted under customary law in respect of self-acquired property it is also theoretically possible for a testator to make a grant of his paramount interest in land to a sole devisee who thus acquires an interest equivalent to that recognized under a system of individual tenure.

In all the above instances, however, where an individual has acquired the paramount title to land either by clearing virgin forest, by purchase, gift, long possession, partition or succession, there is always the possibility that the land could some day revert to family or communal ownership. Conversion to family tenure is more likely because of the customary rules of intestate succession which provide for inheritance of self-acquired and individually owned property by the deceased's nuclear family as a group. Such property could only revert to communal ownership in case of abandonment or extinction of the family – immediate or extended – or the line of succession of the individual owner.

It is not feasible to conduct a survey of the amount of land that has thus actually come under individual ownership in the Provinces of Sierra Leone but all indications gathered from informants and from personal observations by the writer point to the fact that it is a fast developing trend, particularly in the urban areas.

CHAPTER 8

THE NATURE OF INTEREST IN LAND HELD BY CERTAIN ENTITIES UNDER CUSTOMARY LAW

8.1 BACKGROUND TO INTEREST IN LAND HELD UNDER CUSTOMARY LAW

As has already been stated in this work, the chiefdom is the most important unit in the administrative and socio-political structure of the Provinces. Socially, though it is not a kinship group, for the purposes of rights in land under customary tenure it does constitute a closed and well-defined unit, membership of which is acquired only by birth. Politically, it is an autonomous and independent unit occupying an identifiable and specific land area over which the paramount chief exercises absolute jurisdiction and authority for the maintenance of social and political order.

From the point of view of judicial authority, the chiefdom possesses its own internal and independent judicial institutions exercising jurisdiction throughout the territory, and applying therein a distinct body of rules of customary law. But most importantly, the chiefdom, for our present purposes, is at the centre of the system of customary land tenure because no group or individual may claim to be entitled as of right to any lands save those which are within the territorial limits of the chiefdom of their origin.

Though the chiefdom can and does constitute a unit for the purposes of customary land tenure, yet the interests in land within the unit are held by two basic entities within the chiefdom, which, to a large extent, symbolize the chiefdom. These are the chiefdom council and the paramount chief. First to be considered is the position of the chiefdom council in relation to interests in land within the chiefdom.

8.2 INTEREST IN LAND HELD BY THE CHIEFDOM COUNCIL

8.2.1 Features of the Chiefdom Council

The chiefdom council is a rather peculiar institution in the socio-political and legal framework of the chiefdom. In its present form, it is a statutory body established under the Chiefdom Councils Act, Cap. 61, but as regards its membership, and its role in the social set-up of the chiefdom, it is an institution of customary law – especially as it derives most of its power from customary law.

The Act itself takes into account this rather ambivalent status of the chiefdom council. The Act lays down that its membership shall comprise:

> *"the Paramount Chief, the (sub or section) chiefs, the councilors and men of note elected by the people according to customary law".*

In practice, chiefdom councils vary in size and composition from chiefdom to chiefdom. However, apart from the paramount chief, sub-chiefs and chiefdom speakers who more or less qualify automatically for membership of the council, the rest of the membership is invariably made up of other title-holders in the chiefdom such as court chairmen and town or village headmen. It is also traditional to ensure that the heads of all the principal land-owning families in the chiefdom serve as members of the council.

8.2.2 Powers of the Chiefdom Council in Land Matters

Section 4 of the Chiefdom Councils Act, Cap. 61 provides that, for the fulfilment of its duties under the Act, a chiefdom council shall exercise such powers as are conferred on it by statute or by any customary law. The statutory powers of the chiefdom council in relation to land are spelt out principally in the Chiefdom Councils Act, Cap. 61, and in the Provinces Land Act, Cap. 122. The provisions of Cap. 122 are discussed in detail in subsequent sections of this chapter.

With regard to the powers conferred on the chiefdom council by customary law, these could best be explained by making an analogy between the chiefdom council, as established by statute, and the rather amorphous body recognized under customary law and which, for want of a more precise designation, can be termed "the Chief-in-Council". This body traditionally comprised the paramount chief and his closest advisers, the key title holders and principal members of the chiefdom. Together with the paramount chief they were responsible for the day-to-day administration of the chiefdom before the setting up of the statutory body known as the Tribal Authority.

In actual fact, the body which corresponds most closely with the Chief-in-Council, particularly in respect of land matters, is the chiefdom committee, also established under the Chiefdom Councils Act, Cap. 61. This committee consists of the paramount chief as chairman, the senior speaker as vice-chairman and five other leading councillors. This is the body on which the paramount chief mainly relies for advice and consultations in the exercise of his traditional powers, conferred by customary law, in land matters. The full body of councillors meets on average only four times a year, mainly to ratify important decisions taken by the chiefdom committee, or to act as an electoral college to fill a vacancy in the office of the paramount chief.

8.2.3 The Nature of the Chiefdom Councils' Interest in Lands

A useful starting point in analysing the position of the chiefdom councils vis-à-vis interests in lands within the chiefdom is the Provinces Land Act, Cap. 122, the preamble to which declares that:

> *"all land in the Provinces is vested in the Chiefdom Councils who hold such land for and on behalf of the native communities concerned".*

It is significant and rather odd that the only statutory provision dealing with the status of land in the Provinces is couched in such a vague and imprecise manner. This is even more so when one takes into consideration that the preamble is that of an Act whose object is "*to make provision relating to the tenure of land by non-natives in the Provinces*". It is also not clear whether it was the intention of the legislature by this preamble to thus declare all provincial land to be henceforth vested in the chiefdom councils, or whether the preamble was simply meant to put in statutory form what was already an accepted and recognized principle under customary law.

Moreover, it is impossible to ascertain, taking the preamble in isolation or reading the statute as a whole, what exactly was being vested in the chiefdom councils. Is it the legal title to provincial land, or is it merely the right to control and administer provincial land generally? The use of the words "*who hold such land for and on behalf of the communities concerned*" would tend to suggest the existence or creation of a trust. However, despite the fact that certain powers relating to the control and management of land in the Provinces are conferred on chiefdom councils by the Provinces Land Act, Cap. 122 and the Chiefdom Councils Act, Cap. 61, the vesting of title to provincial land is still governed basically by customary law.

It can be concluded, therefore, that the statement in the preamble to the Provinces Land Act, Cap. 122 has not altered the status of provincial land. This view is substantiated by the fact that, apart from those express powers conferred by statute on the chiefdom councils, the rights in and over provincial land, vested in these entities, derive from, and are exercised in accordance with, the relevant customary law.

8.2.4 Powers of the Chiefdom Councils under The Provinces Land Act, Cap. 122

The correctness of the above proposition can be challenged on the ground that some of the statutory powers of chiefdom councils in relation to land were formerly vested either in the paramount chiefs personally or in the chief-in-council. The first and most obvious example is the power to control the alienation of land to persons from outside the chiefdom, that is, to strangers. Section 3(1) of the Provinces Land Act, Cap. 122 provides that no land in the Provinces shall be occupied by a non-native (defined in the Act as a person not entitled by birth to rights in land in the a Province) unless he has first obtained the consent of the chiefdom council.

Traditionally, the right to control the disposition of land to strangers, both natives and non-natives, has always been vested in the chief-in-council under customary law. In the case of family land held under family tenure, only the concurrence of the paramount chief, or other traditional rulers, was required before a stranger could be allowed to occupy land within the chiefdom. However, where the land was held under communal tenure, the consent of the chief-in-council was always a prerequisite for such dispositions, even when the land had already been appropriated or otherwise occupied by a family or an individual member of the chiefdom. The position at customary law has therefore been altered by the Act to require the consent of the chiefdom council in all cases where a non-native stranger wishes to occupy land in any chiefdom, whether the land is held under communal, family or individual tenure.

Another statutory provision which has modified the customary law relating to rights in land in favour of chiefdom councils is that contained in section 10(1) of the Provinces Land Act, Cap 122. This provision vests in the chiefdom councils the reversion in all fixtures, buildings and economic trees on lands occupied by non-natives under the Act. Prior to the enactment of this provision, under customary law, any improvements made on land by a stranger would, prima facie, enure for the benefit of the original grantors or their successors when they retake possession of the land.

8.2.5 The Chiefdom Councils Act, Cap. 61

In addition to the above powers and rights conferred on chiefdom councils by the Provinces Land Act, Cap. 122, there are certain others which clearly did not exist under customary law. Thus, section 16(1) of the Chiefdom Councils Act, Cap. 61, for example, provides that chiefdom councils may make bye-laws dealing, inter alia, with the:

> *"setting aside of land in or near a town for development of the town and the general benefit of inhabitants of that town and its villages".*

In theory, this involves the right to expropriate even members of the chiefdom, a right which is unknown under customary law. In practice, when the chiefdom council needs land for development, or for any public purpose, and the land required is in private ownership, the council secures its surrender by offering the owner, in exchange, another parcel of land within the chiefdom, on the understanding that the land surrendered will revert to the original owner if it is no longer needed by the chiefdom council.

Finally, there are statutory provisions which enable the chiefdom council to institute action, in its own name, in land matters, for example, in boundary disputes with other chiefdoms, or to recover possession of land within the chiefdom from a non-native.[223]

223 Chiefdom councils were formerly known as Tribal Authorities. The change was ef-

8.2.6 Powers of the Chiefdom Councils Derived from Customary Law

In addition to the above statutory provisions vesting powers and rights in chiefdom councils, in relation to land within their respective chiefdoms, there are certain rights in land enjoyed by chiefdom councils which are not expressly provided for by the general law. Since the only other law applicable to land tenure in the Provinces is customary law, the logical inference is that such rights are derived from customary law. In fact, an analysis of the non-statutory rights in land currently enjoyed by chiefdom councils indicates that these tend to correspond with those formerly enjoyed by the chief-in-council under customary law.

These rights would seem to be derived basically, not from the fact that the paramount title to land in the Provinces is vested in chiefdom councils, but because they or rather the entity which they have replaced, that is the chief-in-council, holds certain interests in land within the chiefdom recognized by customary law. These interests could be identified as those of control, supervision and management. Under the interest of control could be classified the rights to allocate and freely dispose of certain lands within the chiefdom to both members and non-members of the chiefdom.

In the case of lands in areas under family tenure the right of user and disposal vested in the chiefdom council is limited to unappropriated lands, such as reclaimed swamp or abandoned lands. In the case of lands under communal tenure, this right extends, in theory, to any land other than lands in actual possession of the family, or individual member, of the chiefdom.

This right of disposal formerly enjoyed by the chief-in-council under customary law has received judicial sanction in two leading cases, namely *Sitia Tribal Authority v. Official Administrator of Intestate Estates,*[224] and *Kamanda Bongay v. F.S. Macauley.*[225] In the *Sitia Tribal Authority* case the Tribal Authority (now chiefdom council) had instituted an action for a declaration that, by virtue of the Protectorate Ordinances of 1924 and 1933 (now the Provinces Act, Cap. 60) and the Protectorate Land Ordinance of 1927 (now the Provinces Land Act, Cap. 122), a certain piece of land in the Bonthe District, Southern Province formed part of the then Protectorate

fected by Act No. 12 of 1964; see also section 18 of the Chiefdom Councils Act, Cap. 61 and section 2 of the Summary Ejectment (Provinces) Act, Cap. 50.

224 (1937–49) ALR S.L. 411.

225 (1932) 1 W.A.C.A. 225.

and was therefore vested in the plaintiffs as Tribal Authority of Sitia Chiefdom. They also sought to recover possession of the land.

In the course of his judgment Boeku-Betts, J. set out in full "*the special case*" as agreed upon between the parties and found as a fact, inter alia, that:

> "*by a conveyance dated August 27, 1879, the land the subject-matter of the action was conveyed by Sorri Yarn, Chief of Sherbro, to Solomon Benjamin Macfoy, a British subject*".

No attempt was apparently made during the trial to challenge the validity of the said conveyance, which according to Beoku-Betts, J., "*granted freehold land to the predecessor in title of the defendant*". The use of the word "*freehold*" by the learned Judge, to describe the interest in the land acquired by the defendant's predecessor in title is, in the opinion of the present writer, rather misleading as the concept of "freehold" has always been foreign to customary land tenure. Presumably, Beoku-Betts, J. was adopting, rather inappropriately, the exact terminology used in the conveyance, which, no doubt, had been prepared in accordance with English form.

However, despite this misdescription of the interest thus granted by the conveyance, the learned Judge was in doubt as to the right of the grantors to dispose of the same, for he went on to hold that it would have been inequitable

> "*to deprive the defendant of land with which the plaintiff's predecessor had voluntarily parted for valuable consideration*".

In Kamanda Bongay v. F.S. Macauley[226] the action had been instituted by the "Paramount Chief of the Big Bo Chiefdom for himself and on behalf of the Tribal Authority of the Big Bo Chiefdom" claiming from the defendant, a non-native, land which had been granted to him by the then paramount chief of Bo Chiefdom in 1892. According to the terms of the grant, the land was to remain the property of the defendant for as long as he cultivated it "in accordance with the conditions as to cultivation subject

226 Above.

to which the land was granted". The West African Court of Appeal held that, from the evidence, the defendant had forfeited his grant by flouting the authority of the paramount chief, contrary to customary law, and ordered possession to be delivered to the Tribal Authority.

What emerges from these two cases is that the grant in each case had been made by the paramount chief, not alone and acting independently, but in collaboration with his body of advisers which can be equated with, at least, the present chiefdom committee, if not the whole chiefdom council. Beoku-Betts, J. confirmed this view when he referred to the grantors in the Sitia Tribal Authority case as "the then Tribal Authority", though at the date of the grant in 1879 Tribal Authorities had not yet been established by statute. Similarly, in the Kamanda Bongay case, there was evidence, which was accepted by the Court, that the land in question had been granted to the defendant by "the Chief and representative men".

The conclusion, therefore, which could be drawn from these and other authorities, is that the chief-in-council had a right to dispose of certain lands within the chiefdom to strangers. That this right has been transferred to the chiefdom council is confirmed by evidence gathered from informants and from an inspection of registered documents such as leases and even English-type conveyances in which varying degrees of interests in land have been transferred to the State, commercial houses or even individuals, with only the chiefdom council named therein as grantor.

Even where the land in question was owned by some other entity, such as a family or an individual, and such entity is in effect making the grant, it is the usual practice to have any document prepared relating to the grant executed by a chiefdom councillor on behalf of the chiefdom council.

Another related practice, which might be an incidence of the chiefdom council's jurisdictional authority over all lands within the chiefdom, is the payment direct to the chiefdom treasury of a one-third share of all rent accruing from property leased to non-natives. This privilege is shared with the paramount chief who traditionally also receives a share, the final one-third share going to the landowners. It would appear that where the land in question is leased directly by the chiefdom council, as sole lessor, the entire sum is paid into the chiefdom treasury without any deductions in favour of the paramount chief.

8.2.7 Other Interests of the Chiefdom Council in Provincial Lands

With regard to the other interests in land within the chiefdom, such as the interests of supervision and management, and which are based on the jurisdictional authority of the chiefdom council over all lands within the chiefdom, there tends to be a great deal of overlapping between the chiefdom council per se and the paramount chief, in the exercise of the rights thereunder. This stems mainly from the fact that the paramount chief is the chief executive of the chiefdom council and it is not always easy to differentiate between rights exercised by virtue of his status as paramount chief and those exercised in the name of, and on behalf of, the chiefdom council as an entity. Examples of the exercise of these rights include the restriction sometimes imposed by the paramount chief against farming or fishing on particular days; the control of the commencement of harvesting or bush firing; the annual allocation of farming lands in areas of communal tenure; and the general charge for and control of access to sacred bushes.

In conclusion, it can be said that despite the suggestion in the preamble to the Provinces Land Act, Cap. 122, that all land in the Provinces is vested in the chiefdom councils, which hold such lands for and on behalf of the native communities concerned, it is only in very exceptional circumstances, for example, in the case of unappropriated or abandoned lands within the chiefdom, that the paramount title to land could be said to be vested in chiefdom councils. On the other hand, chiefdom councils do have certain statutory and non-statutory powers and rights in land deriving from various interests that fall short of the paramount title to land.

8.3 THE PARAMOUNT CHIEF AND PROVINCIAL LAND

8.3.1 Introduction

The institution of chieftaincy is recognized and protected both by statute law, as part of the general law, and by customary law. However, unlike those of the chiefdom council, all the rights and interests in land associated with the office of chieftaincy derive exclusively from customary law. The paramount chief is the political head of the chiefdom with a number of subordinate or section chiefs answerable to him. In that capacity, he has absolute jurisdiction over the entire chiefdom and commands allegiance, not only from his subjects, as members of his chiefdom, but from all persons settled or otherwise resident within his area of jurisdiction.

Apart from political authority, the paramount chief also possesses a certain number of legislative and quasi-judicial powers. His legislative authority is exercised mostly through the chiefdom council by the making of bye-laws and the issuing of orders relating to matters affecting his chiefdom. As discussed in Chapter 3, the judicial authority of chiefs generally is now restricted only to the process of informal customary arbitration, based on the consent of the parties to the dispute. However, in that capacity, chiefs still play an important role in the legal system, as many disputes only end up in the courts after an attempt at settlement through arbitration has failed to satisfy one or both of the parties. As "chief executive" of the chiefdom council the paramount chief also plays a leading role in the exercise of the rights and powers conferred on that body both by statute and by customary law. He is, in many respects, the alter ego of the chiefdom council.

8.3.2 The Nature of Interests in Land Held by the Paramount Chief

What then is the position of the paramount chief in relation to interests in land within his chiefdom? First and foremost, it is essential to make a distinction between lands held under communal tenure, and those held under any other types of tenure. As already discussed in Chapter 7, in the case of lands under communal tenure, the title thereto is vested in the paramount chief, in a representative capacity, on behalf of the whole community. Various expressions have been used to describe the position of the chief vis-à-vis title to communal lands. Probably the commonest, and least appropriate, is that which states that the chief is the owner of the communal lands.

This notion that chiefs owned communal lands was encountered quite frequently during interviews, particularly those conducted in Kono chiefdoms. It is significant that the interviewees came from not just one particular class of the community, but included persons from various walks of life, a few of whom had had the benefit of formal education. They were in a position to elaborate on their perception of ownership. What emerged from such attempts to give a precise interpretation of the term "ownership", as used by most interviewees, was that it was not an absolute and beneficial ownership, but one based on a conception similar to that of the trust under English law, with the "trustee" himself in this case being one out of countless beneficiaries. However, on closer examination of the relation of the chief to communal lands, the analogy with the trust concept must be limited. One basic difference between the two is the absence of any strict liability to account on the part of the chief as "trustee". Other and, in many ways, more appropriate expressions encountered to describe the chief's position were those such as "custodian" or "caretaker". Whatever expression is used to describe the chief's position in relation to communal lands, the fact remains that such title as is vested in him, and the rights and interests deriving therefrom, are not by virtue of his status as chief or in his personal capacity but, primarily, as traditional head of the community.

This latter distinction is best illustrated by contrasting communal lands in the Provinces of Sierra Leone with stool lands in the Akan states of Ghana. In the Provinces of Sierra Leone, the rights and interests of the paramount chief in communal lands are not attached to the office of chieftaincy so as to make the lands "chieftaincy lands" in the same way that lands held by the occupant of the stool of the Akan states are stool lands. In the case of communal lands in Sierra Leone, the emphasis is on the community, and title to the lands is only vested in the paramount chief in a representative capacity by virtue of his traditional headship of the community.

However, the paramount chief combines those interests in land deriving from the vesting in him of the paramount title to communal lands, such as the interest of management, with other interests such as the interests of control and supervision which are based on his political authority over the entire chiefdom. These latter interests in land, based on the paramount chief's jurisdictional authority, are held even in lands which are subject to family or individual tenure.

Where title is vested in him, though in a representative capacity, the paramount chief can exercise all the rights associated with absolute ownership, subject to the major qualification that he must act for the benefit, and in the general interest, of the community as a whole. The welfare and interest of the community are safeguarded by the requirement that the paramount chief must exercise those rights in collaboration with other principal members of the chiefdom.

In this regard, the paramount chief never acts alone, but only after due consultation with his leading advisers who invariably are themselves title-holders such as speakers, section chiefs, village headmen or heads of families whose interests may be directly or indirectly affected by the proposed action. In the same way, the paramount chief would never take a decision to dispose of any piece of communal land, whether by sale, gift, lease or mere loan to a stranger without first consulting the traditional head of the area where the land is located. In fact, as described later in this work, the necessary negotiations usually start at the local level, and end up with the paramount chief only making or ratifying the final decision. The same process of consultation is encountered even when the paramount chief exercises his right to allocate portions of communal lands to families or individual members of the community. In the case of unappropriated or abandoned lands in areas of non-communal tenure, the right to dispose of such lands to strangers, or to allocate them to members of the chiefdom, is exercised by the paramount chief on behalf of and in the name of the chiefdom council.

8.3.3 The Paramount Chief and Title to Provincial Land

Some writers tend to suggest that since the paramount chief was formerly considered as owner of all lands within the chiefdom he had absolute powers of appropriation and disposal thereof. For example, Little,[227] a sociologist, writing about Mende chiefdoms, argues that, after the British domination of the former Protectorate, agriculture replaced warfare as the principal factor in the economy and "*interest in the holding of land was naturally enhanced*". He continues by stating that the settled conditions gave rise to uninterrupted tenure, "*and claims to local ownership came up for ratification*". Little concludes that the fact that the authority of the chief was diminished as a result of the pacification of the country "*limited his powers of appropriation and disposal* [of lands] *and led, in turn, to his being regarded more as a 'caretaker'*".

This view is supported by Collier, a Sierra Leonean jurist,[228] who asserts that "*originally the chief was not merely regarded as the custodian of the people's land but as the actual owner*".[229] Collier based his argument on the fact that the treaties of cession and other dispositions of land to Europeans and other non-natives were originally executed and made by the chiefs in their capacity as beneficial owners of the lands. However, there is no known authority, legal or otherwise, to support this contention. A closer analysis of these treaties and other such dispositions of land would

227 Op. cit., p. 90.
228 Gershon Collier, *Sierra Leone Experiment in Democracy in an African Nation.*
229 Ibid., p. 80.

reveal that they were all made by the chiefs in a representative capacity. This is evident from the fact that the signatures or marks of the chiefs were always accompanied by those of other representatives of the native communities concerned.

As stated earlier in this chapter, there is no evidence to suggest that there have ever been any "chieftaincy lands" as such in Sierra Leone, nor any lands owned by chiefs merely by virtue of their political office. The general understanding is that a chief occupies and uses land within his chiefdom on the same basis as any other member of the chiefdom. Either he could hold the paramount title to land in his private capacity as his self-acquired individual property, or he may personally hold a lesser interest in communal land or inherited family land by appropriating a portion thereof.

If and when a chief requires more land in addition to what he holds in his personal capacity as a member of a community or a descent group, he is expected to acquire title to such land, or an interest therein, in the same way as any other individual member of the chiefdom, that is, by purchase, gift, loan or "begging", pledge, or, in recent times, by leasing. He has no right of eminent domain arising by virtue of his political office, nor can he arbitrarily expropriate or dispossess any member of the chiefdom of his interests in land within the chiefdom.

8.3.4 Other Rights of the Paramount Chief in Relation to Provincial Land

There are, however, certain residual rights in and over lands within the chiefdom which are enjoyed by the paramount chief by virtue of, and as an acknowledgement of, his political jurisdiction over the chiefdom. Some of these rights are now shared with, and others have been transferred completely to, the chiefdom council. These include the right to control the use of land within the chiefdom for agricultural and other purposes. He can exercise these rights in a variety of ways, such as by promulgating regulations about how particular lands in the chiefdom should be farmed; by decreeing when the various annual operations relating to cultivation and harvesting of crops should begin and end; by granting permission to strangers either to fish or take water in streams or rivers or to cut timber, hunt or tap wine from palm trees on lands within the chiefdom.

Along with these jurisdictional rights go certain privileges and responsibilities. One of the most rewarding and well-established privileges of chieftaincy is the right of the chief to receive tribute, in various forms and circumstances, both from his subjects and from strangers who occupy land within his chiefdom. Thus, it is traditional for the paramount chief and other subordinate chiefs to receive tribute in the form of farm produce from lands cultivated in the area where they reside. In the Mende chiefdoms, in particular, the tradition is to give the chiefs a proportion of all rice and palm oil produced in every *mawe* in the chiefdom. Chiefs also have a right to share in the meat of certain animals hunted and killed in the chiefdom and to extract a small "*dash*" from persons cutting timber or tapping palm wine in the chiefdom.

However, some of these practices seem to be on the wane and, in some instances, have been totally discarded – especially in the larger urban centres of the Provinces. But even in urban areas, certain rights to tribute are still insisted on, in particular, the right of the chief to receive a "*shakehand*" from every stranger who intends to settle or occupy land within the chiefdom. Payment of such tribute, invariably in cash, but sometimes in kind, such as a bottle of gin or other alcoholic drink, serves as a symbolic acknowledgement of the chief's jurisdiction, and a formal indication by the stranger that he is prepared to respect and abide by the laws and customs of the chiefdom.

Reference has already been made to the right of the paramount chief to receive a one-third share of all rents paid by non-natives in respect of lands occupied or leased in the chiefdom. Such occupation or leasing by non-natives, as already established in this work, is regulated by the provisions of the Provinces Land Act, Cap. 122. However, there is nothing in the Act which provides for the paramount chief to receive a share of the rent paid by the non-native. It must therefore be considered as an extension of the chief's customary right to receive annual tribute from all strangers resident in or occupying land within the chiefdom. The legal basis for the right of the paramount chief to share in such rents is sometimes misunderstood due to the fact that the paramount chief, nowadays, invariably joins in making the grant as one of the members of the chiefdom council, the lessors under the Act. The signature or mark of the paramount chief on such documents serves a dual purpose; it signifies the chiefdom council's approval of the occupation as required by statute, and it confirms the right of the landowners to dispose of the interest thereby granted.

Another right or responsibility, depending on how it is viewed, of the paramount chief, involves him acting as a kind of unofficial registrar in respect of all alienations of interest in land within his chiefdom. The paramount chief, or his appointed representative, is a necessary witness to all such transactions. Traditionally, a physical presence was required, either at the site when the land was formally handed over to the grantee, or elsewhere when public acknowledgement was being made by the grantee of the grantor's right to effect the transfer. The modern practice, especially in urban areas where documents are now usually prepared, is for the paramount chief to countersign the document itself, or the site plan of the land, drawn and attached to the document. This is a requirement in any such transaction as it serves as a confirmation to the grantee that the grantor has the right or is otherwise duly authorized to make the grant. The presumption is that the paramount chief will not act as a witness to the transaction unless he is satisfied, on the basis of his own knowledge or of reliable information from local elders, that the grantor is acting bona fide. In this respect, the paramount chief is also acting as a guardian of the interests of the different families and individuals holding interests in land within his chiefdom.

Another aspect of this responsibility to act as guardian of the interests of the members in lands in the chiefdom is that the paramount chief is expected to institute action in his own name, and on behalf of the chiefdom council, in all land disputes involving another chiefdom, whether the land in question is owned by the community as a whole, by family groups or by individuals.

The paramount chief's position in relation to lands in his chiefdom could therefore be summarized as follows: Title to land may be vested in him either in a representative capacity in the case of communal lands, or in his private capacity in the case of self-acquired property. He may also hold an interest in family land as a member of his own ancestral family. He has certain interests in lands within the chiefdom based on his jurisdictional authority that entitle him, for example, to control the alienation of such lands to non-members of the chiefdom or to regulate the use of land generally.

Finally, he has certain rights and privileges to receive tribute from owners and occupiers of lands within the chiefdom, together with corresponding responsibilities to act as overall guardian of the interests held by members in lands in the chiefdom as a whole.

8.4 THE FAMILY'S INTEREST IN PROVINCIAL LAND

8.4.1 Introduction

The family is probably the most important entity as far as interests in land under customary tenure are concerned. The family's interests in land are the most complex and could subsist in one form or another under all three types of tenure, namely communal, family and individual. Thus, even in the case of individual tenure, the family has a potential right to succeed to such of the individual's interests in self-acquired property as may not have been disposed of either *inter vivos* or by will. The family's interests in land will now be analysed from three different perspective: firstly, so as to identify the interests in land held by the family as unit, secondly, to ascertain the position and the role of the head of family in the control and management of family lands and, finally, to define the quantum of rights enjoyed by the individual member in family lands.

8.4.2 The Interests in Land Held by the Family as a Unit

In analysing the interest in land held by the family as a unit it is essential to re-emphasize the essential distinction between family tenure and communal tenure. In chiefdoms where family tenure is the dominant form of tenure, such as the Mende or Temne chiefdoms, title to land is vested primarily in the family as a unit. Moreover, the title of the family to such lands is an original and absolute title not derived from nor dependent on the interests of any other entity, such as the wider community. However, the family's rights to use and dispose of its interests in such family lands is qualified in certain respects such as by the interests held by the paramount chief in all lands in the chiefdom because of his jurisdictional authority as political head.

In contrast, in chiefdoms where lands are basically held under communal tenure, such as in the Kono and Limba chiefdoms, title to communal lands, as has been shown earlier in this work, is vested in the paramount chief in a representative capacity for and on behalf of the whole community. The family's interest in such communal lands is therefore not original or absolute. It is not only derivative but also limited in terms of its quantum and its duration, the latter more in theory than in practice.

8.4.3 The Features of the Family's Interest in Land Held under Family Tenure

One of the main distinctive feature of family tenure, under both Mende and Temne customary law, is that the family enjoys rights over land which are almost equivalent to those of an absolute owner. The interests held by the family in lands under family tenure involve the maximum cluster of rights permitted to exist in and over land under the relevant customary law. Both the quantum and duration of these interests are unlimited. This means that in terms of rights of user and disposal, the family as an entity possesses the fullest competence, just like an absolute owner, to deal with its property in any way it sees fit, subject only to such restrictions as are imposed by law and custom on holders of interests in land generally in their use or disposal thereof.

The fact that the rights of user and enjoyment of family lands are not exercised by the family as a unit, but rather by sub-groups thereof, or by individual members, does not detract from the amplitude of these rights. Such user and enjoyment by sub-groups and individuals are exercised in their capacity as members of the family and, in essence, amount to user and enjoyment by the family itself as an entity. However, as regards disposal of its interests to outsiders, the family always acts as a unit and, in this respect, also enjoys unlimited rights to transfer its interests by sale (within the limits imposed by any local customary law), gift, loan, lease or pledge. These rights are exercised by the family through the head of family or any other authorized member.

The duration of the family's interests in family lands is unlimited. In theory, such interests last in perpetuity unless alienated outright or relinquished by the family itself. In this regard, it should be emphasized that it is a principle of Temne customary law that the total interests of the family in family lands could not be alienated outright to an outsider. Even where there is an apparent outright sale or gift, that is, without express conditions or reservations, there is always implied a condition as to reverter under which the interests transferred could revert to the granting family in the event that the grantee dies without heirs or effectively abandons the land. However, the family's interests in family lands could well be extinguished under the general law, that is, in cases where the courts could appropriately apply such equitable principles as laches, acquiescence or proprietary estoppel. Under customary law the family's interests in family lands could not be lost by prescription or adverse possession.

8.4.4 THE FEATURES OF THE FAMILY'S INTEREST IN LAND HELD UNDER COMMUNAL TENURE

On the other hand, the nature and extent of the family's interests in communal lands are limited in almost the same way that an individual member's interests in family or communal lands are limited. The interests of the family in communal lands are sometimes described as a "*usufructuary title*".[230] It is submitted that the concept of usufruct – borrowed from Roman law, and implying a right of user and enjoyment of the fruits of property belonging to another without destruction or waste – could not be appropriately applied to a member's interests in communal lands. This is because the member, whether a family unit or an individual, is an integral part of the community and therefore possesses an inherent and potential right to use and enjoy any portion of the communal lands.

Bentsi-Enchill[231] suggests the use of the expression "*proprietary occupancy*" to describe such interests in contrast with what he terms "*permissive or contractual occupancy*", the latter designating the broad category of interests which arise by unilateral assent or by agreement. This expression, "*proprietary occupancy*", comes near to embracing all the essential features of the interests of the family or an individual in communal lands. However, it has the weakness of assuming that such interests vest only when the holder is in actual occupation of a portion of communal lands. The emphasis on occupancy fails to take into account the potential right of families or of individual members to use and enjoy the benefits of communal lands without necessarily being in actual occupation of any specific portion. Indeed, such interests may involve the exercise of certain rights, such as the right to cut timber, fish or take water from a stream on communal lands without actually going into occupation of the same.

These interests could not be adequately described by using terminology borrowed from English law. However, it is possible to describe them by stating in what respect they differ from those of the paramount interest in land, such as that held by family in family lands. Thus, in terms of quantum, both the rights of the user and the disposal of the family's interests in communal lands are limited. A family can only make use of such communal lands as have not already been allocated to or appropriated by another member of the community. Once a member is in possession

230 See, for example, the dicta of Lord Haldane in *Amadu Tijani v. Secretary, Southern Nigeria*, above at 403–5.

231 Above (1965) J.A.L. 115.

of communal lands, even if he is not in actual occupation, he has a right to exclude not only strangers, but also other members of the community. This is subject to the right of all members of the community to share in the enjoyment of those fruits and benefits of the land which always enure for the community as a whole even when a particular member is in possession, such as the right to fish and take water from any stream on communal lands.

The right of the family to alienate its interests in communal lands is also restricted, and is limited to the disposition of such improvements and developments on the land by the family as a group, such as farms, plantations or buildings. In this regard, a distinction is made under customary law between, on the one hand, the land itself, that is, the surface soil and things found naturally under, on or above the surface, such as minerals and wild plants and trees, and on the other, things planted or brought on to the land by the industry of man.

The family's interests in communal lands are also limited in their duration in the sense that its rights to user and enjoyment are determinable in certain circumstances. Thus, the family's interests in a particular portion of communal lands, or rather its immediate rights to use and enjoy the same, could be extinguished, for example, by an outright transfer to a stranger, of the community's paramount title to that portion of communal lands effected on its behalf by the competent authorities. In another sense, a family's right to immediate possession of a particular portion of communal lands may be lost in the event of effective abandonment of that land by the family. Finally, in the unlikely event of the entire family dying out, then its interests will disappear with the last member.

In any case, whether the family's interests are in land held under family or communal tenure, the right to control the user thereof or to alienate the same, where this is permitted by customary law, and the responsibility for the management of family lands in general, are all vested in the head of the family whose role in this regard we shall now consider.

8.4.5 The Position of the Head of Family

The position of the head of family under customary land tenure is unique. Though the title to family lands is not vested in him, he plays a prominent role in the control and management of the family's interests in lands both under family tenure and under communal tenure. In rural areas where the family's only asset is the land itself, and where the majority of the people live off the land, the influence of the head of family is sometimes even stronger than that of the political title-holders such as town chiefs or village headmen.

The position of headship of the family is traditionally held by the oldest male member of the descent group. In principle, the office is held for life, though deposition in cases of serious and exceptional misconduct is not unusual. It is not an elective office, but succession to it is not automatic either. According to Mende and Temne custom, a new head is normally chosen by consensus after consultations among the principal members of the family. By tradition, the oldest surviving male member of the family is the favoured candidate. However, he may be by-passed in favour of a younger, more dynamic, and these days, a more educated member of the family who has demonstrated personal qualities of leadership and industry. Among the Mende, either a male or a female member could be chosen as head of the family.

8.4.6 The Role of the Head of Family in Dealing with Family Lands

Once chosen, the head of family takes charge of the protection, control and management of all lands in which the family holds any kind of interest. These are invariably his only duties though in some chiefdoms it is not unusual to find farms and plantations exploited by the family as a joint enterprise under the management of the head of family. In Sierra Leone, unlike in Ghana and Nigeria, the concept of family property does not extend much beyond the land itself and interests therein.

It is rare to encounter family investments not concerned with the land. In addition, if assets such as money are held at all, it is only as a temporary measure possibly awaiting distribution. Thus, the primary duty of the head of family is to ensure the well-being of the family as a whole by protecting its interests in its lands, and to foster and promote the spirit of kinship solidarity among members of the group in the use and enjoyment of the family property.

The most important duty of the head of family is the allocation of portions of family lands to individual members. This may be done either on a long-term basis, or annually, depending on the use to which the land is put and the size of the family holdings. The head of family has wide discretionary powers in the matter of allocation, but in this and other functions he is always assisted by the principal members of the family with whom he is obliged to consult before making any important decision relating to the family property. In the exercise of his discretion in allocating family lands, the head of family is influenced by such factors as the age and status of the member of the family and the size of any family holdings the member may already be entitled to. Preference is normally shown for older and more established members of the family, such as those with a large household consisting of many dependants. This explains why it is not unusual to find, in the rural areas, a young man still remaining in his father's household even after he has married and started his own family. His chances of having a good portion of fertile land, especially in areas where cultivable land is scare, are thus enhanced.

Since descent among virtually all the communities of the Provinces is patrilineal, every individual, both male and female, who can trace his or her descent through the male line, is, in principle, entitled to have a portion of the family lands allocated to him or her. However, in practice, the claims of females are invariably postponed to those of males. The usual way for a female to make use of her rights in family lands is by continuing to reside in the paternal household even after marriage. This is also not an unusual occurrence among the Mende and Temne communities living in the rural areas.

Another role of importance performed by the head of family is in relation to any alienation of the family's interests in its lands to an outsider. Though title to the land is vested in the family as a unit, it is only through the head of family that effect is given to the family's corporate will as far as disposal of family lands is concerned. In this regard, the head of family acts as an agent for the entire group and only he, or persons authorized by him, can lawfully alienate the title of the family to family lands. However, the head of family cannot act in isolation or arbitrarily. He is obliged by customary law to seek the consent and concurrence of the family by consulting with the principal members. In principle, an individual member can only dispose of any improvements or developments he has made on family land. The view of most family elders interviewed is that the consent of the head of family is required before such a disposal can take place. However, a minority of interviewees restrict the requirement to one of simply informing the head of family about the transaction. Even though the head of family may not withhold his consent as such, he may discourage any disposal which might tend to jeopardize or risk the family's paramount interests in the land in question. For example, in the case of a proposed pledge of a farm cultivated on family land by an individual member, the head of family would normally attempt to have the loan raised within the family before giving his consent or concurrence to the pledge.

The head of family is also in a predominant position in the distribution of the fruits and benefits accruing from family lands. If there are proceeds from the sale or lease of family land, it is usual for the head of family to allocate to himself a large share before distributing the rest to the principal members as representatives of the various branches of the family. There is no fixed proportion for such distribution, and the practice varies from family to family, depending largely on the size of the family and the personal influence of the head. The same principle also applies in the distribution of income from other sources, such as royalties paid for cutting timber or operating mines on family lands.

8.4.7 The Accountability of the Head of Family

The liability of the head of family to account for funds derived from the use and disposition of family lands is generally accepted. However, this obligation is not normally enforced by legal sanctions such as court action. The usual practice appears to be to seek relief through the process of customary arbitration in which the chief plays a leading role. Failure to abide by the decision of the chief, or recidivism on the part of the head, might lead to his deposition by the family. Preference for the process of customary arbitration, as opposed to formal litigation, does not, therefore, indicate that the head of family is clothed with any immunity in respect of misappropriation of family property.

Finally, the head of family has a duty as well as a right to protect and defend family property both against misuse by members and against trespass by outsiders. The head of family is the proper person to sue and be sued in respect of any dispute involving the family's title to or interests in family lands. This role may be delegated to another member of the family where the head of family is unable or unwilling for any reason to act.

Apart from the privileges discussed above, the head of family is entitled to the same rights of user and enjoyment of family lands as any other member. Any self-acquired property to which he is entitled is held and kept apart from family property, and this does not merge with that of the family on his death intestate.

8.5 THE INDIVIDUAL'S INTERESTS IN FAMILY LANDS

8.5.1 Introduction

An analysis of the nature of the interests held by the family in family lands cannot be complete without a definition of the rights enjoyed by the individual member in family lands. This is because, as has already been discussed, though the paramount title to family lands is vested in the family, as a corporate unit, and the rights of control and management of the family's interests therein are vested in the head of family, the actual use and enjoyment of the largest proportion of such land is not by the group together, but rather by individuals in separate and distinct parcels of family lands.

8.5.2 The Individual's Right of User and Enjoyment of Family Lands

These rights of the individual are among the main incidents of his membership of his descent group and vest in him automatically from the moment of birth into that particular group. The most common, and also the most effective way, in which these rights are enjoyed is by the occupation and exploitation of a portion of family land. This could be achieved by any of the following methods:

i. By appropriation of any unoccupied family land, for example, by clearing virgin forests or by taking possession of land abandoned by a former occupant;
ii. By allocation of a portion of family land made by the head of family or the individual's head of household;
iii. By transfer to him of another member's right to immediate possession either *inter vivos* or by succession on the death intestate of a relative, such as a father or brother.

Once an individual has asserted his inherent right to occupy a portion of family land what then are the incidents of his possession of this portion? As long as he continues in effective possession his rights of user remain exclusive and independent of the overall interests of the family and its other members. Thus, the family cannot dispossess an individual member of the family in occupation of family land no matter how long that occupation may be. This rule is, of course, subject to the exception that, upon abandonment by the individual, or the end of effectual occupation and user, the land may be repossessed by the family and re-allocated to another member.

8.5.3 The Principle of Abandonment under Customary Tenure

There is no generalized principle of customary law as to what constitutes abandonment. It is, however, said to occur when the occupier vacates his holding for an unreasonably long time and does nothing to show an intention to continue or resume occupation. The answer to the question, how long a period of absence would be sufficient to extinguish the individual's exclusive right of occupancy, will vary depending on the demand and availability of land within the family and also on the particular type of use to which the land had been subjected. Thus, the existence on rural farm lands of permanent crops and economic trees will serve as an indication of an absent individual's intention to continue his right of occupancy. Similarly, the construction of a house or other permanent structure on urban land will serve the same purpose even if the building is not occupied by the individual member himself.

A difficult situation frequently arises where the practice of shifting cultivation necessitates an individual leaving a portion of land to lie fallow and apparently unoccupied.

The general rule encountered in most chiefdoms is that no other member may repossess a portion of family land left fallow by the previous occupier, unless that portion has reverted to secondary bush without any effective reoccupation and user for a prolonged period. This rule is now subject to variations and modifications in areas where, because of the increasing scarcity of fertile lands within the family, its members are obliged to revert to fallow lands much earlier than desirable for an effective yield of crops. It is, however, usual for the occupier, in order to avoid giving the impression that the land is abandoned, to plant secondary crops such as groundnuts and cassava which are occasionally harvested during the period of fallow. In this way, fallow land may be regarded as being in the continued occupation of the previous occupier though not under active cultivation.

8.5.4 Duration of the Individual's Right of User of Family Lands

In theory, the interest thus acquired by the individual member through his occupation of a portion of family land only lasts for as long as the member retains effective possession or until his death. For, while a member is free to choose from among any other members for the purpose of alienation of his interest in family land *inter vivos*, he has no such power to choose the successor to his interest in the event of his demise. As a matter of strict law, his interest automatically lapses on his death, but in practice, it usually passes to his heirs according to an order of priority determined in accordance with the relevant rules for succession to self-acquired property on intestacy.

As the successors must themselves be members of the same ancestral family, they become entitled to occupy that specific portion of family land not only by virtue of their right as successors of the deceased, but also by virtue of the inherent right flowing from their own membership of the family. In this way, specific portions of family land may become tied to members of a particular branch within the family, to the exclusion of other members, in a manner indistinguishable from lands inherited as self-acquired property of an individual.

This is particularly true where the land in question has been developed by the erection of a permanent structure or by the cultivation of permanent cash crops or economic trees. This practice was judicially sanctioned in *Tongi v. Khalil*,[232] a case on appeal from the then Supreme Court of Sierra Leone, in which the West African Court of Appeal held that land which had been allocated to an individual and developed by him was transmissible on his death to his heirs, meaning thereby members of his immediate family as opposed to the wider descent group.

8.5.5 Alienation of the Individual's Right of User of Family Lands to Non-Members

However, the right of the individual member to alienate his interest in family land to a non-member is much more restricted. In this regard, there is the usual customary law distinction between the individual's interest in the land itself, and the improvements made on the land by the individual's effort and industry. The general principle seems to be that the individual's interest in the family land itself is not alienable *inter vivos*

232 (1953) 14 W.A.C.A. 331.

by way of sale, lease, pledge, gift or otherwise to a person who is not a member of the family. Only the family, as a corporate unit, acting through its legal representative, the head of the family, is competent to make such dispositions of family land. It is a corollary of this principle that the individual member cannot make a testamentary disposition of his interest in the land itself to a non-member. This restriction extends even to devises in favour of members of the family.

On the other hand, the right of the individual to freely alienate crops, permanent trees, houses and other developments on family land, as opposed to the land itself, is fairly well established. As pointed out earlier, there is no certainty as to whether such alienations could be made by the member without the consent and concurrence, or even without the knowledge, of the head of family. As far as farm products are concerned the general practice is that annual crops grown on family land, and still attached thereto, may be disposed of by a member of the family even without reference to the head of the family. This is understandable because the purchaser of such crops only acquires a licence to enter upon the land to harvest the produce, but acquires no proprietary interest in the land as such which may be viewed as a qualification on the family's paramount title thereto.

This situation is, however, different and much more complex where the subject matter of the alienation is a plantation, house or other permanent structure. The nature of such attachments to the land is such that any disposition thereof whether by sale, pledge or gift implies, at least as a matter of fact, if not of law, a transfer to the grantee of a right to the exclusive user of the land in question for a more or less indefinite period. Though the legal theory may be that the grantee only acquires a proprietary interest in plantations, crops and structures on the land, as opposed to the land itself, in practice, the residual rights of the family are often kept in abeyance indefinitely. This is because they are made dependent upon the unlikely contingency of the extinction of the development or the abandonment of the land itself. This presumably is the reason why, among the Mendes, the prior consent of the head of family is required before an individual member can alienate permanent cash crops or buildings and other structures affixed to family land.

However, among the Temnes and other ethnic groups , such as the Kono, such alienations were essentially regarded as private transactions between the family member and the purchaser and no prior consent of the head of family is required. The only requirement to be satisfied in these areas is that, where the prospective grantee is a stranger to the chiefdom, he must first of all be presented to the head of family and subsequently to the village headman, sub-chief or paramount chief, depending on the importance of the grant. The stranger is expected on such a presentation to pay the customary tribute or "*shakehand*", as an acknowledgement of the superior title of the family, and of the political authority of the paramount chief or other traditional ruler. It is, thus, theoretically possible in such chiefdoms for such alienation to take place even without the knowledge of the head of the family in cases where the grantee is a member of the same chiefdom.

The only known judicial authority on this particular issue in Sierra Leone is the case of *Kormoh v. Coosah and Lamin*,[233] in which Cole, J., as he then was, accepted expert evidence that according to Mende customary law,

> *"the prior consent of all*[234] *the relatives was necessary before there could be an out-and-out transfer of a house built on family land".*[235]

A document which the plaintiff had signed, purporting to convey all his rights and interest in a house built on family land in Luawa Chiefdom in the Kailahun District, was held invalid because of such lack of prior consent. It is ironic that in the *Kormoh* case, the plea of lack of consent was raised by the plaintiff/vendor as a ground for avoiding the purported sale. However, it is respectfully submitted that while the learned Judge may have correctly stated the basic principle relating to prior consent for such dispositions affecting family land, in the present writer's humble opinion, he extended the ambit of the rule too far in stating that the prior consent of "*all the relatives*" is required for such a transaction to be valid. The view commonly expressed at interviews with chiefs and other elders in several chiefdoms was that the only consent and concurrences required were those of the head of family and other principal members of the family. Other interviewees were content to limit the rule to a requirement of the consent of just the head of family.

The issue of consent was canvassed before the Court of Appeal by counsel for the defendant/respondent in *Alhaji Foday Sawaneh v. Alhaju Murray*

233 (1960–61) 1 SLLR 68.
234 Emphasis supplied.
235 Above at p. 68.

Bayoh.[236] In that case the plaintiff/appellant had instituted proceedings in the High Court claiming specific performance of an agreement with the defendant/respondent for the sale of a house in Koidu Town in the Kono District. The defendant/respondent in his defence sought to rely on a document allegedly signed by himself and certain members of his family in which he had acknowledged that the said house was built on family land and was, therefore, not to be sold without the consent of the signatories to the said document. However, both the High Court and the Court of Appeal declined to express an opinion on the question of consent, as the finding of fact by the trial Judge, which was upheld on appeal, was that the document tendered as proof of family ownership of the house and land was in fact a forgery. The Court of Appeal, in the circumstances, found for the plaintiff/appellant which implies, it is submitted, that it found that a valid contract of sale existed.

The Court, however, exercised its discretion against granting specific performance without giving any particular reasons, thus leaving it open to speculation whether the question of lack of consent was a factor taken into consideration in the exercise of its discretion.

The power of an individual to make a testamentary disposition to a non-member of the family of crops, economic trees or any permanent structure grown or erected on family land is, however, potentially the same as his capacity to make such dispositions in respect of other self-acquired property. Although, technically, he is quite free to act without let or hindrance from his family in disposing of such self-acquired property, such devises will only be given effect to in exceptional circumstances, for example, where the family is satisfied that the gift was voluntary and otherwise valid in the eyes of customary law, and that the testator had strong and cogent reasons for disinheriting his traditional heirs. Besides, acceptance of such a devise imposes an obligation on the devisee to recognize the paramount title of the family to the land itself and to respect all the obligations that flow from the deceased member's right of occupation including the performance of any customary services. It is not surprising, therefore, that such devises are only made on rare occasions and, invariably, to benefit a person who though not technically a member of the testator's family had a very close personal or other affinity with the testator himself. This brings us to the next form of interest to be considered which is that of the individual in self-acquired property.

236 Civ. App. 12/77, judgment of the Court of Appeal, unreported.

8.6 INDIVIDUAL TENURE UNDER CUSTOMARY LAW

8.6.1 Introduction

The factors that have led to the individualization of tenure in all of the chiefdoms of the Provinces and the various methods by which an individual can acquire the paramount title to land have already been examined earlier in this work. The analysis which follows focuses on the nature of rights and interests that could subsist in and over those lands that are now held under individual tenure.

8.6.2 The Nature of the Individual's Interest in Land Held under Individual Tenure

The first point to note is that, where individual ownership has come to be accepted, either as a matter of practice or as an integral principle of customary law, such ownership could safely be described as "absolute" or "allodial", in the sense that the individual is vested with the maximum permissible rights in and over the land in question. This principally involves the right of exclusive user, independent of the interests of the family groups or community to which the individual may belong, and the competence to deal with the land in every way permitted by the *lex situ*.

The right of user includes the right to build on the land, the right to grow any crops or trees of his choice (within limits prescribed by the local customary law); the right to sell or otherwise alienate the land at will (also within prescribed limits); the right to cut timber and to tap palm trees, to hunt and to fish in streams and ponds within or adjacent to his land; the right to extract minerals from the earth within the limits permitted by statute or any other law and, above all, the right to keep everyone else away from the land in question. However, despite such extensive rights, an individual owner, whether or not he is a native of the chiefdom where the land is situated, cannot divorce his ownership of the land from the complex framework of socio-political controls which is such a characteristic feature of all forms of customary tenure. Thus, it is doubtful whether any of the rights listed above could in fact be exercised free from some form of local control.

However, such control or restriction imposed on the individual's right of user and power of alienation is not inherent in the fact of individual ownership but is an integral part of the rights of supervision and control vested by statute or customary law in certain socio-political entities. These include the chiefdom councils, paramount chiefs, sub-chiefs, town or village headmen, and in some cases even the family as a unit. Thus, as an illustration, under Temne customary law, the outright sale or other disposition of land so as to deprive the family of its reversionary rights as original owner is not recognized. Therefore, though individual ownership of land in Temne chiefdoms implies the right of free alienation, such alienation is always subject to the original owning family's contingent reversionary rights. These rights exist in perpetuity, and therefore necessitate the grantee's acknowledgement of such rights each time there is a transfer of title to the land either *inter vivos* or by will.

Another example of qualification of the individual owner's rights by customary law is seen where a lease is granted to a stranger who is a non-native. The prevailing custom in all chiefdoms is that the rents, or other proceeds, are shared by the land-owner both with the chiefdom council on behalf of the whole community, and with the paramount chief personally. This applies whether the landowner is an individual or is a corporate entity, such as a family. The right of the paramount chief to share in the proceeds of a lease to a non-native stranger is quite separate from his entitlement to receive customary tribute in the form of farm produce from rural lands or the traditional "*shakehand*" payable by the grantees when any form of disposition of land takes place. These latter privileges the paramount chief shares with the other traditional rulers such as section chiefs and town and village headmen, depending on the location of the land within the chiefdom.

Although, in principle, an individual may dispose of his self-acquired and individually owned property by will or other testamentary form to any person or persons of his choice, the exercise of this right is, indirectly at least, subject to several restrictions and conditions. The making of a written will is foreign to customary law and is only a recent innovation among literate natives. However, the various customary laws have always given recognition and effect to testamentary dispositions made orally in the form of a death-bed declaration of the individual's intention regarding the distribution of his self-acquired property after his demise. The basic presumption is that a man will not, without good cause, disinherit his traditional heirs. Therefore, very strong and cogent evidence of a contrary intention is required to rebut this presumption, and the evidential burden is on the devisee or appointee. Such death-bed declarations are invariably regarded as merely indicative of a personal preference rather than as a legal directive.

The destination of a man's self-acquired and individually owned property, on an intestacy, depends on the relevant rules governing the devolution of an intestate's property in accordance with his personal law. Prior to the enactment of the Devolution of Estates Act, No. 21 of 2007, the general principle of customary law, applicable to all the ethnic groups in Sierra Leone, is that upon a person's death intestate, his self-acquired property vests in his proximate next of kin, either individually or as a group, but does not form part of his ancestral family's property.

The persons entitled to succeed to an intestate's self-acquired property were chosen by virtue of their degree of proximity to the deceased as determined by his personal law, and not necessarily because they belong to the same descent group as the deceased. As a general proposition, we can state that under the customary law of all the principal ethnic groups of Sierra Leone, the right to succeed to a man's self-acquired property now vests in his children as of right, failing which the right devolves on other close relatives such as the deceased's brothers and sisters, his father, his brother's children and so on in an ever expanding circle. It is a fundamental rule found among all these ethnic groups that such property does not become family property to be inherited in the same way as family lands are inherited by the wider descent group as a whole. This would appear to be in stark contrast with the customary law principles applicable in neighbouring countries like Ghana and Nigeria as may be gathered from a study of their case law and legal literature. For example, Ollennu writing on the same subject in relation to Ghana asserts that:

> *"the correct statement of the law is that upon a person's death intestate, his self-acquired property vests in his ancestral family, which includes the immediate, the head and elders of the whole family".*[237]

The same author later sought to clarify this assertion by stating that "*it is the entire family, and not a branch of it … that succeeds*" to such property.[238] This, according to Ollennu, is "*the first principle of the customary law of succession applicable to all tribes in Ghana*".[239] This principle was applied

237 *Principles of Customary Land Law in Ghana*, 1962, pp. 153–4.
238 *The Law of Testate and Intestate Succession in Ghana*, p. 123.
239 Ibid., p. 70. For a different view, see Kludze, op. cit., pp. 269–80.

by the West African Court of Appeal in the Ghanaian cases of *Larkai v. Amorkor*[240] and *Amorfio v. Ayorkor.*[241]

8.7 SUMMARY OF INTERESTS IN LAND UNDER CUSTOMARY LAW

One of the most important factors that emerges from the analysis in this chapter is that title to land, as well as the various forms of lesser interests that could subsist in land in the Provinces, are still governed almost exclusively by customary law. The fundamental basis of customary land tenure in the Provinces has so far survived despite the introduction of the received English law and accompanying legal concepts and ideas. Besides, the impact of local statutes such as the Provinces Land Act, Cap. 122 and the Chiefdom Councils Act, Cap. 61, has been virtually negligible.

Thus, although the preamble to the Provinces Land Act, Cap.122, declares all land in the Provinces to be vested in the chiefdom councils, it has been demonstrated that title to the bulk of land in the Provinces is in fact vested in various other entities, such as paramount chiefs on behalf of the community, families and individuals depending on the form of tenure under which the land is held. Because of this preservation of the traditional position, and because also of the inherent complexity and uncertainty of customary law in general, and customary land tenure in particular, it becomes extremely difficult, if not impossible, for any person, who wishes to enter into a transaction relating to land in the Provinces, to know precisely where the title lies or who holds what interests in any particular piece of land.

Another factor that emerges from our analysis is the marked absence of the State among the various entities that have original interests in land in the Provinces of Sierra Leone. This is a relict of the British colonial policy involving the exercise of sovereignty but not *dominium* over the former Protectorate, and minimal interference with the traditional land rights of the indigenous peoples. Unlike some other former British Colonies, such as Tanzania, which have introduced legislation to assert State ownership over customary land, there has so far been very little or no legislative intervention in the field of customary land tenure in Sierra Leone.

However quite apart from the Public Lands Act, Cap 116 which was originally enacted to enable the Colonial Government to acquire land

240 (1953) 1 W.A.C.A. 323.
241 (1954) 14 W.A.C.A. 554.

compulsorily in the former Colony, there are a number of statutes which provide for compulsory acquisition of land for public purposes throughout the country.[242]

Thus section 36(1) of the Mines & Minerals Act, No. 12 of 2009, expressly provides as follows:

> *"The Minister may by order published in the Gazette compulsorily acquire private land or rights over or under private land or use by the holder of a large-scale mining licence"*

Though this Act makes provision for the payment of compensation for such compulsory acquisition, it is doubtful whether the mechanism for the assessment and payment of such compensation is in consonance with the letter and spirit of section 21(1) of the Constitution Act, No. 6 of 1991 relating to protection from deprivation of property.

242 These include the Sierra Leone Roads Authority Act, No. 2 of 1992 and the National Power Authority Act, No. 3 of 1992.

CHAPTER 9
THE ACQUISITION OF INTERESTS IN LAND HELD UNDER CUSTOMARY TENURE

9.1 BACKGROUND TO ACQUISITION OF INTEREST IN LAND HELD UNDER CUSTOMARY LAW

In the previous chapter, this work focused on the nature and the incidents of the various interests in land which could subsist under customary law. The present chapter is devoted to a consideration of the methods by which such interests could be acquired, either by express grants or by operation of law. Although land held under customary law can be transferred in accordance with the general law, the ensuing analysis will be concerned with acquisitions and transfers that take effect in accordance with customary law. In addition, the provisions of the Provinces Land Act, Cap. 122, which govern leases of provincial land granted to non-natives will be examined.

9.2 *INTER VIVOS* TRANSFERS OF INTEREST IN LAND UNDER CUSTOMARY LAW

Interest in land held under customary law could be transferred by sale, gift or various forms of customary tenancies or as a result of a pledge. Each of these methods of transfer will now be discussed in turn, our focus being on the necessary formalities and the legal effect of such transactions under customary law.

9.3 LEGAL AUTHORITY IN SUPPORT OF SALE OF LAND UNDER CUSTOMARY LAW

The question whether or not land held under customary tenure can be alienated outright by sale has always been a central theme of any discussion of the customary law of indigenous African communities. Among certain writers, there prevails a theory of the inalienability of land under strict customary law, based on the perception that native lands in Africa are held under a kind of sacred trust linking the past, present and future generations.

Thus, writing on customary land tenure in Nigeria, Elias states categorically that:

> *"There is perhaps no other principle more fundamental to the indigenous land tenure system throughout Nigeria than the theory of inalienability of land".*[243]

There are also a number of judicial dicta in support of this view, of which the following by Kingdom, C.J. in a dissenting opinion in the Nigerian case of *Balogun v. Oshodi*[244] is typical:

> *"Under native customary tenure an individual cannot alienate the land he occupies; consequently the rights of his descendants are safeguarded and cannot be realized by him".*[245]

In contrast to this theory of inalienability, the view has always been held by certain writers and supported also by judicial dicta that land has always been saleable under customary law, though for a variety of reasons sale was unknown or at least not very common. The main reason frequently advanced for the rarity of alienation of land by sale is the fact that land was in plentiful supply, and in consequence, it had little or no commercial value. For this reason, there was no incentive to sell land.

Another aspect of this same argument is that, because of a certain magico-religious attitude to land, which was believed to be a spiritual heritage received from the ancestors to be handed on intact to posterity, there has always been a general unwillingness to sell. Yet, this should not necessarily lead to the inference that outright alienation was positively forbidden by strict customary law. Indeed, according to Bentsi-Enchill,

243 T.O. Elias, *Nigerian Land Law*, 4th edn, p. 147.

244 (1931) 10 N.L.R. 3 at 58.

245 See also dicta of Lord Denning in *Oyekan v. Adele* (1957) 1 W.L.R. 876 at 884, in which he dilated on the theory of inalienability of land under strict customary law.

> *"there can be no doubt that sales of land were rare in former times; but it would seem desirable to distinguish between lack of willingness to sell land and lack of capability to do so".*[246]

However, whatever might have been the position under customary law before the introduction of English law, there is now general support among both judges and other jurists in most African countries for the view that modern customary law recognizes the outright alienation of land by sale. This development was thus explained by Weber, J. in *Balogun v. Oshodi*:[247]

> *"The chief characteristic feature of native law is its flexibility – one incident of land tenure after another disappears as times change – but the most important incident of tenure which has crept in and become firmly established as a rule in and become firmly established as a rule of native law is alienation of land".*

Thus, in Ghana and Nigeria there are now innumerable instances of the courts upholding the alienation of land held under customary tenure. The legal literature of these countries also tends to confirm that such alienations are now a regular feature of customary land tenure.[248]

9.3.1 Literature on the Sale of Land under Sierra Leone Customary Law

In the case of Sierra Leone, though one can categorically state that alienation of land under customary tenure is an established fact, there is a dearth of both judicial authority and legal literature to support such a proposition. The earliest and probably the most authoritative view recorded on the subject is that of Maxwell who, writing in 1912, stated that:

246 K. Bentsi-Enchill, *Ghana Land Law*, p. 44.

247 Above, at p. 53.

248 See for example Elias, op. cit., p. 149; S.N. Chinwuba Obi, *The Ibo Law of Property*, p. 124; and Bentsi-Enchill, *Ghana Land Law*, op. cit., p. 44.

> *"As a general rule land was not sold or pledged. The inference has sometimes been drawn that these forms of transfer are entirely alien to natives. However true this may be of other people of West Africa, it is not the case in the Protectorate of Sierra Leone in as much as both sale and pledging between natives have been observed".*[249]

A similar view was expressed in 1925 by Goddard,[250] though his opinion was obviously not based on independent observation as he relied heavily on Maxwell for the part of his work dealing with customary land tenure. Fenton, writing a little later, in 1932, makes reference to Maxwell's claim that instances of sale and pledges of land had been observed and then suggests that:

> *"it is possible that such sale was to another member of the same chiefdom and with the consent of the family 'owning the land'".*

Indeed, Fenton maintained emphatically that "*land cannot be sold*".[251] Fenton does not state the source of the latter proposition nor does he cite any authority in support thereof. It cannot therefore be accorded much weight, especially as Fenton's treatment of Sierra Leone customary law on the whole tends to be superficial.

Another writer, Meek, in dealing with the subject of alienation of land under customary tenure in Sierra Leone, noted the earlier view that sale and pledging of land were formerly unusual. He, however, attributed this to the fact that "*there was no market for land as there was sufficient land for all*".[252]

9.3.2 Judicial Authority on the Sale of Land under Sierra Leone Customary Law

Most of the available judicial authorities on this issue deal with the sale of houses built on communal or family land. They do not take into account

249 J.C. Maxwell, *Notes on Land Tenure in Sierra Leone*, p. 4.
250 T.N. Goddard, *The Handbook of Sierra Leone*, p. 89.
251 J.S. Fenton, *Outline of Native Law in Sierra Leone* , p. 34.
252 C.K. Meek, *Land Law and Custom in the Colonies*, 1946, p. 199.

the distinction made under customary law between the land itself, that is, the surface soil and things found naturally on or under it, and things planted or affixed to it by the industry of man.

The earliest of such authorities is *Kormor v. Coosah*,[253] decided by the former Supreme Court. The trial judge, Cole, J., implicitly recognized the right of a native to sell a house built on family land, when he declared that the sale of the house in question was invalid only because "the prior consent of all the relatives of a native was required before there could be an out-and out transfer".[254]

Next in line there is a more clear-cut authority, this time of the Court of Appeal, in *Sheriff & Ors v. Sheriff*,[255] declaring that where communal land has been allocated to a native and the latter builds a house on such land he has a right to sell that house as his self-acquired property. In that case the land had been allocated to one Kalilu Sheriff by the paramount chief of Nongowa Chiefdom, Kenema District. Sheriff built a house on the land and later sold it with the approval of the paramount chief to the plaintiff/respondent, but he was allowed to remain in occupation of the house until his death. After his death the defendants/appellants refused to hand over possession of the house to the plaintiff/respondent on the ground that the house was family property and could not have been sold without their approval. The Court of Appeal rejected the contention that the house was family property and held that it was in fact the self-acquired property of the deceased. In the circumstances, the sale to the plaintiff/respondent was held valid.

This right of a native to sell a house built on communal or family land was confirmed by the Court of Appeal in *Jah v. Deen*.[256] In delivering the judgment of the Court, During, J.A., dispelled any doubt as to the correctness of the above proposition when he asserted that:

> *"It is clear and settled native customary law that a member of the tribe [sic] to whom land has been allocated has a right to sell or pledge a house owned by him situated on such land and in my view there is no need to adduce*

253 (1960–61) 1 SLLR 66.
254 Ibid., at 68.
255 Civ. App. No. 28/69 decided by the Court of Appeal in July 1970, unreported.
256 (1970–71) ALR S.L. 171.

evidence to prove such customary law even though it may be unwritten."[257]

The Supreme Court has also recognized the right of an individual to sell a house built on communal land in the case of *Alhaji Foday Sawaneh v. Alhaji Murray Bayoh.*[258] The action had been instituted in the High Court by the appellant, who sought specific performance of an agreement with the respondent for the sale of a house situated in Koidu Town in the Kono District. The trial Judge refused to grant the decree because he found that there was insufficient evidence of a valid binding contract. The Court of Appeal reversed this finding of fact and found for the appellant but held that in all the circumstances of the case an award of damages would meet the ends of justice better than an order for specific performance.

Despite this refusal to grant the decree sought, it was clear that the Court was satisfied as to the validity of the contract for the sale of the house, thus impliedly recognizing the right of the respondent under customary law to undertake such a transaction.

Moreover, the Court rejected the contention of the respondent that he could not sell the house because it was family property. The matter was taken on appeal to the Supreme Court by the appellant, who argued that the Court of Appeal had exercised its discretion arbitrarily in refusing to grant an order for specific performance of the contract.

Though this point was not argued before the Supreme Court because of a technical objection successfully raised by counsel for the respondent, the Court went on to uphold the finding of the Court of Appeal that there was a valid binding contract for the sale of the house by the respondent.

It is significant that all the cases mentioned so far were instituted in the High Court which, as has been observed earlier in this work,[259] lacks original jurisdiction in proceedings to determine the title to land situated in the Provinces other than leaseholds granted under the Provinces Land Act, Cap. 122. The issue of the Court's jurisdiction was raised in the case of *Sheriff & Ors v. Sheriff.*[260] In the view of the President of the Court of Appeal, Bankole Jones, J.A. the sale of a house is not a matter that touches and concerns title to the land itself so therefore the Court was not deprived of jurisdiction to try that particular case – which was essentially an action

---

257 Ibid., at 174.

258 Civ. App. No. 6/79 decided by the Court of Appeal in July 1980; unreported.

259 Above, p. 30.

260 Above.

for possession of a house. Moreover, in the opinion of the President of the Court, title to land in the Provinces could not be claimed by individuals as such title was by statute "*vested in the Tribal Authority for and on behalf of the natives concerned*".

The reasons given by the Court of Appeal for assuming jurisdiction could be criticized on at least two grounds. As to the first reason given by Bankole-Jones, J.A. to justify the High Court's assumption of jurisdiction this argument could only be tenable if the learned Justice of Appeal was applying the customary law distinction between the land itself and things planted on or affixed to it by man since there is no such distinction made under the general law. Section 4 of the Interpretation Act, No. 8 of 1971, defines land to include "*any house, building or structure whatsoever and any estate, interest or right in, to or over land*". If this meaning of land had been applied by the Court, then it could not, with respect, have properly held that the matter before the Court, that is the sale of a house, did not touch and concern title to land.

The second reason advanced by Bankole-Jones, J.A. was not necessary for the decision in the instant case. Besides, it would seem to be based on a wrong premise. As has been argued earlier,[261] despite the wording of the preamble to the Provinces Land Act, Cap. 122, which, presumably, the learned Justice of Appeal was relying on, under customary law, title to land in the Provinces could indeed be vested in entities other than the chiefdom councils (formerly Tribal Authorities). It is submitted that if the High Court did in fact correctly assume jurisdiction to try these cases, it could only have been done on the basis that the actions were essentially for possession of the houses in question. An action for possession of land or a building thereon could be determined without necessarily going into the question of ownership. Where in fact the issue of possession could not be decided without going into the question of title, then the High Court lacks jurisdiction.

The case of *Kebbie v. Bernard Kamara*[262] is the nearest the High Court has come to pronouncing on the alienability of provincial land itself, as opposed to a house or other improvement on the land. Unfortunately, the Court did not rule specifically on the validity of the particular transaction, which involved the sale of a plot of building land situated in the Bo District, Southern Province, as the appellant's claim for possession of the

261 See above, p. 162.

262 Decided by the Local Appeals Division of the High Court sitting in Bo, Southern Province on 10 March 1978; unreported.

land was rejected on the ground that the document which he relied on to prove the sale was held inadmissible in evidence for failing to comply, inter alia, with the provisions of the Stamp Duty Act, Cap. 274.

The Court left open the question whether the sale would otherwise have been upheld. It is submitted, however, that the Court would not have considered the question of the admissibility of the document evidencing the sale, if it was of the view that such a transaction was void in any event. It is also significant that both the Local Court where the action had been initiated, and the District Appeal Court, upheld the transaction, though the latter Court found against the appellant on the ground that there was no evidence that the sale had been finalized as required by customary law.

Extensive searches of Local Courts records throughout the Provinces failed to reveal any cases dealing directly with the question of the alienability of customary land per se. This is, however, not too surprising when one considers that the practice of outright sale of land held under customary tenure became widespread with the expansion of the district headquarters and other provincial towns. Information gathered by the present writer during interviews in several chiefdoms in fact revealed that landowners were still reluctant to acknowledge the fact that the land itself could be sold outright. However, when confronted with documentary evidence of such transactions, such as copies of registered conveyances, most informants conceded that land was in fact sold but emphasized that the practice was limited to the sale of building plots in the urban areas.

A closer scrutiny of registered conveyances in respect of sale of provincial land has tended to confirm the contention that land in the rural areas is not normally sold. In fact, in certain chiefdoms where there are no large urban centres, or where the population is sparse because there is relatively little economic or commercial activity, no sale of land has ever been recorded.

The phenomenon becomes understandable when one takes into account the main factors that have contributed to the increase in sales of land under customary tenure. The most significant of these include the increasing demand for land by an ever increasing urban population and the ensuing rise in the price of land, for example, in Koidu Town in the Kono District after the discovery of diamonds; the introduction of the market economy; and the influence of English law and English legal ideas generally. The impact of these factors has tended to be more significant in the urban areas where, because of the greater mobility of the population, there is opportunity for customary law to be modified in response to external forces of change.

9.3.3 Preliminaries for a Sale

The next matter to be examined is how a sale transaction is conducted under customary law. In any such transaction the first, and probably the most important, issue about which the purchaser has to satisfy himself is the capacity of the vendor to make the proposed disposition. In other words, who is entitled to sell land under customary law? Capacity to sell land under customary law depends, to a large extent, on the type of tenure under which the land is held, that is, whether it is communal land, or family land or individually owned land, and also on the nature of the interest in the land held by the proposed vendor.

9.3.4 Capacity to Sell Communal Land

In the case of communal lands the power to deal with a potential purchaser is vested in the paramount chief by virtue of the fact that title to such lands is vested in him on behalf of the community as a whole. This power could be delegated, and is in fact often delegated, to subordinate traditional rulers such as section chiefs, town chiefs and village headmen in respect of land within their respective localities. In each case, the actual decision to sell could not be taken without the concurrence of the community as a whole as expressed through its principal members.

The choice of persons who must be consulted depends on the level at which the transaction is taking place. At the highest level, that is where the paramount chief himself is handling the proposed sale, the usual practice is for him to consult the chiefdom committee and the local traditional rulers of the area where the land is located. The head of any family which claims to have any interest in the land will also be consulted. At the other extreme, that is at the village level, the headman of the village must consult with all heads of landowning families in the village who together invariably constitute the village council. However, at whatever level the consultations take place, the decision to sell must be ratified by the paramount chief.

In this regard, it could be said that no valid sale of communal lands could take place without the consent or concurrence of the paramount chief. The requirement for consultation and consent is designed to protect the interests of the community against any clandestine disposal of communal lands. It also ensures that the interest of future generations will not be easily defeated without full discussion by all the members concerned.

9.3.5 Capacity to Sell Family Land

The position regarding capacity to alienate family lands is slightly different due mainly to the fact that the title to all family lands is vested not in any individual but in the family as a unit. It follows, therefore, that the power of alienation is vested in the family itself. However, as the family is a corporate body, its power in this regard is exercised by its authorized agent, namely, the head of family. Thus, unlike the paramount chief who has the power of alienation of communal lands vested in him, albeit in representative capacity, the head of family has to acquire the requisite authority to make any disposal of family lands. Where, for any reason, the head of family is unable or unwilling to act, such authority may be conferred on any other member of the family. However, under normal circumstances, the head of family is the only authorized vendor of family lands.

Though it is generally agreed that the head of family cannot alienate family lands without the authority of the family, there are conflicting views as to when, how and by whom such authority may be conferred on behalf of the family. Some elders from landowning families who were interviewed expressed the view that the head of family was obliged to seek specific authority for each separate transaction, whilst others held the view that a standing or general authority covering not just one but all transactions of a particular type could be conferred on the head of family. Even if the latter view is correct, the head of family invariably consults with other members of the family in respect of each transaction. In fact, representatives of the family are necessary witnesses for every transaction involving the alienation of family land.

As to the manner of conferring the requisite authority opinion was also split between those informants who maintained that it was necessary for competent members of the family to specifically give their unqualified consent, and the others who thought that authority could be conferred by mere concurrence, or that it may even be implied from conduct, as in a situation where those entitled to object know of a proposed sale transaction by the head of family but do nothing to express their objection.

In any event, the emphasis is on prior consultation. Whether the requirement is one of consent or concurrence, it is a basic principle of customary law that the head of family can only dispose of family land with the authority of the family obtained after prior consultations with all the competent members concerned. Although the consultations usually take place at a meeting of the family, it need not be as formal as that. It is sufficient if each competent member is consulted separately.

More important, perhaps, is the question of the number of persons whose consent or concurrence is required. There seems to be widespread support for the view that this is limited to the principal or important members of the family. The concept of "principal member" cannot be exhaustively defined but, in practice at least, it includes all heads or other senior representatives of the constituent branches of the family.

In smaller families, all the adult male members available at the time of the proposed sale will usually be consulted. In certain Mende and Temne chiefdoms, the modern practice is even to consult influential female members of the family.

The opposite view, that is, that the consent or concurrence of all the members of the family is required, seems to attract little support, even though this view would seem to be backed by judicial authority. Reference has already been made to the dictum of Cole, J. in *Kormoh v. Coosah*[263] to the effect that "*the prior consent of <u>all the relatives</u> is required for the sale of a house built on family land*".[264]

Two observations ought to be made on this proposition. Firstly, it will be noted that the learned Judge used the word "relatives" as opposed to the expression "*members of the family*". It is more usual to use the word "*relatives*" to describe members of a person's nuclear or extended family as opposed to the ancestral family which is the unit that owns family lands as understood under customary land tenure. It is also significant that the transaction in question involved the sale of a house which, though built on family land, is usually considered as self-acquired property. The only persons who have any potential interest, that is, a *spes successionis* in such property which gives them a moral, if not legal, right to object to its alienation are members of the owner's immediate family. It is submitted that a requirement under customary law that the consent of all the members of the ancestral family must be obtained for a valid disposal of what is in effect self-acquired property would be impracticable to comply with. The

263 Above.
264 Emphasis added.

principle of consent as laid down in the *Kormoh* case is, therefore, in our humble opinion, much too wide.

9.3.6 Capacity to Sell Land Held under Individual Tenure

Finally, where the land in question is held under individual tenure the power of alienation is vested in the individual owner.

One of the characteristic features of individual ownership of land, now recognized by customary law, is the capacity of the owner to freely dispose of all his interest in the land without any restriction from the family or community to which he belongs. The power of alienation may in certain circumstances be subject to external restrictions but these do not affect the capacity of the vendor per se.

9.3.7 Formalities for the Sale of Land

The formal requirements for a valid sale of land under customary law are basically the same whether the sale is of communal land, family land or individually owned land. There were slight local variations observed in the procedure which we are about to describe but the basic pattern is the same throughout the Provinces.

The first requirement is for the intending purchaser, having earmarked the piece of land that he wishes to purchase, to ascertain the person or persons competent, not only to negotiate the terms of the proposed transaction, but also to effect a valid transfer of title. This aspect of the sale transaction has already been dealt with in discussing the capacity of the vendor. In this regard, the principle of *caveat emptor* could be said to apply under customary law with much more force than it does under English law. The purchaser is normally expected to make extensive oral enquiries in the locality where the land is situated, and such enquiries should be particularly directed to the town or village headman, other elders and the owners or occupiers of any adjoining property.

After preliminary negotiations with the competent vendor, the intending purchaser, if a stranger to the area, is formally presented to local traditional head, such as the town or village headman. It is traditional at this stage for the purchaser to pay the customary tribute or "*shakehand*"[265] to the traditional head by handing over a bottle of gin or some other

265 In Mende the word is *famalui* and in Temne, *Gborah*. The practice was recognized by the court in *Agip (SL) Ltd v. Edmask* (C.A.) (1970–71) ALR S.L. 332.

alcoholic beverage, or, increasingly, a small sum of money, the amount varying depending on the importance of the transaction and the status of the stranger. This serves as an acknowledgement of the chief's jurisdiction over the territory involved and as an indication of the stranger's willingness to abide by the local laws and customs. This is the reason why a purchaser who is a local kinsman or a stranger who is already resident in the area is not required to pay such tribute.

The next stage is a visit to the site by the vendor and the purchaser during which, in the presence of their respective witnesses, the boundaries of the land agreed to be sold are demarcated. In semi-urban or rural areas, the demarcation is often done visually, with the parties selecting and agreeing on prominent or other suitable landmarks such as perennial trees, anthills, large rocks and streams. Where no suitable landmarks could be found in the vicinity, a clearing is usually made in the bush and trees are planted at intervals along the agreed boundary line. Where the area is relatively small, the distances may be measured or merely estimated, and a rough sketch plan prepared indicating such distances and any other features that might help to locate and identify the property. In the larger urban centres, where plots of land are now sold mostly for building purposes, the demarcation is usually undertaken by professional surveyors making use of some of the latest techniques in the field.

After all the negotiations have been concluded the transaction is finalized at a ceremony during which the vendor formally hands over the land to the purchaser. This ceremony must be attended by a certain number of witnesses from both sides. There is no fixed number but the greater the better. In the case of sale of communal or family land, it is essential and advisable for the witnesses to include principal members of the community or the family. It is the custom for the purchaser to mark the occasion by providing drinks and food, to be consumed by all the participants.

There is no particular legal significance to be attached to this act of the purchaser though it is one which is performed almost as a rule in every such ceremony. Witnesses who may be required to give evidence of the transaction in the future are less likely to forget a ceremony at which they had been particularly well entertained.

Even where the transaction has been thus finalized, there is still a need to have it authenticated by the paramount chief, if he was not already a party thereto. The custom is for the vendor and the purchaser together to acquaint the paramount chief or his representatives of the essential details of the agreement concluded and, in the case of communal land, to have the agreement ratified by the paramount chief. Where any documents relating to the transaction have been prepared they must be executed by the paramount chief, either as a party or witness thereto. Any plans drawn and attached to such documents must also be countersigned by the paramount chief. For the purchaser this serves as further confirmation of the vendor's authority to sell, for the presumption is that the paramount chief would only give his blessing to a sale transaction where he is satisfied that it has been undertaken by a vendor duly authorized in accordance with the relevant laws and customs.

9.3.8 The Use of Written Documents in the Sale of Land

As already indicated, in recent times the parties now tend to depart from the traditional procedures, and in particular, make use of writing at various stages of the transaction, and for different purposes. Thus, payment of a deposit or of the full purchase price may be evidenced in writing by a receipt issued by the vendor or his agent. It is also usual to keep a written record of the essential details of the transaction in the form of a memorandum. Many people who have been involved in land transactions in the Provinces have learnt from bitter and costly experience that the memory of witnesses at such transactions could not always be relied on. A prudent purchaser would now seek to supplement this traditional method of proof by preserving essential evidence of land transactions in written form. The transfer itself is now very often affected by a document such as a conveyance, in English form, executed by the vendor and duly attested by a sufficient number of witnesses. In such a case the parties invariably dispense with most of the traditional formalities described above, especially the final handing-over ceremony.

The question that arises in such cases, where the parties have used writing at some stage of the transaction, or where the transfer itself has been effected by deed, is whether the transaction is still to be considered as being governed by customary law. In practice, such a question is unlikely to arise at the time of the transaction as the parties invariably would not have considered such matters. The issue, however, takes on an added significance if any dispute arises out of, or in connection with, the transaction. It is then for the court seised of the matter to make a choice between the application of customary law or the general law in the particular case. According to the existing statutory rules this should depend on the intention, expressed or to be implied from all the circumstances, of the parties to the transaction.

However, without going into any detailed discussion of the choice of law rules at this stage, it would appear that the attitude of the courts so far has been to apply the general law whenever the parties have made use of writing, regardless of their unexpressed intention, and irrespective of the purpose which the document was intended to serve. For example, in *Kebbie v. Bernard Kamara*[266] the document in question read as follows:

> *"we the undersigned people have received the sum of Le60/00 from Mr. J.J. Kebbie being [the] cost of one town lot on [the] Bo-Kenema Road near Havanna building. Full arrangement for the use of the land will be made at the native Administration Office Yamandu, later".*

It is obvious that the above document was a mere receipt acknowledging payment of the purchase price. It was in fact treated as such by the Local Court where the action was initiated. The Local Court, therefore, treated the transaction as one governed by customary law and ordered the defendants to fulfil their obligation thereunder by handing over the land in question to the plaintiff. This was also the case when the matter went on appeal before the District Appeal Court in Bo. However, when the matter came before the Local Appeals Division of the High Court, the decision of the Court turned squarely on the validity and admissibility in evidence of the said document as determined in accordance with the general law. Apparently, apart from the fact that the document was not duly stamped as required by the Stamp Duty Act, Cap. 274, it also failed to comply with section 2 of the Illiterate Protection Act, Cap. 104, which stipulates that all documents prepared for execution by illiterate persons should be certified as to their authenticity by the author thereof. For these reasons, according to Williams, J. who decided the appeal, "*the document was a worthless piece of writing*".

In *Alhaji Sawaneh v. Alhaji Bayoh*[267] the trial Judge held that the plaintiff could not enforce a contract which was for the sale of a house in Kono District, Eastern Province, merely because a document which had been tendered in evidence by the plaintiff, as proof of the agreement, did not comply with one of the requirements of section 4 of the Statute of Frauds 1677, in that it was not signed by the respondent or his agent. The document, which was clearly intended by the parties to serve only as

266 Above.
267 Above.

a receipt for the purchase price paid by the plaintiff, was in fact thumb-printed though there was no means of identifying the mark thereon. It is, however, significant that the defendant himself did not deny receiving the purchase price or entering into an agreement with the plaintiff for the sale of the house. His defence rested mainly on the fact that the house was family property and could not therefore be sold. As stated above,[268] both the Court of Appeal and the Supreme Court rejected this latter contention by holding that there was a valid and enforceable contract. The Court of Appeal came to the conclusion that the contract was enforceable by accepting evidence to the effect that the document had in fact been thumb-printed by the respondent. However, right up to the Supreme Court the transaction was treated as one governed exclusively by the general law.

9.3.9 Effect of a Sale under Customary Law

The general rule is that a sale of land under customary law operates to transfer all the interests held therein by the group or individual vendor. In principle, this means that the purchaser takes the absolute title to the land in question. He thus becomes entitled to exercise all the rights and enjoy all the incidents of absolute ownership subject only to such general restrictions as may be imposed by the customary law applicable in the area where the land is situated. Where the purchaser is an individual, the land could thereafter be classified as self-acquired property, independent of the rights of his ancestral family as the tenure of the land changes to one potentially held under individual tenure.

The general rule stated above is subject to the qualification that, under Temne customary law, a purchaser cannot obtain the absolute title to family land, as outright alienation of land so as to divest the family of its paramount interest is not recognized. Therefore, in every contract of sale under Temne customary law, there is always implied a condition that the original landowning group retains a sort of reversionary interest in the land conveyed. This entitles the landowning group to repossess the land if the grantee's line of succession becomes extinct or the land is abandoned. This residual interest of the original owners is protected by the requirement that every person who succeeds to the interest of the purchaser must acknowledge the paramount title of the original owners by the payment of customary tribute to the latter before taking over possession. This custom is strictly applied in the case of agricultural land frequently alienated by

268 Above, p. 196.

way of gift. It is doubtful whether it is rigorously followed where the land has been sold for building purposes in urban areas.

9.3.10 The Right to Challenge the Validity of a Sale

A question that needs to be considered is whether, and on what grounds, the sale of group-owned land may be challenged by members of the group. The question is likely to arise where the vendor has failed to hold prior consultations, or to obtain any requisite consent or concurrence or where he simply lacked the capacity to make the purported transfer. It could be said outright that, where an individual member of the community, or the family, purports to transfer the paramount interest in communal or family land, no title passes. However, where the transfer is expressed to be made "*for and on behalf of*" the community or the family the validity of the grant will depend on the status of the vendor. Thus, as has been explained earlier, since the paramount chief is the person to make alienations of communal lands, any alienation of communal lands without him as a party is prima facie void. However, where the sale of communal land is by a subordinate chief, or other traditional ruler, it is not necessarily void. In the latter case, if the transfer is expressed to be made for and on behalf of the community a voidable title passes to the purchaser. The paramount chief has the option of either avoiding the sale or taking action against the vendor to get him to account for the proceeds. Where a satisfactory account of the proceeds is rendered to the paramount chief it is usual for him to ratify the sale unless there are other reasons militating against such a decision, for example, the fact that the vendor had made other unauthorized sales in the past. It would appear that where the paramount chief himself disposes of communal land without consulting the principal members of the community no right of action lies at the instance of an individual member of the community to impeach the sale. It is explained by informants that this is not because the paramount chief enjoys a general immunity from process, but because there are often more effective sanctions, other than judicial action, that could be applied against a paramount chief who disposes of communal lands as his personal property, or who otherwise acts against the general welfare of his subjects. The ultimate and most extreme form of such sanctions is deposition. Where this sanction is applied, the new paramount chief has a discretion either to confirm the disputed grants made by his deposed predecessor or take action to avoid them.

In the case of a sale of family land by the head of family without the authority of the family as conferred by its principal members, the general view of all informants is that such a sale is voidable at the instance of the family. Since such transactions were formerly conducted exclusively in accordance with the formalities laid down by customary law involving maximum publicity, the chances of unauthorized and clandestine dispositions by the head of family or any member were negligible. As a result, there are virtually no recorded cases where action has been taken by the family to avoid an unauthorized sale. However, now that transfers of land held under customary tenure are frequently effected by deed, without the attendant publicity which characterizes dealings in land under customary law, the likelihood of such actions being initiated is bound to increase.

However, the emphasis now seems to be on the duty of the head of family to account for the proceeds of any disposition of family land. This is illustrated by the case of *Kamara v. Tarawallie,*[269] in which the plaintiff, a senior female member of a Temne landowning family, took out a summons against the defendant, head of the family, for allegedly selling portions of the family land without the knowledge of the plaintiff and other members of the family. The defendant admitted in evidence that he had made the sale but contended that he had been granted a standing authority to effect such sales at a family meeting held some time earlier.

The chairman of the Local Court in giving the decision of the Court significantly failed to rule on the question of the validity of the sale. He simply reminded the defendant of his obligation, as head of the family, to account for the proceeds of such sales and to share the same among all the branches of the family. He went on to order the defendant to make a payment to the plaintiff of a sum of eighty Leones out of the total purchase price of three hundred and sixty Leones.

In an interview with the Court Chairman the present writer raised the question of the validity of such a sale which had been made without the knowledge and authority of the family. The Court Chairman confirmed the general principle that an unauthorized sale of family land by the head of family did not bind the family, who had a right to institute an action to avoid the transaction. He, however, insisted that, in practice, the line usually followed by the family is to proceed against the head of family by way of customary arbitration or judicial action, and in very serious cases to

---

269 Case No. 16/81 decided in May 1981 by the Local Court No. 1 in the Bombali Shebora Chiefdom, Bombali District.

have him removed from his most coveted office. This attitude could only be explained by the fact that there have so far not been many instances of large scale-alienation of family land by way of sale. There is no doubt that as the practice of sale becomes more widespread, with families facing the risk of losing their entire holdings, the emphasis is bound to shift towards judicial action to set aside unauthorized sales.

9.4 GIFT OF LAND UNDER CUSTOMARY LAW

9.4.1 Introduction

This is probably one of the oldest methods of transferring interests in land under customary law. There are many families whose title to land in the Provinces originated from this source. The practice of making gifts of land is now on the decline due to the relative scarcity of land and the increase in its commercial value.

There are many similarities between a sale and a gift of land under customary law in terms of both the formalities required for effecting the transfer and the legal effect of the transaction. The competence of the donor to make the gift is determined on virtually the same basis as the capacity of the vendor in the case of a sale. The requirements relating to prior consultations, consent or concurrence apply with equal force to a donor as to a vendor of communal or family land. However, where the gift is to another member of the community or family there is no need for any consent as such. This, presumably, is because such a donee has already a vested interest in the land in question, and the real effect of the gift is that the donor merely transfers his right to the exclusive possession and use of the particular piece of land to the donee. Thus, a father may make an *inter vivos* disposition of his interest in communal or family lands to his children without the need to obtain the consent or concurrence of the chief or the head of family. This frequently happens where the donor has made improvements or developments on portions of communal or family land. However, in principle, any land which has been allocated to or appropriated by an individual member could be transferred as a gift to another member.

9.4.2 Formalities for a Gift of Land

The procedure for making a gift under customary law is substantially the same as for a sale. The main requirement for its validity is that the gift should be adequately publicized. This is traditionally ensured by the presence of an even larger number of witnesses at the ceremony than in the case of a sale when the land is actually handed over by the donor to the donee. Unlike the position under the customary laws of Ghana and Nigeria, there is no legal requirement in Sierra Leone that a gift of land under customary law must be formally accepted.

Though, as in the case of a sale, the donee would normally mark the occasion of the handing over of the land to him by providing drink and food, a gift of land will not be invalidated merely because the donee fails to formally accept the gift by, for example, "*rendering thanks with a thank-offering or presents alone or coupled with an utterance or expression of appropriating the gift*" as required under Fanti customary law.[270]

9.4.3 The Legal Effect of a Gift

On the assumption that a gift is valid under customary law two questions of fundamental importance are relevant in considering its legal effect. Firstly, what is the exact nature and extent of the interest acquired by the donee? Secondly, does the donor have any right to revoke a valid gift?

The answer to the first question will depend on the capacity in which the donor acts in making the gift and the nature of the interest which he held in the land. Where the gift is made by a donor acting for and on behalf of the community or the family, then the totality of the interests held by the group passes to the donee. Any intention to transfer a lesser interest must be expressed at the time of the grant. In principle, therefore, an outright gift operates to transfer the absolute title to the land to the donee in the same way, and subject to the same restrictions, as in the case of a sale. Thus, under Temne customary law the donee takes his interest subject to the reversionary interest of the original owners. Where the gift is made by a donor, acting in his own personal capacity, the donee can only take such interest as the donor himself holds in the land. In the case of individually owned land, the presumption is that the absolute title passes to the donee, the obligation being on the donor to rebut this presumption

270 See Sarbah, *Fanti Customary Law*, 2nd edn, p. 81.

by showing that the intention at the time of the grant was to pass on a lesser interest.

In the case of a gift of family or communal land to a non-member, the onus is upon the donee to show what interest the individual donor intended to transfer to him. Thus, unless there is a clear intention of transferring a specific interest, independent of the paramount interest of the landowning group, the gift will fail. However, where the donee is also a member of the same community or family, the presumption is in favour of his taking all the interest of the donor including the latter's interest in any improvements or developments made on the communal or family land.

Some aspects of the nature and extent of the interest acquired by a donee who has been granted land by a land owning family were considered in *Fulla v. Kondawa*.[271] In that case, the land had been granted to the donee by a Mende family in consideration of marriage. According to the opinion expressed by the three Assessors – one of whom was a paramount chief – who assisted the Court of Appeal, it is a fundamental principle of Mende customary law that, in the case of such gifts, the grant is to the husband for his use and benefit for life and thereafter to his issue. It is, therefore, always implied in such a grant that if the donee dies without issue the land reverts to the donors. The reasoning behind this principle is that the grant is made to ensure that access to land is guaranteed for any children of the marriage who would not otherwise be entitled to rights in their mother's family lands in a patrilineal community. However, another principle of Mende customary law that emerged from Kodowa's case is that in the event of the wife dying without any issue, the husband will still be allowed to use and occupy the land provided he continues, in the words of one of the Assessors, "*to be friendly*" or to "*give respect*" – presumably by the giving of presents and the showing of customary courtesies – to his deceased wife's family. The Assessors also went on to suggest that even where the donee marries into a family other than that of the deceased wife he may continue to use and occupy the land and pass on his right to any issue of the second marriage. This appears to be at variance with the position under Temne customary law.

According to a decision of the Group Local Appeal Court of Kambia District in the case of *Momoh Kamara v. Santigie Lamina*,[272] under Temne

271 (1970–71) ALR S.L. 300.

272 Case No. 90/72 decided by the Local Court in Kawula Masungbala Chiefdom, Kambia District in February 1972.

customary law, only the children of the original marriage are entitled to inherit land granted in consideration of marriage.

9.4.4 Right of the Donor to Revoke the Gift

As a general rule, a donor has no power of revocation in the case of an outright gift of land under customary law. There is, however, nothing to prevent the donor from reserving the right to revoke the gift under certain circumstances. In such a case, the grant is in effect a conditional gift and this should be made known to the donee at the time of the transfer. However, there are certain circumstances in which the power of revocation arises by operation of law even without any express stipulation to that effect. Thus, even in the case of unconditional gifts the grantors always retain a sort of contingent reversionary interest which entitles them to repossess the land upon its effective abandonment by the donee or on his death without heirs.

What constitutes effective abandonment was considered by the Group Local Appeal Court of Kambia District in the case of *Bockarie Saio v. Kambie Yellie.*[273] The facts of the case were that land had been granted by the appellant to the respondent's uncle. After some time the donee returned to his chiefdom of origin, leaving the land unoccupied for a period of seven years. The respondent subsequently took possession of the land and started to cultivate it, laying claim thereto as the successor in title of the donee. At this stage, the appellant repossessed the land whereupon the respondent instituted an action against him for "*trespass*". The respondent's claim was upheld by the Local Court but on appeal it was held by the Group Local Appeal Court that since the evidence disclosed that the donee had no intention of returning to the chiefdom his conduct in leaving the land unoccupied for seven years amounted to abandonment. The appellant was therefore entitled to repossess the land.

273 Case No. 11/70 decided by the Local Court at Numeia, Tonko Limba Chiefdom, Kambia District in October 1970.

9.5 TENANCIES UNDER CUSTOMARY LAW

9.5.1 Introduction

Under the broad heading of customary tenancies fall various forms of grants made under customary law where the intention of the grantor is to convey to the grantee an interest much less than the absolute title to the land in question. Such tenancies may be classified according to their duration. They may range from a seasonal grant, valid for only one farming season and conferring no proprietary interest in the grantee, to a grant for an indefinite duration under which the grantee acquires an interest which is even transmissible to his heirs. A distinction could also be made between those customary tenancies granted for no consideration and those which are subject to payment of some form of economic rent or the furnishing by the grantee of some other consideration in lieu of rent.

In former times, this was the commonest way by which strangers in the chiefdom and persons who were not entitled as of right to access to land acquired land for agricultural or building purposes. The process is sometimes described by the use of the terms "*begging*", and "*loan*". A person in need of the land was expected to "*beg*" for it from the chief or a landowning family and the latter would "*loan*" the land in accordance with well-established practices and principles of customary law. Though this institution could not be equated precisely with the landlord-tenant relationship under English law there are certain similarities and nowadays it is sometimes difficult to differentiate between a customary tenancy and a tenancy created under English law.

9.5.2 Formalities for the Creation of a Customary Tenancy

As far as the capacity of the grantor to create a customary tenancy is concerned, this is regulated in much the same way as the capacity of a vendor or donor under customary law. Traditionally, it was not common for this type of a grant to be made by individual grantors as any surplus lands in the chiefdom were invariably communal or family lands. However, with the trend towards individualization of tenure it is now theoretically possible for such a grant to be made by an individual owner. There is usually also much more flexibility with regard to the requirement as to consent or concurrence since the object of such grant is not to alienate outright the paramount interest of the community or of the family.

However, the need for prior consultation with the principal members of the group is just as important as in the case of a sale or outright gift. The procedure and formalities leading up to the actual grant are more or less the same as for other dispositions of land under customary law. The process starts with the prospective tenant declaring his intention to use or occupy a piece of communal or family land and the payment of the usual customary tribute or "*shakehand*" to the chief or the head of family.

Once a decision has been taken by the landowning group to make the grant the land is formally handed over to the tenant in the usual way in the presence of witnesses. Particular emphasis is laid on the need for a sufficient number of witnesses – especially those representing the group making the grant. Since this type of grant has, by tradition, been made strictly in accordance with customary law the use of writing is not usually contemplated by the parties. The absence of writing is still one of the main features that distinguishes a customary tenancy from one created in accordance with the general law.

9.5.3 Incidents of a Customary Tenancy

Apart from stipulating the purpose for which the land is granted, the duration of the tenancy and the form of payment, if any, there are normally no other express terms or conditions stipulated by the parties. However, certain terms are always implied in such grants by law and custom. The following are among the most important terms usually implied in a customary tenancy:

i. That the grantee may not alienate his interest without the consent of the grantors;
ii. That the paramount title to the land always remains vested in the owner/grantor irrespective of the duration of the tenancy. The corollary of this condition is that a customary tenant cannot acquire the absolute title by prescription;
iii. That the grantor reserves a right to forfeit the tenancy on breach of any term or condition, whether express or implied, of the tenancy. The grantor may not otherwise arbitrarily determine the tenancy.

Before considering the legal effect of some of these implied terms and conditions it is necessary to describe the nature and the extent of the interest acquired by the grantee under a customary tenancy. In this regard, we can classify such tenancies into two categories, viz. short-term tenancies, such as the seasonal tenancy or other grants for a fixed period on the one hand, and long-term tenancies, that is those granted for a long or indefinite period on the other.

9.5.4 Incidents of a Short-Term Tenancy

In the case of a short term customary tenancy, such as one granted for one farming season only, the tenant only acquires a right to occupy and use the land for a specified purpose and for a limited duration. This right is in nature more usufructuary than proprietary. The tenant acquires no interest in the land itself which he can either dispose of *inter vivos* or transmit to his heirs on his death. However, he has a disposable interest in any crops he is permitted to grow on the land or in any other improvements made thereon pursuant to the grant. He may sell or pledge such crops or any other disposable property he lawfully has on the land.

However, his interest lapses immediately the tenancy is determined by effluxion of time or otherwise, though in the case of a seasonal tenancy of agricultural land, the tenant is usually allowed a reasonable time after the determination of the tenancy to harvest any late crops. Anything planted, grown or affixed on or to the land contrary to the express terms of the grant and without the permission of the grantor enures for the benefit of the grantor. Thus, in a seasonal tenancy of farm land the tenant may not grow anything other than annual crops. If, for example, he plants any economic trees, title to such trees vests automatically in the grantor. Unless specifically permitted to do so, a short-term customary tenant may also not cut timber or tap palm trees growing on the land.

Finally, as to duration, though the tenancy determines automatically at the end of the farming season or other specified period, such tenancies are, in principle, renewable either by express agreement or by tacit mutual consent. Factors which might be taken into account for or against renewal include the conduct of the tenant and the extent of his generosity in expressing gratitude to the grantor. Thus, even though the tenancy is gratuitous, it would not normally be renewed if the tenant fails to make the customary gifts of produce from the farm at the end of the season.

9.5.5 Incidents of a Long-Term Tenancy

In the case of long-term customary tenancies, though the interest of the tenant in the land could also be described as a right of usufruct, yet the incidents of such tenancies are much wider in range, and the tenant often acquires more than a mere right of occupancy and user. Much depends on the purpose for which the land is granted. Thus, in the case of land needed for building purposes, the customary tenancy is often granted to endure in perpetuity. Such a right to occupy land in perpetuity has the semblance of ownership and the customary tenants in these cases often regard themselves, and are regarded by others, as "*owners*" of the land.

There are conflicting authorities on the question of whether, and if so how, the interest of a customary tenant under a long-term or perpetual tenancy is transmissible on his death. According to the opinion expressed by their Lordships of the Privy Council in the Nigerian case of *Oshidi v. Dakolo*[274] a customary tenant has the right to transmit his holding to his issue. Another view is that upon the death of a tenant his heirs are supposed to obtain the consent of the grantors to continue in occupation though, in practice, such consent is neither formally requested nor given. This was the unanimous view expressed by the expert witnesses and accepted by the West African Court of Appeal in the Sierra Leone case of *Bongay v. Macauley.*[275] However, according to the Court, "*such a nebulous 'right' cannot be construed to give the appellant an 'estate of inheritance'*".

However, no matter how substantial the rights of a long-term customary tenant may be, as pointed out earlier, these cannot normally ripen into ownership, and so long as the grantor's reversion has not been extinguished in favour of the tenant, it continues to be enforceable no matter how long the tenancy might have been in existence. It does not matter that the tenant has come to regard himself as owner, or that the grantor has ceased for many years to keep in touch with the tenant, or that the landowner has thereby encouraged the tenant to regard the land as belonging to the tenant absolutely. This basic principle of customary law was upheld in *Bongay v. Macauley*[276] and the comment of Macquarrie, Ag. C.J. in this regard is significant for, according to him:

274 (1930) A.C. 667 per Lord Dunedin at 668.
275 (1932) 1 W.A.C.A. 225.
276 Ibid., per Macquarrie Ag. C.J. at 236.

> *"The appellant, who was granted and holds no more than a usufructary right for his lifetime but alienable and defeasible upon conditions, is asserting and attempting to enjoy the incidents of absolute ownership which is a conception quite foreign to the respondent's ideas ... and one which neither the grantors not their successors ever for one moment contemplated".*[277]

At the trial in the Circuit Court the appellant, who had settled on the land in question as a customary tenant for over thirty years prior to the action brought against him by the paramount chief for forfeiture of the tenancy, as part of his defence, had contended, inter alia, that he was the absolute owner of the land; that he could sell it and keep the proceeds, and that he could dispose of it by will to whomsoever he wished. It was also contended at the trial in the Circuit Court that the plaintiff had acquiesced in the claim of the defendant. The trial Judge, Tew, C.J. considered the circumstances in which such a grantor's title could be extinguished due to acquiescence and explained the application of the doctrine as follows:

> *"The doctrine of acquiescence in equity as applied to a case of long possession of land means, in the case of communal land in this country, that the person to whom the control and disposition of the land is vested has allowed the occupier to remain in possession under the mistaken belief that the land is his own absolutely, or at least that he has a better title than that which he actually has, and has allowed [him] to spend money or do some other act on the faith of that mistaken belief".*[278]

In the circumstances of the instant case, the trial Judge held that there was in fact no evidence to justify the application of the doctrine.

It is, however, well established and has been so held in several cases, that despite the fact that there is no such thing in customary law as a prescriptive title, and that "*mere use and occupation for some time cannot of itself oust an original title*",[279] by the application of the equitable doctrines of acquiescence and/or laches or estoppel the original owner may be

277 Ibid., at 234.

278 *Bongay v. Macauley* (1920–36) ALR S.L. 212 at 227.

279 Per Watson, J. in *Agyeman v. Yarmoah* (1913) D and F 1911–16, 56.

barred from maintaining an action for the recovery of his land against the occupier.[280]

In practice, a long-term customary tenant is allowed to remain in occupation for as long as is provided for in the grant or in perpetuity in cases where no specified period is indicated. However, the tenancy may be determined in certain circumstances, such as by notice, by forfeiture for breach of one of the terms of the grant or by operation of law.

9.5.6 Need for Notice to Determine a Customary Tenancy

It is a principle of customary law that a tenancy granted for an indefinite duration cannot be determined arbitrarily by the grantor. This principle of customary law was applied by the Local Court of Bagbo Chiefdom and confirmed by the District Appeal Court in the case of *Abdul Momoh & Ors v. Mattia Amie &Ors.*[281] The appellants had sought to evict the respondents without cause or due notice from land which had been "*loaned*" to them by the appellants' ancestors. The unanimous opinion of the Assessors who sat with the learned Magistrate was that the appellants could not "*drive the respondent from the land merely because he was a stranger*". According to the Assessors, under Mende customary law,

> *"where a person has been given land on loan and he has built on that land and remained there undisturbed for a fairly long period, he is assumed to be the owner of the bush [sic]."*

No doubt the word "*owner*" was being used by the Assessors in a loose sense for, as we have maintained, the absolute title in such cases always remains vested in the original grantors.

The Court of Appeal has also applied this principle as one of Temne customary law in the case of *Ibrahim Kargbo v. Amadu Kanu.*[282] The facts of this case were that land had been "*loaned*" to the appellant's father by the respondent's grandfather. After the death of the original grantee the land was inherited by the appellant without any objection from the respondent's family. Subsequently, and without any valid reason, the respondent entered

280 See *The Bokitsi Concession Case* (1902) Sar. F.L.R. 159; *Akpan Awo v. Cookey Garn* (1913) 2 N.L.R.

281 Appeal decided in December 1975.

282 Civ. App. 7/72 decided by the Court of Appeal on 2 December 1977, unreported.

the land and prevented the appellant from farming it and handed it over to the *Porroh*, a secret society. The appellant thereupon brought an action against the respondent for "*trespass*". The Local Court at Koya Chiefdom, Port Loko District, as well as both the District Appeal Court and the Local Appeals Division of the High Court, found for the respondent on the ground that the appellant could not maintain an action for trespass against the respondent who was his overlord and owner of the absolute title. The Court of Appeal reversed this decision, holding that a customary tenant in lawful possession of land has the right to exclude everybody else there from, including the grantor and that until the tenancy has been lawfully determined the grantors have no right whatsoever to enter upon the land without the permission of the tenant.

There is no fixed rule as to how much notice is required to terminate a customary tenancy. The general view is that the notice should be reasonable. Reasonableness is a question of fact and will depend on such factors as the length of time the tenant or his predecessors in title have been in possession and the purpose for which the grant was originally made. In any case, the notice must allow the tenant sufficient time to remove any improvements that he had lawfully made on the land or to arrange for their disposal.

9.5.7 Forfeiture of Customary Tenancies

This is the usual mode by which a customary tenancy may be determined. A breach of any of the tenant's obligations under the tenancy renders him liable to forfeiture and eviction. However, the grounds that are usually relied on for forfeiture under customary law are the following:

i. Alienation without the consent of the grantor;
ii. Impugning the grantor's title;
iii. Misconduct; and
iv. Using the land for a purpose other than that for which it was granted.

9.5.8 Alienation without Consent of the Grantor and Impugning the Grantor's Title

These two grounds for forfeiture overlap. Any alienation or even attempted alienation by the tenant is viewed as a threat to the grantor's title. According to de Comarmond, S.P.J. in the Nigerian case of *Onisiwo v. Fagbenro*[283] it creates the danger that

> *"if it is not promptly detected, the overlords may one day be faced by an occupier who would aver that the overlords have acquiesced in or tolerated acts adverse to their title".*

In certain cases, where the alienation involves the creation of a sub-tenancy without the consent of the grantor, this might involve a challenge to the grantor's rights of ownership. This happened in the case of *Bongay v. Macauley*[284] where the tenant created a sub-tenancy without permission and instructed his sub-tenants not to pay any settler's fees or other customary tribute due to the grantors as owners of the land.

9.5.9 Misconduct

Though there are several judicial dicta to the effect that "*the rights of the customary tenant under native law custom are limited to occupation during good behaviour*"[285] there is no fixed principle regarding what constitutes misconduct so as to justify forfeiture of a customary tenancy.

It would seem to involve a violation by the tenant of the local customs and traditions of the community or a flouting of the authority of the traditional rulers. Thus, according to one of the expert witnesses at the retrial of the case of *Bongay v. Macauley* "*the basic principle of land tenure in this* [Sierra Leone] *Protectorate is loyalty to the Chief and the Tribal Authority*".[286] The witness went on to define disloyalty, entailing forfeiture of right over land, as including:

> *"treason, continued refusal to pay tribute, any attempt to set up [an] imperium in imperio, or continual flouting of the authority of the Paramount Chief in any way".*[287]

283 (1954) 21 N.L.R. 3 at 7.
284 (1920–26) ALR S.L. 212.
285 Per de Comarmond S.P.J. in *Onsiwo v. Fagbenro*, above, at 5.
286 Above.
287 Ibid., at 222–3.

9.5.10 Using the Land for Other Purposes

As to the fourth ground of forfeiture, since customary tenancies are usually granted for a specific purpose, such as for farming and/or building, it is a breach of the tenant's obligation, entailing forfeiture of his rights, to use the land for any other purpose without the consent of the grantor. In *Bongay v. Macauley*[288] this was one of the grounds relied on by the plaintiff for forfeiture of the tenancy. The land had been granted to the defendant for the purpose of farming, and according to the agreed terms, he was to cultivate the land in accordance with the implied conditions of cultivation subject to which the land was granted. Evidence was given at the trial that one such condition was that a customary tenant who wished to plant economic trees had to obtain the permission of the grantor, in this case, the paramount chief. According to the trial Judge, Tew, C.J., this was

> *"presumably because the planting of anything but annual crops would lend colour to a claim to a more permanent title than that which was actually possessed or could be possibly possessed".*[289]

However, the fact that land had been granted for one specific purpose does not exclude its use for any other purpose incidental to the main purpose. Thus, it is the custom to allow a long-term customary tenant to build a farm house, or other shelter, on land granted for farming only. In the Nigerian case of *Akinrinlow v. Anwo*,[290] the piece of land in question was granted solely for agricultural purposes, but the tenant built on part of it. An action for trespass brought by the grantor failed, for according to the Court, the building did not constitute a permanent injury to the land.

9.5.11 Determination of Customary Law Tenancy by Operation of Law

Under customary law, when a tenant abandons the land possession thereof reverts to the grantors. As stated earlier in this work,[291] what amounts to effective abandonment will vary according to the circumstances of each

288 Ibid.
289 Ibid., p. 225.
290 (1959)W.R. N.L.R. 178.
291 See p. 182.

case. The intention of the tenant in going away, the length of time he has been away and the circumstances surrounding his absence must all be taken into account. However, the fact that the tenant himself is not in occupation for a prolonged period does not amount to abandonment provided he retains the right of possession during his absence and the occupation of the new occupier is not based on contract so as to be construed as an alienation of the tenant's rights. Finally, where a customary tenant of a fixed-term tenancy dies before the expiry of his term and leaves no heir the land reverts to the original grantor. Even where there are heirs, their right of succession is not automatic and may be lost by the refusal of the grantor to allow the continuation of the tenancy.

9.6 PLEDGE OF LAND UNDER CUSTOMARY LAW

9.6.1 Introduction

A customary pledge[292] is a transaction whereby land or an interest in land is transferred from one party to another as security for a debt already due or to become due. From this definition there appears to be a basic similarity between a customary pledge and an English-type mortgage in that they both provide for the use of land as security for the payment of a debt. However, as will be shown below, there are several fundamental differences between the two transactions in respect of their modes of creation, form and legal incidents.

9.6.2 Formalities for the Creation of a Customary Pledge

Since customary law does not require the use of writing for any transaction whatsoever a customary pledge is traditionally always created orally. However, like other transactions in land which we have already considered, a customary pledge may now be evidenced in writing or may even be effected by deed. Apart from this modification, the fundamental rule of customary law relating to the capacity of the pledgor, the requirements for prior consultations and any necessary consent or concurrence still apply. These latter rules are strictly applied because, traditionally, the average pledgor is an individual seeking to use his interest in communal or family lands, such as a farm, a plantation or a building thereon, as security for a relatively small personal debt. However, the customary pledge has now assumed an important financial dimension being means whereby an owner

292 Also referred to as a "customary mortgage" or a "native mortgage".

of land can raise credit on its security in order to finance some business or commercial undertaking.

Despite this new trend, the bulk of customary pledge transactions are still entered into by individuals because there are hardly any corporate community or family undertakings that might necessitate the pledge of communal or family lands by the group as a unit. Since the central feature of a customary pledge is that the pledgor takes possession of the subject matter of the pledge, and this invariably involves the occupation and use of the land itself, there is always the apprehension that the paramount interest of the community or the family may be prejudiced or compromised in the hands of the pledgee who is usually a stranger to the group. For this reason, there is always a great emphasis and insistence on the need for a member seeking to pledge his interest in such lands to obtain the appropriate authority and/or consent before embarking on the transaction. In practice, such consent will only be given where the group is not able to satisfy the immediate financial needs of the individual member that obliged him to make use of a pledge. When consent is given the group ensures the protection of its paramount interests in the land by appointing representatives to act as witnesses to the transaction.

9.6.3 Legal Effect of a Customary Pledge

The generally accepted view is that the legal effect of a customary pledge is the vesting in the pledgee of the right to possession of the land with the right to use and enjoy the profits accruing from it for his own benefit without any reduction of the debt or any liability to account to the pledgor. However, the pledgee acquires no proprietary interest in the land pledged, ownership or title to which remains vested in the pledgor or the landowning group. The right of alienation of the benefit of the pledge is limited under customary law.

There is however authority for the proposition that the pledgee may create a customary tenancy in respect of the pledged land provided he obtains the consent of the pledgor or other persons competent to authorize the same.[293] The interest of the pledgee is however transmissible on his death to his heirs without the need for the consent or approval of the pledgor. In terms of duration, the interest of the pledgee subsists as long as the debt and any interest due remain unpaid. The general rule is that

293 See *Amoo v. Adigun* (1957) 2 W.L.N.R. 55.

upon payment of the amount due by the pledgor or his successors or assigns the right to possession immediately revests in the pledgor or other person entitled under or through him. The pledgee may be allowed sufficient time to harvest annual crops or such perennial crops as are ripe and ready for harvest.

The question sometime arises as to whether the pledgee is entitled to be compensated on redemption for any improvements made on the land by him during the time he was in possession. The strict rule of customary law is that the pledgor or the person redeeming in his stead need only pay the precise amount of the loan plus any interest due. It seems, however, that this strict rule may be modified in a case where the pledgee has not only made improvements to the property but used his own resources to maintain it, as, for example, by preventing a building from falling into ruins or by resuscitating a farm or plantation, as happened in the case of *Momoh Gbewar v. Musa Lamin.*[294] In that case a cocoa plantation was pledged to the appellant. Soon after the appellant had spent his own money and other resources to revive the plantation the respondent purported to redeem the pledge by the payment of only the outstanding amount due on the loan. Deciding the matter in the District Appeal Court the learned Magistrate held that it would be "*unjust and inequitable*" to allow the respondent to redeem in those circumstances without compensating the pledgee for his expense in reviving the plantation.[295]

9.6.4 Redeemability of a Customary Pledge

This brings us to the question of the redeemability of a customary pledge. It is a cardinal principle of customary law that a pledgor can redeem his property at any time no matter how remote. This principle seems to apply in the customary law of most West African countries where the system of customary pledge exists. Thus, in the Ghanaian case of *Agbo Kofi v. Addo Kofi*[296] the West African Court of Appeal held that the successors of a pledgor who had given certain lands as security for a loan made in 1869 were still entitled to redeem them notwithstanding the lapse of some sixty years.[297] Moreover, the West African Court of Appeal held

294 Decided by the District Appeal Court in Kenema in December 1980.

295 See also Ollenu, *Principles of Customary Land Law in Ghana*, op. cit., p. 100.

296 (1933) 1 W.A.C.A. 284.

297 See also *Ebiassah v. Ababio* (1946) 12 W.A.C.A. 106; and *Kuma v. Kofi* (1956) 1 W.A.L.R. 128.

in *Dapaah v. Poku*[298] that the imposition in the pledge agreement of any condition restricting the right of the pledgor to redeem is inconsistent with customary law and therefore void.

The doctrine of the perpetual redeemability of a customary pledge is part of the general principle of customary law that no permissive occupation of land owned by another can ever ripen into ownership in the occupier and operate to oust the title of the real owner. Since the pledgee's occupation is by definition permissive no prescriptive title can be based upon it nor, because of the circumstances of his possession, can he rely on the equitable doctrine of acquiescence or estoppel against the pledgor.[299]

The only practical limitation on the right of the pledgor or his successors to redeem arises where the pledge is in the traditional form, in which case all evidence relating to the true nature of the original transaction would have been recorded only in the memory of witnesses. In most cases, it becomes difficult after a considerable lapse of time for the pledgor or his successors to prove the exact nature of the transaction – either because the witnesses are no longer around or because their memory has grown too dim. Moreover, the pledgee's position is often strengthened by the fact that he would over the years have acted as the reputed owner of the land enjoying the fruits and profits therefrom and not paying any rent or tribute which would otherwise have served as an acknowledgement of the owner's title. However, the onus would seem to be on the party seeking to show that the transaction was of a different nature from a pledge to adduce sufficient evidence to support his contention. Thus, in *Agbo Kofi v. Addo Kofi*[300] the defendant had contended in answer to the plaintiff's claim that the original transaction between his predecessor in title and the plaintiff was a sale and not a pledge. Neither the plaintiff nor the defendant could adduce sufficient evidence of their respective contention, yet the Court found for the plaintiff and held that the defendant's possession must have arisen from a pledge.

As stated above, this is no longer a problem encountered with modern types of customary pledges which are normally recorded in writing and are increasingly taking on the form, if not the essence, of English-type mortgages.

---

298 Decided by the Ghana Court of Appeal on 13 June 1950, unreported. Cited by Ollennu op. cit., p. 173.

299 See *Ebiassah v. Ababio*, above.

300 Above.

9.7 ACQUISITION OF INTEREST IN LAND BY WAY OF SUCCESSION UNDER CUSTOMARY LAW

9.7.1 Introduction

When a man dies possessed of an interest in land held under customary law, the devolution of such property will depend on several factors, such as the following:

i. Whether the deceased died prior to the coming into force of the Devolution of Estates Act, No. 21 of 2007;
ii. Whether the deceased died testate or intestate;
iii. Whether the property in question is self-acquired property as opposed to communal and/or ancestral property; and
iv. The relevant rules of his personal law prescribing the order of succession upon an intestacy.

9.7.2 The Devolution of Estates Act 2007

A significant development in the law of succession in Sierra Leone is the recent enactment of the Devolution of Estates Act, No. 21 of 2007, which came into force on 26 July 2007. Section 1 of the 2007 Act provides as follows:

> *"(1) This Act shall apply to every person who dies leaving property in Sierra Leone irrespective of religion or ethnic origin;*
> *(2) Subject to subsection (3), the distribution of estates of persons dying testate or intestate on or after the coming into operation of this Act shall be done in accordance with this Act;*
> *(3) This Act shall not apply to family property, chieftaincy property or community property held under customary law;*
> *(4) For the avoidance of doubt, this Act shall not apply to any claim that is statute-barred by virtue of the Limitation Act, 1961."*

9.7.3 The Legal Effect of Subsection (1)

The legal effect above is that the provisions of the Act apply throughout Sierra Leone irrespective of the location of the assets of the deceased and the personal law of the deceased. Subject to subsection (3) it is no longer important to know where the asset is located. Thus, the assets comprising the estate of the deceased, apart from those listed in subsection (3), will henceforth be dealt with in accordance with the provisions of the statute irrespective of his religious or ethnic background or the type of marriage, if any, that the deceased had contracted. As a result, section 38 of the 2007 Act provides for the repeal of the following enactments:

i. Section 26 of the Christian Marriage Act, Cap. 95 allowing the personal law of both parties to a marriage under that Act to govern their respective property rights.
ii. Section 9(2) of the Mohammedan Marriage Act, Cap. 96 dealing with the order of priority for the grant of Letters of Administration where the deceased had contracted a marriage in accordance with Muslim law.
iii. The Second Schedule to the Administration of Estates Act, Cap. 45, dealing with the rules of distribution of the residual assets of an intestate whose personal law was the general law.

It is submitted that there has also been an implied repeal of the provisions of section 43(1) of the Administration of Estates Act, Cap. 45, which provided that where a deceased dies leaving property in the Western Area and he was a member of one of the ethnic groups and, as a result, his personal law was customary law the applicable rules of distribution of that portion of his estate would be those laid down by the customary law of the ethnic group to which he belonged.

9.7.4 The Legal Effect of Subsection (2)

The importance of subsection (2) above is to reduce the significance of the distinction between testate and intestate succession. As will be shown below, prior to the enactment of the 2007 Act, a testator in Sierra Leone enjoyed unlimited testamentary freedom and provided his will complied with the relevant statutory provisions governing the validity of wills no one could challenge any dispositions made by the testator. According to section 22 of the 2007 Act an aggrieved dependant is now able to challenge dispositions made by a testator in his will on the grounds of unreasonableness.

9.7.5 The Legal Effect of Subsection (3)

The provisions of subsection (3) above which state that the Act shall not apply to family, community and chieftaincy property preserve the position under customary law as far as succession to interests in land held under communal or family tenure is concerned. However, as has been argued earlier in this work,[301] the interest of an individual in family land and communal land per se as distinct from developments made thereon or thereto is not transmissible to his heirs by way of succession. The same no doubt is true of other forms of property belonging to the group as opposed to the individual. The legal effect of subsection (3), it is submitted, is that the devolution of all individually owned property, including any type of self-acquired interest in land, whether held under the general law or customary law, will henceforth be in accordance with the provision of the 2007 Act.

9.8 THE DISTINCTION BETWEEN TESTATE AND INTESTATE SUCCESSION

Under strict customary law, there is hardly any distinction between testate and intestate succession. A man's heirs would be known in advance and any disposition purporting to vary the order of priority among his successors or to exclude any of his beneficiaries from the list of successors would only be recognized as valid if it was made to take effect during the lifetime of the grantor.

The nearest customary law comes to recognizing the right of testamentary disposition of a man's property is the practice of giving effect to oral death-bed declarations. Sometimes, a dying man would indicate by a death-bed declaration how his property was to be distributed after his death. Such a declaration is regarded by custom as merely indicative of the deceased's preference as to the destination of his property and, though it will invariably be given effect to by the family out of respect for the

301 See p. 181.

deceased, yet it does not have the same binding legal force as a valid devise made in a will under English law. A declaration which disinherits a man's traditional heirs in favour of a stranger will only be given effect to if made before credible witnesses and on good and sufficient reasons being shown by the declarant to justify the disinheritance of his traditional successors. Moreover, the person in whose favour such a declaration has been made does not thereby acquire an enforceable right to have the property in question transferred to him.

However, a new dimension was added to the distinction between testate and intestate succession under customary law with the prevalence of the use of writing to record a preference which would traditionally have been expressed only in the form of a death-bed declaration, and by the adoption of the form of English-type wills.

The question of which law should govern such instruments, the general law or customary law, raises issues of conflict which are discussed later in this work. However, although written wills were unknown under customary law, every Sierra Leonean, irrespective of his ethnic or religious affiliation, has the capacity under the general law to make a will which will be recognized and given effect to provided it complies with the legal requirement for validity of such a will under the general law. The governing statute is the English Wills Act 1837 which, as part of the received law, applies throughout Sierra Leone. If there was any doubt as to the capacity of a Muslim to make a will this was dispensed with by the enactment of the Mohammedan Marriage (Amendment) Act, No. 10 of 1988 which amended the principal Act, Cap. 96, by inserting a new section 10 immediately after section 9 providing as follows:

> *"Every Muslim, whether married under the provisions of this Act or howsoever married, or unmarried, if of the age of not less than twenty-one years, may make a will in accordance with any enactment in force in Sierra Leone regulating the making of wills."*

According to Section 3 of the Wills Act, it is lawful for every person to devise, bequeath or dispose of by his will, executed in the manner laid down by the Act, all real estate and all personal estate to which he is entitled either at law or in equity at the time of his death. This provision not only endows every Sierra Leonean adult of sound mind with capacity to make a will in English form but, apparently, allows him complete testamentary freedom over the entirety of his self-acquired property.

Thus, in theory, any interest in land which could be freely alienated by an individual *inter vivos* could also be the subject of a testamentary disposition. It also follows that those interests in land which an individual cannot dispose of *inter vivos* without the consent and/or concurrence of the head and principal members of his family or other group could not, by the same token, be disposed of by any form of testament whether or not such disposition confirms or alters the recognized order of succession on an intestacy under customary law.

The next point to note is that any rule of customary law which directly or indirectly restricted the freedom of testamentary disposition conferred on an individual by the general law would be inapplicable by the courts on the ground of its incompatibility with the provisions of the Wills Act 1837. This flows from the statutory definition of customary law contained in the Local Courts Act 1963 which has been cited earlier in this work. However, it must be emphasized that the capacity conferred on the individual to make an unlimited testamentary disposition does not endow him with any additional right or power to make any alienation of interest in land held under customary law that would otherwise not be open to him under the relevant customary law.

In essence, in respect of land held under customary tenure, the unlimited testamentary freedom mentioned above only relates to an individual's self-acquired property which may or may not involve the paramount interest in land. A testator may not by the mere act of making a will under English law vary the nature and quantum of an interest in land that he held under customary law: *nemo dat quod non habet*. Moreover, it has been suggested that:

> *"a person cannot divest himself of the character and status he has of being a member of the family. Such membership affects his capacity to make a will. He cannot change that of his own volition".*[302]

302 Per Linglay, J. in *Andoh v. Franklin*, Land Appeal No. 50/1950 decided by the Land Court of Cape Coast, Ghana, unreported, cited by Allott, *Essays in African Law* (1960), pp. 263–4.

9.8.1 Testate Succession to Land under Customary Law

What then is the power of testamentary disposition of interests in land available to an individual as a result of the status and character of the land and the individual's relationship thereto? Firstly, as has seen shown in the previous chapter, the individual's interests in land held under communal tenure being dependent and derivative, his power of alienation both *inter vivos* as well as by will is subject to restrictions under customary law intended to protect the paramount interest of the entire group. This is reflected in the rule that an individual may divest himself by will of his interest in communal land in favour of another member of the group but the consent and concurrence of the head and principal members of the group is required before any disposition affecting communal land could be made to a stranger. Even this right of an individual to make alienation in favour of another member of the group is restricted in the sense that it must take effect in the grantor's lifetime. This is because, in principle, the interest of an individual in communal lands lapses on his death and reverts to the community as a whole. He cannot by making a testamentary disposition purport to extend his interest beyond his lifetime as if it were an absolute interest and thus deprive the community of its right to the *reversion* of the land in question.

The situation is completely different where the interest which the member purports to alienate is self-acquired and is therefore held independently of his membership of the community and detached from the paramount interest of the community in communal lands. An example of such self-acquired and independent interest in communal lands will be a plantation made or a house built thereon. The power of disposition of the individual over such improvements and developments on communal land is not restricted as it does not necessarily affect the paramount title of the community to the land itself.

Since the interest of an individual in family land is similar in nature and quantum to that of his interest in communal lands, it is to be expected that the same kind of restrictions will be placed on his power of alienation both *inter vivos* and by will. This expectation is fulfilled for, even though such an interest is transmissible primarily to his heirs, meaning his next-of-kin or immediate family as opposed to his extended or ancestral family, yet his power of alienation of his interest to other members of his family is limited to *inter vivos* transfers. He has no right under customary law to make a testamentary disposition of his interest in family land per se even to another member of his family. This is because each member's interest in family land is an incident of birth derived from the fact of membership itself based on patri-descent (or matri-descent where the community is matrilineal). The right of a deceased member's heirs to succeed to his interest in family land in priority to other members of the same ancestral family is only an additional right based on a pre-determined order of succession recognized by customary law. In theory, every member of a deceased's ancestral family is a potential successor to his interest in family land but, in practice, the right to succeed is exercised according to the degree of sanguinal or affinal proximity to the deceased. It follows from the above analysis that for the purpose of succession a distinction must be made between an individual's interest in family land per se and his self-acquired interest in his own family land or any other land. At times, this distinction is hard to perceive or to justify but it is one that actually exists and permeates the entire system of customary land tenure and must always be borne in mind in order to comprehend what would otherwise appear to be conflicting rules of the same customary law.

Another limitation placed on the powers of an individual to freely dispose by will of his interest in land is that imposed not by customary law but by statute. By limiting the nature and quantum of the interest which a non-native can hold in provincial land to that of a leasehold for a term not exceeding fifty years, the Provinces Land Act, Cap. 122, makes it impossible for a landowner to make an outright devise of his paramount interest in provincial land to a non-native.[303]

9.8.2 Intestate Succession to Land under Customary Law

Two separate aspects of the law of intestate succession relating to land held under customary tenure come up for discussion under this heading. Firstly, it is intended to determine what persons are entitled to succeed to rights and interests in and over land according to the customary law rules of the various ethnic groups. Secondly, we shall analyse the nature and the quantum of the rights and interests to which such persons may succeed under the various forms of customary tenure.

303 Cf. section 5(1) of the Non-Citizens (Interest in Lands) Act, No. 30 of 1966 which allows an assent of a freehold in favour of non-citizen entitled under a will or on an intestacy.

9.8.3 Who May Succeed?

Traditionally, the choice of successors on an intestacy under customary law is made from two broad categories of heirs, namely, relatives of the deceased traced either patrilineally or matrilineally. However, this distinction is not very important for our purpose because, as this work has shown, virtually all the ethnic groups of Sierra Leone practise a system of patrilineal succession. A more useful distinction is that to be made between communal and family lands on the one hand and self-acquired interests in the lands held by individuals on the other. As far as the devolution of deceased's interests in communal and family land is concerned, succession to those interests is potentially by all the surviving members of the deceased's ancestral family.

9.8.4 The Traditional Rules of Succession

However, in the choice of his actual successors preference was given under the traditional rules to the eldest brother of the deceased. The position of such a successor is not one of an absolute or exclusive beneficiary but is more akin to that of a discretionary trustee, holding the deceased's interest for the benefit, primarily, of the infant children, and secondarily, for the other dependants of the deceased. Thus, under the traditional system, children did not succeed directly to their deceased father's interest in family or communal lands. If a father failed to make allocations of specific portions of family and communal lands in his possession or occupation to his children *inter vivos*, there were only two ways such children could gain access to such lands. They could either appropriate any unoccupied portion of such lands in exercise of their own inherent right of occupation and user as members of their father's ancestral family or of the wider community. Alternatively, they could look to their paternal uncle or any other relative *in loco parentis* to allocate to them portions of the lands that were in their deceased father's exclusive possession or occupation.

Succession by a man's children to his interest in family or communal lands was therefore neither direct nor automatic. It was either by a positive act of appropriation or allocation. However, succession by the brother to the deceased's interest in family or communal lands was viewed by the average native and recognized by customary law as a kind of indirect succession by the deceased's immediate family. Vis-à-vis the deceased's children, such a successor stood *in loco parentis* and vis-à-vis any surviving spouse, he stood *in loco viri*.

However, the continued occupation and use by any wife of any portion of family or communal lands held by the deceased husband was and is still considered as purely permissive and depends entirely upon such wife staying within the family of the deceased. Re-marriage outside the deceased's family automatically deprived her of even this limited right of occupancy and user. Children, on the other hand, continued to look to their father's brother or his other successors in much the same way as they would have looked to their father for access to and for the occupation and user of their father's portion of family or communal lands. Where the deceased has apportioned any family or communal lands under his control amongst his various households, his successor was expected to respect such division and each wife and her children would normally continue occupying and using the portion allotted to them. Once all the children of each household become full grown adults they could either insist on further partitioning per capita or, as is more usual, would postpone partitioning indefinitely depending on the extent of the holding and the needs of each individual child.

Where no apportionment has been made by the deceased during his lifetime, this was done by his successor among the deceased's children, not according to the various households, but per capita, and based on factors such as age, sex, status and individual needs within the family. The eldest son would normally have the right to first refusal of the occupation and use of the most fertile parts of his deceased father's portion of family or communal land. He might, however, find himself postponed to a younger brother whose status has been more advanced due to personal industry or whose personal needs are greater, for example, as a result of an early marriage. Daughters were always postponed to sons and their right to the occupation and use of family or communal lands suspended during marriage and cohabitation with their husbands.

If the deceased died without leaving any issue, the order of entitlement to occupy and use a portion of family or communal land held by a deceased male was traditionally as follows:

i. Brothers of the whole blood;
ii. Half-brothers by the same father;
iii. Nephews or nieces;
iv. Parents, that is father or paternal grandfather;

v. Sisters of whole blood;
vi. Half-sister by same father.

In default of all of these groups, the choice of successors was made from the next nearest paternal relative in an ever expanding circle down to the remotest patrilineal descendant of the deceased. The above order, subject to relatively minor variations, was the traditional one for succession to the family lands practised until recently by all the major ethnic groups of Sierra Leone.

Within these general practices, there are a number of ethnic variations. Firstly, according to Finnegan,[304] the Limba have always regarded a man's children as his direct successors to his interest in family or communal lands. Succession is by all the children, with the eldest son acting as a sort of trustee or caretaker of the deceased's interests. It is only during the minority of the children that the role of trustee and interim administrator is entrusted to the deceased's brother or other senior male relative. As soon as a son or, in recent times, even a daughter is old enough to manage the estate, control and management are transferred to him or her.

Another slight variation in the usual traditional order of succession is noted among the Konos. Though succession was traditionally by any brother of the deceased in respect of other property, only uterine brothers were permitted to succeed to the deceased's interest in family or communal lands. However, this has now given way to the modern practice, adopted by all the ethnic groups alike, of allowing the eldest son or daughter of full age to succeed in priority to the brother or any other relative of the deceased.

9.8.5 Modern Trends in the Order of Succession

The traditional order of succession to a man's interest in family or communal lands has been abandoned in all but the most conservative rural areas. However, one may safely say that among all the ethnic groups the general practice now prevailing is for the children of a deceased male to succeed directly to their father's interest in family and communal lands, as well as in other self-acquired property. Some instances were even quoted by interviewees in communities where the wife had been allowed to succeed as the sole heiress of her husband's self-acquired property. These were obviously exceptional cases and should be treated as such.

304 *Survey of the Limba People of Sierra Leone* (1965), pp. 57–8.

In this regard, the practice of allowing a wife to succeed as sole heiress to rights in land held under customary law is not sufficiently widespread for it to be categorized as a modern rule of customary law. Indeed, the practice is limited to educated and detribalized persons whose personal law is customary law who by contracting monogamous marriages have adopted a new mode of life, distant from their traditional roots, and in keeping mainly with so-called Western civilization and Christian practices. Even before the enactment of the Devolution of Estates Act 2007, it was doubtful whether this practice would have gained recognition in the typical ethnic communities for, no matter how improved the wife's status might have become under customary law, she remained a stranger to her husband's ancestral family. As long as rights in land continued to be based on descent traced patrilineally, the wife's right to her deceased husband's interest in family or communal land always remained restricted to a mere "*licence*" to occupy and use the same subject to such conditions as are imposed by the landowning group. On the other hand, the trend towards a man's children as his successors was not inconsistent with the principle of patri-succession, and as such, can easily be reconciled in the minds of even the most conservative and ardent defenders of the traditional customary law rules relating to succession to rights in land.

On the question of the succession to interests in land held by females, in principle there is no rule of customary law prohibiting a woman from holding an interest in land as a *femme sole.* As a member of a family or community she has potentially the same inherent right to a portion of family or communal lands for exclusive occupation and user and, a fortiori, she could also be the owner of self-acquired property in her own right independent of her husband and her ancestral family.

However, the socio-cultural realities of life in the Provinces do not often permit an individual female to acquire a separate interest in family or communal lands. A woman is expected to look towards her husband for the provision of land needed for her immediate family. However, it often happens that a woman who belongs to a family owning extensive lands may have a portion of her family's land allocated to her, even though she has married into another family. Where a deceased female was at the time of her death in occupation of family or communal lands her interest therein lapses and the land reverts to the general pool for re-allocation by the head of family or group. However, illegitimate children of the deceased who had been adopted by the deceased's family are entitled to succeed to her interests in such family or communal lands in this same way and to the same extent as children of a deceased male.

9.8.6 Succession to the Interest of a Minor

Succession to the interest in land of a minor follows more or less the same pattern as that of adults. However, there are variations to be encountered where the interest is in self-acquired property. In this case, the parents of the minor take to the exclusion of all other relatives. A female minor who was married at the time of her death is treated under customary law for the purpose of succession to her self-acquired property as an adult.

9.9 THE NATURE OF INTERESTS IN LAND TRANSMISSIBLE BY SUCCESSION UNDER CUSTOMARY LAW

The distinction between an individual's self-acquired interests in land and those held in communal or family land is again of importance here. This is mainly due to the fact that, as we have already noted, among the ethnic groups of Sierra Leone, the concept of family development of property is not very common as family land consists basically of undeveloped ancestral land.[305] In the case of self-acquired property, the nature and quantum of the interest in land capable of being transmitted to successors depends on the form of tenure under which the land is held. Thus, where the deceased owned the paramount interest in land subject to individual tenure a similar interest is transmissible to his heirs. It is submitted that the title of the successors, if more than one, is held jointly.

Though the right of the successors is derived from their membership of the deceased's immediate family they do not succeed to the property as self-acquired property but each one inherits an individual share co-extensive with the paramount title held by the deceased. The fact that the property is held in undivided shares by the several successors does not necessarily stamp it with the character of family property. Each successor has an individual interest that can be alienated even before partition. That such partition is seldom undertaken does not detract from the fact

305 Cf. the Akans of Ghana and the Yoruba of Nigeria. Under their respective customary laws the presumption is in favour of family property as individual ownership of the land is limited to the acquirer's lifetime after which it becomes family property if the purchaser dies intestate.

that each successor has a legal right to demand one. Where, however, the property is held jointly by the successors and is passed on as such to their descendants it might appear to take on the character of family property but, in essence, no matter how numerous and diversified the persons who are eventually beneficially interested therein, each one has a separate and divisible interest distinct from their interest held in ancestral land per se.

On the other hand, where the deceased's self-acquired property is dependent on an interest in family or communal land the nature and quantum of the interest transmissible to his immediate heirs is not as extensive as that in land held under individual tenure. A house built on family land or a plantation made on communal land by an individual's personal effort and industry may be classified as self-acquired property. However, since his interest in such property is dependent on and derived from the paramount title of the family or wider community to the land itself the right of the successors to such self-acquired property is not absolute, but qualified. They take their interest subject to all the limitations inherent and prescribed by the system of tenure under which the deceased held his. Thus, they may not alienate a self-acquired interest in family or communal land to a stranger without the consent and/or concurrence of the head and other principal members of the group. In some instances, their right might be limited to a mere "*licence*" or, at most, a "*right of occupancy*" entitling them to enjoy the fruits and profits of the self-acquired interest of the deceased as opposed to vesting in them any proprietary rights in the land per se. In this way, it is possible for even a stranger to the family or group to succeed to the interest in self-acquired property held by a deceased in family or communal land.

The right to use and enjoy buildings, economic trees and other fixtures attached to or planted on family or communal lands is dependent upon the group's paramount interests but could be transmitted to a successor as part of the deceased's self-acquired property.

On the other hand, the interest of the individual member of a family or community in family or communal land per se is one which is shared jointly with other members of the family or group. Thus, it is not capable of isolation for the purposes of transmission by succession. However, where an individual member has realized his interest by the exercise of his right of appropriation or allocation of a portion of family or communal land he thereby acquires a right of exclusive occupation and user for as long as he lives.

The right of exclusive occupation and user is transmissible to his heirs, not as part of the deceased's personal inheritable property, but as part of the ancestral heritage and to which all members of the family or group are also potentially entitled. Unlike an individual succession to a deceased's self-acquired property, a successor to a deceased's interest in family or communal land itself does not have a separate or divisible share but only an interest that entitles him to participate in the exercise and enjoyment of the joint and corporate ownership rights.

9.10 STATUTORY PROVISIONS GOVERNING THE ACQUISITION OF INTEREST IN PROVINCIAL LAND

9.10.1 Introduction

As already shown in this chapter and elsewhere in this work, under customary law there is hardly any restriction in acquiring an interest in land in the Provinces. Land could be granted to anyone, whether to a member of the chiefdom or a stranger. The expressions "native" and "non-native" were unknown to customary law. Besides, a customary tenancy could be granted for any duration, ranging from a short-term or seasonal tenancy, such as a tenancy granted for the purpose of growing seasonal crops, to one for a longer term or one of even indefinite duration. In addition, land could be "*begged*" or "*gifted*" or "*pledged*" for agricultural and other purposes.

On the other hand, access to provincial land by non-indigenous persons and entities came to be restricted and regulated for the first time soon after the declaration of the Protectorate over the territory adjacent to the Colony. These restrictions were imposed mainly by means of two local statutes, the Concessions Act, Cap. 121 and the Provinces Land Act, Cap. 122, both to be found in the 1960 edition of the Laws of Sierra Leone, 1960. The main feature of these statutes was the distinction made between "natives" and so-called "non-natives" for the purposes of access to land in the Protectorate This dichotomy was not limited only to landholding but was extended to other areas such as marriage, divorce, succession and right of residence in certain parts of the Provinces. This frequently led to a great deal of confusion, particularly in relation to access to land, on the part of inhabitants of the Colony who did not belong to any of the indigenous tribes, and even within the Colonial Government itself.

As a result, it became necessary in 1961, just before independence was granted by the British to the Colony and the Protectorate, to insert a provision in the Provinces Land Act, Cap. 122,[306] to the effect that for the purposes of the Act "*the expression non-native shall not include the Government*". A further attempt was made in 1972[307] to clarify the distinction between "natives" and "non-natives" by inserting a definition of a non-native in the interpretation section of Cap. 122 to the effect that a non-native means a person who is not entitled by customary law to rights in land in one of the Provinces. The offshoot of the 1972 definition of a non-native is that, by virtue of the provisions of the Concessions Act, Cap. 121 and the Provinces Land Act, Cap. 122, all persons who are not indigenous to the Provinces and all companies and other non-natural persons, classified as non-natives, have only restricted access to land in the Provinces. The machinery to regulate access to provincial land by non-natives that was thus introduced during the colonial era still remains in full force and effect.[308] However, as explained below, very little or no use has been made of the Concessions Act, Cap. 121, since independence for this purpose.

9.10.2 The Concessions Act, Cap. 121

This statute was enacted for the express purpose of regulating the rights in land which natives can grant to non-natives (with the consent of the Governor) by way of concessions for mining or agricultural purposes.

Concessions under the Act could be granted for as long as ninety-nine years and could cover an area of one thousand acres and above. However, the procedure for the grant of a concession is very complicated and time consuming, and not cost-effective. Not only must the grant be validated by a Concession Court established under section 11 of the Act, but if the extent of the concession exceeds five thousand acres the Governor (now the President) must give his assent subject to the approval of Parliament.[309]

Though the Act remains in the statute book, and was even amended in 1976 to exclude mining concessions from its provisions, the Act has

306 This was done by Act No. 15 of 1961.

307 See the First Schedule to Act No. 29 of 1972.

308 Apparently the provisions of the Provinces Land Act, Cap 1222 are currently being reviewed by the Law Reform Commission and are likely to be significantly amended in the near future.

309 See section 6 of the Act.

not been invoked in recent times for the purposes of granting access to provincial land for agricultural purposes.

9.10.3 The Provinces Act, Cap. 122

In contrast to the situation regarding the Concession Act, Cap. 121, the Provinces Land Act, Cap. 122, which was enacted during the colonial era[310] also for the express purpose of regulating access to land in the Protectorate by non-natives, is still regularly invoked and is the only formal means by which non-natives can gain such access.

A useful way to analyse the provisions of Cap. 122 is to examine the powers vested in certain entities and officials by the Act and their respective roles in regulating access to provincial land by non-natives. What emerges from this analysis is that there are virtually no powers vested in the actual landowners, nor is their role in the whole process defined by the Act. The major players are the following:

i. The chiefdom council consisting of the paramount chief and other traditional rulers and elders in the chiefdom;[311] and
ii. The district officer (now the chief administrative officer of the district council).

9.10.4 The Role of the Chiefdom Council in Creating Leases under the Provinces Land Act, Cap. 122

The first and most important role of the chiefdom council in creating leases under Cap. 122 may be gleaned from the interpretation section of Cap. 122 which states that:

> *"lease means a grant of possession of land by the Chiefdom Council, as lessor to a non-native, as lessee, for a term of years or other fixed period with the reservation of a rent".*

This definition and the other powers vested in the chiefdom council by the Act have led to the misconception that the council has a beneficial interest

310 Cap. 122 was enacted in August 1927 as the Protectorate Lands Ordinance.

311 These may or may not include the actual landowners depending on the type of tenure under which the land is held.

in all Cap. 122 leases. Indeed, it is now generally an accepted practice for the chiefdom council to share in the proceeds of rent derived from leases granted under the Act.

Based on the definition of a lease in the Act, it could be argued that the chiefdom council alone should be named as lessor in the lease. However, though the Act does not make any provision for the landowning families or communities (or even individuals), to be joined as parties to Cap. 122 leases, the common practice is for the representative(s) of the community or the family, as the case may be, to be joined as parties to the lease.

9.10.5 The Power and Rights of the Chiefdom Council in Respect of Cap. 122 Leases

Section 3(1) of the Act provides that no land in the Provinces shall be occupied by a non-native unless he has first obtained the consent of the chiefdom council. Before the enactment of Cap. 122, the right to control the grant of land held under communal tenure to strangers, both natives and non-natives, was vested in the chief-in-council under customary law. In the case of family land held under family tenure, only the concurrence of the paramount chief, or other traditional ruler, such as a section chief, was required before a stranger could be allowed to occupy land within the chiefdom. However, where the land was held under communal tenure, the consent of the chief-in-council was always a prerequisite for such dispositions, even when the land had already been appropriated or otherwise occupied by a family or an individual member of the chiefdom.

The position at customary law has therefore been altered by the Act to require the consent of the chiefdom council in all cases where a non-native stranger wishes to occupy land in any chiefdom, whether the land is held under communal, family or individual tenure.

Another statutory provision which has modified the customary law relating to rights in land in favour of chiefdom councils is that contained in section 10(1) of the Provinces Land Act, Cap. 122. This provision vests in the chiefdom councils the reversion in all fixtures, buildings and economic trees in lands occupied by non-natives under the Act. Prior to the enactment of this provision, under customary law, any improvements made on land by a stranger would, prima facie, edure for the benefit of the original grantors or their successors when they retake possession of the land.

9.10.6 The Role and Responsibilities of the Paramount Chief under a Cap. 122 Lease

Cap. 122 does not expressly define the role of the paramount chiefs in the grant of leases under the Act. The only reference to the paramount chief in the Act is as a member of the chiefdom council. However, in view of the prominent position of the paramount chief within the chiefdom council, he plays a most significant part in any grant of a lease under Cap. 122. As "chief executive" of the chiefdom council, the paramount chief also plays a leading role in the exercise of the rights and powers conferred on that body both by statute and customary law. He is, in many respects, the alter ego of the chiefdom council.

In this regard, the paramount chief never acts alone. He only makes grants after due consultation with his leading advisers, who invariably are themselves title-holders such as speakers, section chiefs or village headmen. He would invariably consult with heads of families whose interests may be directly or indirectly affected by the proposed grant. In the same way, the paramount chief would never take a decision to dispose of any piece of communal land, whether by sale, gift, lease, or even by loan to a stranger without first consulting the traditional head of the area where the land is located. In fact, as described earlier in this work, the necessary negotiations usually start at the local level, and end up with the paramount chief only making or ratifying the final decision.

The same process of consultation is encountered even when the paramount chief exercises his right to allocate portions of communal lands to families or individual members of the community. In the case of unappropriated or abandoned lands in areas of non-communal tenure, the right to dispose of such lands to strangers, or to allocate them to members of the chiefdom, is exercised by the paramount chief on behalf of and in the name of the chiefdom council.

Even where the land in question belongs to a family or an individual, as opposed to the whole community, the paramount chief has a role to play in the grant of land to any stranger to the chiefdom, native or non-native. The right of the family or an individual to use and/or dispose of its land is always subject to the jurisdictional interest of the paramount chief in all lands in his chiefdom. This is because of his authority as the political head of the chiefdom. In all cases, the seal of approval of the paramount chief is necessary to validate the transaction.

Thus, the paramount chief not only executes all Cap. 122 leases as a member of the chiefdom council but also countersigns any survey plan attached to the lease. This serves as a confirmation to the grantee that the landowner has the right or is otherwise authorized to make the grant. The presumption is that the paramount chief will not validate a transaction unless he is satisfied, of his own personal knowledge or based on reliable information from local elders, that the grantor is acting bona fide.

9.10.7 The Role of the District Officer (now Chief Administrative Officer of the District Council) and Other Government Officials in the Creation of Cap. 122 Leases

In addition to the system of native administration in each chiefdom of the Provinces, there exists at the district and provincial level a system of local government administration (formerly under the direct control of the Ministry of Local Government and Internal Affairs) which also has a major role to play in land matters generally and in the machinery for making land grants to non-natives under Cap. 122 in particular.

Prior to the enactment of the Local Government Act, No. 1 of 2004, the head of this local administration at the district level was originally the district commissioner, later re-designated district officer. These civil servants worked under the direct supervision of the provincial secretary for each province. The political head of the local government administration in each province is the Resident Minister. However, the latter has never had any direct role or responsibilities in land matters.

Both the Provinces Land Act, Cap. 122 and the Provinces Act, Cap. 61 vest tremendous powers in the district officers and provincial secretaries in land matters generally, and particularly in regulating access to provincial land by non-natives.

Thus, section 3(2) of Cap. 122 provides that:

> *"any non-native who shall occupy land in the Provinces without the approval of the District Officer shall be a tenant at will within the meaning of this Act."*

A tenancy at will is defined in the interpretation section of the Act as a tenancy in which the lessee holds at the will of the lessor, and which may be determined without notice by either the lessor or the lessee.

Section 7 of Cap. 122 provides that all tenancies which according to the Act are to be created by agreement under seal, that is, tenancies for a term exceeding three years,[312] shall, unless they are under seal and have the consent of the district officer endorsed thereon, shall be construed as creating only a tenancy from year to year.

The district officer also has an oversight role in respect of the performance by the chiefdom council of its statutory obligation under Cap. 122. Section 9, for example, provides, inter alia, that unless a Cap. 122 lease is executed on behalf of the chiefdom council before the district officer and the latter has endorsed therein a certificate that the execution was done in his presence, the lease is voidable at the instance of either party.

A Cap. 122 lease is equally voidable under section 9 of the Act unless it provides that the lessee shall not sublet or assign his interest thereunder except with the consent of the chiefdom council with the approval in writing of the district officer, provided that such consent shall not be unreasonably withheld.

One of the most important powers of the district officer in relation to a Cap. 122 lease is the power to have the rent revised every seven years subject to a right of appeal to the provincial secretary.[313] This is made subject to a proviso that no increase in rent shall be sanctioned by the district officer by reason only of improvement made by the lessee or his predecessors in title. According to section 9 of the Act, this is one of the stipulations set out in the Rules in the Schedule to the Act that must be included in every lease if the same is not to be rendered voidable at the instance of either party.

However, in practice, such revisions are always done in consultation with the head or other authorized representatives of the family in the case of family land, and with the paramount chief, representing the chiefdom council, in the case of land owned by the community as a whole. As in the case of fixing the original rent, the paramount chief does not act alone. The consultation is with the paramount chief, the chiefdom speaker and other leading members of the chiefdom council.

312 See section 6 of Cap. 122.
313 See section 5(1) of Cap. 122.

9.10.8 Power of the President to Make Rules under Cap. 122

Cap. 122 vests in the Governor in Council (now the President) the power to make rules, inter alia, for the following purposes:

> *"(a) ….*
> *(b) Prescribing the terms to be embodied in leases.*
> *(c)….*
> *(d) Prescribing the procedure in submitting deeds of lease for revision of rent.*
> *(e) Specifying the person to whom rents shall be paid and the … manner in which such rents shall be brought to account.*
> *(f) Generally for the more effectual carrying out of the provisions of the Act."*

The rules contained in the Schedule to the Act, last amended in 1932, are still in force.

9.10.9 The Role of the Magistrate for the District

A minor role is also played in the process by the magistrate for the district. He has the duty to ensure that the non-native lessee executes the lease in his presence followed by his endorsement of a certificate to that effect on the lease. According to section 9 of Cap. 122 failure to comply with this requirement renders the lease voidable at the instance of either parties.

9.11 OTHER RELEVANT PROVISIONS OF CAP. 122

9.11.1 Duration of Cap. 122 Leases

The duration of a Cap 122 leases has remained unaltered since 1927 when the statute was first enacted. This is so, despite several representations from stakeholders, including paramount chiefs, landowners and other development-oriented persons and entities.

Section 4 of the Act provides that "*No non-native shall acquire a greater interest in land in the provinces than a tenancy for a term of fifty years; but nothing in this section shall prevent the insertion in any lease of a clause providing for the renewal of such lease, for a second or further terms not exceeding twenty-one years*".

Needless to say, this provision is one of those that act as a hindrance to access to land for development purposes generally, especially as Cap. 122 leases are the only means by which non-natives can gain access to Provincial land.

9.11.2 The Status of Landowners and the Role of the Head of Family in the Grant of Cap. 122 Leases

As stated above, Cap. 122 is silent on the status of, and the role to be played by, the actual landowners in the grant of a lease to a non-native. It has been submitted that where the land is held under communal tenure the person who has capacity to authorize the grant is the paramount chief acting in consultation with the principal men of the chiefdom, such as the chiefdom speaker and other elders such as the section chief for the area where the land is situated.

In the case of land held under family tenure, the head of family has a very prominent role to play. Though title to the land is vested in the family as a unit, it is only through the head of family that effect is given to the family's corporate will as far as disposal of family lands is concerned. In this regard, the head of family acts as an agent for the entire group and only he, or persons authorized by him, can lawfully alienate the title of the family to family lands. However, the head of family cannot act in isolation or arbitrarily. He is obliged by customary law to seek the consent and concurrence of the family by consulting with the principal members. In principle, an individual member can only dispose of any improvements or developments he has made on family land. The view of most family elders interviewed is that the consent of the head of family is required before such a disposal can take place. However, a minority of interviewees restrict the requirement to one of simply informing the head of family about the transaction. Even though the head of family may not withhold his consent, he may discourage any disposal which might tend to jeopardize or risk the family's paramount interests in the land in question. For example, in the case of a proposed pledge of a farm cultivated on family land by an individual member, the head of family would normally attempt to have the loan raised within the family before giving his consent or concurrence to the pledge.

The head of the family is also in a predominant position in the distribution of the fruits and benefits accruing from family lands. In case of proceeds from sale or lease of family land, it is usual for the head of family to allocate to himself a large share before distributing the rest to the principal members as representatives of the various branches of the family. There is no fixed proportion for such distribution, and the practice varies from family to family, depending largely on the size of the family and the personal influence of the head. The same principle also applies in the distribution of income from other sources, such as royalties paid for cutting timber or operating mines on family lands.

9.11.3 The Role of Landowners in Practice

Despite the absence of any express or specific role assigned to landowners by Cap. 122, heads of families and, where appropriate, individuals, are regularly involved in the negotiations for a Cap. 122 leases. This is so with particular reference to the following matters:

- i. In the absence of any documentary evidence of title, the provision of sufficient assurance of their entitlement to possession of the land and their right to make the grant;
- ii. Assisting the lessee's surveyor in ascertaining the precise boundaries of the land;
- iii. Fixing of the initial duration of the term granted;
- iv. Fixing of the initial lease rent;
- v. Fixing of the formula and interval for the revision of the lease rent;
- vi. Determination of what additional consideration should move from the lessee, for example, by way of infrastructural development and compensation for environmental degradation of the land granted to the lessee;
- vii. The formula for the distribution of rent proceeds among all the interested parties;
- viii. Express provision for the exclusion of the usual customary law grounds for forfeiture of a customary tenancy;
- ix. Satisfactory provisions for dispute resolution.

9.11.4 Ascertainment and Demarcation of Boundaries

Of particular significance is the demarcation of the boundaries of land subject to a grant. As noted above, all Cap. 122 leases for a term exceeding three years must be by deed, failing which the grant will be construed as a yearly tenancy. Under the provisions of the Registration of Instruments Act, Cap. 256 as amended by Act No. 6 of 1964, all deeds made after the 1 June 1964 shall be void if not registered within the time limit prescribed by the Act. Section 12 of Cap. 256 further provides that such a deed submitted for registration shall have annexed thereto a plan of the land affected signed by the surveyor who prepared the same. This provision is to be read together with section 15 of the Surveys Act, Cap. 128 as amended. Such a plan must be countersigned by the Director of Surveys and Lands, but only after verification that, technically, it has been prepared in the manner prescribed by the Director.

This imposes an obligation on the landowners to give all possible assistance to the surveyor in ascertaining the precise boundaries of the land in question. Needless to say, in the absence of documentary evidence of their title such an exercise takes on major importance.

9.11.5 The Legal Status of Cap. 122 Leases

The whole objective of the Provinces Land Act, Cap. 122, at least when it was enacted in 1927, was to regulate the occupation of Protectorate lands by settlers from the adjacent Colony and to safeguard the interest of the indigenous communities in their land. The statute was enacted at a time when the landowners would invariably have been in a weaker bargaining position because of their inability to match the superior economic and educational strength of the so-called non-natives from the Colony. In view of the improved social and economic conditions now prevailing in the Provinces generally, and the urgent need to make provincial land more freely accessible for development and other purposes, it is doubtful whether there is any justification for maintaining such statutory restrictions on the freedom of the parties to negotiate appropriate terms of such leases for their mutual benefit and protection. In the absence of such contractual freedom the provincial landowners could end up being in a stronger position than the lessee since there is nothing in the Act to prevent them from importing into a Cap. 122 lease those terms and conditions which would ordinarily be implied in a customary tenancy and which could render the position of the non-native lessee even more precarious. An example is the condition which provides for forfeiture of a customary tenancy on the ground of misconduct by the tenant.

9.12 CONCLUSION

The foregoing exposition and analysis of the rules governing the transfer of interests in land held under customary tenure have served to reveal the complexities inherent in any system of customary law, and the difficulties likely to be faced by a person involved in any transaction under customary law in ascertaining the relevant rules. These problems are further aggravated where the possibility exists of choosing between customary law and another system of law, in this case the general law, but without definite and clear-cut guidelines on the choice of the applicable law. As land becomes increasingly commercialized in the Provinces, and as transactions involving the transfer of land and interests therein continue to become a common occurrence, there is bound to be greater interaction between the two systems.

PART 4

THE LEGAL EFFECT OF THE DUAL SYSTEM OF LAND TENURE

CHAPTER 10

PROBLEMS ARISING FROM THE INTERACTION OF THE TWO SYSTEMS OF TENURE

10.1 BACKGROUND TO THE PROBLEMS ARISING FROM THE INTERACTION OF THE TWO SYSTEMS OF TENURE

The brief examination of the Sierra Leone legal system in this work has indicated that its most striking feature is the duality between the general law, which consists basically of the received English law, and customary law. In Parts 2 and 3 it has been demonstrated how this duality is reflected in the land law which is in force in the Western Area and the Provinces respectively. The implication of this exposition and analysis of the land law is that there exist in Sierra Leone two mutually exclusive categories of lands: those held under English tenure in the Western Area and those held under customary tenure in the Provinces.

Though it is possible to divide up the country in this way, according to the system of land tenure in each geographic area,[314] it could not be said that each area does not permit any interaction between the two systems. In this Chapter, this work will examine the extent of the interaction between the two systems in the Western Area and in the Provinces as well as the problems arising from such interaction.

10.2 THE EXTENT OF INTERACTION BETWEEN THE TWO SYSTEMS

The distinction between the Western Area and the Provinces is once more of marked significance. Each region will receive separate treatment.

---

314 Cf. Allott, *Essays in African Law*, p. 258 where he argues that it is impossible to divide up a country physically on the basis of the tenure under which land is held in any particular area.

10.2.1 Interaction between the Two Systems in the Western Area

The possibilities for interaction between the two systems in the Western Area are limited. This is because land tenure in this part of the country is governed almost exclusively by the general law, and there is only limited opportunity for the application of customary law, or any other system of law.

Moreover, the only courts which have jurisdiction in the Western Area are the English-type courts whose basic or primary law is the general law. Though these courts are empowered to apply customary law, or Mohammedan law in certain circumstances, such applications are in fact exceptions to the basic principle that only the general law applies in the Western Area. The main rules governing the application of customary law by the English-type courts is contained in section 76(1) of the Courts Act 1965. These specifically provide for the application of such law when the courts are determining matters arising in the Provinces in their civil jurisdiction.

The only statute which authorizes the application of customary law in the Western Area is the Administration of Estates Act, Cap. 45. According to section 43(1) of this Act, where any native dies intestate leaving assets (defined in the Act to include both real and personal property) in Sierra Leone, which are not within the jurisdiction of any Local Court, the distribution of such assets shall be according to customary law. Since Local Courts do not have jurisdiction in the Western Area, this means that customary law is to be applied when a native dies intestate leaving real or personal property in the Western Area.

The possibility of applying yet another system of law in the Western Area existed where the situation envisaged in section 9(1) of the Mohammedan Marriage Act, Cap. 96, arose. This section provides that:

> *"If any party to a Mohammedan marriage and being at the date of his death a Mohammedan, or if any person being unmarried and being at such date a Mohammedan, shall die intestate, the estate real and personal of such intestate shall be distributed in accordance with Mohammedan law".*

Thus, it could be said that it is only in the area of intestate succession that there is room for interaction between the two systems in the Western

Area. The problems likely to arise in this regard will be examined later in the chapter.

10.2.2 Interaction between the Two Systems in the Provinces

Unlike the case of the Western Area, there exists much greater room for the interaction between the two systems within the Provinces. This is due to several factors. Firstly, as has already been established in Chapter 3, both the traditional courts and the English-type courts have jurisdiction in the Provinces. However, the two systems of courts are not integrated but rather co-exist in parallel. In such a situation, no matter how well defined their areas of competence are, there are bound to arise cases where their respective jurisdictions either conflict or overlap.

The second, and probably the most important factor, is the fact that the two systems of law, that is, the general law and the customary law, apply concurrently throughout the Provinces. Though there are certain restrictions imposed by statute on the application of customary law generally, for example, it might be excluded because of repugnancy or incompatibility; these restrictions are not particularly significant in the field of provincial land tenure, where customary law remains the basic law. At the same time, subject to only one qualification, due to the provision of section 8(1) of the Interpretation Act 1971, which stipulates that certain statutes enacted before 1 July 1953 do not apply to the Provinces, the general law applies throughout the Provinces. Though the primary law of the traditional courts is customary law, and that of the English-type courts is the general law, both courts may apply either system of law subject to any relevant statutory restrictions. This inevitably gives rise to certain problems involving the choice of law that the courts are to apply in determining cases coming before them in the Provinces.

Thirdly, even outside the field of litigation, there exist possibilities for an interaction of the two systems as a result of the influence of English legal ideas and concepts which have been introduced into various aspects of customary land tenure by both professional lawyers and laymen alike. Thus, a person wishing to transfer an interest in land which is held under customary tenure in the Provinces can either use one of the traditional modes described earlier in this work, or employ an English-type document such as a conveyance, lease, mortgage or will. These parallel possibilities are also bound to give rise to innumerable choice of law problems. In most cases, it is necessary to decide which of the two systems of law is to govern not only the particular transaction, but also the interests in land which have been created or transferred thereby. Some of these conflictual problems and the machinery that exists for their resolution are examined in the next section

10.3 PROBLEMS OF INTERNAL CONFLICTS OF LAW ARISING FROM THE DUAL LAND TENURE SYSTEM

The term "*internal conflicts of law*" has been used by Allott[315] to refer to a situation (identical to the one outlined above) where there is a plural system of law involving the overlap between one system of law and another and, in particular,

> *"to cases where a judge is required to choose between two or more systems or bodies of law which are not territorially distinct that is which apply concurrently and without spatial separation within a single territorial jurisdiction".*[316]

The concept of internal conflicts of law is thus used in antithesis to "*external conflicts of law*" which arise only when a court is required to choose between one national or territorial system and another. Allott[317] also suggests that such internal conflicts may involve either a choice of courts or a choice of laws. However, for present purposes this analysis is limited to those cases of internal conflicts that involve a choice of law rather than a choice of courts. In the field of land tenure in Sierra Leone, there are three situations where such problems of internal conflicts of law are most likely to arise, albeit to a different extent in the Western Area and Provinces. These are in cases of *inter vivos* transfer of interests in land, testate succession and intestate succession.

10.3.1 Internal Conflict of Laws in the Western Area

In the Western Area, problems of internal conflicts of law are only likely to arise in cases relating to intestate succession. There appears to be no doubt that any apparent conflict between the general law, and any other

315 Op. cit. p. 110.
316 Op. cit., p. 112.
317 Ibid.

system of law, arising from dispositions, either *inter vivos* or by will, of interests in land in the Western Area will inevitably be resolved in favour of the general law.

The law is so clear on this particular point that the issue is seldom raised before the courts. The only known case where the possibility of conflict was discussed is that of *In Re Allie (Deceased)*.[318] The relevant facts of this case are that a testator whose personal law was customary law, and who also happened to be a Mohammedan, purported by his will to create a charitable trust in respect of his landed property in the Western Area. In an action before the High Court (former Supreme Court) to determine the validity of the devise, counsel for one of the beneficiaries suggested that Mohammedan law should be applied by the Court instead of the general law. Smith, C.J. rejected this suggestion in no uncertain terms as follows:

> *"I do not consider that I can do this. The properties concerned are in tenures under English law... Although as the testator was a native, Mohammedan law might become applicable to distribute his estate on intestacy, the fact that he made a will in the form recognised by English law leads me to conclude that I must apply English law in determining its validity and effect".*[319]

However, as the learned Chief Justice rightly pointed out, in the case of intestate succession in the Western Area, a choice might have to be made between one of several systems of law to govern the distribution of the residual assets of the intestate. As stated above, for intestacy occurring after the coming into operation of the Devolution of Estates Act 2007, on 26 July 2007, no choice of law problems are likely to arise as only the provisions of that Act will apply. However, for intestacies occurring prior to the enactment of that statute the old law is still applicable and is set out below.

10.3.2 Deaths Occurring prior to 26 July 2007

318 (1950–56) ALR S.L. 338.

319 Ibid., at 340.

A choice might have to be made from among three relevant statutes. These are:

i. The Administration of Estates Act, Cap. 45;
ii. The Christian Marriage Act, Cap. 95; and
iii. The Mohammedan Marriage Act, Cap. 96.

10.3.3 The Administration of Estates Act

Where the provisions of section 43(1) of the Administration of Estates Act, Cap. 45, apply, the choice is between the general law and customary law. There is, however, very little guidance in the Act itself as to the choice of the applicable law in any particular case. The section merely provides that where a native dies intestate leaving property situated in the Western Area, the distribution of his assets should be in accordance with customary law, without even defining the term "*native*".

As has been shown in this work, the term "*native*" is used in several other statutes with a different connotation in each case, as for example in the Provinces Land Act, Cap. 122, where a non-native is defined as a person not entitled by birth, that is under customary law, to rights in land in a Province. Similarly, in the Diamond Industry Protection Act, Cap. 199, a native is defined as

> *"a member of a race, tribe or community settled in Sierra Leone other than a race, tribe or community which is or European or Asiatic origin".*

The only statute which defines a native in a general way is the Interpretation Act 1971. Though, in theory, this definition is intended by the legislature to serve for all purposes, it is submitted that its application in the context of the provision of section 43(1) of the Administration of Estates Act would not be appropriate for several reasons.

Firstly, this definition of a native in the Interpretation Act 1971, has now been extended to include all Sierra Leoneans as a result of the amendment effected by section 29 of the Sierra Leone Citizenship Act 1973. The 1973 Act defines a native as:

> *"A <u>citizen of Sierra Leone</u> who is a member of a race, tribe or community settled in Sierra Leone other than a race, tribe or community which is of European and Asiatic or American origin" [emphasis added].*

In theory, this means that even the Creoles, who do not belong to any indigenous tribe, may now be classified as natives since they are citizens of Sierra Leone and are members of a community settled in Sierra Leone.[320] If this definition were to be applied for the purposes of the Administration of Estates Act this would mean in effect that the estate of Creoles who die intestate leaving property in the Western Area would have to be distributed according to customary law. This would be impracticable for the simple reason that there is no customary law applicable to the Creoles. Besides, as has been pointed out earlier, customary law is defined by statute to mean any rule, other than a rule of the general law having the force of law in any chiefdom of the Provinces.

Secondly, it is to be assumed that the intention of the legislature, in enacting section 43(1) of the Administration of Estates Act, Cap. 45, was to make provision for the devolution of an intestate's estate according to his personal law, the presumption being that the personal law of a native is customary law and that of a non-native is the general law or any other applicable law. If this assumption is correct, then the issue of whether an intestate was a native or non-native would depend, in each case, on what was the particular deceased's personal law, and not on any fixed statutory definition of the term native.

Where the deceased was also a Creole, there is an almost irrebuttable presumption that his personal law was the general law. This presumption could only be rebutted by strong and cogent evidence that the deceased had adopted some other law as his personal law. Though there is also a presumption that the personal law of a member of one of the indigenous ethnic groups is customary law, it is much easier to rebut this presumption as such a person could more readily have opted out of customary law in his personal relationships. Thus, though a person only acquires membership of a particular ethnic group by birth, and such membership prima facie determines his personal law, he may, by adopting a different mode of life through marriage, religion or otherwise, voluntarily alter his personal law.

---

320 Prior to the amendment, a native was defined in the Interpretation Act, No. 8 of 1971, to exclude any member of a community settled in the Western Area so the Creoles had always been classified by statute as "non-natives".

In such a case, it is the intention of the individual that is the determining factor.

In other cases, certain factors, independent of the intention of the individual himself, may contribute to rebutting the presumption that his personal law is that of the ethnic group to which he belonged by birth. One such factor is the possibility of the individual being of mixed parentage, for example, of a Creole mother and a Temne father. The choice of personal law in such a case may depend, for example, on whether he was legitimate or illegitimate at birth, and the system of law under which he was raised. The situation might also arise where either or both parents have altered their personal law acquired by birth and therefore cannot transmit this to their children, even though the children could, for other purposes, be classified as members of their parents' respective ethnic group.

Even where it has been determined that customary law should govern the devolution of the estate of the deceased, a choice might still have to be made between several bodies of customary law. Where the deceased was in fact born in the Provinces the practice is to apply the customary law in force in the chiefdom of his origin. Where, however, the deceased was born elsewhere, and could not be identified with any particular chiefdom of the Provinces, then the choice of the applicable customary law becomes difficult, if not impossible to make, and is in practice often made arbitrarily by the administrator. This situation frequently arises as there are several communities settled in the Western Area whose members are linked by language, culture and tradition to one or other of the indigenous ethnic groups, but for whom the Western Area has always been their domicile.

10.3.4 The Mohammedan Marriage Act

Another statutory provision which might give rise to problems of choice of law in the case of intestate succession in the Western Area is that contained in section 9 of the Mohammedan Marriage Act, Cap. 96, the text of which has already been cited in this work.[321] Where this provision applies, a choice might have to be made between customary law or the general law on the one hand, and Mohammedan law on the other. The wording of the section would tend to suggest that the provision applies to two categories of intestates, that is, those who had contracted a Mohammedan marriage and were at the time of their death still Mohammedans, and those who never contracted such marriage but were at the time of their

321 See above, p. 230.

death Mohammedans. In effect, the provision applies to any person who was at the time of his death a Mohammedan whether he was a party to a Mohammedan marriage or not. The crucial test is whether the deceased was a Mohammedan at the time of his death. Where this is established, then, according to the Act, "*the estate real and personal of such intestate shall be distributed in accordance with Mohammedan law*".

There are no other guidelines in the Act itself to assist the court or an administrator in determining which system of law should apply where the deceased's personal law is either the general law or customary law. Problems of conflict are likely to arise because, apart from the provisions of this Act, Mohammedan law is not otherwise in force in Sierra Leone. Where, therefore, the intestate is a Sierra Leonean, his personal law would normally be either the general law or customary law, depending on whether or not he was a member of one of the ethnic groups whose customary law is in force in the Provinces. The question that arises in such a case is whether, because of the provisions of the Act, Mohammedan law should prevail over either system of law. It is submitted that, prima facie, this question should be answered in the affirmative for two reasons. Firstly, since Mohammedan law does not otherwise apply in Sierra Leone, it is to be assumed that the intention of the legislature was that such law was to apply as against the general law and customary law only in cases falling within the provisions of the Act. Secondly, provided it has been established that the intestate was at the time of his death a Mohammedan, then application of Mohammedan law is not made subject to any other condition imposed by the Act or any other statute.

In practice, however, the decision to apply Mohammedan law, as opposed to the general law or customary law, is not usually based on any of the above considerations, as the choice of law is often influenced, to a great extent, by the application for a grant of letters of administration. Since such applications are invariably dealt with as part of the non-contentious business of the High Court, it usually suffices for the applicant to declare on oath that the deceased was at the time of his death a Mohammedan for the balance to be tipped in favour of the application of Mohammedan law. The decision in such cases is based on such practical considerations as the relative advantages or disadvantages to be gained by potential beneficiaries from the application of Mohammedan law as opposed to the general law or customary law. Thus, without going into the details of the rules of distribution of property on an intestacy under Mohammedan law, it is obvious that a wife, who as a Koranic heiress, would be entitled to a fixed share of her deceased husband's estate would prefer the application of Mohammedan law, as against customary law, under which, traditionally, the widow would not have any legal right to succeed to any portion of her husband's property on his death intestate. It should, however, be noted that the fact that the deceased was married according to Mohammedan law does not per se alter the law governing the distribution of his estate on an intestacy.

10.3.5 The Christian Marriage Act

The same is true where the deceased was married in accordance with the provisions of the Christian Marriage Act, Cap. 95. Section 26 of this Act expressly provides that where a marriage is celebrated under the Act, and one of the parties thereto is a native, the marriage shall not have any effect on the property of such native, and if both parties are natives, their property shall "*be subject in all respects to the laws and customs of the tribe or tribes to which the parties respectively belong*".

These provisions may lead to certain disparities in cases of intestate succession, especially where the parties do not have the same personal law. This could be illustrated by the example of a marriage between a non-native woman and a native man. If the husband predeceases the wife, the latter may find herself unable to benefit from the distribution of her deceased husband's estate where customary law is applied as his personal law to effect a distribution.

According to the modern trend, the wife of the deceased may be allowed to continue in occupation of the matrimonial home subject to certain conditions, such as her remarrying into the same family or staying unmarried. The fact that the property involved is land, held under English tenure in the Western Area, would seem to make no difference as such property would also have to be distributed in accordance with the relevant rules of customary law as provided by section 43(1) of the Administration of Estates Act, Cap. 45. In contrast, on the death intestate of the non-native wife, the application of the general law as her personal law enables the husband to inherit her entire estate (irrespective of the location of any real property) in accordance with the rules of distribution laid down in the second Schedule to the Administration of Estates Act, Cap. 45.

The position of a surviving spouse on an intestacy is completely different where the general law is applied as the personal law of the husband. In such a case, the wife may be entitled to take either a one-third or a half share of the husband's estate depending on whether or not there are any surviving issue of the marriage.

10.4 INTERNAL CONFLICT OF LAWS IN THE PROVINCES

Because both the general law and customary law apply in the Provinces, and there is much more room for the two systems of law to interact, problems of internal conflict of law are likely to be encountered in all the situations discussed in this work, namely, on the transmission of interests in land, whether *inter vivos,* by will or on an intestacy. In the case of a disposition made *inter vivos* or by will, the choice of the applicable law is between the general law and customary law. But in the case of intestate succession, the choice may be between general law, customary law and Mohammedan law, or simply between two different customary laws.

10.4.1 Statutory Rules to Resolve Internal Conflicts of Laws

Where a choice has to be made between the general law and customary law either in relation to an *inter vivos* or a testamentary disposition of an interest in land there are certain guidelines provided by section 76(2) and (3) of the Courts Act 1965. The usefulness of these guidelines depends to a large extent on the interpretation of these provisions, the exact text of which is as follows:

> *76(2) "Subject to subsection (3) ... customary law shall, except where the circumstances, nature or justice of the case shall otherwise require, be deemed applicable in all causes of matters where it shall appear to the Court that substantial injustice would be done to any party by a strict adherence to the rules of any law other than customary law."*
>
> *76(3) "No party shall be entitled to claim the benefit of any customary law if it shall appear either from the express contract, or from the nature of the transaction out of which any cause or matter may have arisen that such party agreed that his obligations in connection with such transaction should be governed exclusively by any law referred to in*

> *section 74 [that is, the received English law] or any Act of Sierra Leone; and in cases where no express rule is applicable to any matter in controversy, the court shall be governed by the principles of justice, equity and good conscience".*

The first observation which could be made on the above provisions is that they are only intended to assist a court actually seized of a cause or a matter in determining which of the two systems of law should be applied to the particular case before it. The Act does not offer any assistance in resolving any conflict that may arise as to which of the two systems are to govern a particular transaction or relationship in the absence of any dispute between the parties thereto. Even where a dispute has arisen involving litigation, the provisions of the Act could only be of assistance where the proceedings are instituted before the English-type court, for the definition of a "court" in the interpretation section of the Act clearly excludes Local Courts.[322] Though the Local Courts Act 1963, which regulates Local Courts, gives such courts authority to apply both the general law and customary law, neither that Act, nor any other statute, provides any choice of law rules to assist these courts in resolving conflictual problems.[323]

The next pertinent observation is that from the wording of section 76(3) these provisions could only be of assistance in the case of a dispute arising out of a bilateral transaction and where the parties to the dispute are the same as the parties to the transaction. Thus, in the case of a dispute involving persons who were not parties to the original transaction, or where the dispute has arisen out of a unilateral act such as a disposition of land made by deed of gift or by will, the provision of section 76(3) could not be of any assistance to a court in determining which system of law should be applied in the particular case.

Another, and probably the most important, observation in this discourse, is that the choice of law rules contained in section 76 tend to be too vague and general, so that the question of choice of law ends up being, to a very large extent, a matter for the court's discretion. This makes it difficult to predict, in advance, which system of law the courts are likely

322 Section 2 defines "court" as "*any court of law in Sierra Leone other than a court martial or a local court*".

323 Cf. the former Western Region Customary Courts Law 1957, which contained specific provisions for the resolution of conflict between English received law and customary law.

to apply to any particular transaction or relationship, or a dispute arising therefrom.

10.4.2 Factors Affecting the Choice of Law

Having thus examined, in a general way, the provisions for the application of customary law by the English-type courts and the rules for the resolution of problems of internal conflict of laws, this work will now consider more closely the factors that affect the application of either system of law in particular cases.

Firstly, there is the basic presumption that each type of court has its own system of primary law which is prima facie applicable in a case before it. Thus, where an action is commenced in the Local Courts, customary law will be deemed to apply unless the case is one which could only be tried under the general law. On the other hand, where the action is instituted in the English-type courts, the general law is prima facie applicable.

One factor which will affect the application of either system of law by the English-type courts is the personal law and/or ethnic origin of the parties, that is, whether any or both of the parties are subject to customary law. Though this is not clearly stated in the statutory provisions, the inference could be drawn from the wording of subsection 2 of section 76 of the Courts Act 1965, that customary law is to apply in any cause or matter where both or at least one of the parties has customary law as his personal law. The court is, however, given the discretion to apply any law other than customary law where "*the circumstances, nature or justice of the case shall otherwise require*". Thus, where the parties have throughout their lives regulated their dealings in accordance with the general law, it would be unjust for one of the parties to insist on the application of customary law merely because he is a native. On the other hand, where there is no clear indication of the parties' intention, or where their conduct and the manner of their dealing would permit the application of either system of law, then the court is bound to apply customary law if it shall appear "*that substantial injustice would be done to any party by a strict adherence to the rules of any law other than customary law*".

Another factor that might affect the choice of law is the nature of the transaction. Sometimes it is clear that the transaction in question is one known only to the general law or only to customary law, as the case may be. Thus a transaction which leads to the creation of a customary pledge, or a customary tenancy, is one which could only be governed by customary, law whereas a will in English form in which the testator creates a settlement or a trust for sale is clearly to be governed by the general law. The difficulty arises, however, where the transaction may be described as "mixed" in character, that is, one which fundamentally or substantially belongs to one system of law but with features and incidents belonging to a different system (as where land held under customary tenure is conveyed in fee simple but with a condition totally prohibiting alienation by the grantee), or one which it is impossible to allocate to any one system, such as an unattested written will.

One development that has led to the prevalence of these so-called "mixed" transactions is the increasing use of writing in all aspects of the transfer of interests in land held under customary tenure. The present trend in the Provinces is that every party to a dealing in land, whether literate or illiterate, will endeavour to secure at least some record of the transaction in writing. The legal question that arises in each case is this: To what extent does the use of writing per se affect the nature of the particular transaction and help to determine which system of law should be applied thereto? Existing judicial authorities would tend to indicate that the attitude of the Sierra Leone courts is to apply the general law whenever any particular form of writing has been made use of in the transfer of interests in land. Reference has already been made to the receipt cases such as *Kebbie v. Kamara*[324] and *Sawaneh v. Bayoh.*[325] However, it is doubtful whether these cases could usefully serve as a guide for the resolution of conflictual problems in general, especially as there is no evidence that the possibility of applying any system of law other than the general law was ever canvassed or taken into account by the court in either of those cases.

It is submitted that it is impossible to maintain that the mere use of writing is sufficient indication of the intention of the parties to a transaction involving an interest in land held under customary law to exclude the application of such law. Much depends on the purpose for which the writing has been used. Thus, where land has been transferred in accordance with customary law but the parties subsequently reduce their agreement into writing so as to record in a permanent form matters which might later be in dispute – such as the description of the land conveyed, the amount paid as purchase price, whether the transaction is a sale or a pledge, or the terms of a tenancy – the presumption is that the transaction is still governed by customary law unless there is some other evidence of

324 Above.
325 Above.

the intention of the parties to the contrary. On the other hand, where the document prepared in respect of the transaction is not a mere record, but is in fact the instrument through which the transfer is effected, so that it has the same binding force as a deed under the general law, then prima facie the parties may be taken to have intended that the transaction should be governed by the general law.

Where, however, the parties have expressly agreed that their rights and obligations in respect of any particular transaction should be regulated by the general law, then the court is enjoined to exclude customary law irrespective of the nature of the transaction. This is in effect the choice of law rule laid down in section 76(3) of the Courts Act 1965. In practice, this rule is not of very much assistance as the parties invariably would not have even considered the question of which law should regulate their relationship. Moreover, this rule could not be applied in cases where the transaction involves a unilateral act, such as a testamentary disposition.

The provisions of section 76 of the Courts Act 1965, as analysed in the foregoing paragraphs, only relate to problems of conflict between the general law and customary law arising in cases before the English-type courts. There also exist possibilities of conflict between customary law and Mohammedan law in cases involving the administration of the estate of persons who have died intestate leaving property situated in the Provinces held under customary law. According to section 13 of the Local Courts Act 1963, the Local Courts have exclusive jurisdiction where the administration of the estate of an intestate is governed by customary law. However, the only way one can determine whether the Local Courts ought to exercise jurisdiction in a particular case is by first settling the choice of law problem. Unfortunately, there are no existing statutory provisions comparable with those contained in section 76 of the Courts Act 1965, which could at least serve as a guide to the Local Courts. Ironically, there have so far not been any cases where the Local Courts have had cause to resolve such conflictual problems, as the usual practice is for disputes relating to the administration of a native's estate to be settled by the process of customary arbitration. The present approach of the Local Courts in such matters has been summed up by Joko Smart writing on customary family law in Sierra Leone:

> *"When inheritance issues go before these courts, it has always been the practice for them not to investigate the details of administration and distribution but merely to advise*

> *the members of the family of the deceased to appoint an administrator, and if there is any disagreement among the family as to who the administrator should be, to request the Paramount Chief, section chief, town chief or an elder to carry out the administration and distribute the estate to the persons entitled under customary law. More often than not, details concerning the persons entitled and distribution are settled within the family. It is not, therefore, surprising that there is a dearth of contentious cases".*[326]

However expedient this approach may be, it cannot always be relied on, especially as the traditional spirit of family cohesion which facilitated such settlements is slowly disappearing and giving way to a new spirit of individualism that might give rise to cases where these courts are obliged to perform their proper role as adjudicating bodies.

326 Joko Smart, op. cit., p. 205.

PART 5

MAKING OF A LAND POLICY: CRITIQUE AND PROPOSALS FOR REFORM

CHAPTER 11
THE MAKING OF A LAND POLICY

11.1 THE STATE AND FORMULATION OF A LAND POLICY
11.1.1 Background

It is most important that Government should evolve and adopt a comprehensive policy for effective land administration and management. This is so because of the several matters that need to be addressed if maximum advantage is to be taken to exploit the potential that land represents, firstly, to the State as a valuable resource for national development, secondly, to the average landowner as a vehicle for his economic empowerment, and thirdly to the entrepreneur as a channel for safe and profitable investment in the fields of agriculture, mining, property development and many more.

Over the years since Sierra Leone attained independence in 1961, with the former Colony and Protectorate coming together to form a unitary State, the need for a land policy has been highlighted in several reports and studies commissioned by the Government of Sierra Leone and various agencies of the United Nations such as the Food and Agriculture Organization, the World Bank, regional bodies such as the EU, and States such as Great Britain through its Department for International Development, and many others interested in the overall socio-economic development of Sierra Leone.

As far back as 1983, the following opinion was expressed on the issue of the advantages of a system of registration of title:[327]

> *"In view of the urgent need for revision and reform of our land law and the system of land administration in general the reader might justifiably be wondering whether the Government of Sierra Leone has any identifiable and clearly defined land policy.*

327 A.R.D. Renner-Thomas, "A Dual System of Land Tenure, The Sierra Leone Experience", unpublished thesis for the degree of PhD in Law, London University.

> *The simple, if rather surprising, answer is that no comprehensive land policy is discernible in the various development programmes that have been prepared since independence. This is particularly surprising especially when one considers that, for most young and developing nations, the adaptation or modification of the existing land tenure system to ensure an adequate and economic use of all land resources is normally a key feature of their development programme.*
>
> *In most African countries also, the traditional attitude to land as embodying the spirit of the ancestors and as a sacred heritage which must be preserved for all posterity is being abandoned in favour of policies which favour the marketability of land. At the same time, the notion that the landowner should be left free to use his land in the way he chooses is now gradually yielding to a new thinking more progressive and socially oriented, namely that the [State] should assume greater regulatory control over the use of land for various reasons such as to ensure better planning, a proper and adequate economic use and a greater productivity for the whole community. This change of attitude has come about because of development in other fields [such] as the social, economic cultural and environmental areas of life. In such circumstances, a comprehensive and articulate land policy becomes an essential requirement of any well coordinated development programme. In Sierra Leone, though there have been clear signs of changes in the social, economic and cultural life of the people necessitating reform of the land law and the system of land administration in particular, it is fair to say that the Governments' response to such changes has been negative".*

That was in 1983. What then is the background to current attempts to formulate a national land policy?

11.2 THE BASIC INGREDIENTS FOR A LAND POLICY

The formulation of any national land policy and indeed its implementation presupposes the existence of an institutional framework for giving effect to such policy and, the existence of established guidelines and regulations applicable throughout the country to ensure, inter alia:

i. An effective land administration and management system;
ii. Machinery for facilitating land transactions such as a system of registration of title to land;
iii. An improved land adjudication system;
iv. Easy access to land for development and other purposes;
v. Machinery for effective land use planning, regulation and control, and protection of the environment.

This work has already examined some of the matters listed above and will be making proposals for addressing the current problems being encountered in the process of land administration because of the absence of a well-defined policy thereon. This part of the work will analyse actual efforts that have been made or are currently under consideration to formulate a policy on all these matters raised above.

11.3 ACCOUNT OF VARIOUS LAND POLICY INITIATIVES SO FAR

11.3.1 Initiatives prior to the Year 2000

Before 2000, much of the focus was largely on the Western Area. For example, in the planning sector, a structure plan for Freetown was prepared as far back as 1982 as a Study Project of the Institute of Planning Studies, University of Nottingham, in the United Kingdom. One of the senior officials of the Ministry of Lands and the Environment, Mr. Johnson, was a member of the study team.

Among other things, the team proposed four alternative strategies for the development of Freetown:

i. control of growth through regional decentralization;
ii. intensification of existing land use;

iii. equitable distribution of land use activities; and
iv. relief of central area congestion by the provision of employment opportunities near residential areas.

The next major initiative in the planning sector was a project for the preparation of a structure plan and an investment programme for Greater Freetown undertaken in 1996 under the direction of the Sierra Leone Road Authority, acting on behalf of the Sierra Leone Government, and financed by the World Bank under an IDA Reconstruction and Import Credit arrangement. In July 1996, Sir Alexander Gibb & Partners of the UK, in association with Techsult and Company Ltd, leading a team of local consultants, was commissioned to undertake the multi-disciplinary studies leading to the preparation of the structure plan for Greater Freetown .

The team commenced the studies, prepared an Inception Report and held a Workshop on the Structure Plan in December 1996. Both the Inception Report and the Workshop Report contain some valuable material that could be relevant in the formulation of a policy for the country as a whole. An example is this extract from the Workshop Report on the state of development planning and development control in Freetown:

> *"At present, the development planning function of the Ministry is limited to the preparation of plot layout schemes and not comprehensive urban development plans. The performance of duties is constrained by inadequate staffing and facilities and lack of coordination with lands and surveys [division of the Ministry], utility delivery agencies and [those responsible for] economic planning. The development control practice, caught in a situation without development guidelines is focusing its activities on the inspection of single development sites of one house plots [and] not on land use control in general. In addition to the need for training staff is [sic] unable to effectively discharge [its] duties due to lack of supporting services and facilities. There is no coordination mechanism with lands and surveys nor with development planning or utility agencies. Litigation activity is constrained by lack of staff and legal advisory services."*

Unfortunately, the team could not complete its work as it was overtaken by the events following the military coup of May 1997. Up to the time of writing, the project has not been revived.

11.3.2 Environmental Aspects

From the environmental perspective concerns were first highlighted in 1980 with the submission of the Report to the Government of Sierra Leone on Environment Protection Policy Administration and Legislation funded by the United Nations Environment Programme. The report contained recommendations for appropriate legal and institutional arrangements for environmental protection. Action on these recommendations led to the creation of an environmental ministerial division originally under the Ministry of Lands Housing and Environment, later moved to the Ministry of Transport and Communications in April 1996, and by November of the same year to the Ministry of Agriculture Forestry and Environment and currently as part of the Ministry of Lands and Country Planning and the Environment. A National Environmental Policy was proposed in 1974 and this was followed by the National Environmental Action plan (NEAP) approved by Government in February 1996. An Environmental Protection Act was drafted in 1995 but only became law in the year 2000 as Act. No. 2.

In the interpretation of section of the Act "environment" is defined to include:

> *"land, air, water and all plants, animals and human beings living therein and the inter-relationship which exists among these or any of them".*

Section 9 of the Environmental Protection Act imposes on the Minister of Environment responsibility for, inter alia:

> *"the setting of environmental goals and objectives and proposing and developing policies on all aspects concerning environmental protection and management; and reviewing the progress made in the implementation of the national Environmental Action Plan and issuing such directive[s] as are necessary".*

11.3.3 Policy Initiatives on Access to Land

Similarly, much has been said and written about the need for easy and equitable access to land, particularly in the Provinces, for development and other purposes. Such access has been hindered by the present dual system of land tenure and in particular by the negative impact of the Provinces Land Act, Cap. 122, to which reference has already been made in various parts of this work. The Act restricts access to land in the Provinces for so-called "*non-natives*", a term which ironically includes a registered company or any other corporate body even if its members are exclusively "*natives*" within the meaning of the Act. In the past, the subject was taboo and successive governments have consistently refused even to make a policy statement on the issue mainly because of the political undertones surrounding the subject and the emotions it arouses.

The need for a clear-cut national policy on land tenure could not have been ignored for too long as the systems of land tenure in force, the laws providing for the acquisition of title and other interests in land and the machinery for facilitating land transactions are essential features of any legal and regulatory framework of land use administration and management in Sierra Leone.

11.3.4 The Draft National Land Policy 2005

It is against this background that the Ministry of Lands Country Planning and the Environment published a draft National Land Policy in February 2005. In the foreword by the then Minister,[328] he acknowledged that this was:

> *"the first time in the history of [Sierra Leone] that a comprehensive land policy was being formulated. Hitherto, land had been managed through various legal instruments and customary practices through the court system. This approach to land did not provide the basis for a comprehensive overview to assess the social and environmental implications of the dynamics of land ownership, acquisition procedures and the use to which land is put."*

328 Dr. Alfred Bobson Sesay, Minister of Lands, Country Planning and the Environment, Freetown, 8 February 2005.

According to the Minister, the draft National Land Policy was to provide the foundation for the review of the existing laws and the enactment of new ones to create the enabling environment to accommodate the rapid socio-economic development programmes and plans of government, in general, and specifically, to regulate and streamline access to, and the use of, land in order to ensure the development of a sustainable environment.

The Minister went on to state that the draft National Land Policy sought to address some of the fundamental problems associated with land management in the country. According to him, these problems include many that we have highlighted in this work such as:

> *"general indiscipline in the land market characterized by land encroachments, falsification of documents, multiple land sales and registration, unauthorized use of land, haphazard development, improper survey practices, indeterminate local authority and chiefdom boundaries, resulting from lack of reliable maps and plans, rampant encroachment on , and illegal acquisition of large tracts of Government land which have either not been surveyed, registered and otherwise protected, or have not been utilized; a weak land administration system and conflicting land uses."*[329].

What then are the main features of the 2005 draft National Land Policy? It may be summarized as follows:

i. the policy framework – this consists of the guiding principles, the aims and objectives of the policy and the legal and institutional mechanism that should ensure the accomplishment of the aims and objectives of the various policies;
ii. the policy guidelines; and finally
iii. the policy actions.

329 Ibid.

11.3.5 The Guiding Principles of the Draft National Land Policy 2005

The guiding principles are both to be found in pages 7 and 9 of the draft policy document issued by the Ministry. Of these attention ought to be focused on three principles in particular:

i. the principle of optimum usage for all types of land uses including human settlements, industry and commerce, agriculture, forestry and mining, the protection of water bodies and the environment in the long-term national interest;
ii. the principle of Government facilitating equitable and reasonable access to land within the context of national land use planning;
iii. the principle of fair access to land and security of tenure.

Among the objectives outlined in the draft National Lands Policy the following may be highlighted:

i. To ensure that every socio-economic activity is consistent with sound land use practices through sustainable land use planning in the long-term national interest.
ii. To facilitate equitable access to and security of tenure of land based on registered land.
iii. To instill order and discipline into the land market to curb the incidence of land encroachment, unauthorized development schemes, multiple or illegal land sales, falsification and multiple registration of land documents, land speculation and other forms of racketeering.
iv. To minimize, and eliminate, where possible, the sources of protracted land boundary disputes, conflicts and litigation in order to bring their associated economic costs and their potential for socio-economic upheaval under control.
v. To create and maintain effective institutional capacity and capability at the national, regional, district, and where appropriate community levels for land service delivery; and promote community participation and public awareness at all levels in sustainable land management and development practices to ensure the highest

and best use of land, and thereby guarantee optimum returns on land.

11.3.6 The Draft Lands Commission Bill 2005

There was provision for a legal and institutional framework that was to be utilized for the implementation of the draft National Land Policy once it was put in place.[330] There was to be a Lands Commission to be established by a proposed statute for which a draft Bill was published at the same time as the draft National Lands Policy.

The focal point of the proposed legislation is the creation of a new statutory body, the Land Commission. Among the key functions of the proposed Commission are the following:

i. On behalf of Government to manage State lands and any land vested in the Republic of Sierra Leone by the Constitution or by any other law or any lands vested in the Commission itself.
ii. To advise Government, local authorities and traditional rulers on the policy framework for the development of particular areas of Sierra Leone to ensure that the development of individual pieces of land is co-ordinated with the relevant development plan for the area concerned.
iii. To formulate and submit to Government recommendations on a national policy with respect to land use and capability.

In addition to the above functions, clause 4 of the draft statute states that there shall be no disposition or development of any State land (and presumably of lands within any chiefdom) unless the Commission or the Local Authority where the land is situated has certified that the disposition or development is consistent with the development plan drawn up or approved by the Planning Authority for the area concerned. This clause is to be read together with clause 6 which stipulates that there shall be within each region branches of the Commission to be known as "District/Town Councils Lands Commission". These regional Lands Commissions shall perform the functions of the Commission at the local level.

The implications of the above provisions have been far reaching because, as has been explained already in this work, the power of alienation of any

330 For the full text see Appendix 6, p. 367.

land is one of the incidents of ownership under both the general law and customary law. If, as is proposed in clause 2, one of the functions of the Commission would be to manage State lands, then one can envisage it giving consent for and concurring in the disposal of the same. However, in the case of provincial land, there does not exist any concept of Chiefdom lands as is mentioned in the heading of clause 4 of the draft statute. If this is a new concept that is being introduced by the legislation, this must be so stated very clearly. Indeed, the draft statute presupposes not only the revision of existing customary law rules relating to disposal of provincial land, but also the repeal or amendment of statutes such as the State Lands Act 1960 and the Provinces Land Act, Cap. 122. Clause 28 of the draft statute lists a number of enactments including the last two mentioned that are to continue to have effect with such modifications as may be necessary to give effect to the proposed statute. However, the draft legislation fails to stipulate expressly the extent of such modification. This, it is submitted, does not make for clarity.

11.3.7 Machinery for the Implementation of the Proposed Legislative Changes

As stated in paragraph 4.0 of the draft national policy, the policy guidelines detailed at pages 10 to 16 of the draft are mere policy statements derived from the policy objectives and intended to guide policy action and implementation. What is of crucial importance is to identify the most effective mechanism for the implementations of the policy actions listed in pages 16–19 of the draft national land policy. Quite clearly, the most obvious method is by enacting a series of new pieces of legislation or amending and consolidating existing ones. Though there are several pieces of relevant legislation in the statute book, there has been lack of action to implement their provisions and to ensure compliance therewith. In particular, the provisions of the Unoccupied lands Act, Cap. 118, the Freetown Improvement Act, Cap. 66, the Town and Country Planning Act, Cap. 81, (as amended) and the Foreshores Act, Cap. 149 have remained dormant since independence in 1961. While it is correct that some of the existing statutory provisions and regulations made thereunder may be inappropriate in certain respects, such as lack of clarity (for instance as to who should initiate action under the statute), quite frequently what is lacking is simply the political will to implement these statutory provisions.

Unfortunately, not only was the draft not adopted by the previous Government, but very little or nothing was done in concrete terms to attain the declared objectives of the policy document.

11.3.8 The Land (Acquisition and Commercial Use) Bill 2005

A much more comprehensive piece of legislation yet to be adopted is the draft Land (Acquisition and Commercial Use) Act 2005,[331] drafted by the Law Reform Commission in 2005 and reproduced in this work for ease of reference as Appendix 7. This Bill also adopts the idea of the establishment of a land commission. More importantly, it provides for equitable access to land throughout the country for all Sierra Leonean citizens and repeals the much decried Provinces Land Act, Cap. 122, thus making it possible for the holding of freehold interest in provincial land by both citizens and non-citizens.

However, some of the obnoxious provisions of the Provinces Land Act, Cap. 122 are to be retained for no apparent reason. Thus, irrespective of who is the lessor in respect of a provincial lease, the chiefdom council is still given the power to revise the lease rent every seven years. Ironically, there is only an implied repeal of the restriction on non-citizens holding other than a reserve leasehold of 21 years in the Western Area imposed by the Non-Citizen (Interest in Land) Act, No. 30 of 1966. The draft statute provides that any person, which clearly includes a non-citizen, may acquire a lease of land in any part of Sierra Leone for a term not exceeding 90 years.

The draft also contains provisions dealing with mortgages. Again, if these provisions, which are very scanty, are enacted, there would be an implied repeal of the provisions of the Conveyancing Act 1881 which, as part of the received English law is still in force in Sierra Leone, and which has more detailed provisions regulating such matters as the exercise by the mortgagee of the power of sale and other rights and remedies of both parties to the mortgage.

The provision in the draft that would allow

> *"a trespasser actually in possession of land who has the intention to be in possession by excluding all others, including the landowner, from the land by means other than the use*

331 For the full text of this draft statute, see Appendix 7, p. 380.

> *of force, and has maintained adverse possession for not less than twelve years"*

to be entitled to be a registered owner thereof is, in our considered opinion, a recipe for chaos and confusion. One wonders what means other than force the draftsman envisages the trespasser would use to exclude all others including the true owner.

It is hoped that the piece of legislation drafted by the Law Reform Commission, apparently after extensive consultations with all interested parties throughout the country, will not be jettisoned outright by the new administration but will be revisited with a view to adopting some of the more acceptable draft provisions contained herein.

11.3.9 Post-2007 Moves to Develop a National Land Policy

The Government which came into office in September 2007 has been actively considering various methods to address the several issues surrounding land tenure discussed in this work The present administration seems to be doing so from a development perspective, focusing mainly on restoration of sanity to the land market and on land use control, the facilitation of access to land throughout the country by both citizens and non-citizens, the introduction of measures leading eventually to a system of registration of title so as to eradicate the uncertainties presently surrounding title to land generally and it is to be hoped, the enactment of appropriate provisions that will address the problems caused by the existing dual land tenure system.

This approach is not surprising especially taking into account that, for most former colonies and developing countries generally, the reform or modification of the existing land tenure system to ensure maximum economic use of all land resources is normally a key feature of their development programme. In most African countries, the traditional attitude to land as embodying the spirit of the ancestors and as a sacred heritage which must be preserved for all posterity is being abandoned in favour of policies which facilitate the marketability of land. At the same time the notion that the landowner should be left free to use his land in the way he chooses is now gradually yielding to a new thinking, more progressive and socially orientated, namely that the State should assume greater regulatory control over the use of land for various reasons such as to ensure better planning, proper and adequate economic use and greater productivity for the whole community. This change of attitude has come about because of developments in other fields such as the social, economic and cultural areas of life. In such circumstances, a comprehensive and articulate land policy becomes an essential requirement of any well co-ordinated development programme.

One very important aspect of land administration that any policy document must address is the current absence of any system for a modern, comprehensive and systematic land survey in Sierra Leone. The present facilities for the survey of land are outlined in the Survey Act, Cap.128. The Act provides for surveys to be undertaken both by private licensed surveyors and by officials of the Department of Surveys and Lands of the Ministry of Lands, Country Planning and the Environment. Though there is a registry in the Department of Surveys and Lands where records of all survey plans deposited with the Department are kept, there is no obligation on private landowners to have their land surveyed. Prior to the amendment of section 15 of the Surveys Act, Cap. 128, by Act No. 14 of 1960 there was no obligation to have a survey plan produced by a private licensed surveyor countersigned by the Director of Surveys and Lands or to even deposit copies of plans with the Department of Surveys and Lands. Section 15 of Cap. 128 simply provided that a licensed surveyor who has prepared a plan may submit the same to the Director of Surveys and Lands for countersignature. Even now that the countersignature of the Director is mandatory for the authentication of a survey plan, as long as the Director of Surveys and Lands is satisfied that the technical details of the survey plan are correct and that the land in question is not Sate land he is obliged to countersign the plan and retain a copy for record purposes. It is the practice for officials of the Department of Surveys and Lands to record the details such as the serial or LS number of each plan submitted for countersignature on the master plan or Ordnance Survey map for the area where the land is located.

However, since the Director of Surveys and Lands is not empowered by the Act to reject any plan submitted for countersignature, except on the grounds of technical inaccuracy, it is not unusual for there to be overlapping and encroachment that would not be evident except on a physical inspection of the respective sites. Another weakness of the present system is that no publicity is given to the fact that a survey plan in respect of a particular piece of land has been deposited with the Director of Surveys and Lands for countersignature. Invariably, most private landowners never bother to prepare a survey plan of their land except when they intend to enter into a transaction which would entail the preparation and registration of a deed or some other instrument, such as a mortgage, lease or sale of the land or part thereof. On such occasions, they often find that when they get round to doing so some unauthorized person, frequently unknown to them and laying a false claim to the same land, had already prepared a survey plan thereof and succeeded in obtaining the countersignature of the Director of Surveys and Lands. In fact, this is the way most landowners first learn of any adverse claim to their title. The problem for the landowner is often compounded by the fact that very often he is unable to take any legal action as the competing survey plan has been prepared in the name of a fictitious person in whose name a Statutory Declaration or a Conveyance has been prepared, executed and registered.

As was pointed out in Chapter 6, even the State is not immune from the effect of such fraudulent practices. Instances abound where persons who have been able to have survey plans in respect of State land prepared in their names have even had the audacity to sue the State for a declaration of title in respect of such lands. This is made possible mainly because the Department of Surveys and Lands does not have any accurate records relating to State lands nor is there any reliable means of identifying the same.

11.3.10 Report of the Presidential Task Force to Examine the Reasons for the Delay in the Administration of Justice and Other Related Matters

In October 2007, soon after President Bai Koroma assumed office, he set up a Presidential Task Force under the chairmanship of the Vice-President to examine the reasons for the delays in the justice sector and other related matters. The President was concerned about the inordinate delay in both the criminal and the civil justice system. The Task Force was mandated, inter alia, to ascertain the reasons for the delay in the conduct of cases generally and to examine the possibility of establishing fast track courts to handle commercial and land cases, which constituted the great majority of case in the courts' calendar.

The Task Force examined the possibility of setting up fast track courts to deal with the increasing number of land cases that the regular courts had to handle. It concluded that the establishment of such courts would not necessarily reduce the number of land cases that reached the courts. This was because the present machinery for processing survey plans of State lands and private lands under the Survey Act, Cap. 128 and the inadequacies of the existing system of deeds registration under the Registration of Instruments Act, Cap. 256 tended to facilitate the making of false land title documents leading to the multiplicity of land cases. The Task Force recommended that the ideal solution was the introduction of a system of title registration to replace the present system of registration of deeds.

However, the Task Force recognized that the introduction of a system of land title registration, the enactment of a modern law on registration of title and the establishment of the prerequisite lands adjudication tribunal was a medium- to long-term measure that required important financial, manpower and other resources. It therefore recommended that, as a short-term measure, machinery for the handling of survey plans under Cap. 128 and the procedures for the allocation of State lands should be reviewed by the Ministry of Lands, Country Planning and Environment as a matter of urgency.

11.3.11 The Task Force to Review and Propose Revision to Land Laws

As a follow-up to the findings and recommendations contained in the Report of the Presidential Task Force another Task Force was set up under the auspices of the office of the Attorney-General and Ministry of Justice with the following mandate:

> *"(i) to review existing land statutes and make recommendations for ... amendments thereto, if necessary;*
> *(ii) to review and finalize any draft legislation that is already available and work with relevant authorities to prepare the same for presentation to cabinet and Parliament; and*
> *(iii) to make further recommendations for the origination of any new piece of legislation deemed necessary to support the overall desire to improve access to investment and use of land in Sierra Leone."*

The Task Force is yet to publish a report.

11.3.12 The Investment Climate Facility (ICF) for Africa Land Registration Project

In early 2009, the International Climate Facility, a public-private partnership between governments and business that aims to help African countries create a more attractive business environment, funded a Land Registration Project aimed at establishing the foundation for developing an effective land registration and administration system for the Western Area of Sierra Leone. The project was implemented by a private firm providing the technical expertise working in collaboration with officials of the Ministry of Lands, Country Planning and Environment and other stakeholders.

The terms of reference of the project included the following:

i. A review of the current land use cadastral survey;
ii. Design and installation of a spatial database (LRMAP) to be compatible with a title-based land administration system;
iii. The Central Unit and two satellite stations to be linked by Local Area Networks (LANs);
iv. Establishment of an intranet at each station;
v. Installation and configuration of relevant software and related licences;
vi. Setting up mechanisms for inputting data into the databases at each station;
vii. Design and installation of a simple, easy-to-use computerized system to automate the work flow of procedures in the land registration process;
viii. Design and deployment of an Internet Web Portal for the Land Registration Project;
ix. Creation of a Geographical Information System (GIS)-based land use cadastral survey of the Western Area of Sierra Leone using the latest satellite imagery;
x. Digitization and mapping of existing land records against the background of the cadastre; and
xi. Implementation of the cadastral survey as a system for verification of land availability and current use.

The project was intended to be the precursor to one for the introduction of a land title registration system for which there are already indications that funds could be made available by the World Bank and other related agencies. It is expected that the planned project activity as detailed above will complement any future transition to a title-based registration system through improved data quality and portability. Thus, for the time being the Deeds Registration system will continue to exist but it will be integrated with a new Cadastral Map Index to provide a parcel-based Deeds Registration system. Meanwhile, the office of the Registrar-General is embarking on a rapid computerization of the Deeds Register and Index, including the scanning of complete individual deeds and accompanying survey plans, where these exist, thus creating a property registration database to be linked to the new Cadastral Registration Index Map in the office of the Director of Lands and Survey.

The new Cadastral Map Index System (LRMAP) will be based on a geodatabase linked to a new Geographical Information System (GIS). Eventually, the Cadastral Map Index System could become a vital decision support tool for land use planning and natural resource management as more and more data and mapping are entered into the system. Ultimately, it is hoped, the public should also be able to have access to the system to verify the status of a land transaction.

11.3.13 Extension of the Innovations of the Land Registration Project to the Provinces

Though the above project was limited to the Western Area, it is proposed to replicate its benefits in the Provinces. Indeed, there is a growing urgency for the production of modern survey plans demarcating the precise boundaries of lands held under communal, family or, in recent times, individual ownership in the Provinces. When land was plentiful, in proportion to the population, and was of very little or no commercial value, the need to demarcate boundaries with precision was not so acute. However, the traditional system of relying on natural landmarks to demarcate boundaries cannot give the necessary security and certainty required of a modern title. Most land disputes in the rural areas of the Provinces today, especially inter-chiefdom disputes, arise because of imprecision in the demarcation of existing boundaries. Apart from the expense and futility of boundary disputes they also halt much needed agricultural production because of the traditional practice of "flagging" the area over which there is a dispute.

11.3.14 The 2009 Initiative of the Ministry of Agriculture, Forestry and Food Security

In January 2009, as part of its drive to promote private-sector investment in agriculture in Sierra Leone the Ministry of Agriculture, Forestry and Food Security issued a document[332] pertaining to, inter alia, access to provincial land by potential investors in the agricultural sector. The document correctly states that access to such land could only be by way of a statutory lease for a maximum duration of 50 years with an option for a further period not exceeding 21 years. This is as provided for in the Provinces Land Act, Cap. 122.

The document further states that:

> *"If necessary or required, Government will serve as intermediary between the landowners/host communities and the foreign private investor. For that purpose, the Government will lease the land of interest to the foreign private investor from the land owners and, in turn, sub-lease it to the investor under terms stipulated in [the] document."*

It is submitted that such a policy would infringe the provisions of the Provinces Land Act, Cap 122, because, although the Government can properly acquire unlimited leasehold interest in land in the Provinces, until the Act is amended all grants of an interest in provincial land to a non-native must be made subject to the Act. In contrast, the new formula[333] proposed in the document for the distribution of the rent proceeds from such lease could be applied without more as this matter has never been regulated by law.

11.3.15 Comprehensive Study of Land Policy Issues Commissioned by the Ministry of Lands, Country Planning and the Environment

The latest initiative in the formulation of a national land policy by the Ministry of Lands, Country Planning and Environment was a Land

332 The document is entitled "The Investment Policies and Incentives For Private Sector Promotion in Agriculture in Sierra Leone".

333 The new formula would give 50% to the landowners, 20% to the chiefdom administration, 20% to the district council and 10% to the central government.

Tenure Reform Issues Scoping Study which it commissioned in July 2009 under the aegis of the United Nations Development Programme in Sierra Leone. The objective of the Study was to examine the opportunities and threats to development, poverty eradication and peace which are posed by existing land management practices and land disputes. The Government has given its approval for the Report of this Study to form the basis of a comprehensive national land policy.

Following Government acceptance of the Scoping Report the Ministry of Lands, Country Planning and Environment hosted a meeting in February 2010 to launch the National Land Policy Formulation and Implementation Process. At this meeting the Minister[334] disclosed that the envisioned national land policy should lead to the realization of the Ministry's key aspirations which he outlined as follows:

- *"Retaining the multi-form land tenure system, whilst improving the customary and statutory tenures to become drivers of economic development;*
- *Ensuring that all Sierra Leoneans (including the poor, women, youth) have a reasonable opportunity to gain access to land with secure rights, in order to fulfil their basic needs for housing and productive livelihoods;*
- *Clearly defined property rights supported by an effective judicial and 'governance' system, which ensures that all citizens have access to a fair, equitable and accountable land administration system;*
- *Secure forms of long-term land tenure which enhance agricultural investment so as to ensure livelihood security, reduced food imports, expanded agricultural exports and improved agro-industrial development;*
- *Secure and well regulated land rights for domestic and foreign investments in all sectors to promote inter-sector linkages and increased growth, productivity and employment, while protecting landowners' rights;*
- *Effective land use planning and regulation system which promotes optimal land utilization in all sectors;*
- *Mining concessions which are ecologically sustainable and provide adequate benefits to local populations;*

334 The meeting was hosted in Freetown on 23 February 2010 by Dr Denis M. Sandy, Minister of Lands, Country Planning and the Environment.

- *The effective management of urban lands for the development of sustainable infrastructures (transportation, energy, and communications), housing and other approved developments;*
- *Effective management of land and associated natural resources and ecosystems to realize requisite ecological services and sustainable tourism."*

According to Sam Moyo, one of the consultants who prepared the Scoping Report, the key issues in the formulation process are centred around:

- Access to land for foreign investment;
- Access to land for domestic investment and the poor;
- Sustainable land use;
- Land conflicts and disputes management; and
- Social and equity issues in land access and use.

It is envisaged that the process of formulation of the National Land Policy will involve four phases. The first phase will be devoted to analysis and approval of the Scoping Report prepared by the consultants. Thereafter, three structures, a Steering Committee, a number of Technical Working Groups and a Coordination Unit are to be established.

The second phase will involve research, consultation and policy decision-making during which the issues highlighted above will be reviewed, consultations will be held with all stakeholders and the reform proposals will be drafted by the Steering Committee for eventual approval by the Government.

The third phase will cover revision and enactment of relevant legislation, reform of the adjudication facilities and the upgrading of the administration and technical framework of the Ministry.

It is envisaged that the entire process of formulation of the National Land Policy will be under the guidance of the Steering Committee which will be responsible for:

1. Direction and co-ordination of the National Land Policy formulation process;
2. Organization of public consultations and communication;
3. Drafting of the National Land Policy;

4. Collation and analysis of public reaction;
5. Commissioning and review of studies and technical reports;
6. Preparation for cabinet approval; and
7. Monitoring and evaluation process.

11.4 CONCLUSIONS

The above account discloses that this is the first attempt at a systematic process of formulating a national land policy. Apart from the process which was started by the Government in 2002 and which resulted in the formulation of the draft National Land Policy in 2005, virtually all the other initiatives have been donor driven. The common feature of these initiatives is that they have all tended to focus on short-term solutions to land tenure problems relevant to investment in private-sector activities in specific sectors such as agriculture, tourism, mining, housing and urban development. While it is true that the formulation of a comprehensive national land policy is a prerequisite for sustainable national economic development, because land is such a sensitive political issue, the process of land policy formulation, as well as its implementation, should not only be development oriented , but also be inclusive and consultative. The need for inputs from all stakeholders, including those at the grassroots, particularly the poor and landless members of society, such as rural women for whom access to land is such an important and strategic factor in the struggle for economic emancipation and sustainable human development, cannot be over-emphasized.

CHAPTER 12
CRITIQUE AND PROPOSALS FOR REFORM

12.1 INTRODUCTION

This work has highlighted various aspects of the substantive land law, and discussed problems relating to the dualism of tenure, and the system of land administration, which are in urgent need of review and reform. This concluding chapter focuses on one particular aspect of the problems highlighted earlier in this work, that relating to uncertainties surrounding the ownership, acquisition and transfer of title to land in Sierra Leone.

Therefore, the ensuing critique is undertaken from the perspective of the private landowner and other entities who may want to enter into a land transaction of one type or another. From this perspective, there follows an examination and assessment of the adequacy and effectiveness of the facilities available for assuring titles to land. This critique is followed by some proposals for the reform of the existing system

In the second part of this chapter there is a review of the existing system of land administration and an evaluation of the role of the State in ensuring that the system is made to serve the requirements not only of individual landowners but of the community as a whole.

12.2 CRITIQUE OF THE PRESENT FACILITIES FOR ASSURING TITLES TO LAND

12.2.1 Introduction

Probably one of the most fundamental requirements of the average private landowner, under any system of land administration, is the need for some effective machinery for assuring the title to his land. This is needed to protect his rights of ownership against wrongful claimants, as well as to facilitate whatever transactions he might desire to enter into with respect to such rights. The same applies to persons dealing with the landowner, such as potential purchasers, lessees or mortgagees, whether local or foreign investors, or banks and other financial institutions to whom the land may be offered as security for any transaction. Such persons need to be assured, by some independent means, that whatever interest they are acquiring from the landowner will vest in them free of any unexpected competing claims.

It has been suggested that the ideal solution would seem to be a machinery which provides

> *"an authoritative record, kept in a public office, of the rights to clearly defined units of land as vested for the time being in some particular person or body, and of the limitations, if any, to which these rights are subject"*[335]

This implies a system of registration of title. In Sierra Leone at present, the only facilities available for achieving the above objectives are the Deeds Registry and the law governing the registration of instruments in general.

12.2.2 The System of Registration of Deeds

The present Deeds Registry is set up under the General Registration Act, Cap. 255, which established a General Registry for the whole country. The Act also provides for the appointment of a Registrar-General and for other procedural matters relating to the production of registered documents in court proceedings In short, the Act is mainly concerned with establishing and regulating the office of the Registrar-General. However, the Act is intended to be read together with the Registration of Instruments Act, Cap. 256, which effectively provides for the registration of instruments generally, and of those affecting land in particular, as well as stipulating the legal consequence of non-registration of certain documents.

12.2.3 The Operation of the Registration of Instruments Act, Cap. 256

The main provisions relating to the registration of instruments affecting land are contained in sections 4, 5 and 6 of the Registration of Instruments Act, Cap. 256. As will be argued below, this system affords very little protection to landowners or persons dealing with interests in land, partly because of the inherent limitations of any such system of registration of

335 Simpson, *Land Law and Registration*, pp. 15–16.

deeds and partly because of the peculiar inadequacies of the Sierra Leone legislation as revealed by an examination of the relevant provisions.

Section 4, which is the most important as far as the registration of instruments affecting land is concerned, provides as follows:

> *4(1) "Every deed, contract conveyance ... so far as regards any land to be thereby affected, shall take effect, as against other deeds affecting the same land, from the date of its registration ... Provided that every such instrument shall take effect from the date of its execution if registered within any of the periods limited for registration as follows ... [the specified periods depend on the place of execution, that is 10 days if executed in Freetown, 60 days if executed elsewhere in the country and one year if executed abroad.]".*

> *4(2)(a) "Every deed, contract, or conveyance executed after the 1st of June 1964, shall be void, so far as regards any land to be thereby affected, unless it is registered within the appropriate period limited for such registration under the provision of subsection(1)".*

There then follows a proviso to section 4(2)(a) to the effect that any person aggrieved by the avoidance of any transaction under the provision of the subsection may apply to a judge of the High Court for permission to register the document out of time. Such permission will be granted if the judge is satisfied that the failure to register was not due to the applicant's fault, or if all the circumstances of the case are excusable. Thereafter, the transaction in question:

> *"shall be deemed never to have been avoided and shall take effect as against other transactions affecting the same land from such date as shall be just".*

Invariably, the judges have failed to exercise the discretion thus granted to them to fix a just date for the transaction to take effect by simply ordering that it be deemed to take effect from the date of execution.

Section 5 of Cap. 256 prescribes the date that wills executed after 1837 are to take effect, so far as regards any lands to be thereby affected. As against any other documents affecting the same land, such a will takes effect at the date of registration. However, this is made subject to a proviso that such will:

> *"Shall take effect from the death of the testator if registered within any of the periods limited for registration, as follows, that is to say—*
>
> *a) of any person dying in the Western Area or the Provinces within two months next after the death of the testator;*
> *b) of any person dying elsewhere ... if registered within eighteen months next after the death of the testator."*

Finally, according to section 6, where a memorial of judgment affecting land is registered under the Act such judgment shall take effect as against other instruments affecting the same land from the date of their registration. These, in essence, are all the statutory provisions relating to the registration of instruments affecting land and the consequences of non-registration.

12.2.4 The Period of Grace Provision

The initial observation relating to these provisions is that there is a so-called period of grace provision. According to this provision, if a deed, contract or conveyance is duly registered within the specified periods, then it is to take effect as against other instruments affecting the same land from the date of its execution or, in the case of a will, from the death of the testator; otherwise it takes effect as against other instruments from the date of registration.

The period of grace provision is not objectionable per se, and is to be found in statutes of some other countries providing for the registration of instruments.[336] What may be criticized in this particular version of the period of grace provision is that, on registration during the period of grace, the document still takes effect from the date of execution. It is submitted

336 See, for example, section 24, Ghana Land Registry Act, 1962.

that such a provision opens the door to fraud. This could be illustrated by the following hypothetical cases:

A can convey his interest in land by deed to **B**, he can then connive with **B** to cheat **C**, a subsequent buyer of the same land from **A**, by causing **B** to delay registration until just before the expiry of the period of grace. Meanwhile, a search of the Register by **C** would not reveal anything about the earlier deed which, though registered subsequent to **C**'s deed, is in effect in priority to **C**'s deed because of the period of grace provision.

A second example of a fraudulent dealing that could be facilitated by the period of grace provision is where **A** conveys an interest in land to **C**, then **A** connives with **B** to cheat **C** by giving **B** a deed with an earlier date of execution than that of the deed he had given to **C**. In either case provided **B** registers his document within the prescribed period, including the grace period, the Act gives priority to **B**'s document over that of **C**.

Such a loophole in the legislation could have been avoided by the inclusion of a provision that

> *"every registrable document shall take effect, as against other instruments affecting the same land from the date of its registration, and not from the date of its execution".*

The same objective can also be attained by a provision to the effect that every registrable instrument shall be of no effect until it is registered.[337]

Another pertinent observation is that the impact of the 1964 amendment to the Act, which renders all deeds, contracts and conveyances void unless registered within the specified period limited for registration under the Act, is substantially reduced by the effect of the proviso to Section 4(2)(a) referred to above, which gives such a wide discretion to the courts to permit registration out of time and thus make a void transaction valid.

12.2.5 The Effect of the Proviso to Section 4(2) of Cap. 256

A blatant example of the arbitrary exercise of this wide discretion granted to the courts by the proviso to section 4(2) of Cap. 256 is to be found in the decision of the Supreme Court in the case of *Grace Johnson v. Yvonne Nicol and Yvette Davies.*[338] The appellant had applied to register, out of

337 Cf section 24(1) Ghana Land Registry Act, 1962.

338 Sup. Ct. Civ. App 1/80 judgment delivered by the Supreme Court on 16 December

time, a conveyance which had been executed six years before the date of the application. The trial judge had found, as a fact, that the failure to register was due to the negligence of the applicant and that, in all the circumstances of the case, it was inexcusable. The reason the applicant, who happened to be a solicitor, had given in his affidavit for the failure to register was that the document had been mislaid by his secretary. The trial judge in the circumstances exercised his discretion against permitting the registration out of time and dismissed the application.

When the matter came before the Court of Appeal the majority held that the trial judge had exercised his discretion under a mistake of law, misapprehension of facts as well as on irrelevant matters and, even though the Court agreed with the trial judge's finding of fact that the failure to register was due to the applicant's fault, the Court proceeded to set aside the judge's order and then exercised its discretion in favour of the applicant.

At the Supreme Court, the majority (Livesey Luke, C.J. dissenting) also upheld the findings of fact of the trial judge but held that the failure to register was excusable, even though, according to Tejan, J.S.C, "*one can say that the applicant was inadvertent or careless. One can even go so far as to say that he was negligent*". Notwithstanding such comment, the Court held that in the light of the applicant's "*misapprehension*[s] *of law and facts*" which in their opinion "*are excusable reasons*", the failure to register was excusable and the application was allowed for the conveyance to be registered so as to take effect from the date of execution as opposed to the date of registration. It is submitted that the Supreme Court unfortunately failed to consider the provision of the statute to the effect that where permission is granted to register out of time then the instrument shall take effect as against other instruments affecting the land "*from such date as shall be just*" (emphasis added).

Thus, for a person wishing to enter into a land transaction in Sierra Leone a search of the Deeds Registry is of little assistance in discovering the existence of any instruments affecting the same land. At the date of the search there may be in existence instruments affecting the same land duly executed but not yet registered. Such instruments may still gain priority over instruments executed and registered after the search, provided that the instruments which were executed earlier are registered before the end of the grace period. Moreover, even where the document has been invalidated for non-registration it might still gain priority over documents

1981, unreported.

registered earlier if, as in the case of *Johnson v. Nicol*,[339] a judge exercises his discretion under the proviso to section 4(2)(a) of Cap. 256 not only to permit registration out of time, but also to order that the document should take effect from the date of its execution, as against other documents affecting the same land.

12.2.6 Disadvantages of the System of Registration of Deeds

What then is the extent of protection both to owners and to purchasers of interests in land conferred by the system of registration of instruments described above? In the first place, it is necessary to reiterate the limited purpose of the system of registration of instruments as far as land is concerned. It is intended merely to provide a public record of land transactions carried out by means of written documents and to deal with priorities among competing documents affecting the same land. It is not concerned with title, nor does it purport to verify the validity or authenticity of any document relating to land. Thus, for the owner of an interest in land, the fact that his title is evidenced in a registered document does not guarantee the validity of that title, nor does it give him a better title to the land than a competing claimant whose title to the same land may be evidenced in a document that was registered subsequently, or was not registered at all, or whose title may not even be evidenced in writing.

Moreover, prior to 1964 when the proviso to section 4 of the Registration of Instruments Act, Cap. 256 was enacted, failure to register any deeds, contracts and conveyances affecting land did not render such documents void as regards other documents affecting the same land. As a result, there may well be a good number of pre-1964 documents which remain unregistered but which may well contain incontrovertible evidence of title to the land affected. Besides, as pointed out by Livesey-Luke, C.J. in Seymour *Wilson v. Musa Abess*:[340]

> *"it is a matter of common knowledge that most lands in the Western Area are based on possessory title and most of them are not covered by title deeds".*

339 Above.
340 Above.

In fact, it is more appropriate to say that most lands in the country as a whole are not covered by title deeds. As between two persons laying claim to the same land, but who do not derive title from the same source, the existence of a prior registered deed affecting the land is not per se conclusive evidence of a better title to the land. The construction put on section 4 of the Registration of Instruments Act, Cap. 256 by the Court of Appeal in *Davies v. Bickersteth*[341] which tended to suggest the contrary to the above proposition was, with respect, clearly erroneous. In the *Bickersteth* case, the appellant relied on a conveyance registered in 1944, and the respondent on a conveyance registered in 1945. Bankole Jones, P., purporting to apply the provisions of section 4(1) of the Act, concluded, merely on the basis of the fact that the appellant relied on a prior registered deed, that "*of the two ... it would appear that the appellant had a better title*", and therefore found for the appellant. Commenting on the Court of Appeal's interpretation of the subsection Livesey-Luke, C.J. had this to say:

> *"If the construction put upon Section 4 by the Court of Appeal in Davies v. Bickersteth is upheld, it would mean that any person [who took] a conveyance of a piece of land after 1964 from a person having no title to the land and duly registered the conveyance would automatically have title to the land as against the true owner holding an unregistered pre-1964 conveyance".*[342]

However, the fact still remains that a landowner in Sierra Leone, whether his title is evidenced in a registered or unregistered document, presently has very little or no protection against fraudulent claims, especially if the land is undeveloped and unoccupied.

Indeed, one can even go so far as to say that, to a certain extent, the present system of registration of instruments does in fact facilitate fraudulent claims to land. This is due to the current practice whereby a persons wishing to lay claim to any piece of land can do so by simply preparing a statutory declaration purporting to establish his possessory title to the land in question and then presenting the same for registration under the provisions of the Registration of Instruments Act, Cap. 256. Despite the doubt expressed by the judge in *Bright v. Roberts*[343] that such

341 (1964–66) ALR S.L. 403.

342 *Seymour Wilson v. Musa Abess*, above.

343 (1964–66) ALR S.L. 156.

documents may not be registrable under the Act, they are routinely being accepted for registration. The argument of Registrars over the years has been that the Act confers only limited power on the Registrar to reject documents presented for registration under the Act.

It has always been contended that it is only in one of the following circumstances that registration could be denied by the Registrar:

i. where the document is defective in form;
ii. where the document is not accompanied by a requisite survey plan;
iii. where the document is not duly stamped in accordance with the provisions of the Stamp Duty Act, Cap. 274; or
iv. where the time for registration has expired.

Even where the Registrar is convinced, on the basis of available evidence, that the document sought to be registered creates an interest inconsistent with that held by a rival claimant as contained in an instrument previously registered and affecting the same land, if the document is not otherwise legally defective, the Registrar may not refuse the registration. The effect is that there are often two or more registered documents purporting to vest title to the same piece of land in completely different persons without the rival claimants being aware of the other competing claims. As a result, all too often the same piece of land is sold by different "owners" to unsuspecting purchasers, who, in their eagerness to buy are prepared to accept any registered document as proof of title. Indeed, it is only when the rival claimants seek to exercise acts of ownership over the land in question that they may become aware of the competing claim.

Thus, for the purchaser of land in Sierra Leone today, the present system of registration of instruments affords only a limited measure of protection. The system fails to assist the purchaser in what is probably his most important task, that is, finding some independent means of assuring himself that he has obtained a good title from the vendor, and that he has not, as is invariably the case in Sierra Leone today, purchased a lawsuit. In most cases, a purchaser ends up with, not even an encumbered title, but no title at all. This is because the vendor simply had no title to the land in question despite being armed, at the time of the sale, with some registered document or other, such as a statutory declaration purporting to vest title to the land in question in him. The gravity of the present situation may be judged from the fact that nine out of every ten land cases currently before the High Court in Sierra Leone involve claims and counter-claims for a declaration of title – with the opposing parties invariably being purchasers who had acquired the land in dispute from two different vendors. Because of the prevailing uncertainty of title to land generally, and in the absence of any other channels for asserting and authenticating claims of ownership, landowners as well as purchasers are obliged to have recourse to a multiplicity of legal actions in an attempt to protect or prove their rights of ownership.

Since it is obvious that the present machinery for the registration of instruments cannot provide the requisite facilities for assuring titles to land this work will now make proposals for the reform of the existing registration system.

12.3 PROPOSALS FOR REFORM

12.3.1 Introduction

Reform of the land law in any country is inevitably a vast and complex exercise, involving not only the law, but other related areas of society, such as the social, economic, cultural and political spheres. The subject increases in complexity when the existing land law is a compound of two fundamentally different systems of law, such as English law and customary law. Much also depends on the objective of the proposed reform. In view of the vastness and complexity of the subject in the case of Sierra Leone, it is impossible for the subject to be treated in very much detail in a work of this nature. These proposals are therefore confined to only two out of the many possible objectives of any proposed reform of the land tenure system in Sierra Leone today. Those objectives that have been selected involve the resolution of the problems arising, firstly, from the uncertainty of title, both under English tenure in the Western Area and under customary tenure in the Provinces, mainly due to the inadequacy of the present system of registration of deeds; and, secondly, from the duality of the land tenure system itself.

12.3.2 Proposals for Eradicating Uncertainty of Title to Land

The need for reform in this area of the land law can be best expressed by adapting the following passage from the report of a United Nations

Housing Mission to Gold Coast (now Ghana), published in 1954, to describe the present situation in Sierra Leone:

> *"It has long been acknowledged that a serious need exists for clearing titles to land in certain areas of [Sierra Leone] and for instituting a system of land registration. These reforms are essential to record the rights of the people to their land, to secure those who have purchased property against eviction and to assure people who build their homes that they can do so without fear and uncertainty. It has been iterated and reiterated that, only when a sound system for buying and selling a property exists, will the fundamental wealth represented by the country's land be brought into use for the benefit of the people.*
>
> *All too often though no one may be disputing ownership to land, the reputed owner is unable to establish his ownership, cannot borrow money with which to develop his land, nor sell it to those able to develop it. A legal mechanism able to define and record his interest is needed to enable him to bring his land to use."*[344]

Indeed, at various stages of this work, the problems created by uncertainty of title to land in both the Western Area under English tenure and the Provinces under customary tenure have been highlighted. The inadequacies of the existing system for the registration of instruments as a means for assuring titles have already been highlighted.[345] There seems to be a consensus among the wide cross-section of jurists who have considered this problem that registration of title is one of the best methods of achieving certainty of title. The basic objective of registration of title is to make title to land certain and simple to prove and easy, cheap and quick to convey. It essentially involves the ascertainment of existing rights in land by a process of adjudication followed by the use of facilities for their recording in an official register which will thereafter become the unimpeachable source of title.

344 See Simpson, *Report on the Registration of Title to Land in Lagos* (Lagos, Nigeria, 1957), para. 20.

345 See, for example, Allott, *The Future of Law in Africa. Record of Proceedings of the London Conference, 28th_December 1959–8th January 1960*, pp. 42–3.

Though there is a great deal of support for the view that title registration is the ultimate solution to the problem of uncertainty of title, there is no uniformity of view as to the various approaches and patterns for the ascertainment of title on first registration and the operation of the scheme thereafter.

The problem is rendered even more complex if the new system is required to cater for registration of titles under two different systems of law. However, registration of title could also be used as a means of reforming the land law by, for example, incorporating in the registration statute some measure of substantive law aimed at uniting the two systems of law governing land tenure in Sierra Leone.

The registration statute to be enacted should therefore combine rules drawn from both customary law and the general law regulating the interests or rights which are to be recognized and the mode of transfer of such interests or rights. Under such a system customary law interests could, as far as possible, be assimilated or equated to their English law counterparts. This could be done without necessarily using English law terminology or expressions such as "fee simple" or "freehold". The register could also provide for the recording of group as well as individual ownership. In the case of a family or a community, the names of those authorized to act on behalf of the group could also be entered on the register. Rights of individual members in family or communal lands could be recorded in a separate register as encumbrances on the ownership of the family or community.

An alternative and more radical approach would be to devise a completely new system of tenure expressed in terms neither of the received English law nor of customary law, but defining in the registration law new forms of ownership and dealings in land. An extreme example of this would be the introduction of the "rights of occupancy" system which is in force in Nigeria and Tanzania. Under such a system, private ownership of land would be abolished and the State would have and exercise the most important incident of ownership, namely the power to control alienation of interests in land, as it is a cardinal principle of the system that no holder of a right or occupancy can alienate without the consent of the State. Whilst it is admitted that such a system can and does contribute towards a simplification of the law, the system cannot, however, do away completely with the complexities of the land law nor can it abolish the present dualism altogether.

In both Northern Nigeria and Tanzania customary law has continued to govern land tenure among the indigenous citizens, subject to the provisions of the statute. The natives of these countries continue to hold their lands under their respective customary laws, and their rights are designated "customary rights of occupancy" in Northern Nigeria and "deemed rights of occupancy" in Tanzania. The main objection to this system is that, no matter how desirable its objectives might be, there would hardly be a sufficient justification for the abolition of private ownership of land, and so bold a departure from the customs and forms at present known to society would not be easily understood by the vast majority of the traditional communities and consequently would not be easy to implement.

Without necessarily adopting such an extreme approach the process of registration of titles could be used as an instrument of government policy in such matters as consolidation, redistribution and control of the use of agricultural land. This was the approach adopted by Kenya,

> *"when in the 1950s the decision was taken, as a matter of government policy, to convert customary tenure to full individual ownership in order to promote the agricultural development which the uncertainty of customary tenure inhibited".*[346]

Though strictly speaking registration of title is a device to give certainty to the ownership of land to enable dealings to be conducted quickly and cheaply, it could also serve as means of effecting changes in the substantive land law and the system of land tenure as a whole.

No matter what approach is adopted or whatever other purpose the process of registration of title may be made to serve there is no doubt of its obvious advantages.

Downson and Sheppard[347] list nine benefits which registration of title confers "*when competently established and efficiently operated*".

Some of the most important benefits are that an inspection of the register shows, at all times, the legal situation of the land; all dealings in land can be effected with security, expedition and cheapness; litigation over land is greatly reduced, and most significantly from the point of view of the Government:

346 Simpson, *Land Law and Registration*, p. 200.

347 Sir Ernest Downson and V.L.O. Sheppard, *Land Registration*, 2nd edn, p. 72.

> *"The administration of every public service and every branch of national activity connected with land is greatly assisted in the execution of its work by the existence of up-to-date and unimpeachable maps and records of landed property throughout the country."*[348]

It must be conceded however that in a developing country like Sierra Leone there are also several factors that tend to militate against the introduction of a system of registration of title, the principal ones being the ignorance, apathy and apprehension of landowners as well as the cost, manpower and other technical difficulties involved in the initial compilation and subsequent maintenance of the register. However, as Simpson has argued,

> *"the question is not whether registration of title can be afforded, but whether any country which recognizes private ownership and allows dealing in land can afford to do without it".*[349]

Indeed in Sierra Leone today, with the present trend towards the increasing commercialization of land throughout the country and the absence of security of titles under the present system, it is difficult to argue against the introduction of a system of registration of title, at whatever cost.

12.3.3 Proposals for Addressing the Problems of Dualism

As discussed earlier in this work, the basic problems arising from the duality of the system of land tenure are the products of the co-existence of two different bodies of law, the general law and the customary law, and the interaction of the two systems of land tenure, English tenure and customary tenure. The problems arising from the co-existence and coincidence of the two systems of laws involve choice of courts and/or choice of law, while those arising from the interaction of the two systems of tenure involve determination of the question of whether there has been

348 Ibid.

349 Simpson, op.cit., p. 174.

conversion of the original form of tenure. There are two possible ways that these problems could be tackled in any scheme for a reform of the system, namely, either by providing more adequate rules for the resolution of the conflictual problems, or by eliminating the cause of the problems itself, that is, by the integration of the two land tenure systems into a single uniform system.

12.3.4 The Advantages of Integration

In making the following proposals for the reform of the dual system, preference is given in this work to an integration of the two systems, as opposed to retaining the dual system with improved facilities for the resolution of conflictual problems. The main reason for this choice is that, irrespective of the provisions made by statute for defining and delimiting the respective areas of operation of the two systems, a certain amount of uncertainty and complexity is inevitable in any pluralistic legal system. Indeed, it could even be said that the existence within the same country of two systems of law of differing origin, nature and temperament is undesirable in itself.

The main advantage of unification of the legal system is that it not only eliminates the choice of law problems and the inevitable uncertainties and complexities of dualism, but it should provide an opportunity to create a single national land law, compounded of rules drawn from the two existing systems, but shorn of the objectionable features in each system, such as the undue technicalities of the rules of the received English land law on the one hand and the uncertainties of the rules of customary law on the other. Thus, for example, the English land law doctrines of tenures and estates, in particular the concept of the fee simple, should have no place under an integrated law. On the other hand, absolute ownership or the concept of freehold as received in Sierra Leone is an established fact in the country as a whole, under both English-type tenure and customary tenure, and this form of ownership could be recognized without any equivocation. The incidents of such ownership could also be clearly spelt out under the integrated law. At the same time all lesser interests permitted to exist in land under the new law could be defined simply and without ambiguity.

Apart from providing an opportunity for reforming the law by redefining clearly the nature of rights and interests which could exist in land, integration would also eliminate the uncertainties created by the multiplicity of forms available for the acquisition and transmission of interests in land under the two systems. In this regard, there is a clear need for harmonization of the law relating to the use of writing in the disposition of interests in land. A provision in the integrated system which makes it compulsory to use written documents in all land transactions would result in greater security of title, by providing evidence of title, which is more reliable and permanent than oral tradition or equivocal acts of ownership, and making it possible for all such transactions to be officially recorded in a public register. Sufficient safeguards against fraud on illiterate parties to such dealing already exist under the Illiterates Protection Act, Cap. 104.

12.3.5 Disadvantages of Integration

A word should also be said about some of the disadvantages of a policy of unification of the existing laws under the two systems. In as much as integration would be achieved by legislation, this would inevitably involve the codification of relevant rules of customary law. The new system would, to that extent, be deprived of the benefit of flexibility which is one of the main characteristics of customary law. In as much as customary law is a "mirror of accepted usage", its rules must continually change with changes in the social practices or usages of the people. Legislation, even when kept under constant review, does not always reflect current practices or usages. Therefore, even after the programme of reform is completed there will always remain the need to keep the law under constant review.

12.4 CONCLUSION

By way of conclusion, one can only reiterate the various proposals for reform suggested throughout this work and more particularly those highlighted in this chapter. The need for urgent statutory reforms to remove the restrictions currently imposed by the Provinces Land Act, Cap. 122, and the Non-Citizens (Interest in Land) Act, No. 30 of 1966 on access to land needed for development purposes by non-native and foreign investors cannot be over-emphasized. If land is to contribute in a meaningful way to the economic development of the country, Government must take immediate action to introduce legislation and other measures with a view to minimizing, if not eradicating, some of the economic and social problems caused, or aggravated, by the inadequacies and anomalies of the present system of land use control. The need for reform is therefore undisputed, but the form which such reform should take could be the subject of much controversy. This is because of the inherent political, socio-economic and cultural implications of any programme of land law reform in a country with a dual land tenure system. However, as proposed above in this work, there is a third option, that of adopting a middle course, retaining a modified form of the two distinct systems of tenure, making each conform to the requirements of the new regime of land use and administration.

To give a brief example, the English land law concept of the fee simple presently utilized for the outright grant of a freehold interest in land should have no place under an integrated system of law. On the other hand, as the concept of absolute ownership is generally recognized throughout the country, both under the general law and customary law, this form of ownership, whether by the community, family or individuals, should be given statutory recognition under the integrated system of land law.

All interests subordinate to absolute ownership such as customary tenancies and statutory leases of provincial land should be clearly defined to render certain their incidents and legal import. A person entering into a land transaction in any part of the country should no longer have to wrestle with the distinction between a mortgage on the one hand and a customary pledge on the other or between a communal tenure and family tenure.

Integration would also provide an opportunity to eliminate the uncertainties arising from the differing modes of acquiring title and interest in land under the two systems. A provision in the integrated system which makes it compulsory to use writing in all land transactions would result in less ambiguity and greater security of tenure, by providing evidence of title which is more reliable and permanent than the oral transactions or equivocal acts of ownership so common under customary law. It would also make it possible for all land transactions to be officially recorded in appropriate public registers. Sufficient safeguards against fraud on illiterate parties to such land transactions already exist under the Illiterates Protection Act, Cap. 104.

The making and keeping of records of all land transactions is one of the ingredients of a system of land registration or registration of title to land. Land registration must be introduced in Sierra Leone as a matter of urgency if we are to reduce the interminable land disputes and eradicate the new phenomenon of land grabbing. Land registration has both a public and a private function. From the point of view of the State it could serve as the basis of an inventory of our national land resources for fiscal and developmental purposes. From the perspective of the owner or occupier of land it enables him to conduct his land transactions safely, cheaply and quickly.

Registration of title could also be used as a means of reforming the land law by, for example, incorporating some measure of substantive law to unite the two systems of law governing land tenure in Sierra Leone. This approach would involve combining rules drawn from both customary law and the general law, and would simplify the system and facilitate land use administration and management. Under such a system customary law interests could, as far as possible, be assimilated or equated to their general law counterparts.

An alternative and even more radical approach would be to devise a completely new system of land tenure expressed in terms neither of the received English Law nor of customary law, but defining in the new registration law new forms of ownership and dealings in land.

Another area in which there is a marked absence of any positive State policy is that of regulation of land use for agricultural and other purposes. So far, in the Provinces, this has been left largely in the hands of the traditional institutions such as the paramount chief and his chiefdom councillors in areas of communal tenure and the head of family in areas of family tenure. In particular the customary practice of allocating land to members of the community or family for agricultural purposes has tended to perpetuate the practice of subsistence farming rather than promote large-scale farming.

On the other hand there is still considerable uncertainty and even difficulty experienced by persons not entitled as of right under customary law to land in the Provinces (whether you call them non-natives, strangers or otherwise) in gaining access to agricultural land. This issue must be addressed urgently by legislation or otherwise.

APPENDICES

Appendix 1

The Imperial Statutes (Law of Property) Adoption Act, Cap. 18

SCHEDULE

Date of Statute and Title.		Extent to which applied.
44 and 45 Vict. c. 41 22nd August, 1881.	The Conveyancing and Law of Property Act, 1881.	The whole Statute except sections 3(2), 6(3), 30, 45, 48, 65, 72 and 73.
45 and 46 Vict. c. 38 10th August, 1882.	The Settled Land Act, 1882.	The whole Statute except sections 3(ii), 4(7), 6(ii), 9, 10, 11, 14, 15, 16, 17, 20(3), 21(iii), (v) and (viii), 25, 26, 27, 28, 29, 30, 31(v), 32, 46(7), (8), and (10), 48, 49, 58(viii), 61 and 65.
45 and 46 Vict. c. 39 10th August, 1882.	The Conveyancing Act, 1882.	The whole Statute except sections 2, 7 and 11.
47 and 48 Vict. c. 8 3rd July, 1884.	The Settled Land Act, 1884.	The whole Statute except sections 7(v) and (vi) and 8.
51 and 52 Vict. c. 59 24th December, 1888.	The Trustee Act, 1888.	The whole Statute.
52 and 53 Vict. c. 36 12th August, 1889.	The Settled Land Act, 1889.	The whole Statute.
53 and 56 Vict. c. 19 25th July, 1890.	The Trustees Appointment Act, 1890	The whole Statute.
53 and 54 Vict. c. 69 18th August, 1890	The Settled Land Act, 1890.	The whole Statute except sections 8, 10, 13, 15, 17, 18 and 19.

55 and 56 Vict. c. 13 20th June, 1892.	The Conveyancing and Law of Property Act, 1892.	The whole Statute.
56 and 57 Vict. c. 21 29th June, 1893.	The Voluntary Conveyances Act, 1893.	The whole Statute.
56 and 57 Vict. c. 53 22nd September, 1893.	The Trustee Act, 1893	The whole Statute except sections 6, 16, 34, 41, 44, 46 and 52.
57 and 58 Vict. c. 10 18th June, 1894.	The Trustee Act, 1893, Amendment Act, 1894.	The whole Statute except section 2.
59 and 60 Vict. c. 35 14th August, 1896	The Judicial Trustees Act, 1896.	The whole Statute.
1 and 2 Geo. V. c. 37 16th December, 1911.	The Conveyancing Act, 1911.	The whole Statute except sections 4(ii)(b) and 13.

Appendix 2
THE STATE LANDS ACT 1960

NO. 19 of 1960

ARRANGEMENT OF SECTIONS

PART 1 – PRELIMINARY

Section No.

PART II – GRANTS

PART III – REMEDIES OF STATE

PART IV – PENALTIES

PART V – MISCELLANEOUS

Appendix 2

An Act to make Further and Better Provision for the Management and Disposal of State Lands

19 of 1960
37 of 1961
18 of 1963

Date of Commencement [5th January, 1961]

Be it ENACTED by the Legislature of Sierra Leone, as follows:-

PART I–PRELIMINARY

Short title and application

1. This Act may be cited as the State Lands Act 1960 and shall apply to the Western Area only.

Interpretation

2. In this Act, unless the context otherwise requires –

"agricultural lease" means a lease for the purposes of agriculture, or for the raising and breeding of cattle, or for the growing and cultivation of any economic product or crop, or for a timber forest;

"building lease" means a lease for building purposes or for purposes connected therewith;

Cap. 193

"State lands" means all lands which belong to the State by virtue of any treaty, cession, convention or agreement, and all lands which have been or may hereafter be acquired by or on behalf of the State, for any public purpose or otherwise howsoever and land acquired under the provisions of the Public Lands Act and includes all shores, beaches, lagoons, creeks, rivers, estuaries and other places and waters whatsoever belonging to, acquired by, or which may be lawfully disposed of by or on behalf of the State;

"Director of Surveys and Lands" includes the Assistant Director of Surveys and Lands;

"grant" means-

(a) Any grant for an estate in fee simple;
(b) Any lease;
(c) Any licence or other document authorising the grantee, his heirs and assigns or any of them to hold and occupy any State lands;
(d) Any licence or other document conferring any right to cut, gather, take and carry away timber, fibre or other natural product within any State lands therein specified;
(e) Any licence or other document conferring any right to search for work and carry away any minerals, gravel or other materials within any State lands therein specified;
(f) Any licence or other document conferring any right to make use of any beach, bank, foreshore or ground adjoining the shore or bank of any sea, creek or river;
(g) Generally, any grant, licence or right whatsoever relating to any State lands which may lawfully be made, given, granted, assigned or otherwise disposed of by or on behalf of the State;

"lease" means the grant of the possession of land by or on behalf of the State as lessor for a term of years or other fixed period with a reservation of rent;

No 8 of 1958, Cap. 144

"mineral oil" has the same meaning as in the Mining (Mineral Oil) Act, 1958;

"minerals" has the same meaning as in the Minerals Act;

"Minister" means the Minister for the time being charged with the responsibility for lands;

"public purposes" means and includes-

(a) For exclusive government use or for general public use;
(b) For or in connection with sanitary improvements of any kind, including reclamations;
(c) For or in connection with the laying out of any new Government station or the extension or improvement of any existing Government station
(d) For obtaining control over land contiguous to any port or airport;
(e) For obtaining control over land required for defence purposes;
(f) For obtaining control over land required for civil aviation purposes; and
(g) For obtaining control over land the value of which will be enhanced by the construction of any railway, road, or other public work or convenience about to be undertaken or provided by the Government.

PART II–GRANTS

Sale of State lands restricted

3. …

Who may make grants

4. The Minister may make grants of State Lands in such manner and subject to such conditions as may be required and as they may deem proper.

5. Every grant shall be executed by the Minister or a public officer authorised by him in that behalf.

Validity of grants

6. Every grant of any State Lands executed in accordance with the provisions of section 5 of this Act shall be deemed to be valid and effectual for the purpose of conferring and assuring any right, proprietary or possessory or as the case may be, thereby expresses or intended to be conferred.

Reservations

7. (1) A grant under this Act shall not, unless express provision to the contrary is contained therein, confer any right to-

The water of any spring, river, lake or stream other than such water as may be required for domestic purposes upon the land which is the subject of the grant;

(a) The foreshore or to the banks of any navigable waterway; or
(b) Any mineral or to any mineral oil.

(2) There is hereby reserved to the State the right to enter upon any land which is the subject of any grant under this Act, and-

(a) To search for, mine and remove any mineral or mineral oil; and
(b) Except in the case of land leased for building purposes only, to remove any stone, gravel, soil or other substances required for the construction or repair of any road, government building or other public work.

(3) The rights reserved under subsection (2) of this section may be exercised by any person authorised by the grantor in that behalf.

Payment of agreed sum for grant

8. (1) Where an agreement has been entered into for the making of any grant under this Act in consideration of the payment of an agreed sum of money and a portion only of such sum has been paid, the land shall vest in the grantee, but the State shall have a lien on the land for the balance of the agreed sum remaining unpaid.

(2) If the balance of such agreed sum is not paid within such other period as may be specified in the agreement, the land shall revert to the State and all money paid by the grantee shall be forfeited.

(3) No grantee shall be entitled to a conveyance, lease or other formal instrument conferring the grant until the whole of the agreed sum has been paid.

Land to be surveyed before grant made

9. …

Implied covenants by grantor

10. In every grant under this Act, there shall by virtue of this Act be implied covenants by the grantor-

(a) That he has full power to make such grant; and
(b) That the grantee, fulfilling the covenants and conditions contained in such grant or implied by virtue of this Act, shall quietly hold and enjoy the premises without any interruption by the grantor or any person claiming under him, except so far as the laws for the time being in force in Sierra Leone may permit.

Implied covenants by grantee

11. In every grant under this Act, there shall by virtue of this Act be implied covenants by the grantee-

That he will pay rent or royalties (if any) thereby reserved at the times and in the manner therein provided;

(a) That he will pay all taxes, rates, charges, duties and other outgoings of whatever description as are or may be imposed, charged or assessed upon the land and upon any buildings which are or may be erected thereon; and
(b) That he will allow the grantor or any person acting under his direction or by virtue of his duty as an officer of the Government, with or without workmen, at all reasonable times to enter into and upon the premises and examine the state and condition thereof.

Idem

12. In every grant under this Act there shall by virtue of this Act be implied, unless such covenants are therein expressly varied or excepted, covenants by the grantee-

(a) That he will not sub-divide, convey, assign, or otherwise alienate the premises or any part thereof by sale, mortgage, transfer of possession, lease or sub-lease, without the consent of the grantor in writing first had and obtained;
(b) That he will cause all conveyances, and assignments of the premises or any part thereof to be registered in the office of the Registrar-general within one hundred and twenty days of the date thereof;
(c) That he will not at any time carry on or commit or cause or permit to be carried on or committed any noisy, offensive or dangerous trade or nuisance;
(d) That he will not fell, cut down or in any other way injure or destroy any mature trees standing or growing on the premises without the consent of the grantor in writing first had and obtained;
(e) That he will at all times fully comply with the provisions and requirements of all such regulations and rules relating to the erection and construction of buildings as are applicable to the premises, or as may otherwise be required.

Implied covenants by lessee in building lease

13. In every building lease granted under this Act, there shall by virtue of this Act be implied, unless such covenants are therein expressly varied or excepted, covenants by the grantee-

That he will erect the buildings specified in the lease in the manner and within the period of time therein provided;

(a) That he will provide drainage and water supply in full compliance with all such regulations and rules relating to the provision of drainage and water supply as are applicable to the premises, or as may otherwise be required;

(b) That he will maintain the buildings erected on the premises in good and substantial repair.

Implied covenants by lessee in agricultural lease

14. In every agricultural lease under this Act, there shall by virtue of this Act be implied by the lessee a covenant that he will improve and develop the natural resources of the land in a prudent and businesslike manner and will abstain from the undue destruction or exhaustion of any timber, trees or plants for the sale or cultivation of which the land is leased.

Covenants binding on person deriving title from grantee.

15. (1) Every covenant, whether express or implied, contained in any grant under this Act, shall, unless an express provision to the contrary is contained in the grant, be binding upon all persons claiming an interest in the land which is the subject of such grant, and whose title is derived through or under the grantee.

(2) Any minor who becomes a grantee under this Act shall be in the same position with regard to his liability and obligation under or in respect of his grant as if he were of full age.

Boundary marks

16. (1) The owner or lessee of any State land sold, granted or leased before or after the coming into operation of this Act shall at all times maintain in repair to the satisfaction of the Director of Surveys and Lands or of such other officer as the Minister may appoint in this behalf all boundary marks or pillars placed or erected to denote the boundaries of the land in question.

(2) Every owner or occupier of land abutting on State land shall define and keep defined the boundary between the land owned or occupied by him and the adjoining State land to the satisfaction of the Director of Surveys and Lands or of such other officer as the Minister may appoint in this behalf, and in default of his so doing the Director of Surveys and Lands or other officer as aforesaid may by notice in writing require such owner or occupier to define such boundary in such manner and within such time as shall be specified in such notice.

(3) Any owner or occupier who fails to comply with the requirements of a notice served upon him in accordance with the provisions of subsection (2) of this section shall be guilty of an offence against this Act, and shall on summary conviction be liable to a fine not exceeding one hundred pounds and in addition to or in lieu of such fine the court shall order him to pay the expenses incurred (if any) by the Government in defining the boundary which he has neglected to define.

Power to erect telegraph poles, etc

17. …

Saving of public thoroughfares

18. All public thoroughfares existing on any land granted under this Act shall be deemed to be and shall be reserved and shall remain free and uninterrupted unless the same be closed or altered by the order of the Minister or by any other competent authority.

Resumption of land for roads, railways, etc

19. …

Revision of rent

20. (1) In every lease granted under this Act, unless express provision to the contrary is contained therein, there shall by virtue of this Act be reserved to the grantor the right to revise and fix the rent for such periods (hereinafter referred to as revision periods) as may be specified in the lease, or, in the absence of such specification, for periods of seven years.
(2) As nearly as may conveniently be to the date of commencement of each revision period, the grantor shall revise and fix the yearly rent which shall be payable during such revision period:

Provided that if for any reason the grantor considers it desirable to postpone the revision of the rent reserved under any lease, the grantor may postpone such revision for such time, irrespective of any revision period, as he shall think fit; but should the right to revise be subsequently exercised the rent then fixed shall be payable for the remainder of the current revision period.

(3) In revising the rent, the grantor shall have regard to the rent obtainable at the time of revision for similar land of similar area and amenities similarly situated, and to all the circumstances of the case, but shall not take into account any increase in the value of the land due to improvements made on the land by the lessee.
(4) The amount at which the revised rent has been fixed by the grantor shall be notified to the lessee.
(5) If the grantor and the lessee are unable to agree as to the revised rent to be paid, the matter shall be referred to an arbitrator to be agreed upon by the grantor and the lessee, or, in the absence of such agreement, by the Chief Justice.
(6) The decision of the arbitrator shall be final and binding on both parties, and unless the revised rent fixed by the arbitrator is less than that originally demanded by the grantor the lessee shall pay any costs incidental to the arbitration.

Penal rent.

21. (1) When in any lease under this Act the lessee has covenanted to develop or effect improvements on the land leased and has committed a breach of such covenant the grantor may at the time of such breach or at any time thereafter, and at expiration of every year thereafter so long as the breach be not remedied, fix a penal rent which shall be payable for one year from the date it is fixed and shall be paid by the lessee in addition to and at the same time and manner as the rent reserved is payable and shall be recoverable as rent. The first penal rent shall not exceed the rent reserved in the lease and penal rent subsequently fixed shall not exceed double the penal rent payable in respect of the preceding year.

(2) Notice of such penal rent being imposed and the amount thereof and the date from which it is payable shall be given in writing to the lessee.

(3) The fact that a penal rent has been imposed shall not preclude the grantor, in lieu of fixing a subsequent penal rent, from taking or directing to be taken proceedings for the forfeiture of the lease by reason of the breach in relation to which the penal rent has been imposed, provided that such proceedings shall not be taken during the period for which a penal rent has been paid.

Rent.

22. The rent reserved or payable under any lease granted under this Act shall be a debt to the State and shall be paid at the office of the Director of Surveys and Lands or at such other office as the grantor may appoint.

Grantor may sue for rents in arrear.

23. The grantor or any appointed by the grantor in that behalf may, without prejudice to the right of the State to recover rent in arrear in any other way, sue for the same, together with the penalty (if any) which may be payable under the last preceding section, and such suit may be instituted in the Supreme Court or in a Magistrate's Court.

Grantor may distrain for rent due.

24. The grantor may, on behalf of Her Majesty, distrain for rent due under any lease under this Act, or under any Act repealed by this Act, and may authorise any person to act for him in this behalf.

General powers of grantor

25.(1) The grantor may accept on such terms and conditions as he may think proper the surrender of any lease or licences granted under this Act.

(2) The grantor may wholly or partially remit, except as otherwise prescribed, all or any of the covenants or conditions contained in any lease or licence granted under this Act in any case where, owing to special circumstances, compliance therewith would be impossible or would cause great hardship to the grantee.

(3) The grantor may extend, except as otherwise prescribed, the time to the lessee for performing the covenants or conditions contained in any lease or licence liable to forfeiture for such period, and upon such terms and conditions, as he may think fit, and the period so extended and the terms and conditions so imposed shall be deemed to be inserted in the lease and shall be binding upon the lessee.

Sale of lease by a Court to be approved by the grantor.

26. No lease under this Act or under any Act repealed by this Act which contains a covenant, whether express or implied, by the lessee not to assign without the consent of the grantor shall be sold by or under the orders of any Court in execution of a decree or otherwise howsoever, except to a purchaser approved by the grantor.

PART III–REMEDIES OF STATE

Power of re-entry on breach of covenant.

27. (1) If there shall be any breach or non-observance by the grantee or by any person deriving any interest in the premises through or under the grantee of any of the covenants or conditions whether express or implied contained in any grant under this Act, the grantor may at any time after such breach or non-observance re-enter into and upon the premises or any part thereof in the name of the whole, and have again, repossess, hold and enjoy the same as in his former estate;

Provided that the power of re-entry authorised by this subsection shall not be exercisable in respect of the breach or non-observance of any covenant or condition express or implied which is capable of immediate remedy (other than a covenant for payment of rent or a covenant against assigning or sub-letting) unless and until the grantor shall have caused to be served upon the lessee a notice specifying the particular breach or non-observance of which complaint is made and requiring the lessee to remedy such breach or non-observance, and, at the discretion of the grantor, to make reasonable compensation in money therefor, and the lessee has failed to remedy such breach or non-observance and to pay such compensation as aforesaid to the grantor. Such notice shall-

(a) Be served personally upon the lessee; or
(b) Be sent to him by registered post to his last known address; or
(c) be published in the *Gazette* and a copy thereof be affixed to the premises.

accruing by reason of the breach or non-observance of any covenants or conditions, whether express or implied, contained in any grant under this Act.

(2) Any right of action or other remedy of the grantor in respect of any breach or non-observance by the grantee or by any person deriving any interest in the premises through or under the grantee of any of the covenants or conditions, whether express or implied, contained in any grant under this Act shall not be prejudiced by the exercise of the power of re-entry conferred upon the grantor by subsection (1) of this section.

(3) The acceptance by or on behalf of the grantor of any rent shall not operate as a waiver by the grantor of any forfeiture

Unoccupied lands

28. (1) Where any land granted under this Act appears to the grantor to have been unoccupied for a period exceeding twelve months, he may cause notice in writing to be given to the grantee that, if within the six months next following the date of such notice the grantee does not appear and afford proof that he intends to use and develop that land to a reasonable extent within a reasonable time, the land shall revert to the State, and all money paid in consideration of the grant of such land shall be forfeited.

(2) Such notice shall be published in the *Gazette*, and a copy thereof shall be affixed to the land, and, if the address of the grantee is known, a copy shall be sent by registered post, to such address.

(3) If the grantee does not appear within the six months next following the date of the publication of such notice in the *Gazette*, or, if having appeared, he fails to afford reasonable proof that he intends to use and develop the land within a reasonable time, the grantor may by notice in the *Gazette* declare the land to be forfeited, and the land shall thereupon revert to the State.

Debt to State not extinguished by forfeiture

29 No forfeiture shall operate to extinguish any debt to the State in respect of any rent or payment to be made by a lessee under a lease forfeited.

Recovery of State lands in unlawful occupation.

30. (1) Without prejudice to any remedy which the grantor may have under any other law, where any person without right, title or licence or whose right, title or licence has expired or been forfeited or cancelled, is in occupation of State land, the Attorney-General or some person appointed by him in that behalf, or the Director of Surveys and Lands, may enter a suit in the Supreme Court or in a Magistrate's Court to recover possession thereof.

(2) If upon the hearing of such suit the defendant does not appear, or appears but fails to establish an absolute right to the possession of the land, the court shall order that the possession of the land sought to be recovered shall be given by the defendant to the plaintiff on behalf of the State, either forthwith or on or before such day as the court shall think fit to appoint, and shall issue such process as may be necessary to carry such order into effect.

Evidence in proceedings.

31. In any action, suit or proceedings against any person for or in respect of any alleged unlawful occupation, use or trespass upon any State Land, the proof that the occupation or use in question was authorised shall lie on the defendant, and in every such action, suit or proceedings and in every action by or against the Government in which title to land shall be in issue the averment that any land is State land shall be sufficient without proof of such fact, unless the defendant prove the contrary.

Right of State to sue not to be barred by limitation.

32. No action or other remedy by or on behalf of the State for the recovery of State Land shall be barred or affected by any Statute, Act or other law of limitation.

Suit for rent not barred by limitation.

33. No action or other remedy for the recovery of rent due under any lease granted under this Act or under any Act repealed by this Act shall be barred or affected by any Statute, Act or other law of limitation.

Right of way not to be presumed against the State.

34. No right of way shall be presumed or allowed to be asserted or established against the State by reason only of user, whether such user commenced before or after the date of the coming into operation of this Act.

Service of notice

35. A notice served personally on the person to be served, or left at or sent by registered post to his last known address in Sierra Leone, or if his address is not known, published in the *Gazette,* shall be deemed to be good service for the purpose of this Act.

PART IV–PENALTIES

Setting fire to State lands.

36. Any person who shall set fire or cause the same to spread to any State Land, unless such person is a lessee of, or holds a licence to occupy and use, the same or is acting under the lawful orders of such lessee or licensee, shall be guilty of an offence and liable, on summary conviction, to a fine not exceeding fifty pounds.

Lessee or licensee allowing fire to spread.

37. Any lessee of, or person who holds a licence to occupy and use any State Land who shall allow any fire to spread from the land so leased or occupied and used by him to any other land, whether such other land be State land or private property, shall be guilty of an offence and liable, on summary conviction, to a fine not exceeding fifty pounds.

Production of licence.

38. Any person who shall be found occupying or using any State Land or cutting wood or felling and removing trees thereon and who shall upon demand being made by any police officer or any other person in uniform appointed for that purpose in writing by the Director of Surveys and Lands, refuse or fail after reasonable time given for that purpose, to produce and show his licence or other authority shall be guilty of an offence and liable, on summary conviction, to a fine not exceeding ten pounds.

Power to arrest

39. Every police officer or other person in uniform appointed for that purpose in writing by the Director of Surveys and Lands may arrest any person who is found cutting wood or thing is felling trees on or occupying or using any State Land, unless such person holds a licence or other authority for that purpose under this Act.

Punishment of persons cutting trees on State Land

40. Any person who cuts or takes any wood or thing from or off any State Land without having a licence or other authority for that purpose granted under this Act, or in breach of any condition of such a licence or authority, shall be guilty of an offence, and liable, on summary conviction, to a fine not exceeding fifty pounds.

Punishment of persons trespassing on State Land.

41. Any person who occupies or uses any State Land unless he holds a licence or other authority for that purpose granted under this Act, shall be guilty of an offence, and liable, on summary conviction, to a fine not exceeding fifty pounds.

Claim of right.

Provided that no person shall be convicted under this section who proves to the satisfaction of the court before whom he is brought that he, or those through whom he claims occupied the land under a *bona fide* claim or right.

PART V– MISCELLANEOUS

Rules

42. The Minister may make Rules for all or any of the following purposes-

(a) Classifying leases according to the purpose of which or the class of persons to whom they may be granted and prescribing the form of any lease;
(b) prescribing the term of years for which any class of lease may be granted;
(c) prescribing the praemia and rents to be paid and providing for the revision of rent;
(d) prescribing the manner in which application for leases shall be made and the fees to be paid;
(e) providing for the Survey and demarcation of State lands to be sold or leased, and fees to be paid for such survey and demarcation;
(f) prescribing the fees to be paid for any instrument issued under this Act;
(g) prescribing the period for which and the conditions under which licences for the temporary occupation of State Land may be issued.
(h) providing for the care, management and protection of unoccupied State land; and
(i) generally for carrying out and giving effect to the purposes of this Act.

Validation of existing grants.

43. No grant of State Land made before the commencement of this Act shall be deemed to be invalid because it has been made or executed or both made and executed by the Minister or by the Director of Surveys and Lands or because it has been so made or executed, it has not been made under the Public Seal.

Repeal of Cap. 53

44. (1) The State Lands Conservancy Act is hereby repealed without prejudice to anything done or suffered thereunder or to any right, privilege, obligation or liability acquired or incurred thereunder.

Cap. 200 (2) The Registration of Instruments Act is hereby amended by the deletion of the definition of "State grant" which appears in Section 2 thereof, and by the substitution therefore of the following definition-

"'State grant' means a grant of land made by the President or by the Minister for the time being charged with the responsibility for lands, or by a public officer deputed by the Minister on behalf of the State".

Passed in the House of Representatives this 24th day of November, in the year of our Lord one thousand nine hundred and sixty.

Appendix 3
THE NON-CITIZENS (INTERESTS IN LAND) ACT 1966

Act No. 30 of 1966

Date of Commencement. [22nd September, 1966.]

BE IT ENACTED by the Queen's Most Excellent Majesty, by and with the advice and consent of the House of Representatives in this present Parliament assembled, and by the authority of the same, as follows:-

Application — 1. This Act shall apply to the Western Area only.

Interpretation — 2. In this Act-

"Board" means a Board consisting of the Ministers responsible for Trade and Industry, Lands, Finance, and Development and the Attorney-General, of which the Minister of Lands shall be the Chairman.

"Non-Citizen" means-
Any individual who is not a citizen of Sierra Leone, and any company, association or body or persons corporate or incorporate-
More than one half of the members of which are persons who are not citizens of Sierra Leone; or
which by any means is controlled whether directly or indirectly by such persons; or
in the case of a company having a share capital, in which more than one half of the share capital is held beneficially by or on behalf of or in trust for such persons;

"reserved leaseholds" means leaseholds of which the unexpired term exceeds twenty-one years.

Non-Citizens not to purchase freeholds.

3. No non-citizen shall purchase or receive in exchange or as a gift any freehold land in the Western Area.

Non-Citizens not to purchase long leases in Western Area without the licence of the Board.

4.(1) No non-citizen shall purchase or receive in exchange or as a gift reserved leaseholds in the Western Area without first obtaining a licence from the Board.

(2) The Board may grant licences to purchase or receive in exchange or as a gift reserved leaseholds to non-citizens on such terms and conditions as it shall think fit and every such licence shall contain a description of the land to which it applies.

(3) At least three weeks before the grant of any such licence the Board shall publish a notice of its intention to grant the licence in the *Gazette* specifying the land and the name of the intending purchaser.

(4) The provision of subsection (3) shall not apply to sales by public auction.

Powers of Board over land received by non-citizens.

5. (1) Any conveyance, lease, grant, transfer, declaration, agreement, settlement or other disposition (other than an assent in favour of persons entitled under a will or on an intestacy) which, apart from the provisions of this Act would have vested-

freehold land; or

reserved leaseholds, where the purchaser has not been previously authorised by a licence issued under Section 4,

in a non-citizen (whether alone or together with any other person) shall vest such land (whether freehold or leasehold) in the Board for the whole estate or interest conferred by, or in virtue of, the instrument and the Board shall cause the Sheriff to sell the same by public auction.

(2) If satisfied that failure to observe the law was due to genuine and excusable mistake or ignorance (whether of law or fact) the Board may either-

Permit the parties to annul the transaction or modify it in such manner as may be approved by the Board and grant such licence as may be necessary in relation thereto; or

cause the Sheriff to sell the property by public auction and if it thinks fit cause to be paid out of the residual proceeds of the sale to the person or persons whose purchase of the freehold or leasehold land caused it to vest in the Board, a sum not exceeding the purchase price stipulated in the disposition which has been avoided (or in the case of a gift or exchange such sum as the Board shall think fit).

(3) The proceeds of sale which have not been disposed of by paragraph (b) of sub-section (2), after deducting-

The costs of the sale and

Any payments which may have become due under a lease, vested in the board by virtue of this section,

shall be paid into the Consolidated Revenue Fund.

Instruments not to be registered unless provisions of this Act have been observed.

6.(1) The Registrar-General shall not register any such instrument relating to freehold land or reserved leaseholds other than an assent in favour of persons entitled under a will or on an intestacy until he is satisfied either-

That a licence covering the transaction sought to be registered has been obtained under section 4, or

That the person to whom the freehold land or reserved leaseholds are being transferred or granted is not a non-citizen.

(2) Where registration of any instrument is delayed on account of enquiries into the citizenship of an applicant, the registration shall be deemed to have been effective for all purposes as from the dated the application was first received by the Registrar-General.

(3) The Registrar-General shall keep a separate register of all such pending applications arranged alphabetically according to the surname of the owners of the properties and shall permit the same to be searched by any member of the public for a fee of twenty-five cents.

Mortgages prior to Act No. 61 of 1962.	7. The following provisions shall apply to a mortgage made before the 17th January,1963, namely- (a) With the exception of the provisions which require a non-citizen purchaser to obtain a licence from the Board, nothing in this act shall in any way affect such mortgage or in any way limit the powers or remedies of the mortgagee of any such property. (b) Notwithstanding the provisions of Section 3, a non-citizen may, after obtaining a licence for this purpose from the board (which shall grant the same unless it shall see strong reason to the contrary) purchase the freehold of such property on a sale by the mortgagee.
Mortgages after Act No. 61 of 1962.	8. The following provisions apply to a mortgage made on or after the 17th of January, 1963, namely- Nothing in this Act shall affect the right to transfer property by way of mortgage; No order of foreclosure shall be made in favour of a non-citizen mortgagee of property unless he has previously obtained a licence from the Board authorising him to take foreclosure proceedings with respect to the property in question. Nothing in this section shall be construed as exempting any non-citizen who purchases or leases property from the mortgagor or mortgagee thereof from complying with the provisions of Section 4.
Act No. 61 of 1962.	9. All licences granted and acts done under the Land Development (Protection) Act, 1962, hereby repealed shall remain in force as if they were granted or done under this Act.

Passed in the House of Representatives this 13th day of July, in the year of our Lord one thousand nine hundred and sixty-six.

Appendix 4
THE PUBLIC LANDS ACT
CHAPTER 116

ARRANGEMENT OF SECTIONS

(3) Postponement of payment of price; parties not notified may appear and claim.
(4) Payment after one year to be complete discharge

PUBLIC LANDS ACT

6 of 1898
12 of 1924
44 of 1924
12 of 1928
24 of 1932
26 of 1945
10 of 1946

P.N. 148 of 1959

An Act to repeal The Public Lands Act, 1896 and to make other provisions in lieu thereof.

[12th April, 1898.]

Short title

1. This Act may be cited for all purposes, as the Public Lands Act.

Interpretation

P.N 148 of 1959

2. In this Act unless the context otherwise requires-
"public work" means any work not coming within the provisions of the Railway Act executed, maintained or repaired, and any measure or undertaking, prosecuted, whether wholly or partly, at the public expense;
"land" includes all land, whether covered with water or otherwise, together with all buildings and erections, if any, thereon, and where such meaning may be inferred, any right to the same;
"Minister" means the Minister charged for the time being with responsibility for the subject of lands;
"Chief Justice" includes any Judge of the High Court of Sierra Leone in its civil Jurisdiction.

PART I –
ACQUISITION OF LANDS FOR THE SERVICE OF THE STATE

Power to enter to survey

3. (1) Whenever Parliament resolves that any land is required for any public work, the President may from time to time, by writing under his hand, authorise any person together with his agents, servant or workmen, to enter as often as may be necessary upon such land, and there to survey and take levels to make boring or trial pits, and to do such other acts as may be necessary with the view to the taking or appropriating of any such land.

(2) The report of any such person, together with a plan of such land, shall be laid before Parliament.

Warrant for acquisition of land

4. When the President, with the advice and consent of the House of Representatives, shall by resolution declare that any land shall be acquired for any public work, it shall be lawful for the President, by warrant under his hand and the public seal of the State , to direct that such lands shall be acquired for the service of the State .

Every such warrant may be in the Form A in the schedule hereto, and shall be published in the *Gazette.*

Service of notice on owners

5. Whenever, by any such warrant, as in the last section mentioned, it is directed that any land shall be acquired for the service of the State , the Director of Surveys and Lands shall cause to be served personally on the person or persons entitled to sell or interested in any lands specified in such warrant, or if he or they cannot be found, shall cause to be left at his or their last usual place or places of abode or business with some inmate thereof, to be given to such person or persons, and in case no such person can be ascertained or found shall cause to be left with the occupier of such lands, or if there be no such occupier, shall cause to be affixed on some conspicuous part of such lands, within eight days from the date of such warrant, a notice in the Form B in the schedule hereto, or as near thereto as possible.

Power to enter and take land.

6. After the lapse of twenty-one days from the publication of any such warrant in the *Gazette* it shall be lawful for the Director of Surveys and Lands, with all necessary workmen and other servants, to enter upon such land, and also to set out, appropriate and take so much of such land as is specified in the said warrant.

Land to be marked out

7. When the Director of Surveys and Lands shall set out, appropriate and take the land specified in any such warrant, he shall cause such land to be marked out, and a notice to be posted in some conspicuous part of such land, and such notice shall be in these words, viz.:-

"Taken for the service of the State ", and shall be signed by the Director of Surveys and Lands. All such land, when so set out, appropriated or taken, shall be vested in the State , free from all other estates and all liens, rights, charges and encumbrances whatsoever.

Plan and certificate to be registered

8. Within eight days any such appropriation, the Director of Surveys and Lands shall cause a plan of the land so set out, appropriated and taken as aforesaid, together with a certificate, under his hand, to the effect that the same has been taken and appropriated for the service of the State , to be registered in the Office of the Registrar General.

Registration to be conclusive

9. When any land has been taken and appropriated for the service of the Colony, whether under the provisions of this or any other Act, the registration of a plan of such land, together with the certificate in the Office of the Registrar General, as in the last section mentioned, shall be conclusive evidence that such land has been set out, appropriated and taken for the service of the State under the provisions of this Act.

Land injuriously affected

10. If any land be so cut through and divided by the taking and appropriation of part of such land for any public works as to leave a portion thereof practically useless to the owner for the purpose for which he had been accustomed to use the land, it shall be lawful for the owner of such land, by notice in writing to be served on the Director of Surveys and Lands, at any time, before an agreement is come to, for the purchase of the land as aforesaid, or before the assessment of the price to be paid for such land under the provisions of this Act, to require the President, on behalf of the State , to purchase not only the land actually taken as aforesaid, but also the land rendered useless as aforesaid by reason of the severance aforesaid, or, if he refuses to do so, it shall be lawful for the Chief Justice, if he shall find as a fact that any portion of the said land has been, by the severance, rendered useless as aforesaid, to adjudge that the President shall purchase the same and determine the price to be paid for the same in the same way as if such land had actually been taken for any public work.

Resale of land

11. It shall be lawful for the Minister to resell any land purchased under the provisions of the last preceding section, and any moneys arising from any such sale shall be carried to, and form part of, the general revenue of the Government of Sierra Leone .

Part of house etc., not to be taken

12. Nothing in this Act shall be deemed to authorise the Director of Surveys and Lands to take a part only of any house, building or manufactory, but where a part of the land on which any house, building or manufactory stands is required for any public work it shall be lawful for the owner of such house, building or manufactory to require the Director of Surveys and Lands to take the whole house, building or manufactory;

Provided that it shall be lawful for the Minister to resell any portion of any such house, building or manufactory that may not be required for any such public work, and any moneys arising from such sale shall be carried to, and form part of the general revenue of the Colony.

Power of the Minister to sell, lease etc. when public or abandoned land is superfluous to requirements

13.Whenever any land which has been acquired under the provisions of this Act for a public work is not required for the purpose thereof, or the said public work has been abandoned, it shall be lawful for the Minister to sell, exchange, lease or in any other manner dispose of such land, and any moneys arising from the said sale, exchange, lease or other disposal thereof shall be carried to, and form part of, the general revenue.

Cases in which the owner, etc. refuses to give up possession

14. If in any case in which, according to the provision of this Act, the Director of Surveys and Lands is authorised to enter upon and take any land, and the owner or occupier or any such land, or any other person, refuse to give up possession thereof, or hinder the Director of Surveys and Lands, his workmen or servants from entering upon or taking possession of the same, it shall be lawful for the President to issue his warrant in the Form C in the schedule hereto, or as near thereto as possible, directed to the Sheriff, ordering him to deliver possession of the same to the Director of Surveys and Lands and upon receipt of such warrant the Sheriff shall deliver possession of any such land accordingly; and the costs accruing by reason of the execution of such warrant, to be taxed by the Master of the Supreme Court, subject to review by the Chief Justice, shall be paid by the person refusing to give possession or hindering the Director of Surveys and Lands, his workmen or servants as aforesaid, and the amount of such costs shall be deducted and retained by the President from the compensation, if any, then payable by him to such person, and if no compensation be payable to such person, or if the same be less than the amount of such costs, then such costs or the excess thereof beyond such compensation, if not paid on demand, shall be levied by distress, and upon application to the Magistrate for that purpose, he shall issue his warrant accordingly.

PART – II COMPENSATION

Compensation to be allowed

15. The owners and occupiers of, and all other persons interested in, any land which may be appropriated, and taken or entered upon as aforesaid, shall be entitled to, and shall receive, compensation for the value of the land so taken and appropriated, and for all damages sustained by such owners, occupiers and other persons, by reason of the exercise, as regards such land, of the powers granted by the Act, the amount of such compensation to be ascertained and determined as hereinafter provided.

Agreed compensation

16. It shall be lawful for the President, for and on behalf of the State , to contract and agree with the owner or occupier or any other person interested in any land which may be appropriated and taken for the service of the Sierra Leone or injuriously affected by the exercise of any of the powers as regards such land granted by this Act, the compensation to be allowed, either in respect of the actual value of the land, or in respect of damages incurred by reason of the exercise of any of the said powers, and any sum or sums so agreed on as last aforesaid, or which shall be awarded under the provisions of this Act, shall be paid by the Accountant General.

Cases of disputed compensation, etc.

17. In all cases in which any land has been appropriated, taken or entered upon under the provisions of this Act, or has been injuriously affected by the exercise of any of the powers granted by this Act, if within twenty-one days after the publication of the warrant in the Gazette that such land shall be acquired for the service of Sierra Leone as hereinbefore provided, no claim shall have been lodged with the Director of Surveys and Lands in respect of such lands, or if the person who may have lodged any claim and the President shall not have agreed as to the amount of compensation to be paid for the interest of any such person, or if any such person shall not have given satisfactory evidence of his alleged interests, or if separate and conflicting claims are made in respect of the same land, the amount of compensation due, if any, and every such disputed interest or title shall be settled in accordance with the following provisions-

Application may be made by motion *ex parte-*

(i) By or on behalf of the Attorney General, or

(ii) In the event of the Attorney General making no such application within eight days after the registration of the plan of any land, and of the certificate of the Director of Surveys and Lands that such land has been set out, appropriated and taken for the service of Sierra Leone in the Office of the Registrar General, either by, or on behalf of, the Attorney General, or of any person or persons claiming to be the owner, occupier, or to be otherwise interested in any such land, to the Chief Justice, who shall have jurisdiction to hear and determine in all such cases as aforesaid.

The Attorney General, or other person or persons applying to the court as last aforesaid, shall cause the records in the Registrar General's Office to be searched in order to ascertain whether or not there are or are not any mortgages or other charges affecting any such land, or any part thereof, and in the event of there being any mortgage or other charge affecting any such land, or any part thereof, shall produce at the hearing of any such application a report of all such mortgages or charges, the nature, the persons interested thereunder or affected thereby, and the court shall thereupon direct that the value of the land so appropriated be ascertained, that the amount of compensation which out to be paid to the several persons interested therein be determined, what notices shall be given or served to enable all persons interested to protect their rights, and the manner in which such notices shall be given or served, and shall further appoint the time and the place at which he will sit to hear and determine the matter, and the Master of the Court shall cause public notice of the time and place so appointed to be published in the *Gazette.*

The Court shall, after hearing evidence in that behalf, assess the amount of compensation to be paid by the Government by the owner of the land the subject of the application, and to all persons having any just right, title or interest in respect of the said land or any portion thereof, and when ever it shall appear that any such land is owned, either wholly or in part by, or that the occupier or any person injuriously affected as aforesaid is an infant, lunatic, or a person who is absent from Sierra Leone , it shall be lawful for the court to appoint a guardian or curator to protect the interest of any such infant, lunatic, or absentee, and every such guardian or curator shall be subject to the control and direction of the court.

On the day appointed for the hearing-

(i) the Attorney General, or any person on his behalf, and every person interested in the land the subject matter of the said application, may appear before the court and may tender such evidence as may be relevant in support of their alleged rights and the value thereof, and may cross-examine any witness produced in any adverse interest, and may produce any adverse testimony;

(ii) The Attorney General, or any person on his behalf, or any person interested as aforesaid, may summon any witness who may be required.

When the owner or any person claiming to be the owner, of such land, or to possess or represent the possessor of any interest therein, shall not appear at the time appointed for the hearing, a decision may be given *ex parte* upon hearing the evidence adduced by the Attorney General, or any person on his behalf, and such decision shall be as effectual as if given after hearing and in the presence of all parties.

The written report of the Director of Surveys and Lands, or any surveyor or engineer nominated by him, as to the value of such land, shall be evidence thereof, but shall not exclude any other evidence of such value. Such report may be proved by a copy thereof under the hand of the Director of Surveys and Lands, or of any such surveyor or engineer as last aforesaid, as the case may be, but any or them may be called to give evidence by any party having interest. Proof of the signature of such copy shall not be required, unless the court sees reason to doubt the genuineness thereof.

Compensation shall not be awarded to any party in respect of unoccupied land. Any land shall be deemed to be unoccupied where it is proved that beneficial use thereof for cultivation or inhabitation, or for collecting or storing water, or for any industrial purposes, has not been made for twelve years next prior to the date or which such land has been set out, appropriated and taken for the service of Sierra Leone under the provisions of this Act.

Matters to be considered in determining compensation

18. (1) In determining the amount of compensation to be awarded for land acquired under this Act, the court shall take into consideration the following matters and no others, namely-

The market value at the date of the publication or the warrant under section 4 of this Act;

Any increase in the value of other land of the person interested likely to accrue from the use to which the land acquired will be put;

The damage, if any, sustained by the person interested at the time of the taking possession of land by reason of serving such land from his other land;

The damage, if any, sustained by the person interested at the time of the taking and appropriation of the land by reason of the acquisition injuriously affecting his other property whether movable or immovable in any other manner or his actual earnings;

If, in consequence of the acquisition, he is compelled to change his residence or place of business, the reasonable expenses, if any, incidental to such change;

The damage, if any, sustained by persons interested by reason of the imposition of any easement or exercise of any other rights of user on the basis of amount by which the value of the land shall have been diminished thereby; and

Where land is, and but for the compulsory acquisition would continue to be, devoted to a purpose of such a nature that there is no general demand or market for land for that purpose, the compensation may, if the court is satisfied that reinstatement in some other place is *bona fide* intended, be assessed on the basis of the reasonable cost of equivalent reinstatement.

(2) For the purpose of paragraph (a) of subsection (1) of this section-

If the market value has been increased by means of any improvement made by the owner or his predecessor in interest within two years before the publication of the warrant under section 4, such increase shall be disregarded if the improvement was made in contemplation of proceedings for the acquisition of the land being taken under this Act;

When the value of the land is increased by reason of the use thereof or any premises thereon in a manner which could be restrained by any court or is contrary to law or is detrimental to the health of the inmates of the premises or to the public health the amount of that increase shall not be taken into account;

The effect of any expressed or implied condition of title restricting the use to which the land may be put shall be taken into account.

Matters to be neglected in determining compensation

19. In determining the amount of compensation to be awarded for be land acquired under this Act the court shall not take into consideration-

The degree of urgency which has led to the acquisition;

Any disinclination of the person interested to part with the land acquired;

Any damage sustained by the person interested which, if caused by a private person, would not be a good cause of action;

Any damage which is likely to be caused to the land or buildings acquired after the date of the publication or the warrant under section 4 by or in consequence of the use to which it will be put;

Any increase to the value of the land or building acquired, likely to accrue from the use to which it will be put when acquired;

Any outlay on additions or improvements to the land acquired which was made after the date of the publication of the warrant under section 4, unless such additions or improvements were necessary for the maintenance of any building in a proper state of repair;

Any increase to the value of the land by reason of any work done thereon by or at the expense of the President prior to the acquisition;

The special suitability or adaptability of the land for any purpose is a purpose to which it could be applied only in pursuance of statutory powers, or for which there is no market apart from the special needs of a particular purchaser or the requirements of the President .

Appeals

20. (1) Any final judgment of the court respecting compensation or in the case of disputed interest or title shall be subject to the like appeal to which other final judgments of any court are subject, including appeal to the Court of Appeal and to the Supreme Court where such appeal is allowed by law.

Notice of Appeal when Court's decision to be final

(2) The party who may desire to appeal against such judgment shall proceed according to any Rules of Court for the time being regulating appeals, and if an appeal is not perfected within the period prescribed, the judgment of the Court of Court Appeal, as the case may be, shall be final.

Postponement of payment of price, parties not notified may appear and claim

(3) The decision of any court having competent jurisdiction, whether original or appellate, where appeal has been taken in the manner above mentioned, respecting compensation, or on any question of disputed interest or title, shall be final and conclusive in regard to all persons upon whom notices have been served or who have appeared and claimed or on whose behalf any person having authority to that effect has claimed any lands or any interest therein:

Proviso

Provided that persons upon whom notices have not been served, and who have not appeared or claimed or on whose behalf no claim has been made, may do so at any time within one year after the date of the final decision.

Payment after one year to be complete discharge

(4) In all cases where any compensation has been awarded, except where a valid written title to the land shall be delivered, payment thereof shall be postponed until the period of one year shall have elapsed from the date of the judgment, or judgment on appeal, whereupon it may be paid over to the person who shall then appear by the judgment of the court to have the best right thereto, and such payment shall, as concerns the Government, operate as a complete discharge and acquittance of such compensation and of all claims in respect of such lands or any interest therein;

Proviso

Provided that such payment shall not hinder any subsequent proceedings at the instance of any persons having or alleging better right thereto as against the person to whom such payment may have been made.

SCHEDULE
FORM A

Section 4

WARRANT THAT LAND SHALL BE ACQUIRED FOR THE SERVICE OF THE STATE

Sierra Leone
(L.S.)

By His Excellency,
....
The President.

Whereas on the ....day of ....19..........., the President, with the advice and consent of Parliament, by Resolution, declared that the land hereinafter described, that is to say [*insert description of land*], should be acquired for a Public Work:

Now, therefore, I do hereby under the provisions of the Public lands ordinance, by this my warrant under my hand and the Public Seal of the State, direct that the said land shall be acquired for the service of the State.

Dated this...............day of ....19..........

FORM B

NOTICE

Notice is hereby given that the following land [*describe land, denoting the boundaries by physical marks wherever practicable*] is to be acquired for the service of the State.

Any person claiming to be possessed of, or to have any right, title or interest in, the said land, or to be injuriously affected by any such acquisition, is required, on or before the day of [*twenty-one-days after the date of publication of warrant in the Gazette*], to forward to the Director of Surveys and Lands a statement of his right or interest, and the evidence thereof, and of any claim made by him in respect of the value of such land or of his interest therein.

The President is willing to treat for the purchase of the said land, but if no such statement is lodged with the Director of Surveys and Lands before the date hereby prescribed, the land is liable to be dealt with as unoccupied land.

Date ....

Director of Surveys and Lands

FORM C

WARRANT TO THE SHERIFF

Section 14

To the sheriff of the Republic of Sierra Leone;

Whereas by a warrant dated the……….day of…………19………, under the hand of the president and the Public Seal of the State, it was directed that the following land [*describe land*] should be acquired for the service of the State;

And whereas twenty-one days have elapsed since the publication of the said warrant in the Gazette.

These are therefore to command you to put the Director of Surveys and Lands, or any person authorised by him in that behalf, in possession of the said land and premises.

Dated the……………..day of…………..19…………………

Appendix 5

THE PROVINCES LAND ACT

CHAPTER 122

ARRANGEMENT OF SECTIONS

Section

16 of 1927.
34 of 1928.
32 of 1933.
1 of 1935.
Rules Nos.
15 of 1930.
24 of 1933

An Act to Make Provision Relating to the Tenure of Land by Non-natives in the Provinces.

[1ST AUGUST, 1927.]

Preamble.

WHEREAS all land in the Provinces is vested in the Chiefdom Council who hold such land for and on behalf of the native communities concerned:

AND WHEREAS it is expedient to make provision regulating the interests in land which such Chiefdom Council may grant to non-natives.

Short title and construction Cap. 60

1. This Act may be cited as the Provinces Land Act, and shall be read and construed as one with the Provinces Act.

Interpretation

2. In this Act unless the context otherwise requires—
"decree book" means any book record of such a nature as those in which, before the passing of this Act, there were entered the terms on which the Chiefdom Council consented to the settlement of non-natives on lands in the Provinces; or any other form of record which the President r shall by Order prescribe;
"deed" means an agreement under seal;
"non-native" means any person who is not entitled by customary law rights in land in a Province;
"Chiefdom Council" means paramount chiefs and their councillors, and men of note, or sub-chiefs and their councillors, and men of note;
"tenancy at will" means a tenancy in which the lessee holds at the will of the lessor, and which may be determined without notice by either the lessor or the lessee;
"tenancy at sufferance" means the tenancy of a person who having originally come into possession of land by a lawful title holds such possession after the determination of his title. Such tenancy may be determined without notice by the lessor;
"term of years" means an interest in land created by lease and subject to a yearly rent payable at regular periodic intervals;
"lease" means a grant of possession of land by the Chiefdom Council, as lessor, to a non-native, as lessee, for a term of years or other fixed period with the reservation of a rent.

For the purpose of the Act …'non native' shall not include the Government.

Conditions on which non-natives may occupy land in the Provinces

3. (1) No land in the Provinces shall be occupied by a non-native unless he has first obtained the consent of the Chiefdom Council to his occupation of such land.

(2) Any non-native who shall occupy land in the Provinces without the approval of the District Officer shall be a tenant at will within the meaning of this Act.

(3) Whenever any non-native shall, with the consent of the Chiefdom Council and the approval of the District Officer, occupy land in respect of which no lease shall be executed by the Chiefdom Council as lessor and the non-native as lessee, a memorandum of the terms of such occupation, consent to which shall have been given by the Chiefdom Council with the approval of the District Officer, shall be drawn up and entered in the decree book or in such other manner as the Governor may by Order prescribe, by the District Officer and shall set out-

The annual consideration to be paid by the non-native for occupation of the land;

The area of the land to be occupied;

The duration of the term, which shall in no case be for more than three years;

Any special conditions (such as an undertaking to establish permanent cultivation of crops, such as rubber, cocoa, etc.) with which the non-native has to comply in consideration of occupying the land without payment or at a reduced annual rental;

whether or not the interest of the non-native may be assigned or, in the case of death, is intended to devolve on his executors, administrators or assigns.

Non-native not to acquire greater interest than lease for 50 years

4. No non-native shall acquire a greater interest in land in the Provinces than a tenancy for a term of fifty years; but nothing in this section shall prevent the insertion in any lease of a clause providing for the renewal of such lease, for a second or further terms not exceeding twenty-one years.

Revision of rents

5. (1) The rent reserved under any lease of land in the Provinces shall be subject to revision by the District Officer – from whom there shall be a right of appeal to the Provincial Secretary – every seven years:

Provision

Provided that no increase of rent shall be sanctioned by the District Officer by reason only of improvements made by the tenant or his predecessors in title.

Indorsement on lease

(2) A note of any such revision of rent shall be endorsed on the lease and entered by the District Officer in the decree book.

Tenancy exceeding three years to be under seal

6. No tenancy for a term exceeding three years shall be created by any agreement not under seal.

Construction of defective lease

7. No tenancy by this Act required to be created by agreement under seal shall, unless it is duly made by deed and unless the District Officer has endorsed thereon his consent, be construed as creating a greater interest than a tenancy from year to year.

Determination of tenancies from year to year

8. Every tenancy from year to year shall be determinable by either party giving three months notice to the other. Such notice shall expire at the end of a current year of the tenancy.

Voidable deed

9. Every deed creating a tenancy of land shall be voidable by either party, unless it—

(a) Is executed in the presence of two witnesses by the lessor before the District Officer of the district in which the land is situated; and is executed, in the presence of two witnesses, by the lessee or his attorney or his agent before a Magistrate; and

(b) Has endorsed upon it certificates of execution in their presence signed respectively by the District Officer and the Magistrate before whom it was executed; and

(c) Provides that the lessee shall not sublet or assign his interest thereunder except with the consent of the Chiefdom Council with the approval in writing of the District Officer, provided that such consent shall not be unreasonably withheld; and

(d) Contains stipulations with regard to all the matters set out in rule 3 to the schedule to this Act.

Record and evidence

10. The terms of all leases to which his consent is required shall be recorded by the District Officer in the decree book, and such record shall be admissible in all courts of law in Sierra Leoneas *prima facie* evidence of the matters therein stated.

Fixtures, buildings and economic trees

11. The reversion in all fixtures affixed to the land by the tenant, whether fences or of whatever other nature soever, and any building erected by him thereon, and of all economic trees, shall, whether the tenancies concerned were created before the date of coming into operation of this Act or not, in the case of a tenant on sufferance, be in the Chiefdom Council; but in the case of a tenancy created by lease, in the absence of any agreement to the contrary contained therein—

Removability

(a) Any [thing] affixed to the land by the tenant, whether fences or of whatever other nature soever, and any building erected by him thereon which is not so affixed or erected in pursuance of some obligation in that behalf or instead of some fixture or building belonging to the Chiefdom Council, shall be the property of and be removable by the tenant before or within two months after the termination of the tenancy:

Rent

Provided that—

(1) Before the removal of any fixture or building the tenant shall pay all rent owing by him, and shall perform or satisfy all other his obligations to the Chiefdom Council in respect to the land:

Care in removal

(2) In the removal of any fixture or building the tenant shall not do any avoidable damage to any other building or other part of the land:

Making good damage

(3) Immediately after the removal of any fixture or building the tenant shall make good all damage occasioned to any other building or other part of the land by the removal:

Notice to Chiefdom Council

(4) The tenant shall not remove any fixture or building without giving one month's previous notice in writing to the Chiefdom Council of his intention to remove it.

Purchase by Tribal Authority

(5) At any time before the expiration of the notice of intention to remove any fixture or building, the Chiefdom Council, by notice in writing given by him to the tenant, may elect to purchase any fixture or building comprised in the notice of intention to remove and any fixture or building thus elected to be purchased shall be left by the tenant, and shall become the property of the Chiefdom Council, who shall pay to the tenant the fair value thereof to an incoming tenant of the land;

Compensation for economic trees.

(b) The Chiefdom Council shall pay to the tenant the fair value to any incoming tenant of the land of any economic trees which shall have been planted by the tenant;

Powers of District Commissioner, etc., at enquiry.

(c) If there is any dispute as to the value of any fixture of building or any economic trees, the District Officer shall hold an enquiry and give his decision thereon. If either the Chiefdom Council or the tenant is dissatisfied with the said decision, there shall be a right of appeal to the Provincial Secretary who shall hold a further enquiry and whose decision shall be final;
(d) For the purpose of such enquiry the District Officer and the Provincial Secretary shall have all the powers conferred upon the Magistrates' Courts by the Courts Act, or any Act amending or substituted for the same.

Definition of economic trees

12. For the purpose of the last preceding section, the term economic trees shall include all trees, shrubs and plants which are grown or cultivated for their intrinsic value.

Settler's fee.

13. Every non-native residing in a chiefdom who does not hold a lease of land within the chiefdom, other than a non-native employed by a person holding a lease and residing on the land held under such lease, shall, in lieu of the customary presents or contribution of labour sanctioned by native law, pay to Paramount Chief, in respect of each year or portion of a year such residence, a settler's fee.

In no case shall the wife or husband or children of a settler who resides with him or her be liable to pay any settler's fee:

Provided that it shall be lawful for a Paramount Chief, with the consent of the Provincial Secretary, to forgo exacting payment of the whole or any part of such fee in the case of a non-native resident within the chiefdom who—
By his knowledge of any special trade or calling, or by his maintenance of any school or other institution, is in the opinion of the Paramount Chief conferring a benefit on chiefdom; or
Is employed by a person engaged in any industrial undertaking.

For the purpose of this section the term "industrial undertaking" shall have the same meaning as in the Employers and Employed Act.

Saving of Cap. 121 and Cap. 230

14. [Deleted by Act No.18 of 1976]

Registration by District Commissioner of existing titles to land

15. (1) Every non-native claiming any title to land in the Provinces shall, before the first day of April, 1929, produce to the District Officer all documents of title upon which he bases such claim, or, in the absence of such documents, a memorandum of the terms of such occupation signed by the lessor and lessee, which documents or memorandum shall be entered by the District Officer in the decree book or in such other manner as the President may by Order prescribe.

(2) The claim of a non-native to a title to any land in the Provinces, documents of title to which or a memorandum as to which have not been produced in conformity with the last preceding sub-section, shall be disallowed by every court in the Provinces.

Power of governor to make rules

16. The President may make rules for any or all of the following purposes—

Fixing the amount payable as settlers' fees either generally or in a particular locality;

Prescribing the terms to be embodied in leases;

Directing the manner in which leases shall be recorded;

Prescribing the procedure in submitting deeds of lease for revision of rent;

Specifying the person to whom rents and settlers' fees shall be paid and the manner in which such rents and fees shall be brought to account.

Generally for the more effectual carrying out of the provisions of this Act;

Provided that until varied or revoked by any such rules, the rules contained in the schedule to this Act shall be in force.

SCHEDULE

Section 16.
Rules 15 of 1930.
24 of 1933

Settler's fee

1. Every non-native residing in a chiefdom who does not hold a lease of land within the chiefdom shall pay to the Paramount Chief a settler's fee of two leones per annum, or ten cents per mensem at the option of the payor during the continuance of his residence in such chiefdom.

Mode of payment of settler's fee

2. Settlers' fees shall fall due in advance on the first day of January in each year in the case of a yearly fee and on the first day of each month in the case of monthly fee:

Provided that a non-native shall not be required to pay a settler's fee in respect of the month in which he took up his residence in the chiefdom.

Terms of deed

3. Every lease required by this Act to be by deed shall state—

(a) The rent;
(b) The term;
(c) The purpose for which the land is to be used;
(d) Whether the interest is assignable;
(e) Where buildings of permanent construction are to be erected, the rights of the parties to and in respect of such buildings at the expiration or determination of the lease;
(f) In cases where the lease is for a longer period than seven years, that the rent is subject to revision every seven years by the District Officer subject to right of appeal to the Provincial Secretary.

Decree book

4. The terms of all leases to which the consent or approval of the District Officer is required shall be recorded by the District Officer in the decree book, in the same manner in which the terms of leases have heretofore been recorded.

5. The District Officer shall keep a rent roll of all rents due to each Chiefdom Council in his district, and all rents in respect of tenancies, whether created before the date of the coming into operation of this Act or not, shall be payable to him. He shall place all moneys so received by him on deposit in the Government Treasury pending disbursement.

Appendix 6

THE LANDS COMMISSION BILL 2004

ARRANGEMENT OF SECTIONS

Section

Part III – ADMINISTRATION AND MISCELLANEOUS PROVISIONS

1. Lands Commission Secretariat
2. Executive Secretary
3. Deputy Executive Secretary
4. Other staff of the Commission
5. Funds of the Commission
6. Accounts and Audit
7. Annual report
8. Access to information
9. Offences
10. Offences by bodies Corporate
11. Regulations
12. Act 123, 124, 125 to have effect with necessary modifications
13. Interpretation

ACT OF THE PARLIAMENT OF THE REPUBLIC OF SIERRA LEONE ENTITLED

THE LANDS COMMISSION ACT, 2004

An Act to establish the Lands Commission, provide for its composition and functions and for other connected purposes.

PART 1 ESTABLISHMENT OF THE COMMISSION

Establishment of the Commission

1. There is established by this Act, a Lands Commission referred to in this Act as "The Commission".

The Functions of the Commission

2. (1) The Commission shall, in co-ordination with the relevant public agencies and Governmental bodies, perform the following functions:

a) On behalf of the Government manage State Lands and any lands vested in the Republic of Sierra Leone by the constitution or by any other law or any lands vested in the Commission;
b) Advise the Government, local authorities and traditional rulers on the policy framework for the development of particular areas of Sierra Leone to ensure that the development of individual pieces of land is co-ordinated with the relevant development plan for the area concerned.
c) Formulate and submit to Government recommendations on national policy with respect to land use and capability;
d) Advise on and assist in the execution of a comprehensive programme for the registration of title to land through Sierra Leone;
e) Perform such other functions as the Minister responsible for Lands may assign to the Commission;

2. (2) The Minister may with the approval of the President, give general directions in writing to the Commission on matters of policy in respect of the management of State lands.

Independence of the Commission

Except as otherwise provided in the Constitution, or in any other law which is not inconsistent with the Constitution, the Commission shall not be subject to the direction or control of any person or authority in the performance of its functions.

Consent and Concurrence in Disposition of State and Chiefdom Lands

4. (1) There shall be no disposition or development of any state land by any person unless the Lands Commission of the Local Authority where the land is situated has certified that the disposition of development is consistent with the development plan drawn up or approved by the Planning Authority of the area concerned.
4. (2) The grant of consent and concurrence by the local Authority Lands commission shall be communicated by it to the Central office of the Lands Commission and the Regional office of the Lands Commission.
4. (3) Where the Regional Lands Commission fails or refuses to give the consent and concurrence under subsection (1) of this section a person aggrieved by the failure or refusal may appeal to the Minister.

PART II – COMPOSITION, QUALIFICATION, APPOINTMENT OF MEMBERS AND RELATED MATTERS

5. (1) The Commission shall consist of the following persons:-

(a) a Chairman, who is neither a Minister nor a Deputy minister;

(b) one representative of each of the following bodies/professions To be appointed by the President

(i) A member of parliament

(ii) A Lawyer

(iii) A Town Planner

(iv) A Surveyor

(v) A representative of each Regional Lands Commission;

(vi) The Ministry/Department responsible for Town and County Planning

(vii) The National Association of Farmers

(viii) The National Association of Fishermen;

(ix) The Environmental Protection Council;

(x) The Ministry/Department responsible for Lands and Surveys.

(xi) The Ministry/Department responsible for Forestry; and for Agriculture.

(xii) A Member of the Public

(xiii) The Chief Administrator of the Lands Commission who shall be the Executive Secretary

5. (2) The Chairman and other members of the Commission shall be appointed by the President acting in consultation with the Cabinet.
5. (3) The salaries and allowances payable, and the facilities and privileges available to the Chairman and the other members of the Commission shall be determined by the President.

<u>Regional Lands Commissions</u>

6. (1) There shall be within each region branches of the Commission to be known as "District/Town Council Lands Commissions" which shall perform the functions of the Commission at the local level.
6. (2) The activities of the District/Town Council Lands Commissions shall be coordinated by the Commission.
7. (1) A District/Town Council Lands Commission shall consist of the following persons appointed by the Minister responsible for lands;

a) A Chairman who is neither a Minister nor a Deputy Minister;
b) One representative of each of the following bodies/professions.

i. The District/Town Council
ii. Each Local Authority/Ward within the District/Town;
iii. The Department responsible for Town and Country Planning;
iv. A Lawyer practicing within the area of the local authority;
v. A Town Planner or Surveyor practicing within the area of the Local Authority.
vi. A representative of the National Association of Farmers/Fishermen within the area of the local authority.
vii. The District/Town Council lands officer.

District/Town Council Lands Officer

8. (1) Each District/Town Council Lands Commission shall have a District/Town Council Lands Officer who shall be a person knowledgeable and experienced in land administration.
8. (2) The District/town Council Lands Officer shall be a member of and the Secretary to the District/Town Council Lands Commission.
8. (3) Subject to the directions of the Executive Secretary appointed under section 6. (2) of this Act and in consultation with the District/Town Council Lands Commissions, the District/Town Council Lands Officer shall perform the functions of the Executive Secretary in the District/Town Council concerned.

Qualification for Membership of the Commission or Regional, (District/Town Council), Lands Commission

9. (1) No person is qualified to be a member of the Commission or a Rregional, (District/Town Council), Lands Commission unless he is qualified to be a member of Parliament;
9. (2) A person shall not be disqualified from being a member of the Commission or a Regional Lands Commission because such person is a public officer;
9. (3) A member of the Commission or of a Regional Lands Commission who has a professional qualification shall cease to be a member of the Commission or Regional Lands Commission if the member is disqualified or suspended from practicing his/her profession by an order of a competent authority made in respect or him/her personally or he/she ceases to be a member of the profession otherwise than at his/her own request.

Tenure of Office of Members of the Commission and Regional, (District/Town Council), Lands Commission

10. (1) The Chairman and members of the Lands Commission and the Chairman and members of a Regional, (District/Town Council), Lands Commission other than the Executive Secretary and the Regional, (District/Town Council), Lands Officer shall hold office for a term of four years and are eligible for reappointment.
10. (2) The office of the Chairman or a member of the Commission or the Chairman or a member of a Regional, (District/town Council),

Lands Commission other than the Executive Secretary and the Regional Lands officer shall become vacant if:-

a. He/she ceases to hold office under subsection (1) of this section;
b. Any circumstance arises that would cause him to be disqualified for appointment under section 9 of this Act; or
c. He/she is removed form office by the President or, in the case of a member of a Regional, (District/Town Council), Lands Commission, by the Minister for inability to perform the functions of his/her office or for stated misbehaviour.

Resignation of Members of the Commission and Regional, (District/Town Council), Lands Commission

11. (1) The Chairman or a member of the Commission may resign his/her office by notice addressed to the President.

(2) The Chairman or a member or a Regional, (District/Town Council), Lands Commission may resign his/her office by notice addressed to the Minister

Removal of Members of the Commission and Regional, (District/Town Council), Lands Commission

12. (1) The Chairman or a member of the Commission may be removed from office by the President for inability to perform the functions of his/her office or for stated misbehaviour.

12. (2) The Chairman or a member of a Regional, (District/Town Council), Lands Commission may be removed from office by the Minister for inability to perform the functions of his/her office or for stated misbehaviour.

Filling of Vacancies

13. (1) Where the Chairman of the Ccommission or the Chairman of a Regional, (District/Town Council), Lands Commission dies, resigns or is removed from office or by reason of illness unable to perform the functions of his/her office, the members of the Commission or Regional, (District/Town Council), Lands Commission shall elect one of their members to act as Chairman until such time as the Chairman is able to perform the functions of his/her office or until a new Chairman is appointed.

13. (2) Where a member of the Commission or of a Regional Lands Commission dies, resigns or otherwise ceases to hold office, or is by reason of illness or any other sufficient cause unable to perform the functions of his/her office, the President or the Minister as the case may be, may appoint another person to act in his/her place until such time as the member is able to resume the performance of the functions of his office or until a new member is appointed to fill the vacancy.

(3) Where a person is elected as Chairman or appointed a member to fill a vacancy he/she shall hold office for the remainder of the term of the previous Chairman or member and may, subject to the provisions of this Act, be eligible for re-appointment, re-election or re-nomination.

Meetings of the Commission

14. (1) The Commission or a Regional, (District/Town Council) Lands Commission shall meet for the despatch of business at a time and place determined by the Chairman but shall meet at least once in every three months.

(2) The quorum at a meeting of the Commission or a regional, (District/Town Council), Lands Commission shall not be less than half of the membership of the Commission or Regional, (District/Town Council), Lands Commission.

(3) The Chairman shall preside at each meeting of the Commission or Regional, (District/Town Council) Lands Commission but in his absence a member of the Commission or Regional, (District/Town Council), Lands Commission appointed by the members present from among themselves shall preside.

(4) A member of the Commission or a Regional, (District/Town Council), Lands Commission who is absent without sufficient reason from three consecutive meetings shall cease to be a member of the Commission or a Regional, (District/Town Council) Lands Commission.

(5) The validity of the proceedings of The Commission or a Regional, (District/Town Council) Lands Commission shall not be affected by a vacancy in its membership or any defect in the appointment or qualification of a member.

(6) Questions before the Commission or a Regional, (District/Town Council) Lands Commission shall be decided by a majority of the members present and voting.

(7) The Chairman or the person presiding at a meeting of the Commission or a Regional, (District/Town Council) Lands Commission shall in the event of equality of votes have a second or casting vote.

(8) The Chairman of the Commission or a Regional, (District/Town Council) Lands Commission shall summon a special meeting of the Commission or a written request for the special meeting signed by not less than four members of the Commission or Regional Lands Commission.

(9) Except as provided in this Act the Commission or a Regional Lands Commission shall regulate the procedure at its meetings.

<u>Power to Co-opt</u>

15. The Commission or a Regional, (District/Town Council), Lands Commission

<u>Appointment of Committee</u>

16. The Commission or a Regional, (District/Town Council) Lands Commission

17. (1) There is established by this Act a Lands Commission Secretariat referred to as 'the secretariat' which shall be the secretariat of Commission.

(2) The Secretariat shall subject to this Act, be responsible for giving effect to the decisions of the Commission and shall perform such function as the Commission may determine.

<u>Executive Secretary</u>

18. (1) The Commission shall have an Executive Secretary who shall be a person knowledgeable and experienced in land administration.

(2) The Executive Secretary shall be appointed by the President in accordance with the advice of the Commission given in consultation with the Public Service Commission.

(3)The Executive Secretary is responsible for the day-to-day administration of the Commission and the implementation of the decisions of the Commission subject to the general directives of the Commission.

(4) The Executive Secretary may delegate any of his function to an officer of the Commission but shall not be relieved from ultimate responsibility for the discharge of the delegated function.

(5) The Executive Secretary shall be responsible for the organisation and control of the employees of the Commission.

(6) The Executive shall act as the secretary to the Commission.

Deputy Executive Secretary

19. (1) The Commission shall have a Deputy Executive Secretary appointed by the President in accordance with the advice of the Commission given in consultation with the Public Service Commission.

(2) The Deputy Executive Secretary shall in the absence of the Executive Secretary perform his functions specified under section 18 of this Act and shall perform such other duties as may be assigned to him by the Executive Secretary.

Other Staff of the Commission

20. (1) The Commission shall have such officers and staff as may be reasonably necessary for the effective discharging of its functions.

(2) The President may delegate to the Commission or any Public officer the appointment of the officers and staff of the Commission.

(3) The officers and staff shall hold office upon such terms and conditions as the Public Services Commission shall approve.

(4) Public officers who have specialized knowledge of the work of the Commission may be transferred or seconded to the Commission or may otherwise give assistance to it.

(5) The Commission may engage the services of consultants and advisers.

21. (1) The funds of the Commission shall include:-

a. Government subventions;
b. Monies received by Commission from any source approved by the Minister for Finance.

(2) The Commission may by legislative instrument levy charges for anything required or authorised to be done by this Act to provide further funds to meet the expenses of the Commission.

Accounts and Audit

22. (1) The Commission shall keep proper books of account and proper records in relation to them and the account books records of the Commission shall be in a form approved by the Auditor-General.

(2) The books and accounts of the Commission shall be audited annually by the Auditor-General or auditor appointed by him/her.

(3) A report on the audit shall be submitted to the Commission by the Auditor-General or the auditor appointed by him/her within two months of the end of each financial year.

Annual Report

23. (1) The Commission shall as soon as possible after the expiration of each financial year but within six months after the end of the preceding financial year, submit to the Minister responsible for Lands an annual report dealing generally with the activities of the Commission and shall include-

a. A copy of the audited accounts of the Commission together with the Auditor-General's report on it; and
b. Such other information as the Minister responsible for Lands may require.

(2) The Commission shall also submit to the Minister responsible for Lands such other reports on its activities as the Minister may require.
(3) A copy of the annual report shall be forwarded by the Commission to the:

a. Office of the President;
b. Minister for Finance;
c. Minister for Town Planning
d. Minister for Forestry, Agriculture and Food Security;
e. Minister for Energy and Power;
f. Minister for Mines;
g. Minister for Education, Science and Technology

h. Minister for Roads, Works and Housing;
i. Minister for Transport and Communications;
j. Minister for National Development and Economic planning
k. Governor, Bank of Sierra Leone
l. The Statistician General, Statistics Sierra Leone

(4) The Minister shall as soon as possible but not more than three months after receiving the annual report cause it to be laid before Parliament.

<u>Access to Information</u>

24.The Executive Secretary and the Regional Lands Officer shall have access to the information and records of any department of state which are reasonably necessary for the performance of their functions under this Act.

<u>Offences</u>

25. Any person who-

a. At the request of the Commission for information deliberately or negligently submits a false or misleading statement; or
b. Refuses without reasonable excuse to give information or provide a document which the Commission may reasonably request for the purpose of its function; or
c. Refuses without lawful excuse to admit an officer or designated agent of the Commission on to the business premises or otherwise obstructs an inspection.

Commits an offence and is liable on summary conviction to a fine not exceeding …….. Leones or to a term of imprisonment not exceeding six months or to both.

<u>Offences by Bodies Corporate</u>

26. (1) Where an offence under this Act or any regulations made under it is committed by a body of persons, the following shall apply-

a. Where the body of persons is a body corporate other than a partnership every Director, Manager, Secretary or an officer of similar status of that body corporate shall also be deemed to be guilty of that offence;

b. In the case of a partnership, every partner or officer or similar shall be deemed to be guilty of that offence.

(2) No persons shall be deemed to be guilty of an offence under subsection (1) of this section if he/she proves that the act in respect of which he/she is charged was committed by another person without his/her consent or connivance and that he exercised all due diligence to prevent the commission of that act as he/she ought to have done having regard to all the circumstances.

Regulations

27. The Minister may in consultation with the Commission by legislative instrument make such regulations as are necessary to give full effect to the provisions of this Act.

Acts to have Effect with Necessary Modification

28. Act No. 19 of 1960, "an Act to make Further and Better provision of the management and disposal of Crown Lands," [otherwise known as the State Lands Act (as amended), the Provinces Land] Act, Cap. 122, Act No. 14 of 1960, the Survey Ordinance, Act No. 42 of 1961, the "Compulsory Acquisition of Property Act", Cap. 116, the "Public Lands" Act, Cap. 117, the "Unoccupied Lands" Act, Cap.118, the "Crown Lands Conservancy" Act, Cap. 119 & 120, the "Defence Lands Acquisition" Act; Cap. 121, the "Concessions" Act, Cap. 66 "The Freetown Improvement Act"; Cap. 81, The Town and Country Planning Act (As amended), and any other enactments relating to land, in force immediately before the commencement of the Act, shall have effect with such modifications as may be necessary to give effect to this Act.

Interpretation

29. In this Act, unless the context otherwise requires-

"Minister" means the Minister responsible for Lands.

Appendix 7

THE LAND (ACQUISITION AND COMMERCIAL USE) BILL 2005

A BILL ENTITLED

Short title. THE LAND (ACQUISITION AND COMMERCIAL USE) ACT 2005

Being an Act to ensure equal access to land anywhere in Sierra Leone for all Sierra Leoneans, to facilitate the commercial use of land by both local and foreign investors; and to provide for other related matters.

ENACTED by the President and Members of Parliament in this present Parliament assembled.

Date of Commencement. [ ]

PART I – PRELIMINARY

Interpretation Cap.225.

1. In this Act, unless the context otherwise requires:-

"**acquire**" means to possess or receive;

"**Commission**" means the Lands Commission established by section 2 of the Lands Commission Act 2005;

"**Community Land**" means provincial land, that is not owned by a family or an individual;

"**district land registry**" means a registry designated as such under the General Registration Act;

"**economic trees**" means all trees, shrubs and plants which are grown or cultivated for their intrinsic value;

"**head of family**" means the eldest member of the family or any member of the family designated as such by all or a majority of the members of his family;

"**interest in land**" include freehold, leasehold, mortgage, concession, licence, and a registered joint venture agreement for the use of land;

"**land**" means the soil, ground or earth, buildings on the land, fixtures attached to the land, mines and minerals and incorporeal hereditaments;

"**Minister**" means the Minister responsible for Local Government;

"**Paramount Chief**" means the Paramount Chief of the Chiefdom in which the land is situated;

"**provincial land**" means land in the provinces;

"**sale of land**" means the sale of freehold interest in land;

"**Sierra Leonean**" means a citizen of Sierra Leone or a Sierra Leonean company or corporation;

"**Sierra Leonean Company or Corporation**" means a company or corporation, as the case may be, registered or established by law in Sierra Leone and wholly owned or owned to the extent of fifty-one percent or more by Sierra Leoneans.

PART II – ACQUISITION OF FREEHOLD INTEREST IN LAND

Acquisition of freehold interest in land

2. Any Sierra Leonean may acquire a freehold interest in land in any part of Sierra Leone.

Contract for sale of land

3. (1) Subject to subsection (2), a contract for the sale of land shall be-

(a) made by deed incorporating all the terms to which the parties have agreed and shall be signed by or on behalf of each of the parties; and

(b) in the case of provincial land, countersigned by the Paramount Chief; and

(c) registered in Freetown or in the district land registry, as the case may be.

(2) A contract for the sale of provincial land under customary law shall be valid notwithstanding that it is not in writing, if,-

(a) the parties have reached agreement in the presence of two witnesses and the Paramount Chief has approved it in writing; or

(b) a memorandum of the agreement incorporating all the terms to which the parties have agreed, is signed by or on behalf of the parties and countersigned by the Paramount Chief;

and a copy of the approval of the Paramount Chief under paragraph (a) or, as the case may be, the memorandum under paragraph (b) is deposited with the Chiefdom Treasury in accordance with section 19.

(3) A contract for sale of land shall also state the purpose for which the land is intended to be used, which shall be compatible with the development plan of the local council of the district in which the land is situated.

(4) Nothing in this section shall prevent a purchaser of provincial land from changing, with the permission in writing of the Chiefdom Council, the purpose for which the land is intended to be used.

Parties to contract for sale of land

4. (1) Parties to a contract for the sale of land shall be-
(a) In the case of family land, the prospective purchaser and, subject to subsection (2), the head of the family that owns the land and who has the capacity to enter into the contract; and if the land is provincial land, the Paramount Chief as countersignatory;
(b) in the case of land owned by an individual, the prospective purchaser and the individual or his representative;
(c) in the case of provincial land which is community land, the prospective buyer and the Chiefdom Council.
(2) The head of the family shall, before entering into a contract for the sale or land, consult the members of the family.
(3) A contract for the sale of land shall be binding on all the parties, including members of the family, and their successors in title, and the Paramount Chief and his successors.

Offence of Chief signing conflicting contracts

5. (1) It shall be an offence for a Paramount Chief to countersign a contract for the sale of family land under paragraph (a) of subsection (1) of section 4, if he has already signed or countersigned another contract in respect of the same land, unless he can show that, despite due care, he was not aware of the defect in the title of the family in the earlier contract.
(2) An offence under subsection (1) shall be punishable by a fine not exceeding twice the purchase price paid under the contract found to be defective.

PART III – ACQUISITION OF LEASEHOLD INTEREST IN LAND

Lease of land

6. (1) Subject to section 7, any person may acquire a lease of land in any part of Sierra Leone for a term not exceeding ninety years.
(2) Nothing in subsection (1) shall prevent the inclusion in any lease of a provision for the renewal of such lease for a second or further term not exceeding twenty-one years or twenty-one years in aggregate.
(3) Section 4 shall apply to the parties to leases, with such modification as may be necessary.
(4) The rent reserved under any lease of provincial land shall be subject to revision by the Chiefdom Council concerned every seven years;
Provided that:-
(a) There shall be no revision of rent by the Chiefdom Council by reason only of improvements made by the lessee or his predecessors in title;
(b) a note of any revision of rent referred to in paragraph (a) shall be endorsed on the lease and entered in the district land registry.

Leases exceeding three years to be under seal.

7. A lease for a term exceeding three years shall be valid unless created by deed.

Construction of defective lease

8. Where a lease longer than three years is created otherwise than by deed, it shall be constructed as a lease from year to year, unless-
(a) it is in respect of provincial land; and
(b) the Chiefdom Council concerned has endorsed thereon its consent.

Determination of defective leases

9. Every lease from year to year shall be determinable by either party giving three months' notice to the other and the notice shall expire at the end of a current year of the lease.

Voidable deeds

10. Every deed creating a lease of land shall be voidable by either party, unless-
(a) it is executed by the lessor and by the lessee or their respective attorneys or agents, in the presence of two witnesses; and
(b) in the case of provincial land, it is countersigned-
(i) by the Paramount Chief; or
(ii) by a Magistrate; and
(c) it provides, in the case of provincial land, that the lessee shall not sublet or assign his interest there under except with the consent of the Chiefdom Council which consent shall not be unreasonably withheld; and
(d) it stipulates-
(i) the rent;
(ii) the term;
(iii) the purpose for which the land is intended to be used;
(iv) whether the interest is assignable;
(v) where buildings of permanent construction are to be erected, the rights of the parties to and in respect of such buildings at the expiration or determination of the lease;
(vi) in the case where the lease is for a longer period than seven years that the rent is subject to right of appeal to the Minister, in the case of provincial land and to the Rent tribunal, in the case of land in the Western Area and;
(e) it is registered in the district land registry within sixty days after its conclusion.

Reversion of fixtures

Provided that-
(a) before the removal of any fixture or building, the lessee shall pay all rent owing by him, and shall perform or satisfy all his other obligations to the lessor in respect of the land;
(b) in the removal of any fixture or building, the lessee shall not do any avoidable damage to any other building or other part of the land;
(c) immediately after the removal of any fixture or building, the lessee shall make good all damage, if any, done to any other building or other part of the land by the removal;
(d) the lessee shall not remove any fixture or building without giving one month's notice in writing to the lessor or in the case of provincial land, the Chiefdom Council, as the case may be, of his intention to remove it.
(2) At any time before the expiration of the notice of intention to remove any fixture or building under paragraph (d) of subsection (1), the lessor may, by notice in writing to the lessee, elect to purchase any fixture or building comprised in the notice of intention to remove and any fixture or building elected to be purchased shall not be removed by the lessee and shall become the property of the lessor who shall pay to the lessee the fair value thereof.
(3) The lessor shall pay to the lessee a fair value of any economic trees which have been planted on the land by the lessee.
(4) If there is a dispute as to the value of any fixture or building or any economic trees, the Provincial Secretary shall hold an inquiry and his decision thereon shall be final.

Amendment of Act No. 30 of 1966

12. For the purpose of section 6, the Non Citizens (Interest in Land) Act, 1966 is hereby amended-
(a) by the repeal of section 4 thereof;
(b) by the repeal and replacement of section 5 thereof by the following:-

"Powers of Board over land received by non-citizens

"(5) (1) Any conveyance, lease, grant, transfer, declaration, agreement, settlement or other disposition (other than an assent in favour of persons entitled under a will or on an intestacy) which, apart from the provisions of this Act, would have vested freehold land in a non-citizen (whether alone or together with any other person) shall vest such land in the Board for the whole estate or interest conferred by, or in virtue of, the instrument and the Board shall cause the Sheriff to sell the same by public auction.

(2) If satisfied that failure to observe the law was due to genuine and excusable mistake or ignorance (whether of law or fact), the Board may either-
(a) permit the parties to annul the transaction or modify it in such manners as may be approved by the Board and grant such licence as may be necessary in relation thereto; or
(b) cause the Sheriff to sell the property by public auction and if it thinks fit, cause to be paid out of the residual proceeds of the sale to the person or persons whose purchase of the freehold land caused it to vest in the board, a sum not exceeding the purchase price stipulated in the disposition which has been avoided or in the case of a gift or exchange, such sum as the Board shall think fit.
(3) The proceeds of sale which have not been disposed of under paragraph (b) of subsection (2), after deducting the cost of the sale, shall be paid into the Consolidated Fund."

(c) in section 6,

(i) by deleting the words "or reserved lease holds" in subsection (1) thereof;
(ii) by deleting the words "or reserved leaseholds are" from paragraph (b) of subsection (10) thereof;

(d) in section 8, by deleting the words "or leases" from paragraph (c) thereof.

PART IV – MORTGAGES

Creation of mortgages.

13. (1) A person may mortgage his land or create a charge over it to secure the repayment of a debt, loan or some other obligation.
(2) The mortgage or charge shall be by deed executed by the mortgagor or creator of the charge in the presence of two witnesses and where the land is provincial land, countersigned by the Paramount Chief.
(3) A deed executed under this section shall contain all the essential terms of the mortgage or charge.
(4) No mortgage or charge shall be created by the deposit of title deed.

Exclusion of equity of redemption invalid

14. Any provision in a mortgage to exclude the equity of redemption shall be invalid.

Mortgagors' right to sell mortgaged property.

15. A mortgagor may, with the consent of the mortgagee, sell the mortgaged property and if the mortgagee refuses to give his consent, a court may grant an order for sale of the property.

Mortgageee in possession and the power of sale

16. (1) A mortgagee of a mortgage or the chargee of a charge created under this Act may take possession immediately upon the creation of a mortgage or charge unless the right has been expressly or impliedly postponed until default.

(2) A mortgagee or chargee in possession shall be strictly accountable for any rents and profits received.

(3) The mortgagee of a mortgage or chargee of a charge created under this Act may, in exercise of his power of sale, sell the mortgaged or charged property at any time he chooses, but he shall have regard to the interests of the mortgagor.

(4) Any money received by the mortgagee or chargee from the sale, after discharge of prior encumbrances shall be held by him in trust to be applied first, in payment of all costs, charges and expenses properly incurred by him as incident to the sale and secondly, in discharge of the loan, interest and costs, and the residue of the money so received shall be paid to the person entitled to the mortgaged property.

Sale by mortgagee to himself void.

17. A sale or purported sale of mortgaged property by a mortgagee to himself or his servant shall be void.

Lenders not to refuse land in provinces

18. A lender shall not refuse to accept land as security for the payment of his loan because the land is provincial land.

PART V – MISCELLANEOUS

Chiefdom Treasuries to provide for custody of land documents.

19. For the purposes of Parts II and III, every Chiefdom Treasury shall appoint an officer and other staff and provide facilities for the receipt, safe custody and processing of documents relating to land transactions required to be deposited with or kept by the Chiefdom Treasury thereunder.

Underutilized land to be taxed

20. (1) Where, after a reasonable time, the buyer or lessee fails to use or begin to use the land for the purpose for which it was acquired, unless he has obtained the necessary permission in writing to delay or alter the purpose, the land shall be subject to tax or levy as underutilized land.

(2) The rate or amount of the tax or levy shall be fixed by the Commission after consultation with the Minister responsible for finance.

Title derived from adverse possession.

21. (1) A trespasser actually in possession of land who has the intention to be in possession by excluding all other, including the landowner, from the land by means other than the use of force, and has maintained the adverse possession for not less than twelve years, shall be entitled to be registered as owner, after he has published notice of intention to register in the Sierra Leone Gazette and a reputable newspaper in Sierra Leone on not less than three occasions three months before registration.

(2) Adverse possession shall not create a valid title to state land in the Western Area or community land in the Provinces.

Joint venture agreement

22. (1) A joint venture agreement for the use of land for a productive purpose shall, in the case of provincial land, be countersigned by the Paramount Chief.

(2) A joint venture agreement made under subsection (1) shall not create an interest in land unless registered.

Chiefdom Councils to administer lands.

23. (1) Subject to this Act, Chiefdom Councils shall be responsible for the administration, in accordance with customary law, of land situated in their respective chiefdoms.

(2) Until registration of title to land is effected in the Provinces, a Chiefdom Council shall compile a list of families and individuals that have freehold estates in land situated in its chiefdom, together with the name and address of each head of such families and individuals.

(3) The Chiefdom Council shall cause the list referred to in subsection (2) to be deposited in its treasury and in the district land registry.

(4) The list referred to in subsection (2) shall be reviewed every three years or earlier, when necessary.

(5) A committee of elders of the Chiefdom and the Court Chairman shall be empanelled by the Paramount Chief to arbitrate in any dispute over the compilation or content of the list, but not in any matter relating to title to or boundary of any lands.

Regulations

24. The Commission may, by statutory instrument, make regulations for carrying into effect the provisions of this Act.

Repeal of Cap. 122

25. The Provinces Land Act is hereby repealed.

Appendix 8
TREATY NO. 1 OF 22ND AUGUST, 1788.

Know all men by these presents that I, King Naimbanna, Chief of Sierra Leone, on the Grain Coast of Africa, by and with the consent of the other Kings, Princes, Chiefs and Potentates subscribing hereto, in consideration of the presents, as by a list annexed, now made me by Captain John Taylor, of His Britannic Majesty's brig "Miro", in behalf of and for the sole benefit of the free community of settlers, their heirs and successors, lately arrived from England, and under the protection of the British Government, have granted, and by these presents do grant and for ever quit claim to certain district of land for the settling of the said free community, to be theirs, their heirs, and successors for ever; that is to say, all the land, wood, water, etc., etc., which are now contained from the bay commonly called Frenchman's Bay, but by these presents changed to St. George's bay, coastwise up the river Sierra Leone to Gambia Island, and southerly of inland from the river side twenty miles. And further be it known unto all men that I, King Naimbanna, do faithfully promise and swear for my Chiefs, gentlemen, and people, likewise my heirs and successors, that I will bear true allegiance to His Most Gracious Majesty George the Third, King of Great Britain, France, and Ireland, etc., etc., etc., and protect the said free settlers, His subjects to the utmost of my power, against the insurrections and attacks of all nations or people whatever. And I do hereby bind myself, my heirs, and successors, to grant the said free settlers a continuance of a quiet and peaceable possession of the land granted, their heirs, and successors for ever.

In witness whereof I and my Chiefs have set our hands and seals this 22nd day of August 1788.

And it is also further agreed by the aforesaid contracting parties that the customs payable by vessels anchoring in St. George's bay shall pay ten bars to the free settlers and subjects of His Britannic Majesty, and the customs paid for watering to be paid to King Naimbanna, his representatives or successors; that is to say, fifteen bars as customary, and if to anchor and not to water the customs as above to be paid to the free settlers of St. George's bay as aforesaid.

In witness whereof to this additional part of these presents, and all others contained herein, we have made our marks and signed our names, with our seals affixed, this 22nd day of August, 1788.

	their
John Taylor	King X Naimbanna
Richard Weaver	James X Dowder
	marks
Thomas Peall	Pabongee
Benjamin Ellett	Dick Robbin
	Abram Elliott Griffith Secretary to the King

Source: J.J. Crooks, *A History of the Colony of Sierra Leone*

REFERENCES

- BOOKS

Allott, A.N., *Essays in African Law*, Butterworth, 1960.

Allot, A.N., *New Essays in African Law*, Butterworth, 1970.

Bohannan, P., *Social Anthropology*, New York, Holt Rinehart & Winston, 1963.

Bentsi-Enchill, K., *Ghana Land Law*, Sweet & Maxwell, 1964.

Clarke, J.T., *Sierra Leone in Maps*, University of London Press, 1969.

Coker, G.B.A., *Family Property Among the Yoruba*, Sweet & Maxwell, 1958.

Collier. G.B.O., *Sierra Leone – Experiment in Democracy in an African Nation*, University of London Press, 1970.

Crooks, J.J., *History of the Colony of Sierra Leone*, Frank Cass & Co. Ltd., 1903, new impression, 1972.

Daniels, W.C.E., *The Common Law in West Africa*, Butterworths, 1964.

Dart, J.H., *Treatise on the Law and Practice relating to Vendors and Purchasers of Real Estate*, 6th edn, ed. W. Barber, R.B. Haldane and W.R. Sheldon, Stevens & Sons, 1888.

Downson, Sir Ernest and V.L.O. Sheppard, *Land Registration*, 2nd edn, HMSO, 1956.

Elias, T.O., *Ghana and Sierra Leone: The Development of their Laws and Constitution*, Stevens, 1962.

Elias T.L., *Nigerian Land Law*, Sweet & Maxwell, 4th edn, 1971.

Fenton, J.S., *Outline of Native Law in Sierra Leone*, Freetown, Government Printer, 1948.

Finnegan, R.H., *Survey of the Limba People of Northern Sierra Leone*, London, HMSO, 1965.

Fyfe, C.H., *A History of Sierra Leone*, OUP, 1962.

Fyfe, C.H., *Sierra Leone Inheritance*, OUP, 1963.

Goddard, T.N., *The Handbook of Sierra Leone*, London, Grant Richards Ltd, 1925.

Hailey, Lord, *An African Survey*, OUP (revised edn), 1956.

Hailey, Lord, *Native Administration in the British African Territories, Part III, West Africa*, London, HMSO, 1951.

Hall, H.U., *The Sherbro of Sierra Leone*, University of Pennsylvania Press, 1938.

Hertslet, Sir E., *Map of Africa By Treaties*, 3rd edn, Vols 1, 20, Frank Cass & Co. Ltd., 1967.

Hussain, M.H., *Report to the Government of Sierra Leone on Customary Land Tenure in the Context of a Developing Agricutural Economy*, Rome, F.A.O., 1964.

Kludze, A.K.P., *Ewe Law of Property*, Sweet & Maxwell, 1973.

Little, K.A., *The Mende of Sierra Leone*, Routledge & Kegan Paul (revised edn), 1967.

Liversage, V., *Land Tenure in the Colonies*, CUP, 1945.

Lloyd, P.C., *Yoruba Land Law*, OUP, 1962.

Maxwell, J.C., *Notes on Land Tenure in Sierra Leone*, Freetown, 1912.

McCulloch, M., *Peoples of Sierra Leone*, London, International African Institute (unrevised reprint), 1964.

Meek, C.K., *Land Law and Custom in the Colonies*, OUP, 1946.

Megarry, R.E. and H.W.R. Wade, *The Law of Real Property*, 4th edn, Stevens, 1975.

Newbury, C.W.,*British Policy Towards West Africa: Selected Documents 1786–1874*, Vol. 1, Oxford, Clarendon Press, 1965.

Nwabueze, B.O., *Nigerian Land Law*, Enugu Nwanife Publishers, 1972.

Obi, S.N.C., *The Ibo Law of Property*, Butterworths, 1963.

Olawoye, C.O., *Title of Land in Nigeria*, Lagos Evens, 1974.

Ollennu, N.A., *Principles of Customary Land Law in Ghana*, Sweet & Maxwell, 1962.

Ollennu, N.A., *The Law of Testate and Intestate Succession in Ghana*, Sweet & Maxwell, 1966.

Park, A.E.W, *The Sources of Nigerian Law*, Sweet & Maxwell, 1963.

Pluncknett, T.F.T., *Concise History of the Common Law*, (5th edn) Butterworths, 1956.

Radcliffe-Brown, R.A. and C.D. Forde, *African System of Kinship and Marriage*, OUP, 1950.

Royal Anthropological Institute of Great Britain and Ireland, *Notes and Queries on Anthropology*, 6th edn, Routledge & Kegan Paul, 1951.Rubin, N.N. and E. Cotran (eds), *Annual Survey of African Law*, Rex Collins, Vol. VII, 1973.

Sarbah, J.M., *Fanti Customary Law* (2nd edn), Frank Cass & Co. Ltd, 1968.

Saylor, R. *The Economic System of Sierra Leone*, Durham, North Carolina, Duke University Press, 1967.

Simpson, S.R., *Report on the Registration of Title to Land in Lagos*, Federal Government Printer, Lagos, 1957.

Simpson, S.R., *Land Law and Registration*, CUP, 1976.

Smart, H.M.J., *Sierra Leone Customary Family Law*, Freetown, Fourah Bay College Bookshop, 1983.

Smart, H.M.J., "Sierra Leone Family Law", unpublished Ph.D. thesis, London University, 1973.

Thomas, N.W., *Anthropological Report on Sierra Leone*, Part I, Harrison & Sons, 1916.

Turay, H., *Land Tenure System in Sierra Leone*, Freetown, 1980.

Williams, J.H. and Yates, W., *The Law of Ejectment*, 2nd edn, Butterworths, 1911.

- ARTICLES AND MISCELLANEOUS PUBLICATIONS

Allott, A.N., "Towards a Definition of Absolute Ownership" (1965) *J.A.L.* 99.

Allott, A.N., "Family Property in West Africa: Its Juristic Bases, Control and Enjoyment" in J.N.D. Anderson (ed.), *Family Law in Asia and Africa*, London, 1968.

Allott, A.N. (ed.), "The Future of Law in Africa", Record of Proceedings of the London Conference, 28 December 1959–8 January 1960.

Bentsi-Enchill, K., "Do African Systems of Land Tenure Require a Special Terminology?" (1965) *J.A.L.* 114.

Biyi, E., "Temne Land Tenure", *African Affairs*, Vol. 12, 1913.

Dorjahn, V.R. and C.H. Fyfe,"Landlord and Stranger: Change in Tenancy relations in Sierra Leone", *Journal of African History*, Vol. 3 No. 3, 1962, pp. 391–7.

Harris, W.T., "Mende Marriage and the Law of Inheritance", *Sierra Leone Bulletin of Religion*, June 1959, 10; December 1959, 34.

Hollins, N.C., "Notes on Mende Law", *S.L.S. (O.S.)*, No. 13, 1929, 29; No. 15, 1929, 57.

Jones, W.S.M., "Law Reform in Sierra Leone", *Aureol Review*, Freetown, April 1969.

Langley, E.R., "The Kono People of Sierra Leone", *Africa*, Vol. 5, 1932, 61.

Langley, E.R., "The Temne, their Life, Land and Ways", *S.L.S. (O.S.)*, No. 22, 1939, 68.

Park, A.E.W., "A Dual System of Land Tenure: The Experience of Southern Nigeria", (1965), *J.A.L.*, 1.

Renner-Thomas A., "Historical Background To The Duality Of Land Tenure In Sierra Leone" *Africana Research Bulletin*, Vol XV, Dec, 1985.

Renner-Thomas A., "Facilities For Assuring Title To Land In Sierra Leone" *Sierra Leone Law Journal*, Vol 1, No.1, Nov 1994.

Renner-Thomas A., "The Case For More Substantial Law Reform In Sierra Leone" *Sierra Leone Law Review* [2000] Vol.1 No.1.

Smart, H.M.J., "The Local Court System in Sierra Leone", S.L.S. (N.S.), No. 22, 1968, 31.

Smart, H.M.J., "The Inheritance to Property in Sierra Leone: An analysis of the Law and Problems involved", *S.L.S. (N.S.)*, No. 24, 1969, 2.

Smart, H.M.J., "Sierra Leone", *Annual Survey of African Law*, London, Rex Collins, Vol. VII, 1973, pp. 77–90.

Index

2527916R00225

Printed in Great Britain
by Amazon.co.uk, Ltd.,
Marston Gate.